GLOBALIZATION AND FOOD SOVEREIGNTY

Global and Local Change in the New Politics of Food

D0040278

In recent years, food sovereignty has emerged as a way of contesting corporate control of agricultural markets in pursuit of a more democratic, decentralized food system. The concept unites individuals, communities, civil society organizations, and even states in opposition to globalizing food regimes.

This collection examines expressions of food sovereignty ranging from the direct action tactics of La Vía Campesina in Brazil to the consumer activism of the Slow Food movement and the negotiating stances of states from the global South at WTO negotiations. With each case, the contributors explore how claiming food sovereignty allows individuals to challenge the power of global agribusiness and reject neoliberal market economics.

With perspectives drawn from Europe, the Americas, Asia, Africa, and Australia, *Globalization and Food Sovereignty* is the first comparative collection to focus on food sovereignty activism worldwide.

(Studies in Comparative Political Economy and Public Policy)

PETER ANDRÉE is an associate professor in the Department of Political Science at Carleton University.

JEFFREY AYRES is a professor in the Department of Political Science at Saint Michael's College in Colchester, Vermont.

MICHAEL J. BOSIA is an associate professor in the Department of Political Science at Saint Michael's College in Colchester, Vermont.

MARIE-JOSÉE MASSICOTTE is an associate professor in the School of Political Studies at the University of Ottawa.

Studies in Comparative Political Economy and Public Policy

Editors: MICHAEL HOWLETT, DAVID LAYCOCK (Simon Fraser University), and STEPHEN McBRIDE (McMaster University)

Studies in Comparative Political Economy and Public Policy is designed to showcase innovative approaches to political economy and public policy from a comparative perspective. While originating in Canada, the series will provide attractive offerings to a wide international audience, featuring studies with local, subnational, cross-national, and international empirical bases and theoretical frameworks.

Editorial Advisory Board

For a list of books published in the series, see page 377.

Globalization and Food Sovereignty

*Global and Local Change
in the New Politics of Food*

EDITED BY PETER ANDRÉE,
JEFFREY AYRES, MICHAEL J. BOSIA,
AND MARIE-JOSÉE MASSICOTTE

UNIVERSITY OF TORONTO PRESS
Toronto Buffalo London

© University of Toronto Press 2014
Toronto Buffalo London
www.utppublishing.com
Printed in Canada

ISBN 978-1-4426-4375-8 (cloth)
ISBN 978-1-4426-1228-0 (paper)

∞

Printed on acid-free, 100% post-consumer recycled paper with vegetable-based inks.

Library and Archives Canada Cataloguing in Publication

Globalization and food sovereignty: global and local change in the new politics of food/
edited by Peter Andrée, Jeffrey Ayres, Michael J. Bosia, and Marie-Josée Massicotte.

(Studies in comparative political economy and public policy)
Includes bibliographical references and index.
ISBN 978-1-4426-4375-8 (bound). – ISBN 978-1-4426-1228-0 (pbk.)

1. Food sovereignty. 2. Agriculture – Economic aspects. 3. Globalization. I. Andrée,
Peter, 1970–, editor of compilation II. Ayres, Jeffrey McKelvey, editor of compilation
III. Bosia, Michael J., editor of compilation IV. Massicotte, Marie-Josée, 1971–, editor
of compilation V. Series: Studies in comparative political economy and public policy

HD9000.5.G585 2014   338.1'9   C2013-907475-9

This book has been published with the help of a grant from the Federation for the
Humanities and Social Sciences, through the Awards to Scholarly Publications Program,
using funds provided by the Social Sciences and Humanities Research Council of Canada.

University of Toronto Press acknowledges the financial assistance to its publishing
program of the Canada Council for the Arts and the Ontario Arts Council.

Canada Council   Conseil des Arts
for the Arts   du Canada

University of Toronto Press acknowledges the financial support of the
Government of Canada through the Canada Book Fund for its publishing activities.

Contents

Contributors

Peter Andrée, Department of Political Science, Carleton University, Canada

Jeffrey Ayres, Department of Political Science, Saint Michael's College, USA

Michael J. Bosia, Department of Political Science, Saint Michael's College, USA

Irena Knezevic, Department of Communication and Culture, York University, Canada

Sarah J. Martin, Program in Global Governance, University of Waterloo, Canada

Marie-Josée Massicotte, School of Political Studies, University of Ottawa, Canada

Martha McMahon, Department of Sociology, University of Victoria, Canada

Philip McMichael, Department of Development Sociology, Cornell University, USA

Michael Menser, Department of Philosophy, Brooklyn College, CUNY, USA

Elizabeth Smythe, Faculty of Arts and Political Science, Concordia University College of Alberta, Canada

Sarah Wright, Discipline of Geography and Environmental Studies, University of Newcastle, Australia

Noah Zerbe, Department of Politics, Humboldt State University, USA

Acknowledgments

Today, the study of food as a political phenomenon has become a hot topic in and outside of academia, with political scientist James Scott, best known for his work on peasant politics, featured in the *New York Times* as much for his scholarship as for his organic farm. Moreover, over the past several years, food prices have skyrocketed in many places around the world, accompanied by expanding food protests and extended policy debates about the health and safety of the food being consumed by the general public. In response to these events, the activists, organizations, and movements behind the call for food sovereignty have won many struggles to put a new vision of food and agriculture on the international public agenda, including on that of some powerful institutions such as the Food and Agriculture Organization of the United Nations.

Because these changes result in part from the constant work and efforts of small farmers, peasants, and food activists, the editors of this collection have turned their attention to the links between food, globalization, and politics. For Peter Andrée and Marie-Josée Massicotte, this project is a direct result of their research in the field and scholarship on peasant politics and food movements as well as the commitments they hold in their lives. For Jeffrey Ayres and Michael J. Bosia, this volume is as much a product of the commitments in their families and communities in the small state of Vermont, with both of their spouses directly involved in local farming and production, as it is a reflection of their own interest in social justice and responses among social movements to global forces. Therefore, we owe our greatest debt to the many local activists and movements involved in food struggles in the North and South, some of whom have been essential sources of analysis, inspiration, and information through exchanges and interviews, for deepening our understanding of the complexities of today's food debates in different parts of the world.

In addition, this volume has been an interestingly evolving and growing collaboration. It began with a panel organized by Ayres and Bosia at the International Studies Association annual meeting in San Francisco in 2008, continued through a short course at the American Political Science Association meeting in Toronto in 2009, where Andrée and Massicotte joined the editorial team and where many of the contributors became more directly involved, and evolved with a panel sequence at the Canadian Political Science Association conference in Montreal in 2010. During this discussion, revision, and healthy intellectual exchange, we have gathered together a thoughtful, innovative, risk-taking, engaged, and provocative set of contributors with strong scholarly credentials. In fact, this is as much a volume by people who conduct research and build theory as it is the collective work of those who care about their world and seek to shape social change.

We also want to thank Daniel Quinlan of the University of Toronto Press for his early enthusiasm and support for this project, for acquiring an advance contract for publication, and for securing excellent anonymous reviewers who provided timely, insightful, and constructive criticism to further strengthen this project's empirical and theoretical contributions. Individually, the editors extend their appreciation to the colleagues, family, and friends who have been so supportive of this project and of our scholarly work and social commitments more generally. The editors also acknowledge individually the support they received for research on this project from their home institutions, including funding for research, conferences, and publication expenses. We gratefully acknowledge that this book has been published with the help of a grant from the Federation for the Humanities and Social Sciences, through the Awards to Scholarly Publications Program, using funds provided by the Social Sciences and Humanities Research Council of Canada.

Finally, the editors wish to thank especially each of the contributors to this volume for their patience in the face of a challenging and changing world, working with us as the process of building this volume has evolved over these past several years. With the opportunity to connect at conferences during the writing and review, the authors have had a chance to meet, share ideas, and exchange drafts of chapters that improved the scope of the work and advanced the dialogue, helping to cement a more theoretically and thematically coherent book. The result is a collection that is as much an internal discussion as it is a conversation with the world of activists and academics beyond our pages. This patient collaboration has provided us with a rich and broad coverage of the politics of food in a period of economic uncertainty, heightened political contestation, and intense debate over what can or should be done to improve agricultural practices, and to promote more just and sustainable food systems in different environs.

GLOBALIZATION AND FOOD SOVEREIGNTY

Global and Local Change in the New Politics of Food

Introduction: Crisis and Contention in the New Politics of Food

PETER ANDRÉE, JEFFREY AYRES, MICHAEL J. BOSIA,
AND MARIE-JOSÉE MASSICOTTE

The evidence speaks for itself. If we turn to the world as a source of nutrition, we see the glaring paradox brought about by a globalizing food system that arose in the industrial and scientific transformation of food production in Europe and the United States and was then exported first to the most proximate agricultural economies, and in the past three decades, carried through a series of structural reforms to every region of the global South. The paradox is evident in a context of increasing food production and access to affordable food for many, especially in urban areas, that has brought land grabs and dislocations, hunger and food shortages, obesity, food contamination, and environmental impacts that threaten the very resources upon which that food production depends. This volume focuses on responses to these paradoxical crises, in which peasants and farmers, consumers and activists, and other social movement and economic actors are coalescing around a toolkit of participatory actions that are variously called "food sovereignty" or "food democracy."

We take the position that the geographically diverse food crises are interrelated and that they can be tied to McMichael's concept of a "globalizing food regime" (McMichael 2011, 805). This view emphasizes the intensification and expansion across borders of the industrial model of agriculture based on capital-intensive equipment, energy-intensive inputs of fertilizers, pesticides, water, and seeds, and favouring large-scale production, often oriented towards export markets. Through increasingly concentrated and integrated processes from local producers to state regulations, large food conglomerates, and global distribution chains, this regime is the product of the historic and ongoing transformation of agriculture in Europe and North America, now dominated by a tiny number of major corporations in the seed, food processing, and distribution sectors. It is this globalizing food regime of production and distribution that these crises reveal as intensely problematic.

Notably, McMichael's concept also emphasizes that this food regime emerged in the context of specific local needs, interests, and pressures, which have diffused across borders and localities; our "globalizing" regime continues to rely heavily on local agency, ecologies, and practices. In other words, as a "globalized localism" (Santos 2006) resulting from the concentrating tendencies of capitalism as well as a range of policies enacted domestically, and then diffusing internationally in recent decades, the globalizing food regime increasingly shapes the transformation of local practices in economic, political, and scientific terms through "localized globalism."

This way of understanding the multiple crises of the global agricultural and food system, and their rootedness in specific local dynamics, suggests the need for researchers to examine how concretely the globalizing food regime is adopted, adapted, or resisted in multiple ways, and with what kinds of impacts. Indeed, globalization, competition, and inclusion for some translate into localization, dispossession, and exclusion for others. As a result, these are contested processes, and small-scale or subsistence farmers are far from disappearing. In fact, some authors (see Douwe van der Ploeg 2010; Schneider and Niederle 2010) examine the resurgence of a new peasantry, or re-peasantization, and attempts to remove food from the commodity system, and the consolidation of alternative, mostly local and regional, markets for small-scale food producers. The chapters in this volume engage the contemporary food system as the authors, following Gibson-Graham (2006), acknowledge and explore some of the multiple alternative practices happening below and beyond monetarized capitalist circuits that are often essential to sustain today's market economy.

The following chapters emphasize the way that sovereignty – expressed as control, autonomy, democratic participation, and agency – has become a challenge to and an organizing principle for individuals and communities, as well as some states, responding to the crises outlined below of the globalizing food regime in the opening decades of the twenty-first century. Our goals are fourfold: first, to emphasize the importance of the critical study of food as a *political* issue that addresses both global and local power dynamics for academics and activists; second, to bring to a political science audience the emerging discussion about food sovereignty and food democracy as alternatives to neoliberal models of agricultural production and food distribution;[1] third, to examine, through detailed case studies, how actors are organizing themselves in relation to the principles of food sovereignty and food democracy in various parts of the world; and finally, to discuss some of the main challenges and opportunities faced by these actors, both North and South, in their struggles for more just, democratic, and ecologically sound models of agricultural development and food system governance. In short, this volume explores the multilayered and more nuanced approach to reclaiming sovereignty in the face of global agribusiness, as emerging movements build bridges between local action and global norms, and between disciplines, theories, and approaches as well as scholarship and activism.

Global Food Crises

From October 2007 to early 2008, the news media reported widespread global anxiety and protests over speculation, rising costs, and declining availability of food. Locales as diverse as suburban Sam's Clubs and Costcos in Southern California, the slums of Port-au-Prince, Haiti, rural Uzbekistan, and cities in West Bengal, Italy, Mexico, Pakistan and Afghanistan, witnessed looting and hoarding sparked by fears of food shortages and soaring prices (McMichael 2009). The skyrocketing grain prices were the outcome of a complex set of intermediate factors predicated on states' adoption of agricultural trade liberalization and the commodification of globalizing, yet locally grounded food production. Price increases were also nurtured by mounting perceptions of upcoming scarcities (fertile land, food, and energy in particular), financial speculation related to the rapid growth of ethanol production as an alternative market for food crops like corn and sugar cane, and wild trading in oil futures in late 2007 (Conceição and Mendoza 2009; Lang 2010; Clapp and Cohen 2009). Observers were moved to describe the "tsunami of need" (Heffern 2008) sweeping across the world, arguing that emerging global food shortages threatened to become one of the new security dilemmas of the twenty-first century. These events also drew the world's attention back to the longer-term trends of hunger and malnutrition. Of course, recent evidence indicates that global climate change will disrupt production, increasing shortages and driving up food costs (Gillis 2011). While a focus on climate change is beyond the scope of this volume, the tensions between the globalizing food regime and food sovereignty movements that will be exacerbated by climate change and the responses to it figure in many chapters.

Despite innovations in technologies and the development of a globalizing food production and distribution system over the last forty years, the United Nations (UN) continues to estimate that over 850 million people – approximately 13 per cent of the world's population – are chronically undernourished and lack enough daily food to sustain a minimally healthy life (Devereux 2006; Haque 2009). With voluntary contributions reduced by a developed world still ensnared in the financial crisis – support for the World Food Programme in 2009 hit a twenty-year low (Vidal 2009; Clapp 2012) – estimates are that the chronically hungry surpassed the one billion mark in 2010. North Korea, Mongolia, Guatemala, Haiti, and wide stretches of East Africa are some of the states and regions suffering the worst from chronic food shortages, with humanitarian crises only expected to worsen into 2015, the year the UN Millennium Development Goals had targeted a 50 per cent reduction in the number of hungry people globally. Thanks to policies that do not directly challenge the political and economic reasons for continued hunger in a world of plenty, this goal is unlikely to be reached.

Meanwhile, growing meat consumption, agro-fuel production, the damaging effects of many forms of modern agriculture and fishing, and a changing climate all appear to be exacerbating the crisis of food access for the poorest of the world. While most analysts agree that farmers and fishers still produce more than enough calories to feed every human being (e.g., Nellemann et al. 2009), future global food security is less certain. Causes include the fact that rich people tend to eat more animal-based protein such as meat, eggs, fish, and cheese, and populations around the world are growing in their levels of wealth. In China, for example, protein demand per person grew by a factor of ten between 1975 and 2005 (though still little more than a third of U.S. protein consumption per person) (Food and Agriculture Organization 2007). The consumption of animal protein places intense pressures on the land that grows the crops to feed these animals.

More emphasis on the use of land to produce agro-fuels may also put future food access in jeopardy. In late 2007, financial speculation about the rapid growth of ethanol as an alternative market for food crops like corn and sugar cane, wild trading in oil futures, and a turn to commodities to hedge against the emerging global financial crisis helped to send the price of staple food grains through the roof (Conceição and Mendoza 2009; Lang 2010; Clapp and Cohen 2009). In terms of resource capacity,

Lester Brown's work (e.g., 2005) has demonstrated over many years that the land and oceans relied on to produce our food are limited, and that a variety of factors associated with industrial agricultural production are placing severe strains on this land and water, despite the fact that these same models have also made food production more efficient, per unit of land (Surgeoner 1990). Soil erosion and water depletion in China and Africa may undermine food production in those regions, for example, while the rapid exhaustion of global fish populations threatens this crucial source of protein for much of the world. We are now also starting to see the effects of global climate change on crop productivity – with the Australian drought of the 2000s that cut its wheat supply to the world in half over several years in a row, and the heat wave that hit the U.S. Midwest in the summer of 2012 that severely damaged its corn crop – threatening to be a sign of things to come.

Among food consumers, what is being called a growing epidemic – a word normally reserved to describe widespread outbreaks of infectious disease – is raising concerns as childhood and adult obesity rates soar, causing numerous long-term medical complications, shortening lifespans, and adding to already overstressed national health-care budgets. We have truly become a world both "stuffed" and "starved," to borrow the title from Raj Patel's incisive 2008 book. According to a 2000 study by the Centers for Disease Control and Prevention (CDC), the number of overweight children tripled in the United States between 1980 and 2000, while the number of obese adults has increased by 50 per cent (Centers for Disease Control Foundation 2009). A recent study by a health economist at Duke University, moreover, suggested that over 42 per cent of adults in the United States will be obese by 2030 (Healy 2012). Changes in food processing over the past decades, including the dramatic increase in the amount of sugar in diets, combined with a still powerful food industry lobby in Washington, DC, and food industry advertising (Nestle 2007), have created what has been called a "toxic environment" for children and adults increasingly susceptible to debilitating diseases such as heart attacks and type 2 diabetes (Brown 2006). First Lady Michelle Obama has even made battling childhood obesity in the United States her signature cause. In February 2009, she launched a new initiative designed to reverse the obesity trends in the United States, while British chef Jamie Oliver brought his healthy eating "food revolution" television series to the United States' most obese city in West Virginia. Yet, dramatically, the high-calorie, low-fibre diet characteristic of the burgers and soda fast food lifestyle embraced for decades is no longer restricted to the developed world. The World Health Organization now reports that obesity rates are increasing at a faster rate in the developing world than the developed, with "globalization and modernization" major culprits in this spreading crisis (Sinha 2010).

Moreover, concerns over the growing connections between long-term obesity and chronic health problems have been matched in recent years by acute fears over the seemingly inexhaustible supply of tainted food products in diets around the world. North Americans, for example, could be forgiven for losing track of the number of food scares and recalls in recent years, as a wide variety of tainted foods have been implicated in sickness and death. Canadians experienced a crisis of confidence in pre-cooked deli meats in the summer of 2009, when a listeria outbreak at one of Canada's largest meat packers, a Maple Leaf plant in Toronto, led to twenty-three deaths coupled with a massive product recall (Canada, Agriculture and Agrifood Canada 2009). Meanwhile, U.S. Department of Agriculture Food Safety and Inspection Service has issued food recalls in a majority of U.S. states for salmonella outbreaks in products as diverse as tomatoes, spinach, peanut butter, pistachios, ground beef, pretzels, potato chips, black pepper, seafood sauce, and vegetable dip (Walsh 2009). After U.S. pet owners began to witness the sudden and mysterious deaths of their cats and dogs, the U.S. Food and Drug Administration issued a major pet food recall in the spring of 2007, implicating melamine – an industrial chemical used to manufacture fertilizers and plastics – as a pollutant that had tainted food additives in pet food produced and exported from China (Food and Drug Administration 2007). The following year in China hundreds of thousands of infants and children were sickened, with some deaths resulting from melamine-contaminated milk and infant formula, which caused kidney damage, highlighted extensive political corruption, and promoted public anger and unrest over the questionable safety of China's food industry and lack of quality control (Branigan 2008). Finally, an especially virulent antibiotic-resistant strain of E. coli swept across Europe in the spring of 2011 – the deadliest on record – raising greater concerns of potential global spread of this bacterium, and once again raised doubts about the safety of the food supply in even the most industrialized of states with purportedly strict food safety regulations (Benedict 2011; Kristof 2011).

Beneath these immediate food scares lay deeper public concerns with modern industrialized methods of food production and processing, including the use of pesticides, genetically modified organisms, and food irradiation. These issues are reshaping markets and the public policy landscape. Consider the food scare in the United Kingdom associated with bovine spongiform encephalopathy (BSE), a brain-wasting disease in cattle that caused at least a dozen people to contract the disease's human equivalent (Creutzfeldt-Jacob disease) in the early 1990s (Levidow 1999). That outbreak of BSE (controlled only after the slaughter and incineration of 80,000 cows) was eventually traced to the use of animal byproducts such as brains and spinal cords in animal feed. That the BSE problem was exacerbated by the industrial food system, that food safety experts did not predict the problem, and that the UK government denied the ties between BSE and the human deaths, all became critical factors in the widespread European rejection of another set of industrial technologies – genetically modified organisms (GMOs) – only a few years later (Andrée 2007). These and other food scares have created growing concerns over the safety of industrialized food production and processing in general, and raised questions about the efficacy of national food regulatory bodies in the face of huge increases in the trade of food globally.

Among small farmers and peasants, these crises are hardly recent phenomena. The impacts of the adoption of an industrial model of agriculture and trade liberalization have been denounced and felt by rural communities across the world for decades. As a powerful symbol of the plight and difficulties faced by so many small producers, one will remember Lee Kyung Hae, a Korean dairy farmer, who committed suicide outside the meeting of the WTO in Cancun, Mexico, in 2003, calling attention to free trade policies that have driven nearly three million Korean peasants from the land. With the promotion of agro-fuel production and the recent waves of land grabbing,[2] small farmers are regularly pushed off their lands, thus destroying their way of life and destabilizing ecological and social reproduction processes.

Small- and medium-scale farmers in the North have also paid the price of a globalizing food system. In Canada, for example, the federal government has emphasized the goal of trade liberalization over farm stability in most agri-food sectors since the early 1970s, thereby furthering farm and industry consolidation, as well as deepening integration of Canadian farms into the North American industrial "grain-livestock complex" (Friedmann 1992). By the 1990s, some farm activists were likening the changes in agriculture taking place in Canada to the structural adjustment programs in the global South that were putting Southern farmers in such a precarious position (Qualman and Wiebe 2002). This

context is useful to begin to understand the growing number of suicides among farmers worldwide, whether in advanced economies like
Australia (Bryant 2006) or India (Patel 2008).

A new global land grab has further magnified the problems of inequality and democracy in agricultural production. In a 2009 report
Olivier de Schutter, UN special rapporteur on the right to food, states
that over a three year period (2006–9) "between 15 and 20 million hectares of farmland, the equivalent of the total surface of France, have
been subject of negotiations by foreign investors" (De Schutter 2010).
Although this phenomenon is particularly acute in the global South,
the growing tendency among foreign governments and private investors to buy massive surfaces of fertile land has long existed and continues in new ways in the global North. For example, in Quebec and other
regions of Canada, a growing number of Chinese groups and individuals are buying lands from farmers who are willing to sell, often because
of acute financial difficulties or because new generations are uninterested or cannot afford the cost of "modern" large-scale installations. In
such cases, foreign buyers see these as good investments, since the land
remains cheaper than in many other regions of the North, and the political and financial environment is considered a secure one.

In the global South, land grabs already threaten the very survival of
poor rural communities and the food security – defined at a national
level as the ability of a country to feed itself[3] – of entire countries. For
example, in Mauritania, where about 50 per cent of the population still
eke out a living from small-scale agriculture, agribusiness is rushing in
from Saudi Arabia and the United States, among other metropoles.
They are displacing whole communities, often without compensation,
and putting a large proportion of the population in a position of near
famine. These processes, as De Schutter indicates, go directly against
the right to food as part of the human rights obligations of states.
Legally in Mauritania, unoccupied land has been nationalized following Islamic rules – if no property rights are exercised for ten years, the
state becomes owner – but the president can lease it to private investors
and conglomerates who want to exploit the soil, whether they are foreigners or citizens, or if it is for mining exploitation or agricultural production. In the latter case, there certainly is no guarantee, and often
little intention, that the output will provide for domestic consumption,
especially given the climate pressures on food production in countries
like China.

Alternatively, a report produced by the Barcelona-based NGO GRAIN,
a recent article in the *New York Times*, and the 2010 World Bank report

on the subject all noted that some of the arable lands bought by foreigners are in fact left unproductive, which might indicate a more speculative than productive interest. In Mauritania, this situation left many refugees who were pushed out of their own country during the border war with Senegal (1989–91) over grazing rights without any legal status to reclaim the land they used to work and live on. With the growing demand for agro-fuels, analysts also fear that further rural community displacement and dislocation will occur (Holt-Giménez and Shattuck 2010). Arable lands that traditionally served for subsistence farming could become speculating areas as the demand for agro-fuel productions has already begun to transform the main purpose of these lands in the North and in the South, with most land availability and rural vulnerability in sub-Saharan Africa, Latin America, and the Caribbean (World Bank 2010).

Looking Ahead: Plan of the Book

Food sovereignty and food democracy, as emerging and contestable structures of resistance, are clearly unsettled frames. So it is in fact too early to offer a settled definition of a growing movement as divergent as that represented by the producers, processors, and consumers around the world who have taken up these frames to respond to the neoliberal food system. Indeed, as the contributors in this volume demonstrate, movements engage with the contemporary food system through a range of strategies, from outright resistance to adaptation and co-option. Instead of conclusions, we lay the seeds for analysis, presenting the variety of arenas in which the study of food sovereignty and food democracy[4] is gaining relevance to scholars and practitioners.

At the same time, we can introduce the contours for the analysis of food sovereignty, which are interrogated, contested, examined, and applied in the chapters that follow. Broadly, food sovereignty is a set of reactions to neoliberal globalization and the industrial food system that is presented as an alternative approach predicated on the dispersal of power. Neoliberalism valorizes the market as the final arbiter of efficient economic policy, as global and national institutions remove larger and larger policy domains from democratic decision-making, walling off powerful economic actors and industrial forces from popular accountability and local responsibility. Food sovereignty valorizes the reverse – localized, accountable, and democratic economic decision-making – and does so in ways that link local communities as part of regional and global movements. But in its local aspirations, food sovereignty is not the equivalent of a more traditionalist movement like Slow Food, though the emphasis on artisanal production and historic agricultural practice among adherents of the latter is also found in the former, nor of those notions of sovereignty that fetishize the state as the ultimate political actor or system of social protection. Food sovereignty instead recognizes the transformative possibilities of community empowerment in democratic processes of economic and social decision-making. Such transformations might sustain rural life or promote the virtues of historical agricultural patterns, or they might seek to sustain rural life through new rural economies. Moreover, the actors who have articulated or invoked food sovereignty (and food democracy) are a disparate lot: farmers and peasants, consumers and producers, as well as distributors, men and women, young and older, entrepreneurs and subsistence farmers, spanning the globe from South to North. This means that food sovereignty is conceived of and deployed as diverse and fungible.

Part One of the book, "Food Sovereignty in Theory and Policy Debates," examines the politics associated with the term *food sovereignty* as used by actors as varied as consumer activists, transnational social movements, and local farmers. In chapter 1, the editors propose specific conceptual and theoretical insights in an effort to offer useful tools for researchers and to demonstrate the necessity to take food more seriously, as a central issue that cuts across social, political, economic, cultural, and ecological domains, and highlight the growing concerns of citizens across the globe calling for substantial changes. In chapter 2, Michael Menser reflects on the paradox of the global food movement projecting itself outside the realm of the state while embracing sovereignty in defence of a popular right to control food policies. Menser argues that food sovereignty practitioners are redefining the notions of self-determination, territory, non-interference, and autonomy normally associated with the absolutes of the Westphalian state system. After tracing the evolution of the food sovereignty concept along this reconceptualization since 1996, Menser compares models of what he calls state-supported and indigenous food sovereignty and considers the challenges still facing advocates of either food sovereignty approach from class and gender inequities.

In chapter 3, Noah Zerbe presents a study of the global fair trade movement, comparing it to the emerging local food movement. Along the way, his chapter offers a historical overview of the global food system from the Second World War to today. While fair trade should have been seen as a corrective to the conventional agribusiness model, Zerbe argues fair trade is limited in two ways: by the size of its spatial scale of production, and by its dependence on the same system of capitalist-based food production it seeks to challenge. Instead, Zerbe argues that the local food movement's embrace of food sovereignty concerns such as trust and reciprocity can provide an important improvement over the compromised fair trade model.

Chapter 4 also discusses the local food movement, but in this essay the perspective is less hopeful about current directions taken by that movement. Martha McMahon, a sociologist as well as a sheep farmer on Vancouver Island, in British Columbia, considers the twin adoption of localism and "food security" by food activists in that province. As an antidote and political counter to the neoliberal consumer approach to local food as well as the administrative discourse of food security, she argues that food sovereignty is more helpful for constructing an alternative conception of agrarian citizenship. McMahon also examines the detrimental effect of governmental regulation on small farmers, often women, which undermines small-scale husbandry and meat production in favour of large systems, again because food safety fears are construed in ways that devalue small-scale networks of trust, reciprocity, and initiative. Drawing on a feminist analysis to encourage radical democratic engagement between local food movements and farmers, she argues that the local food project needs to be reframed through democratic political alliances between peasant and landless people's movements globally and farmers locally.

Part Two, "Food Sovereignty in Comparative Perspective," presents case studies that highlight how individuals and communities in different regions of the world are engaging in this widening political struggle to move their states and locales closer to a food sovereignty framework. In chapter 5, Peter Andrée explores how emerging alternative food networks in Australia – home to one of the most liberalized agricultural sectors in the world – are challenging environmental degradation caused by conventional food and agricultural supply chains. Considering a variety of production and distribution models – from permaculture, organic farming, farmers' markets, and community-supported agriculture – Andrée argues that a new "citizen-farmer" is emerging who embodies specific aspects of a food sovereignty or food democracy response, one that may have a far-reaching impact on forms of governance and collective goals resistant to conventional food system norms. The spreading appropriation of the food sovereignty perspective in Canada is then explored in chapter 6, where Sarah Martin and Peter Andrée study the rural and urban threads being woven together in the People's Food Policy Project, a collaboration between left-leaning farmers, international solidarity, and community food-security activists. Martin and Andrée point out that while Canada is also at the heart of the neoliberal global food system alongside Australia – as one of the world's leading importers and exporters of agricultural products – the embrace of the food sovereignty discourse by urban food-security activists signifies their increased influence within sites of governance and over the governance of food.

Chapter 7 then analyses the embrace of food sovereignty by a social movement in the global South, where MASIPAG, a small farmer network in the Philippines, has improved the quality of life of poor farmers through a farmer-led sustainable agriculture approach. Sarah Wright sees food sovereignty and farmers rights as promoted by MASIPAG as an explicit challenge to the neoliberal mantra of TINA – There is No Alternative – and as an alternative more broadly to the dominant capitalist agribusiness model. How movements "do" food sovereignty is then illustrated in her analysis through the construction of an economy in this small-farmer network in the Philippines that is socially rooted and place-based in local communities and the soil of the farms.

Finally, in chapter 8, Irena Knezevic underscores the contradiction that has emerged between the European Union's emphasis on international trade and free markets in food policy, which constrains the development of food sovereignty concerns and leaves little opportunity for civic participation in food policy creation. Knezevic, herself a native of the western Balkans, notes that the EU policy of enlargement to include the incorporation of Central and Eastern Europe has included a process of reform heavily influenced by the EU's Common Agricultural Policy, which has reshaped food policy and the food economies and upset the cultural and social fabric of "foodways" across this region. However, Knezevic argues that the "foodscapes" of three hopeful future EU states – the western Balkan counties of Bosnia and Herzegovina, as well as Croatia and Serbia – illustrate the contradictions of the EU's neoliberal project, where a subversive food economy has emerged to reclaim sovereign decision-making over food through individual and collective participation through informal markets.

In Part Three, "Food Sovereignty in Contentious Politics," three contributions assess recent achievements, ongoing campaigns, and limitations to popular movements, which draw upon the food sovereignty frame of reference to challenge the dominant capitalist global agribusiness model. Marie-Josée Massicotte argues in chapter 9 that the food sovereignty frame has been an important component to the alter-globalization movement, and has shaped contentious claims-making by various groups on multiple scales for several decades. Massicotte's analysis draws upon feminist political ecology to link the work of Vía Campesina–Brazil and locally rooted Brazilian peasant organizations in the Landless Rural Workers Movement to the Latin American School of Agro-ecology that supports the implementation of food sovereignty. The transformative potential of food sovereignty is illustrated in two ways in this chapter: as a practical means of democratizing the governance of food "from the ground up" through the actions of Brazilian small farmers, rural women, and peasants; and as an alternative analytical framework for rethinking global governance through food sovereignty as a more inclusive process of practices and norms at multiple scales

Elizabeth Smythe in chapter 10 approaches food sovereignty as a means to reclaim lost sovereignty in connection to food policy and local practices across countries and local communities. Smythe notes that food sovereignty is now resonating within a wider arrangement of organizations and local food activists in non-producer groups in the North, as well as within small-scale food producers in the South. Drawing upon case studies of rules on food labelling in Canada and the United States illustrates how the political struggle over the right to know the origins of food should be seen by activists as part of a larger multi-scalar struggle to achieve food sovereignty.

Chapter 11 revisits the potential and limits to commodity-based models of resistance to the global agribusiness model, building on earlier contributions by Zerbe, Andrée, and McMahon. In this chapter, Jeffrey Ayres and Michael J. Bosia compare how activists in France and the United States have in different ways appropriated the food sovereignty frame by focusing on what they call "re-localization." The authors explore how food sovereignty is articulated in local practices in Larzac, France, and the small U.S. state of Vermont, to reject, secede from, or reform the neoliberal food system, and highlight limitations of both the class-based French peasant movement and the consumer-based local-vore movement in the United States. Finally, Philip McMichael's conclusion reemphasizes the breadth of the food sovereignty concept, noting how the chapters in this volume struggle to extend the "elasticity" of food sovereignty while considering whether it remains linked to its rural agricultural roots. Broadly, McMichael reconnects the chapters to the emphasis placed in chapter 1 on the current contradictions of neoliberal globalization, highlighting the phenomenally contentious character of food politics in our time.

In sum, this volume posits that – given the increasing attention to the politics of food as local, national, and global – it is important to incorporate these new arenas of political action much more widely into curriculums and scholarship and focus especially the framework and methodologies of political science on the profoundly political issues raised by the food sovereignty response. As well, with contributors that bridge the divide between theory and practice, we seek to develop the study of food politics as a more engaged arena within the social sciences, where scholarship is informed by and integrated into the variety of new food movements. At the same time, its appeal is broader than the topic of food, reaching out to include scholars in a variety of domains. Contributors to the volume interrogate the question of food as it relates to institutions of global governance and political economy, transnational and local social movements, democratic practice, and questions of state sovereignty, providing new perspectives on classic debates in political science, international relations, political economy, sociology, as well as anthropology and food-related disciplines. The volume provides a comparative perspective that draws contrasts, parallels, and differences on similar issues from North American, European, Asian, and Latin American perspectives. And finally, the volume addresses the topic of food sovereignty through the diverse participation of scholars and practitioners who provide a range of international perspectives in expertise, theoretical and methodological approach, and case studies. As such, this volume should appeal to instructors, practitioners, scholars, and students alike, who will find it useful to consider the critical perspectives and empirical observations of experts on the dynamics, determinants, and impact of food politics as local, national, and global.

NOTES

1 By drawing on political scientists and political theory, we hope to encourage more political scientists to join this debate. At the same time, the diversity of our authors' academic backgrounds and approaches demonstrates in this volume that the study of food movements as political phenomena must include a variety of social science perspectives.

2 See special issue of the *Journal of Peasant Studies* 37, no. 4 (2010).

3 See Martin and Andrée (this volume) for more analysis of the concept of food security.
4 The democratization of the food system is an integral aspect of the food sovereignty framework, but in the United States the food movement tends to use the language of food democracy instead of food sovereignty.

REFERENCES

Andrée, Peter. 2007. *Genetically Modified Diplomacy*. Vancouver: UBC Press.
Benedict, Jeff. 2011. "The Next Outbreak." *New York Times*, 4 June.
Branigan, T. 2008. "Chinese Figures Show Fivefold Rise in Babies Sick from Contaminated Milk." *Guardian*, 2 December 2008. http://www.guardian.co.uk/world/2008/dec/02/china.
Brown, Lester. 2005. "A Planet under Stress." In Dryzek and Schlosberg 2005, 37–48.
Brown, Phyllis. 2006. "Childhood Obesity Caused by 'Toxic Environment' of Western Diets, Study Says." UCSF News Office. http://www.ucsf.edu/news/2006/08/5459/childhood-obesity-caused-toxic-environment-western-diets-study-says.
Bryant, N. 2006. "Australia Drought Sparks Suicides." *BBC News*, 19 October. http://news.bbc.co.uk/2/hi/asia-pacific/6065220.stm.
– 2012. *Hunger in the Balance: The New Politics of International Food Aid*. Ithaca, NY: Cornell University Press.
Clapp, J., and M.J. Cohen, eds. 2009. *The Global Food Crisis: Governance Challenges and Opportunities*. Waterloo, ON: Wilfrid Laurier University Press.
Conceição, P., and R.U. Mendoza. 2009. "Anatomy of the Global Food Crisis." *Third World Quarterly* 30 (6): 1159–82. http://dx.doi.org/10.1080/01436590903037473.
De Schutter, Olivier. 2010. "Responsibly Destroying the World's Peasantry." Project Syndicate. http://www.project-syndicate.org/commentary/deschutter1/English.
Devereux, Stephen, ed. 2006. *The New Famines: Why Famines Persist in an Era of Globalization*. London: Routledge.
Douwe van der Ploeg, Jan. 2010. "The Peasantries of the Twenty-First Century: The Commoditisation Debate Revisited." *Journal of Peasant Studies* 37 (1): 1–30. http://dx.doi.org/10.1080/03066150903498721.
Dryzek, John S., and David Schlosberg, eds. *Debating the Earth: The Environmental Politics Reader*, 2nd ed. Oxford: Oxford University Press.

Food and Drug Administration. 2007. "Melamine Pet Food Recall of 2007," 15 March. http://www.fda.gov/animalveterinary/safetyhealth/recallswithdrawals/ucm129575.htm.

Friedmann, Harriet. 1992. "Distance and Durability: Shaky Foundations of the World Food Economy." *Third World Quarterly* 13 (2): 371–83. http://dx.doi.org/10.1080/01436599208420282.

Gillis, Justin. 2011. "A Warming Planet Struggles to Feed Itself." *New York Times*, 4 June.

Haque, A.N.M. 2009. "The Hungry Billion," *Daily* Star, 4 December. http://www.thedailystar.net/newDesign/news-details.php?nid=116238.

Healy, Melissa. 2012. "42% of American Adults Will Be Obese by 2030, Study Says," *Los Angeles Times*, 8 May. http://articles.latimes.com/2012/may/08/health/la-he-obesity-20120508.

Heffern, Rich. 2008. "Food Riots Underscore 'Tsunami of Need.'" *National Catholic Reporter* 2 May. http://ncronline.org/.

Kristof, Nicholas D. 2011. "When Food Kills." *New York Times*, 11 June. http://www.nytimes.com/2011/06/12/opinion/12kristof.html.

Lang, T. 2010. "Crisis? What Crisis? The Normality of the Current Food Crisis." *Journal of Agrarian Change* 10 (1): 87–97. http://dx.doi.org/10.1111/j.1471-0366.2009.00250.x.

Levidow, Les. 1999. "Blocking Biotechnology as Pollution: Political Cultures in the UK Risk Controversy." Paper presented at "Alternate Futures and Popular Protest" conference, Manchester Metropolitan University, 29–31 March 1999. Centre for Technology Strategy: Open University, Milton Keynes, UK.

McMichael, Philip. 2009. "The World Food Crisis in Historical Perspective." *Monthly Review* 61 (3): 32–47.

– 2011. "Food System Sustainability: Questions of Environmental Governance in the New World (Dis)order." *Global Environmental Change* 21 (3): 804–12. http://dx.doi.org/10.1016/j.gloenvcha.2011.03.016.

Nellemann, C., M. MacDevette, T. Manders, B. Eickhout, B. Svihus, A.G. Prins, and B.P. Kaltenborn, eds. 2009. *The Environmental Food Crisis: The Environment's Role in Averting Future Food Crises.* GRID-Arendal. http://www.grida.no/publications/rr/food-crisis/.

Nestle, Marion. 2007. *Food Politics.* Santa Cruz: University of California Press.

Patel, Raj. 2008. *Stuffed and Starved.* Toronto: Harper Collins.

Qualman, D., and N. Wiebe. 2002. *The Structural Adjustment of Canadian Agriculture.* Ottawa: Canadian Centre for Policy Alternatives.

Santos, Boaventura de Sousa. 2006. *The Rise of the Global Left: The World Social Forum and Beyond.* New York: Zed Books.

GLOBALIZATION AND FOOD SOVEREIGNTY: GLOBAL AND
LOCAL CHANGE IN THE NEW POLITICS OF FOOD; ED. BY
PETER ANDREE.   Paper   376 P.
TORONTO: UNIV OF TORONTO PRESS, 2014
SER: STUDIES IN COMPARATIVE POLITICAL ECONOMY
AND PUBLIC POLICY; 42.
ED: CARLETON UNIVERSITY. NEW COLLECTION COMPARES
FOOD SOVEREIGNTY WORLDWIDE.

   ISBN 1442612282   **Library PO#** GENERAL APPROVAL

	List	34.95 USD
5461 UNIV OF TEXAS/SAN ANTONIO	**Disc**	10.0%
App. Date 4/16/14 GLO.APR 6108-11	**Net**	31.46 USD

SUBJ: 1. FOOD SOVEREIGNTY. 2. AGRICULTURE--ECON.
ASPECTS. 3. GLOBALIZATION.

CLASS HD9000.5   DEWEY# 338.19   LEVEL GEN-AC

YBP Library Services

GLOBALIZATION AND FOOD SOVEREIGNTY: GLOBAL AND
LOCAL CHANGE IN THE NEW POLITICS OF FOOD; ED. BY
PETER ANDREE.   Paper   376 P.
TORONTO: UNIV OF TORONTO PRESS, 2014
SER: STUDIES IN COMPARATIVE POLITICAL ECONOMY
AND PUBLIC POLICY; 42.
ED: CARLETON UNIVERSITY. NEW COLLECTION COMPARES
FOOD SOVEREIGNTY WORLDWIDE.

   ISBN 1442612282   **Library PO#** GENERAL APPROVAL

	List	34.95 USD
5461 UNIV OF TEXAS/SAN ANTONIO	**Disc**	10.0%
App. Date 4/16/14 CLO.APR 6108-11	**Net**	31.46 USD

SUBJ: 1. FOOD SOVEREIGNTY. 2. AGRICULTURE--ECON.
ASPECTS. 3. GLOBALIZATION.

CLASS HD9000.5   DEWEY# 338.19   LEVEL GEN-AC

Schneider, Sergio, and Paulo André Niederle. 2010. "Resistance Strategies and Diversification of Rural Livelihoods: The Construction of Autonomy among Brazilian Family Farmers." *Journal of Peasant Studies* 37 (2): 379–405. http://dx.doi.org/10.1080/03066151003595168.

Sinha, Vidushi. 2010. "Childhood Obesity Epidemic." *Voice of America News*, 27 February. http://www.voanews.com/lao/2010-02-27-voa1.cfm.

Vidal, John. 2009. "Millions Will Starve as Rich Nations Cut Food Aid Funding, Warns UN." *Guardian*, 11 October. http://www.guardian.co.uk/environment/2009/oct/11/millions-starvation-food-aid-cuts.

Walsh, Bryan. 2009. "The Real Cost of Cheap Food." *Time*, 31 August.

World Bank. 2010. *Rising Global Interest in Farmland: Can It Yield Sustainable and Equitable Benefits?* World Bank. http://siteresources.worldbank.org/INTARD/Resources/ESW_Sept7_final_final.pdf.

PART ONE

Food Sovereignty in Theory and Policy Debates

1 Food Sovereignty and Globalization: Lines of Inquiry

PETER ANDRÉE, JEFFREY AYRES, MICHAEL J. BOSIA,
AND MARIE-JOSÉE MASSICOTTE

Introduction

Our approach to food sovereignty as a response among producers and consumers to the global food crises draws on the theoretical traditions of critical political economy, contentious politics, comparative politics, feminist and critical analysis, and the social studies of science. In this chapter, we introduce our views on food sovereignty and food democracy and how these constructs challenge the conventional, globalizing food regime. We then propose four main lines of inquiry, or theoretical lenses, to carry forward into the case studies of this book. The first examines food politics through the lens of neoliberalism, looking at how neoliberalism has shaped the dominant food system and set the context for (and sometimes even defined the content of) resistance. The second line of inquiry adopts the lens of social movement analysis, focusing on the structures, practices, and ideologies of food movements that seek both to resist this neoliberal hegemony and to build an alternative present.

Our third unpacks these food movements further through the concept of "protectionism," not as understood by the World Trade Organization and its acolytes, but rather as forwarded by Polanyi (1957) and his followers when they speak of society trying to protect itself from a too-powerful market. Fourth, we explore food politics through the lens of knowledge as power, to show how the globalizing food system continues to rely on specific assumptions about whose views matter – those of the Western scientist – despite some of its efforts to apparently become more progressive and inclusive. Though each of these lines intersect in the chapters that follow, a fifth area of broad concern is embedded within each thread, as race and indigeneity, gender and class are also key sites of inquiry within neoliberal strategies and resistance, social movements, the prioritization of social over purely economic relations, and power and knowledge.

The Politics of Food Sovereignty and Food Democracy

To the authors of this volume, the vignettes highlighted in the introduction sketch the contours of distinct and yet intertwined crises resulting from an increasingly complex, industrialized, globalizing, and arguably under-regulated food-production, processing, and distribution system. How, as political scientists, should we unpack them? One approach would be to examine these issues from the point of view of the state and key industry actors, and how they respond to (or help to create) these crises (e.g., Clapp 2012; Nestle 2007; Higgins and Lawrence 2005; Winson 1993). A U.K. study found that the state intervened to regulate the food supply chain at least 150 times between the seed and the dinner plate (Lange, Barling, and Caraher 2009). While this level of intervention is certainly not universal, it does suggest that a focus on the role of the state continues to have value, and some contributors to this book do adopt the state as their starting point. In her chapter, for example, Irena Knezevic begins by looking at the way that harmonization with the EU's Common Agricultural Policy (CAP) has reshaped the food economy of countries in the western Balkans. On the whole, however, most authors in this volume start from a different position, rooted in the assumption that to make sense of contemporary food crises we need to challenge our discipline to think more broadly. Even Knezevic follows this alternative route, in fact, as her chapter shifts to examining the resistance movements that are emerging in the Balkans to counter the hegemony of the CAP.

This broader approach starts by recognizing that the more recently publicized conflicts over food are part of capitalist development and contradictions spanning decades, if not centuries, increasingly expressed through the corporatization of agriculture production under neoliberal globalization (Holt-Giménez 2009; McMichael 2009a, 2009b). Building on the classic works of Fernand Braudel, Karl Polanyi, and René Dumont, among others, on the historical development of agriculture and capitalism, we focus here on situating today's food crises within the trend of the last thirty years towards a neoliberal model of agricultural development and globalization. We then look at how resistance to this model has resulted in the emergence of new actors, mobilizations, and food politics in specific locales around the world. We are particularly interested in local, national, and global social movements promoting "food sovereignty," or "food democracy" as the concept is often characterized among activists in the United States.

Food sovereignty, much like the state in the era before neoliberal globalization, is not a universal monolith constituted through similar norms and practices. In fact, food sovereignty has a variety of manifestations that have sought to challenge multinational corporations and global agribusiness processes on multiple levels in pursuit of more decentralized conceptions of sovereignty. While food sovereignty encourages a rights-based approach to international negotiations and dialogue among agricultural actors, it is also explicitly about practices, as sovereignty can be claimed only by those who take their own responsibility for its enactment.

Constantly under scrutiny and open to discussion and redefinition, the concept of food sovereignty emerged in 1996, from a working group of La Vía Campesina – the largest transnational movement of peasant and farmer organizations, to be discussed in subsequent chapters – in order to oppose the neoliberal model of "monocultures" and agribusinesses, and to call for alternatives responding to the agrarian crisis and the needs of small food producers (Nicholson, in McMichael 2011, 80). As it became the main rallying cry of La Vía Campesina, and as it began to be appropriated by other groups and allies, the campaign for food sovereignty increasingly united disparate individuals, localities, and groups that contest the lack of democratic control over their food systems, whether peasants fighting for their rights to grow food sustainably on small plots of land, or consumers fighting for the rights of all to eat sufficient, safe, and healthy food.

McMichael highlights the central elements of food sovereignty, quoting Paul Nicholson, a founding member and leader of La Vía Campesina: "We propose local food markets, the right of any country to protect its borders from imported food, sustainable agriculture and the defence of biodiversity, healthy food, jobs and strong livelihood in rural areas" (McMichael 2011, 806).

When we dig into the details and various usages of the concept, we begin to see different priorities among actors in the campaign for food sovereignty. As the chapters in this volume will elaborate, for some, food sovereignty requires first and foremost stronger and better state regulation over food and agriculture. For others, it is mostly a normative tool and discourse to denounce the impacts of neoliberal policies and of the WTO Agreement on Agriculture on small food producers. For some activists, food sovereignty means community, or even personal, control over their food systems. This position is then connected to the promotion of "buy local," organics, and farmers' markets, often without questioning the capitalist structures of these alternative food networks. For still others, food sovereignty represents a right to be defended and respected, a right to alternative agricultural policies and practices, based on a diversified and sustainable production, as well as social reproduction and ecosystem maintenance (e.g., a right to practise "agroecology" – see Massicotte, this volume) in order to guarantee a healthy life for both rural and urban communities, in the global North and the global South.

These approaches demand an accounting from feminist, postcolonial, and subaltern analyses, calling greater attention within the study of political economies to the agency of marginalized actors as they respond in their own terms and through local strategies to the challenges that globalization has imposed on them. Indeed, food sovereignty often aligns with movements advocating women's empowerment, feminist models of co-production and ecology, and women's knowledge alongside indigenous empowerment and knowledges, as intrinsic to the processes of decision-making for the constitution of sustainable rural communities (Patel 2010). This dimension of food sovereignty broadens claims to rights and expertise beyond the confines of Western norms. At the same time, indigenous nations and peasant movements might not align on the invocation of the geographic nation state as a defence against the neoliberal food system, for example (see Menser, this volume), while class differences remain evident in rates of land ownership within and across communities, and limited access to land ownership and nutrition disadvantages women within households and communities. Such critical analyses (see Fraser 2005) would point to the risks of a strategy that merely affirms rural life without considering the transformations necessary for real empowerment and social justice.

Alongside food sovereignty, we also see increasing calls for "food democracy," a closely related concept. Lang and Heasman (2004) define food democracy as a more inclusive approach to food policy making: "Its ethos is 'bottom-up,' considering the diversity of views and interests in the mass of the population and food supply chain; the needs of the many are favoured over the needs of the few; mutuality and symbiosis are pursued" (279). They contrast food democracy with the "food control" of the few (multinational companies) that currently control global supply chains (279). Building on Lang's work, Alexandria Fisher (2010) of the non-governmental organization Food First in San Francisco sees food democracy as "a right and responsibility of citizens to participate in decisions concerning their food system." She explicitly distinguishes food democracy from the "'vote with your fork' ideology (a prevalent position in the US food movement) which does *not* provide a democratic way to change the food system," since that ideology "means the more money you have – and spend on food – the more votes you have" (1). Fisher's clarification points to an important tension in the food movements of industrialized countries. That she has to explain that food democracy is not the same as the control that consumers have in defining their food systems by their purchasing habits points to the power of the latter point of view, and to the debate between those who advocate for *political* solutions (e.g., most who associate themselves with food sovereignty and food democracy as movements) and those who feel that market-based solutions (as represented by the organic industry and fair trade) can or will help achieve more sustainable and just food systems (see Andrée, this volume).

Another point of tension, this time between the idea of food "democracy" and food "sovereignty," is also important to recognize. In many countries, farmers are the minority, and consumers (which include all of us) a strong majority. This is especially true in advanced industrialized countries, where farmers make up only 1–2 per cent of the population. While La Vía Campesina has been reaching out to consumer organizations in its bid to develop a unified stance on food sovereignty between producers and consumers in recent years (see chapters 1 and 13 in Wittman, Desmarais, and Wiebe 2010), these two class perspectives do not easily see eye to eye, making it more difficult to develop a shared position on what "democratic" food policy means in any given context. Food sovereignty activists – at least those associated with La Vía Campesina – are still generally rooted most strongly in a producer perspective, given the origins of the movement, while food democracy advocates are more likely to be as (or even more) preoccupied with consumer concerns about the dominant food system.[1]

Despite their diversity, both food sovereignty and food democracy clearly challenge the basic conditions sustaining today's dominant food regime. Furthermore, as McMichael aptly points out, all the tenets of food sovereignty agree (and food democracy advocates likely would too) on the need for flexibility, to allow various organizations and citizens groups to adapt the principles of food sovereignty to fight for adequate "agricultural, labour, fishing, food and land policies [and practices] which are ecologically, socially, economically and culturally appropriate" (NGO / CSO Forum for Food Sovereignty, quoted in McMichael 2011, 806) to their context. Over time, interactions between food activists from within the same region or organization, as well as from outside, may lead to changes in priorities and vision of what food sovereignty means, and how it should be implemented to consolidate other, more just, democratic and ecological models of agricultural development and governance. Given this diversity, this volume explores what food sovereignty, or food democracy, is coming to mean in various contexts around the world.

The Political Science of Food

Why take on this subject in the context of political science? Perhaps it is because there is nothing more banal than food, a basic ingredient of life. Seen as quintessentially part of the "private" and not "public" sphere, the politics of the cultivation, distribution, and consumption of food have been largely ignored by political scientists. It is true that questions of agricultural policy might receive attention, and the work of peasants in revolutionary and political processes is a source of persistent controversy, despite Marx's claim that they were nothing more than a "sack of potatoes" (Marx 1963; Moore 1966; Skocpol 1979; Wood 2003). But even after Levi-Strauss equated cooking with culture (Levi-Strauss 1966), and post-structuralist as well as materialist perspectives have refocused attention on the politics of the quotidian and "everyday acts of resistance" (Scott 1985), political science has largely failed to theorize the political aspects of food. The ignorance of political scientists about food as a question of power and contention might be indicative of a crisis in the discipline and in our understanding of the political world, just as the variety of crises evident in the contemporary experience of food are indicative of the tensions and tragedies of today's production and distribution systems.

   This disregard for food as a focus of study and for the peasant as a political and social agent compounds the marginalization of scholarship on gender and social power, especially in terms of women who are central to rural life and to the production and consumption of food. It reinforces the invisibility of women and women's claims in policy strategies directed at rural communities, but also neglects the intersection of gender with race and class analysis. We see, for example, parallels between capitalism's devaluation of women's household work as unproductive from the nineteenth century on – because goods were not produced for market (Folbre 1991) – with both the devaluation of subsistence farming and household economies today. If what counts as work must produce for sale on the market, then both "women's work" within households in terms of food production and peasants' work that is bounded by households and communities cannot be demonstrably integrated in the neoliberal food system. This has been a significant problem in international considerations of economic production when UN standards exclude householding (Waring 1988). Moreover, as neoliberal designs equate citizenship and participation with labour and productive capacity, women peasants and farmers might be excluded from decision-making if their labour is not counted as productive (Pateman 1998). By placing the politics of food on the political science agenda, we are thus also prioritizing the study of those avenues open to women and peasants in agriculture and food production that provide opportunities for capacity building and the development of sustainable rural economies.

Granted, there are analysts who argue that the crises discussed throughout this volume simply reflect the price of progress, or are small problems on the surface of a globalized production and distribution system that is, on the whole, enormously productive and feeding billions of people reasonably well every day. On the issue of land grabs, for example, as countries continue to industrialize, peasants move to the cities and their land is bought or leased by others with the capital to invest in more machinery. This is how Europe developed, in broad strokes. Now the rest of the world is following suit, even if it is a messy and contentious process. Further, the biophysical issues of soil erosion and toxins in food can be solved from within the globalizing food system, with better technology or tighter supply-chain regulation, rather than through the more dramatic rethinking of the model as embodied in phrases like *food sovereignty* and *food democracy*. Dennis Avery (2000) is a strong proponent of this view, arguing that it is high-yield farming (and its reliance on agricultural chemicals, factory farming, and biotechnology), along with trade liberalization, that will both feed the world and "save" the environment.

More moderate than Avery in their views, Paul Collier (2008) and Robert Paarlberg (2010, 2008) are also advocates for *more* of the globalizing industrial food system as an answer to global food challenges, if perhaps a somewhat kinder and gentler version. In his 2008 essay in

Foreign Affairs on the food price spikes of earlier that year, Collier argued that it was three forms of "romantic populism" – a love affair with peasant agriculture, a fear of scientific agriculture, and the desire for U.S. energy independence (which is fuelling the biofuel boom in that country) – that stand in the way of ensuring global food security in an era of rising food prices. A response to Collier's argument is warranted here, both for dispelling the assumptions of those who would tend to side with Collier, and for establishing the need for an alternative approach to the problems he contends with, as undertaken by the authors of this volume.[2]

For Collier, the primary culprits of those price spikes were gradually increasing demand for high-protein food in Asia, combined with supply shocks such as the drought in Australia. While most economists agreed that these factors have affected the longer-term trends in the price of food, missing in Collier's account were the declining value of the U.S. dollar over 2007 and early 2008, a concomitant increase in commodity prices, and growing speculation by large commercial banks on agricultural commodities futures markets (encouraged by regulatory loopholes opened in recent years), which bid up prices sharply. The financial collapse in subsequent months burst the commodity-price bubble, as financial institutions scrambled to liquidate their assets, suggesting that the food price volatility of 2008 was much more a product of financial instability and speculation than changes in supply and demand for food.

Collier's first two proposals for reducing food prices – dropping U.S. biofuel subsidies and increasing GMO agriculture – were presented in his essay as politically appealing because of the way they would balance the interests of Europeans (in seeing the United States drop its biofuel subsidies) and the United States (in seeing the EU open its doors to GMOs). However, in our view, policy prescriptions need to be based on more than just political appeal. On the issue of biofuels, OECD and World Bank reports have confirmed that the rise of these fuels has had a major impact on food prices, so we strongly agree that biofuel subsidies should be re-examined. The impact of growing biofuel production on both food prices and the land-grabbing trend demand it. On the potentially positive role of GM crops, however, the available data simply do not show the productivity benefits that Collier asserts. The only real evidence that Collier provides, on the decline in EU productivity since 1996 (when North American farmers started using GM technologies) was insufficient to back his claim, given the range of factors that affect productivity in the EU.

Furthermore, the GM path entails multiple and significant impacts that Collier did not consider, including new intellectual property rights regimes that raise significant concerns for farmers both in the North and the South, as well as a new technological treadmill that will always require farmers to adopt new seed varieties (often alongside chemical applications) as pests and weeds develop resistance to the ones they used last year. Collier did not consider either the potential impacts of a reduction of biodiversity for human and ecosystem health and maintenance, or the diminishing autonomy and control of producers and consumers in choosing what and how they produce and what ends up on their dinner plates – all fundamental efforts to build food sovereignty. It is these issues with GM technologies and others that led the authors of the International Assessment of Agricultural Knowledge, Science and Technology for Development – a report backed by governments around the world, with the exception of the United States, Canada, and Australia – to be highly cautious in how they described the potential benefits and risks of agricultural biotechnology (see IAASTD 2009). Despite Collier's optimism, a more careful study of these technologies, and continued maintenance of the traditional farming systems that they are rapidly displacing in many parts of the world, is clearly in order.

Collier's (2008) third proposed solution was to enhance the role of "commercial" agriculture in the global South. Unfortunately, it is well documented that the results of the first green revolution in Latin America and Asia (in the 1960s) – while positive in immediate productivity gains for certain crops – came at significant environmental and human health costs, forced millions of people from the land, and is ultimately unsustainable because of its dependence on high levels of fossil fuel–derived inputs. It is for this reason that the International Assessment of Agricultural Knowledge, Science and Technology for Development report noted the need for sustainable agriculture that achieves economies of scale, but also recognized the positive role that small-holder agriculture can play in realizing global food security and combating climate change. Collier's advocacy for commercial agriculture simply ignores the complexity of these issues and the importance of defining a range of productive models that suit local contexts around the world.

One of Collier's most problematic statements – one that we reiterate here because it appears to be the unspoken assumption of those who uncritically accept the globalizing food system as a "solution" – is that "there need be no logical connection between the causes of a problem and appropriate or even just feasible solutions to it" (2008, 68). While efforts to be pragmatic are to be applauded, we believe that it is important to start from the position that the root causes of the food price spikes, along with the root causes of peasant dislocation and toxins in foods, must indeed be unpacked if we are going to avoid repeating these problems in a future that will be only more resource-constrained. Merely cranking up agricultural production without concern for its broader ecological and social consequences will not solve the food crisis, and definitely not in a way that also addresses the exigencies of justice and sustainability. It appears as if Collier and others who would side with him are substituting one romantic vision with another.

This volume starts with a very different set of assumptions, as outlined in the next section. We recognize that the industrial – or "commercial" – agricultural model advocated by Collier and others has led to significant increases in total food production since the development of synthetic fertilizers in the early part of the twentieth century,[3] but this does not mean that this path was unproblematic, or that it will provide a viable model for the twenty-first century without major rethinking. Collier may view us as romantics. We would call ourselves realists who see hope in calls for food sovereignty and food democracy to build food systems that are more sustainable, more inclusive, equitable, and just – and, yes, even more productive – than what the globalizing food system currently has to offer.

Neoliberal Governance and the Contentious Politics of Food

The crises of the food system outlined in the Introduction to this book are inextricably linked to historic shifts in the global political economy in the post–Cold War era, and especially to those of the neoliberal era. In the North, neoliberalism's earliest supporters promoted the tax cuts and state-level deregulated business environment of the Reagan-Thatcher years in the 1980s. Proponents of neoliberalism argued that its policy prescriptions were a necessary corrective to the stagflation, uncompetitive business climate, and seemingly limited effectiveness of Keynesian responses to the economic downturns of the 1970s. However, neoliberalism as a political program also developed over the past four decades to limit what had been in fact the traditional role of the state in providing countervailing pressure against market failures through social welfarism, union-friendly legislation, and social democratic political parties. Over time, neoliberalism became associated with a much larger international agenda, including the liberalization of interstate trade and investment rules, further deregulation of the global economy, cuts in public spending and social services, the opening of financial and capital accounts and the removal of foreign exchange restrictions, privatization of government-owned services, shifts towards voluntary modes of industry self-regulation, the de-legitimization of the trade union movement, and still deeper tax cuts.

In the immediate post–Cold War era, neoliberal prescriptions were pushed further as they became embedded in existing and newly created institutions of global governance. The World Trade Organization, the International Monetary Fund, and the World Bank were shaped by neoliberal principles, through policies of stabilization, structural adjustment, and the promotion of liberalized trade and investment rules. The 1989 Canada-U.S. Free Trade Agreement, and more dramatically the 1994 North American Free Trade Agreement (NAFTA), privileged the rights of corporations vis-a-vis states and civil society and providing "conditioning frameworks" (Grinspun and Kreklewich 1994; McBride 2005) that limited corrective actions by the state. Building on the work of Stephen Gill (2002), Janine Brodie further clarifies the binding power of neoliberal arrangements in her discussion of "new constitutionalism." This concept refers to the decreasing capacity of state officials to regulate and control the policy fields once governments have ratified binding, "constitution-like," yet supra-state agreements, like NAFTA and the WTO. Difficult to amend, such institutional arrangements and the norms that they consolidate are therefore governing mechanisms that "trump decisions of national democratic bodies" (Brodie 2004, 20) in their attempts to regulate regional and global capitalism.

In the food and agricultural sectors of countries of the global North, the neoliberal revolution has been slower to take hold than in other sectors. Vanguard states like New Zealand and Australia committed to trade liberalization, the harmonization of domestic standards with international standards, and the removal of import restrictions on products like milk (to protect their own dairy farmers) only in the 1990s. Furthermore, even in 2012 massive farmer subsidies continue to define the structure of the food systems of the United States, the European Union, and Japan. These subsidies have an enormous impact on communities around the world, preventing farmers elsewhere from exporting into those highly subsidized markets and undermining local agriculture with the dumping of excess products. Still, the framework of neoliberalism is having an impact in the global North, as witnessed by the decline of state regulation to be replaced by industry self-governance, the growing role of civil society (rather than the state) in providing a safety net for the hungry (Koc, Das, and Jernigan 2007), and the ongoing attack on tariff barriers in countries that still maintain forms of supply management to protect their farmers, such as Canada. The latest example in this case is the 2011 Conservative government's decision to dismantle western wheat and barley farmers' single-desk marketing system, contravening its own federal law that guarantees the democratic right of farmers to vote on any change to the Canadian Wheat Board Act. For years now, neoliberal policies have also threatened the agricultural model and livelihoods of small and medium-size farmers in the global North, who cannot compete with agribusinesses that keep growing and getting the lion's share of farm subsidies (Borras, Edelman, and Kay 2008, chap. 1).

In the global South, neoliberal norms usually have had a much more immediate impact, especially in least-developed countries, cutting a swath through state interventionism in the food and agricultural sectors since the 1980s, through structural adjustment policies imposed by the IMF and the World Bank. Recommendations for decades to these states have encouraged a move away from domestic production of food staples, increased dependence on the international market, the production of "foodstuffs" for exports through an emphasis on monocultures in demand in the global North, and the movement of food into the hands of international speculators and commodities markets. For example, it is IMF policies that have contributed to putting Haitian rice farmers out of business by requiring the removal of import restrictions on subsidized Alabama and Louisiana rice in order to access loans. Regional trade agreements like NAFTA, along with U.S. corn subsidies, have further undermined the ability of many Mexican campesinos to grow corn commercially in their own country since 2000. Together, these institutions have attacked states' and citizens' capacity to control agriculture and food distribution, thereby working to normalize a globalizing food regime that is far from "free." Meanwhile, tight collaboration between the biotechnology, chemical, and agribusiness industry around the world further encourages oligopolies and distortions of the food production and distribution system in a way that severely restricts the options available to both consumers and farmers (Patel 2008).

The current crises in the globalizing food system are clearly connected, then, to the persistence of neoliberalism as a motivating ideology legitimating the unfettered commodification of food production and distribution and undermining national and local control over food policies. However, attempts at "de-peasantization" and to convert "the global South into a world farm" (McMichael 2009b) are failing, for now. Indeed, while there were important movements and coalition-building efforts among small producers for many decades (see Edelman 2003; Borras, Edelman, and Kay 2008; Winson 1993), there is a resurgence of food politics, resistance, and re-peasantization, with movements like La Vía Campesina, reclaiming and valuing anew the peasant identity and production methods (see Douwe van der Ploeg 2010; Desmarais, Wiebe, and Wittman 2010; Massicotte 2010). This is due in part to the impact of neoliberalism, and because the global North is now also exporting basic foodstuffs like rice and corn to the South, thus completely destabilizing rural and urban communities in those countries. Building on earlier experiences and networks, peasants have re-emerged since the mid-1990s as key players in alter-globalization movements. Present in the mass demonstrations in 1999 in Seattle and Cancun in 2003, and in the meetings of the World Social Forum, they are rejecting the neoliberal model of development and trade, but also proposing and seeking new ways to put into practice more sustainable models of agriculture and community, that are socially, culturally, and ecologically more sensitive.

What has been unleashed with less than predictable outcomes or political allegiances is a tide of contentious political behaviour seeking to construct countervailing power to the excesses, dislocations, and crises exacerbated by neoliberalism, from the bottom up. Peasants, gardeners, agricultural workers, and environmental justice activists, along with a host of other elements in civil society, are experimenting and reinventing relations between society, the state, and the market, and struggling to expand the space for non-state politics and participatory democratic control (Mittelman 2004). These countless initiatives include peasant movements for food sovereignty in Indonesia, efforts to promote fair trade in Germany, re-localization projects in British Columbia, farmers' protests in Mexico, and a growing movement of "localvores" in the small U.S. state of Vermont (see Ayres and Bosia, this volume).

Moreover, while many promising trends are emerging from peasant organizations, many challenges remain for small-scale agriculture to become a credible alternative and one that can promote and maintain sustainable agricultural practices combined with democratic decision-making processes. Primary among these are the forms of marginalization and disempowerment based on race and gender that, at least, intersect with neoliberal globalization to undercut the stability of communities and undermine the productive capacity of women. The coincidence of preferred industries and production systems with geographic location reinforce postcolonial practices that are concomitant with the racism and sexism that justified exploitation under colonial rule. So it is not just rice farmers who are losing their land, but Haitian rice farmers. And the classification of household work as unproductive not only marginalizes women economically, but reinforces their inequality at home, as well as in the community (Curtis 1986). As a result, it is not just communities that are undermined by neoliberal globalization, but activities and livelihoods that have been the economic sustenance for rural women and families, as capitalism devalues household labour and subsistence farming as intrinsically unproductive, thus affecting in particular the lives of gendered and racialized groups. These dimensions continue to be neglected even within and between rural communities and many peasant organizations. But a growing number of analysts and movements now recognize that not only ecology but also patriarchy and racism will need to be fully interrogated to avoid the continued marginalization and power struggles that present major obstacles in the pursuit of socio-economic justice, food democracy, and food sovereignty (e.g., Patel 2010).

Movements of Peasants, Producers, and Consumers

One starting point for analysing global food crises is therefore to connect the attempts at subjugating peasants and family farmers through the neoliberal food regime to swelling global and regional contentious responses of transnational movements such as La Vía Campesina, or Mexico's coalition of organizations around the campaign "Sin maiz no hay pais" or "No Corn, No Country." As tens of thousands of Mexican farmers and allies march on Mexico City to protest the agricultural section of NAFTA (Bartra and Otero 2009), European dairy farmers converge on Brussels to protest the declining prices of milk, and thousands of South Korean farmers mobilize against the U.S.–South Korean Free Trade Agreement through their "Protect Our Livelihood" campaign. These are a few examples of contentious politics, which we understand as the broad environment of longer-term political struggle outside formal political institutions, where people who lack access to political institutions engage in forms of collective action, claims-making, and / or alternative practices (Tarrow 1998, 2005). The acts of protest can be undertaken on behalf of new or unaccepted claims and in ways that target directly institutions or authorities. They can also reflect efforts to reclaim identities and political spaces encroached upon by the state or market prescriptions.

Moreover, as mentioned in the introduction, the roots of resistance to the upending of traditional food systems and practices date back prior to the neoliberal transformation of the global economy in the 1990s – as far back as centuries of resistance to colonial powers. Here we are focusing on more recent decades of mobilizations and alter-globalization rebellions in order to show the continuities and deepening of the impact of colonial and capitalist models of development and industrialization affecting food production, consumption, and distribution. Yet even more importantly, we want here to test and challenge the idea that after the structural adjustment policies that undermined the sovereignty of states and communities around the globe, there is little hope or opportunity for communities to organize and to foster food sovereignty and food democracy. Rather, we argue that the contours of an important and democratic debate are unfolding, through contentious political action around food and the theme of redistributing power more fairly and equitably in food systems.

Another starting point, equally rooted in contentious politics and responses to neoliberalism, is to examine the growing efforts to re-localize food systems. "Localism" – in the form of the "100-mile diet," the explosion of farmers' markets, community-supported agriculture (CSA), regional food brands, and more – is seen by many consumers as a response to the anonymity and questionable human and environmental impacts associated with long-distance food chains (Renting, Marsden, and Banks 2003). While historically communities were grounded in localized practices, localism reappears today as a way to resist the globalizing food regime, with its variety of innovative pragmatic techniques and a nearly utopian view of rural life.[4] It also has a complicated relationship with neoliberalism, by contesting its offerings but being at the same time entrepreneurial and market-oriented. Together, these features mean that further exploration of local food and family farmer movements allows important questions to surface for analysts of contemporary food politics.

Most recently re-articulated in the popular imagination as "locavore" eating habits, localism can in fact be conceptualized across three domains: an approach to consumer behaviour embedded in social institutions such as the farmers' market and CSAs, which explicitly seek to reconnect urban and rural linkages; government policies and investment strategies emphasizing farm-to-plate infrastructure and more intensely relational distribution systems; and democratic participation in making community-based decisions about food production, distribution, and consumption. Each shares a commitment to cultivating personal relationships, reciprocity, and solidarity as the foundations of healthy community. Idealized as they are realized, theorized at the same time they are applied, locally grounded practices unite dreamers, practitioners, and activists around these common assumptions about "pre-modern" human communities, cultivating a particular bond with the soil that refracts the bond between individuals in a community.

This utopian perspective unites disparate practices around concerns about the appropriate scale of productive activities, but it provides no specific answers. As localism challenges the commodification of food from a position of micro-resistance as a series of oppositional activities in everyday life, some practices associated with the movement offer a sizable challenge to neoliberal globalization. They can reinforce democratic practice in preference to the econometric rationalizations of distant global institutions (Smith 2005; Mittelman 2004). Other locally grounded practices, however, privilege econometric assumptions, just optimized differently from those in the current neoliberal model.

With the word *utopian* we do not intend to deride localism as unattainable or wild-eyed. Instead, we use utopian to indicate a shared set of values uniting the disparate advocates of locally grounded, ecologically sound, and culturally sensitive practices. Based on a vision of rural community often inspired by long traditions of rural collective action and a mythologizing of the commons, it therefore includes local projects under construction and a variety of realized utopian endeavours (see Wright 2010). This vision has a pedigree that includes utopian movements and communities from the nineteenth century like New Harmony and Finnish socialist communities, to the twentieth-century kibbutzim and the back-to-the-land movements of the 1960s.

However, as the variety of practices considered "local" continues to expand, the tension between a consumerist utopianism and a democratic one increases as well. Are farmers' markets inherently democratic, or just potentially more democratic than the supermarket alternative? Does the emphasis on the consumer still privilege consumption as opposed to eating, or will locavore consumers chip away at the global commodification of agriculture? Does government and investor support for local "agrepreneurs" undermine the democratic promise of localist resistance? Where Olson sought to apply market principles to understanding democratic collective action (Olson 1971), in the case of food, we might reverse the question to consider if a consumer-centric collective action at the local level, using preferences and incentive, can revitalize democratic communities that reconnect the needs and hopes of food producers and consumers present and active in rural and urban areas.

In its confrontation with global markets, localism implicitly and explicitly invokes Polanyi's critique of self-regulating commodity capitalism as unsustainable as well as his analysis of the social foundations of pre-capitalist economic activity (Polanyi 1957). This is apparent in the Slow Food movement – an Italian precursor to localism founded in 1986 – which emphasizes traditional artisan practices and the preservation of historically local production and the small trattoria or brasserie, against the disconnected agro-industrial food chains that breed fast food consumption (Miele and Murdoch 2002). In this movement, technique and expertise, cultivated across generations and based in family operations that serve a broad community, stand out as a kind of culturally sensitive and socially integrated system of production and social reproduction.

Fair Trade, another precursor to localism seeking to eliminate intermediaries between small-scale food producers and consumers in dio tant localities attempts to impregnate markets with social values such as justice, autonomy, and environmental sustainability (Linton, Liou, and Shaw 2004; Zerbe, this volume). More recently, the advocates of localism and food democracy condemn the commodification of food, labour, and land, much as Polanyi did land, labour, and money, vividly harkening back to the rural commons as inspiration. For example, Vermont author Bill McKibben, who began the locavore movement in his part of the world with an article in *Gourmet Magazine* about his year eating only local foods, published a popular manifesto that is a critique of the growth-oriented ideology of consumer capitalism as internally and environmentally unsustainable (McKibben 2007). Food activist Raj Patel gives Polanyi effusive credit for the democratic turn in food politics (Patel 2009). Feminist concepts of co-production, which see economic transactions in terms of relationships deeply embodied in time and place, and not as abstracted economic calculations, also reinforce Polanyi's account in gendered terms, drawing from Young's conceptualization of the relationship between consumers and producers in terms of responsibility and solidarity, including her critique of structured power that privileges certain actors in the distribution of goods (Young 1990, 2003). Notably, the transnational peasant movement La Vía Campesina, with its emphasis on local democratic participation in decision-making about the production and distribution of food, the end of violence against women, and women's empowerment in making decisions, is implicitly indebted to critiques of the self-regulating market like Polanyi's, as well as Sen's analysis of development as a relationship between democratic means and economic choice (Sen 2000). This correlation raises the interesting possibility, albeit one fraught with the challenges of unequal power relations and potentially conflicting interests, of finding a balance between the emerging interests of consumers in healthy food and ecosystems and the growing militancy of peasants and small farmers who would like to provide just that, for themselves as well as the society more broadly.

Autonomy, Sovereignty, Protectionism?

Just as Polanyi explained the rise of protectionism as one half of a double movement that included an internal reaction to the implementation and expansion of the self-regulating market, food and agricultural activism today most often is a direct response to the forces of globalization that have impelled the commodification of agriculture and continued a 200-year assault on rural communities and values. We can see this in activism on behalf of protectionist policies and in the invocation of the state as a prominent feature of many local responses. French and Indian peasants, for example, advocate that their respective states impose barriers to the importation of GMO or hormone-laced foods, often because conforming to the global standard undermines local practices, preferences, and products.

Protectionism of a sort is also pursued without the state through programs to promote or preserve rural communities and artisan production. Indeed, whereas Polanyian analyses of the double movement tend to emphasize the largely protectionist *reactions* of civil society forces vis-à-vis the destabilizing penetration of market forces, one also needs to acknowledge the persistence of alternative forms of socioeconomic communities and practices. Too often discredited and marginalized as economically inefficient and unsustainable, or gendered as unproductive, these alternatives have always been present and are still striving to maintain and consolidate themselves, in the cracks of today's globalizing agro-industrial food system. For example, well-known Indian activist-researcher Vandana Shiva was part of a collective initiative to found Navdanya, an organization active in sixteen rural states with fifty-four seed banks, to preserve traditional techniques and distribute native seeds that have been preserved and improved through locally based knowledge and practices, but are increasingly threatened by bioengineered crops and patenting laws.[5] Using traditional techniques and expertise, Navdanya is similar to the way Slow Food connects consumers and producers, not just locally, but also globally in an effort to identify and protect the unique features of culturally sensitive and locally grounded agriculture. These structured initiatives to preserve agricultural diversity and communal life have an informal counterpart, as evidenced by the farmers in Hardwick, Vermont, who have joined in cooperative and informal networks of mutual support to share ideas, equipment, and money (Hewitt 2010). Together, these examples present important questions about the future role of the state, versus that of local communities themselves, in creating and maintaining food sovereignty or food democracy.

Increasingly, these "protectionist" innovations suggest not just an economic fortress, but most importantly a return to grassroots and participatory practice across geographies, race, and gender, emphasizing immediate democratic control over markets and the environment, and valuing relationships of trust based in mutual benefit and reciprocity over profit (Menser 2008; Patel, Balakrishnan, and Narayan 2007). Feminist scholarship on the formative dimensions of women's work in individual and social development (Luxton 1997) and the creative capacity of women's sociability (Eisler and Montouri 2007) illustrates that movements based on trust and creativity can be gendered in unique ways, as they combine productive strategies with the nurturing of unmonetized social or relational strategies typically valued in households. The food democracy movement in the United States, and La Vía Campesina globally, have organized around initiatives to counteract the commodification of food and the global threat to rural communities. These more direct alternatives have gone beyond mere traditionalism to embrace an expanded notion of local participation and rural life, making explicit efforts to recognize the role of women in agriculture, the importance of rural youth in production and community life, and an intersection of food politics, women's rights, and human rights (Desmarais 2008; Patel, Balakrishnan, and Narayan, 2007). Such efforts have emphasized a commitment to environmental protection and ecological sustainability, theorized by ecofeminism and feminist political ecology, as Massicotte demonstrates in her chapter.

Contemporary food movements also raise questions about the role of consumers in the new politics of food. While many of the activists discussed above often seek state support or promote local initiatives or stronger community organizing, some of the localist efforts are brazenly capitalist in their reliance on "agrepreneurialism" and consumer preference as a foundation for sustainable communities. In response to the locavore movement, for example, many restaurants are touting their close and cooperative relationships with farmers. In California, the farm-to-table movement was pioneered by Alice Waters at Chez Panisse, whose staff includes a professional "forager." New York chef Dan Barber operates a restaurant at the unique agricultural "think tank" known as the Stone Barns. Community Supported Agriculture coupons enable consumers to invest directly in a farm's harvest, providing literal seed money for the produce they will eat throughout the growing season and often into the winter.

A movement of investors known as "Slow Money" – to parallel Slow Food's emphasis on durable practices – has been a key force in financing local agrepreneurialism. With an investment strategy that focuses on social capital and long-range returns, Slow Money has been a partner in the growth of value-added agriculture businesses that target local economies in struggling rural communities through the identification and cultivation of niche-oriented products for regional or specialty markets. While minimizing the role of local consumers and relying on broader distribution systems, these businesses hope to plow profits from regional markets back into their communities.

Nevertheless, the nexus of investor capital, government support, and entrepreneurial risk-taking might undermine the democratic aspirations of agrepreneurs and empower typical actors in ways that reinforce marginalization on the basis of gender, class, and race. Indeed, the rise of a community of organic and artisan producers in Hardwick, Vermont, faces criticism from within the community, including those families that have been farming in the region for generations and the back-to-the-land utopians who arrived after the 1960s. Though this emerging food economy has been heralded in the popular media and within both national and global activist networks, and despite their internal commitment to reciprocity and mutual support, some in Hardwick are concerned about where these growing businesses with their regional-scale and specialty products will take the community (Hewitt 2010).

Knowledge and Power

Agriculture by definition invokes concepts of expertise and knowledge, whether formal or informal, and challenges to the commodification and globalization of food include contestation over knowledge, expertise, and accreditation. Not only, "Whose knowledge counts?," but, as feminist political ecology poses the questions, "Whose knowledge is seen?" and "What counts as knowledge?" These concerns cut across processes of production and distribution, and demand an analysis of how disparities between empowered actors and small communities across global regulatory systems not only reinforce racial and gender hierarchies, but impose the racial and gender divisions between productive and unproductive, public and private, household and market that enable the singularity of Western knowledge (Rocheleau, Thomas-Slayter, and Wangari 1996). As neoliberal globalization advantages Western knowledge, and the construction of knowledge becomes entwined with market institutions or government regulation, these inequalities are reinforced when alternative sites of knowledge production (and the gendered and racialized subjects who produce such knowledge) are rendered invisible (Santos 2006). In this section, we illustrate how two forms of expertise in food empower specific economic actors to the detriment of democratic communities, and thus how the politics of knowledge and its production figures centrally in food politics: the first is associated with the use of knowledge to increase yield, and the second with the standardization of practices to promote outcomes that many might consider optimal or beneficial.

The globalization of agriculture can be traced through colonial processes, within the trade winds that carried ships laden with spices and slaves and later through the Opium Wars and the British desire for tea. For our purposes, scientific knowledge became privileged first with the rise of industrial agriculture in the West and later its export to the Third World in the first Green Revolution. Scott's work on rural transformation in Southeast Asia in particular, and agricultural transformation more generally, clearly illustrates not only the tensions and dislocations precipitated by the Green Revolution, which tore at the fabric of rural life and promoted the exodus of the rural population to the growing megalopolis, but also the high-modernist logic behind the export of a scientific agricultural model from North America (Scott 1985, 1999). Focusing on a kind of Western expertise lacking common sense as it is applied to revolutionize food production, Scott reveals how an agriculture model predicated on a temperate climate faced disaster when transported to more arid or tropical climates. As well, he reveals the scientific arrogance that inhibited cooperation, as indigenous knowledge was undermined and discounted by "Western expertise."

Despite the shortcoming of the first Green Revolution, a second has emerged, this time focused squarely on Africa. Spearheaded first by global agribusiness with patent-protected GMO seeds, this effort has been reorganized and philanthropized by the Bill and Melinda Gates Foundation. Their Green Revolution Redux claims to have learned the lessons of failure from the first, as it seeks to apply more contemporary and sensitive technology to a process of apparently shared learning. But the Gates Foundation's agricultural initiatives raise more questions than they answer. The Program for African Seed Systems, for example, is sensitive to the differences in climate and food cultivation, and the program has identified local talent and expertise. But the focus is still on improvements in seed, pest control, and fertilizers along the lines of the modern industrial agricultural system, and Gates himself has at times revealed a broader support for GMO seeds and other technologies than the foundation cares to admit (Philpott 2009). Furthermore, while the Gates Foundation presents itself as working in close partnership with farmer organizations, the power of the foundation to define the projects – rather than the farmers themselves – cannot be underestimated.

The Gates Foundation argues that it has learned the lessons from the first Green Revolution and is now closely focused on the needs of small farmers. One of the first answers to frequently asked questions on its website reads, "We focus on small farmers – most of whom are women – and are committed to listening so that our work helps meet their needs" (Bill and Melinda Gates Foundation 2010, 1). However, an effort to map the relationships of the Gates Foundation by Kenny and Fransescone (2010), which included several interviews with representatives of organizations funded by the foundation, revealed that "farmers and low-level implementation organizations are not given the opportunity to create and develop alternatives that are 'farmer-based'" (26). Rather, the Gates Foundation is ultimately focused on a model of development "that is aligned with that of the [first] Green Revolution: It is mainly participating in projects and funding institutions that are primarily Western science-based" (26). While farmers are involved in some projects, Kenny and Fransescone (2010, 26) add, "the emerging trends ... are that the model itself is [financial] input and not farmer driven, which affects the ways projects are structured and organizations and projects are able to operate. The agenda for agricultural development has been set by the Foundation (and other powerful players like USAID) and the freedom for smaller organizations, and producers to act, even if funded by the foundation, is severely restricted as a result."

That the new Green Revolution for agriculture is not driven by the guidance of farmers, though it makes some awkwardly feminist claims, and that it is focused on an input-intensive model of agriculture (GMOs) should raise concerns. In addition to the environmental questions raised by such practices, the experience with GMOs elsewhere in the world, including India, suggest that indigenous knowledge about soil quality, climate, and growing practices – often produced and reproduced by women in everyday experience – is undermined by the expansion of a patent-protected GMO seeds coupled with the microfinance mechanisms necessary for cash-poor farmers to buy them (Shiva 2005). In these circumstances, declining yield – or yield less than promised in the promotion of the seeds – leads to a cycle of increasing debt and often the loss of land, though the seed distributors refuse to acknowledge the practical knowledge of the farmers as they attempt to cultivate the new products. Indeed, the Gates Foundation promotes not only the development of specialized seeds and fertilizer use through an intellectual hybrid that still privileges Western approaches, but also the very microfinance mechanisms needed to provide short-term purchasing power (and concomitant indebtedness) to farmers, countering current efforts to foster greater food sovereignty.

While the second Green Revolution seeks seed improvement to end world hunger, expanding commodity markets penetrate the same terrain to foster South to North production and distribution systems, transforming both the types of crops cultivated and the how they are grown and accounted for. Freidberg points out that increasing worry over food safety in Britain, coupled with patterns of deregulation, have allowed supermarkets to impose their own requirements in the form of "best practice" on producers in Zambia and Kenya, often overriding or undermining local practices and experience (Freidberg 2007). As well, the increasing governmental and quasi-governmental regulation of labelling has brought the imposition of new standards on food produced for global distribution, from the beneficial effects of fair trade licensing based in civil society organizations – which, of course, has its own costs in licensing procedures and local practice – to the government takeover of organic and other forms of origin labelling that have actually imposed new standards and procedures on local farming to meet global demand, often beyond the means of small local producers. In this volume, Smythe shows how these systems have been construed to undermine the ability of consumers to learn more about their food. As well, governments promote local urban-rural and other divides that can coincide with gender.

Together, these Green Revolutions (both the original one and its newest iteration in Africa), with their reliance on specialized seeds and increasing inputs, coupled with the new systems of regulation and authorization, create added pressures on many communities as they gender and racialize local knowledges in order to render them invisible – to adapt to new forms of regulation as well as new practices and mechanisms, to adopt new financial mechanisms to meet the costs of added inputs and patented products, as well as the costs associated with licensure and authentication. While local knowledge might be appreciated in some of these systems, it is valued only as recognized and invoked, and it is central to neither the process nor to the mission. Whether seeking to increase production for local consumption, transform production for global markets, or encourage environmentally and socially sustainable practices, the mechanisms employed rely first and foremost on Western priorities, desires, and technological insights, and only next on a local "buy-in." Moreover, the reliance on expertise in the new Green Revolution and the North-South market breeds an emphasis on capitalist measures of efficiency in productive systems that currently depend on human labour and community support, transforming village life and resulting in the dislocation of now surplus labour to increasingly clogged urban centres, where industrial development has not kept pace with agricultural transformation. Such a process flips the urbanization imperative experienced by much of the West.

Conclusion

This chapter has outlined the importance of food as a source and example of crisis in the neoliberal market system, and suggested the global distributions of power that enforce and define that system. We have called attention to the points of inequality and contention, sensitive to the fact that the politics of food within a commodified system of production and consumption is neither closed nor complete, but instead a subject of controversy and ongoing resistance. This globalizing food system is structured through an econometric paradigm as well as a scientific one, and these two forms of knowledge – as they work separately and in conjunction – often work to disempower local social organization and production based on indigenous knowledge and values. The result is a wide variety of conflicts, where diverse communities and actors have responded to the logic of food as commodity with one of food as community. But even these responses differently illustrated within the food sovereignty rubric, in the assortment of positions occupied by proponents and in their different responses to questions of reform or transformation, have generated contentions and controversy within the same vanguard that is leading the response to the neoliberal imperative.

Together, the following chapters in this volume suggest the points of resistance to commodified food as well as tensions within these diverse movements. However, we know these suggestions are neither exhaustive nor complete. Our collective goal, as authors and editors of this volume, is to draw attention to food as a focal point of global inequality, local and transnational political struggles, and therefore a central political concern both academically and normatively. Given the questions of power and participation essential to the globalization of a specific food paradigm, as well as the intensity of famine, starvation, underemployment, displacements, and malnutrition at the all too redolent margins of the current globalizing food regime, food as an aspect of the quotidian should not be overlooked but instead focused upon, because in the very ordinariness of consumption and deprivation lies its importance and power. In addressing these lacuna in political science in particular, and bringing the expertise of colleagues from outside the discipline into the conversation, this volume specifically focuses on the expression of food sovereignty and food democracy as politicized concepts linked to a variety of practices, norms, and contexts. Emphasizing the role of gender, international institutions, transnational movements, culture, economic structures, and agency, contributors provide unique perspectives drawn from research and experience in the West and in the global South, from the Americas, Europe, and Asia, to Australia.

Finally, despite outlining these specific conceptual approaches here, this chapter makes no claim to a definitive paradigm for the study of food politics. Rather, we hope it, combined with the other chapters in this volume, encourages a broader conversation about the politics of food and agriculture across the social sciences, including practitioners and policymakers, and situating analyses and experience from the local to the global. In our view, this conversation should pay special attention to actors often ignored by mainstream political science – including peasants, farmers, community gardeners, chefs, and fair trade activists, hence the selection of chapters in this volume – but this list is by no means exhaustive. The contributions on gender, race, and indigenous peoples in this volume point to the need for much more attention both in research and in theoretical development within the food sovereignty frame and as affected by neoliberal globalization. Nonetheless, we have begun to highlight how such actors, we believe, are indeed preparing the ground for a future beyond neoliberalism through their calls for, and daily practices of, food sovereignty and food democracy.

NOTES

1 Several chapters in this volume thus examine what happens in these efforts to unite producer and consumer perspectives, including McMahon, Andrée and Martin, Ayres and Bosia, and Zerbe.
2 This response to Paul Collier's analysis is based on a letter to the editor of *Foreign Affairs* initially penned by Peter Andrée and Jennifer Clapp in December 2008.
3 For a comprehensive review of the productivity gains associated with the industrial revolution in agriculture on a global scale, see Evans (1998).
4 Thanks to an anonymous reviewer for this clarification.
5 See Navdanya, http://www.navdanya.org /.

REFERENCES

Avery, Dennis T. 2000. *Saving the Planet with Pesticides and Plastic: The Environmental Triumph of High-Yield Farming*. 2nd ed. Washington, DC: Hudson Institute.

Bartra, Armando, and Gerardo Otero. 2009. "Contesting Neoliberal Globalism and NAFTA in Rural Mexico: From State Corporatism to the Political-Cultural Formation of the Peasantry." In *Contentious Politics in North America: National Protest and Transnational Collaboration Under Continental Integration*, edited by Jeffrey Ayres and Laura Macdonald, 92–113. Houndmills, U.K.: Palgrave Macmillan.

Bill and Melinda Gates Foundation. 2010. "Agricultural Development Overview." Accessed 22 November 2010. http://www.gatesfoundation.org/agriculturaldevelopment/Pages/overview.aspx.

Borras, Saturmino, Marc Edelman, and Cristóbal Kay, eds. 2008. *Transnational Agrarian Movements Confronting Globalization*. New York: Wiley-Blackwell.

Brodie, Janine. 2004. "Globalization and the Social Question." In *Governing under Stress: Middle Powers and the Challenge of Globalization*, edited by Marjorie Cohen and Stephen Clarkson, 12–30. London: Zed Books.

Clapp, Jennifer. 2012. *Hunger in the Balance: The New Politics of International Food Aid*. Ithaca, NY: Cornell University Press.

Collier, Paul. 2008. "The Politics of Hunger." *Foreign Affairs* 87 (6): 67–79.

Curtis, Richard. 1986. "Household and Family in Theory on Inequality." *American Sociological Review* 51 (2): 168–83. http://dx.doi.org/10.2307/2095514.

Desmarais, Annette A. 2008. "The Power of Peasants: Reflections on the Meanings of La Via Campesina." *Journal of Rural Studies* 24 (2): 138–49. http://dx.doi.org/10.1016/j.jrurstud.2007.12.002.

Desmarais, Annette A., Nettie Wiebe, and Hannah Wittman, eds. 2010. *Food Sovereignty: Reconnecting Food, Nature and Community*. Toronto: Brunswick Books.

Douwe van der Ploeg, Jan. 2010. "The Peasantries of the Twenty-First Century: The Commoditisation Debate Revisited." *Journal of Peasant Studies* 37 (1): 1–30. http://dx.doi.org/10.1080/03066150903498721.

Edelman, Marc. 2003. "Transnational Peasant and Farmer Movements and Networks." In *Global Civil Society 2003*, edited by Mary Kaldor, Helmut Anheier, and Marlies Glasius, 185–220. London: Oxford University Press.

Eisler, Riane, and Alfonso Montouri. 2007. "Creativity, Society, and the Hidden Subtext of Gender: Toward a New Contextualized Approach." *World Futures* 63 (7): 479–99. http://dx.doi.org/10.1080/02604020701572681.

Evans, L.T. 1998. *Feeding the Ten Billion: Plants and Population Growth*. Cambridge: Cambridge University Press.

Fisher, Alexandria 2010. "What Is Food Democracy." *Food First*, 7 April. http://www.foodfirst.org/en/node/2868.

Folbre, Nancy. 1991. "The Unproductive Housewife: Her Evolution in Nineteenth-Century Economic Thought." *Signs* 16 (3): 463–84. http://dx.doi.org/10.1086/494679.

Fraser, Nancy. 2005. "Reframing Justice in a Globalizing World." *New Left Review* 36:69–88.

Freidburg. 2007. "Supermarkets and Imperial Knowledge." *Cultural Geographies* 14 (3): 321–42. http://dx.doi.org/10.1177/1474474007078203.

Gill, Stephen. 2002. "Constitutionalizing Inequality and the Clash of Globalizations." *International Studies Review* 4 (2): 47–65. http://dx.doi.org/10.1111/1521-9488.00254.

Grinspun, Ricardo, and Robert Kreklewich. 1994. "Consolidating Neoliberal Reforms: 'Free Trade' as a Conditioning Framework." *Studies in Political Economy* 43:33–61.

Hewitt, Ben. 2010. *The Town That Food Saved: How One Community Found Vitality in Local Food*. Emmaus, PA: Rodale.

International Assessment of Agricultural Knowledge, Science and Technology
for Development (IAASTD). 2009. *Synthesis Report.* Washington, DC:
Island. http://www.unep.org/dewa/agassessment/reports/IAASTD/EN/
Agriculture%20at%20a%20Crossroads_Synthesis%20Report%20(English).pdf.

Higgins, V., and G. Lawrence, eds. 2005. *Agricultural Governance: Globalization
and the New Politics of Regulation.* Abingdon: Routledge.

Holt-Giménez, Eric. 2009. "From Food Crisis to Food Sovereignty: The
Challenge of Social Movements." *Monthly Review* 61 (3): 142–56.

Kenny, Meaghan, and Kirsten Fransescone. 2010. *Mapping the Bill and Melinda
Gates Foundation: Agricultural Development and Power.* Report prepared for
Food First: San Francisco. Authors' collection.

Koc, M., R. Das, and C. Jernigan. 2007. "Food Security and Food Sovereignty
in Iraq: The Impact of War and Sanctions on the Civilian Population." *Food,
Culture and Society* 10 (2): 317–48.

Lang, Tim, and Michael Heasman. 2004. *Food Wars: The Global Battle for
Mouths, Minds, and Markets.* London: Earthscan.

Lang, T., D. Barling, and M. Caraher. 2009. *Food Policy: Integrating Health,
Environment and Society.* Oxford: Oxford University Press.

Levi-Strauss, Claude. 1966. "The Culinary Triangle." *Partisan Review* 33 (4):
586–95.

Linton, April, Cindy Chiayuan Liou, and Kelly Ann Shaw. 2004. "A Taste
of Trade Justice: Marketing Global Social Responsibility via Fair Trade
Coffee." *Globalizations* 1 (2): 223–46. http://dx.doi.org/10.1080/
1474773042000308587.

Luxton, Meg. 1997. "The UN, Women, and Household Labour: Measuring and
Valuing Unpaid Work." *Women's Studies International Forum* 20 (3): 431–9.
http://dx.doi.org/10.1016/S0277-5395(97)00026-5.

Marx, Karl. 1963. *The Eighteenth Brumaire of Louis Bonaparte.* New York:
International Publishers.

Massicotte, Marie-Josée. 2010. "La Via Campesina, Brazilian Peasants, and
the Agribusiness Model of Agriculture: Towards an Alternative Model of
Agrarian Democratic Governance." *Studies in Political Economy* 85 (Spring):
69–98.

McBride, Stephen. 2005. *Paradigm Shift: Globalization and the Canadian State.*
Halifax: Fernwood Publishing.

McKibben, Bill. 2007. *Deep Economy: The Wealth of Communities and a Durable
Future.* New York: Times Books.

McMichael, Philip. 2009a. "Market Civilization and the Neo-Liberal Food
Regime's Global Food Crisis." Paper presented at the annual meeting of the
International Studies Association, 15 February, New York.

– 2009b. "The World Food Crisis in Historical Perspective." *Monthly Review* 61 (3): 32–47.

– 2011. "Food System Sustainability: Questions of Environmental Governance in the New World (Dis)order." *Global Environmental Change* 21 (3): 804–12. http://dx.doi.org/10.1016/j.gloenvcha.2011.03.016.

Menser, Michael. 2008. "Transnational Participatory Democracy in Action: The Case of Via La Campesina." *Journal of Social Philosophy* 39 (1): 20–41. http://dx.doi.org/10.1111/j.1467-9833.2007.00409.x.

Miele, Mara, and Jonathan Murdoch. 2002. "The Practical Aesthetics of Traditional Cuisine: Slow Food in Tuscany." *Sociologia Ruralis* 42 (4): 312–28. http://dx.doi.org/10.1111/1467-9523.00219.

Mittelman, James. 2004. *Whither Globalization? The Vortex of Knowledge and Ideology*. New York: Routledge.

Moore, Barrington. 1966. *Social Origins of Dictatorship and Democracy: Lord and Peasant in the Making of the Modern World*. Boston: Beacon.

Nestle, Marion. 2007. *Food Politics*. Santa Cruz: University of California Press.

Olson, Mancur. 1971. *The Logic of Collective Action: Public Goods and the Theory of Groups*. Cambridge, MA: Harvard University Press.

Paarlberg, Robert. 2008. *Starved for Science: How Biotechnology Is Being Kept out of Africa*. Cambridge, MA: Harvard University Press.

– 2010. *Food Politics: What Everyone Needs to Know*. Oxford: Oxford University Press.

Patel, Raj. 2008. *Stuffed and Starved*. Toronto: Harper Collins.

– 2009. *The Value of Nothing: How to Reshape Market Society and Redefine Democracy*. New York: Picador.

– 2010. "What Does Food Sovereignty Look Like?" In *Food Sovereignty: Reconnecting Food, Nature and Community*, edited by Annette Aurélie Desmarais, Nettie Wiebe, and Hannah Wittman, 186–96. Halifax: Fernwood Publishing.

Patel, Rajeev, Radhika Balakrishnan, and Uma Narayan. 2007. "Transgressing Rights: La Vía Campesina's Call for Food Sovereignty/Exploring Collaborations: Heterodox Economics and an Economic Social Rights Framework/Workers in the Informal Sector: Special Challenges for Economic Human Rights." *Feminist Economics* 13 (1): 87–116. http://dx.doi.org/10.1080/13545700601086838.

Pateman, Carol. 1998. "Contributing to Democracy." *Review of Constitutional Studies/Revue d'études constitutionnelle* 4 (2): 191–212.

Philpott, Tom. 2009. "Bill Gates Reveals Support for GMO Ag." Grist. http://grist.org/article/2009-10-21-bill-gates-reveals-support-for-gmo-ag/.

Polanyi, Karl. 1957. *The Great Transformation: The Political Origins of Our Time*. Boston: Beacon.

Renting, H., T.K. Marsden, and J. Banks. 2003. "Understanding Alternative
   Food Networks: Exploring the Role of Short Food Supply Chains in Rural
   Development." *Environment & Planning* 35 (3): 393–411. http://dx.doi.
   org/10.1068/a3510.
Rocheleau, Dianne, Barbara Thomas-Slayter, and Esther Wangari, eds. 1996.
   Feminist Political Ecology: Global Issues and Local Experiences. London:
   Routledge.
Santos, Boaventura de Sousa. 2006. *The Rise of the Global Left: The World Social
   Forum and Beyond.* New York: Zed Books.
Scott, James. 1985. *Weapons of the Weak: Everyday Forms of Peasant Resistance.*
   New Haven, CT: Yale University Press.
Scott, James C. 1999. *Seeing Like a State: How Certain Schemes to Improve the
   Human Condition Have Failed.* New Haven, CT: Yale University Press.
Sen, Amartya. 2000. *Development as Freedom.* New York: Knopf.
Shiva, Vandana. 2005. *India Divided: Diversity and Democracy under Attack.* New
   York: Seven Stories.
Skocpol, Theda. 1979. *States & Social Revolutions: A Comparative Analysis of
   France, Russia, and China.* New York: Cambridge University Press.
Smith, Jackie. 2005. "Response to Wallerstein: The Struggle for Global Society
   in a World System." *Social Forces* 83 (3): 1279–85. http://dx.doi.org/10.1353/
   sof.2005.0047.
Tarrow, Sidney. 1998. *Power in Movement: Social Movements and Contentious
   Politics.* 2nd ed. Cambridge: Cambridge University Press. http://dx.doi
   .org/10.1017/CBO9780511813245.
− 2005. *The New Transnational Activism.* Cambridge: Cambridge University
   Press. http://dx.doi.org/10.1017/CBO9780511791055.
Waring, Marilyn. 1988. *If Women Counted: A New Feminist Economics.* San
   Francisco: Harper San Francisco.
Winson, Anthony. 1993. *The Intimate Commodity: Food and the Development of the
   Agro-Industrial Complex in Canada.* Toronto: Garamond.
Wittman, Hannah, Annette A. Desmarais, and Nettie Wiebe, eds. 2010. *Food
   Sovereignty: Reconnecting Food, Nature and Community.* Toronto: Brunswick
   Books.
Wood, Elisabeth. 2003. *Insurgent Collective Action and Civil War in El Salvador.*
   New York: Cambridge University Press. http://dx.doi.org/10.1017/
   CBO9780511808685.
Wright, Eric Olin. 2010. *Envisioning Real Utopias.* New York: Verso.
Young, Iris Marion. 1990. *Justice and the Politics of Difference.* Princeton:
   Princeton University Press.
− 2003. "From Guilt to Solidarity: Sweatshops and Political Responsibility."
   Dissent (Spring): 39–44.

2 The Territory of Self-Determination: Social Reproduction, Agro-Ecology, and the Role of the State

MICHAEL MENSER[1]

First formulated in 1996 by a transnational association of peasants called La Vía Campesina, food sovereignty is "the right of all peoples, their nations, or unions of states to define their respective agricultural and food policies" (La Vía Campesina 1996; Wittman, Desmarais, and Wiebe 2010b, 2–14). The concept of food sovereignty is a direct response to the failure of the UN Food and Agriculture's Organization's "food security" framework to protect the interests of small farmers, peasants, and consumers in the face of the neoliberal restructuring of agriculture that commenced in the 1970s. But the emergence of this remarkably diverse transnational subject and its attractive political project was made possible by some of these same forces of regional and global institution-making and state restructuring.[2] Thus food sovereignty is not just a reaction against neoliberalism, it is a project *for* the democratization of the food system that also aims to restructure the state and remake the global economy. Just like many of its partners and fellow travellers in the global justice movement, La Vía Campesina is both a counter-hegemonic, contentious politics and a constructive one. And its constructive project is not a single issue but multidimensional: it is a food movement and a democracy movement, it fights for gender equality alongside resource conservation. Food sovereignty is not just about "farmers and food," but the nature of work, the scope of politics, and the meaning of social and ecological sustainability; it is about participatory democracy, dignity, solidarity, and social inclusion.

In this chapter, I trace the development of food sovereignty through a transnational movement coordinated through and with La Vía Campesina. But food sovereignty (and the food democracy variant, as discussed in the previous chapter) are broadly used outside this movement, even when the program is not fully adopted. My focus is on the ways in which the concept of food sovereignty draws upon but departs from the traditional notion of state sovereignty as it is defined in political philosophy and articulated in the Westphalian system of states. Most of what follows attempts to operationalize the idea to better understand its conceptual intricacies and to know what it looks like in practice, its strengths and limitations, and its implications for our understanding of neoliberalism, the politics of an "alternative economy," and the relationship between states and social movements.[3]

From Crisis to Project

Epidemics of obesity and type 2 diabetes. One billion people without enough food, another two billion malnourished. Mass extinction, marine dead zones, potable water shortages. One-fourth of all greenhouse gas emissions. The destruction of rural communities, cultural heritages, ancestral homelands, and ancient forests. The proliferation of urban slums. These are some of the consequences of the current global food system.[4] To make it truly sustainable will require significant transformation at the national and global levels, but local and regional territories are the primary venues for the production of alternative models. As a result, such a transformation will lead to an "extreme makeover" of the Westphalian system of sovereign states and hypermobile multinationals and to the actualization of sustainability that integrates and democratizes the economic, political, and social spheres. This encapsulates the position of those advocating a type of sovereignty prefaced with a most unexpected adjective. Food sovereignty is a threat to the interstate system in both its traditional and current forms for three reasons: it challenges the legitimacy of states, changes the meaning of *territory*, and grounds the practice of self-determination outside the state apparatus in the terrain of ecological-cultural.

Yet in this age of transnational cosmopolitanism, international economic globalization, global human rights, and militarist neo-imperialism, why adopt the sovereignty rubric? However amended, the concept of "sovereignty" is under attack by theorists and activists for reasons both pragmatic and normative. Given the proliferation of so much inter- and trans-nationalism (both hegemonic and / or counter-hegemonic), some question whether sovereignty can be effectively institutionalized. Others argue that even if it could, it *should not*, because sovereignty promotes nationalism and xenophobia, undermines global cooperation, impedes cultural cosmopolitanism, and further fosters a Hobbesian interstate system marked by resource hoarding, violent conflict, and cultural, racial, and class-based exploitation. Environmentalists in particular bemoan the persistence of state sovereignty and the interstate system because, they claim, addressing ecological crises requires post-national perspectives and cross-border collaborations, and the interstate system is ill equipped to manage such problems for both structural and normative reasons (Eckersley 2004, 1–17, 53–84; Litfin 1998, xi, 8–16).

Given these moral, political, and institutional difficulties, it seems perplexing that a transnational social movement that explicitly grounds itself *outside of the state* would appeal to the concept of sovereignty. Yet the growing popularity of the concept suggests otherwise: the International Planning Committee for Food Sovereignty counts more than 800 member organizations, and Vía Campesina comprises more than 100 organizations with more than 200 million members (Wittman, Desmarais, and Wiebe 2010b, 5–7; Martínez-Torres and Rosset 2010, 165).[5] In this chapter, I argue that food sovereignty advocates deploy the sovereignty rubric to place the notions of non-interference and autonomy at the forefront of their political project. But these two concepts – so central to the tradition and current instantiation of the interstate system – function very differently in the food sovereignty frame, which redefines the notions of self-determination and territory. Indeed, what constitutes autonomy, and thus "interference," can be understood only via these more basic political notions. I will argue that food sovereignty defines self-determination as "maximal democracy" (Menser 2008), and territory as the space of ecological-social (or eco-social) reproduction. The next section offers a brief historical and philosophical discussion of sovereignty, followed by a reconstruction of the notion of food sovereignty as it has evolved since 1996. The two sections that follow examine two different models in order to better understand what food sovereignty requires, how it relates to the state, and what it looks like in practice at multiple scales. The first example looks at Cuba, where the state has played a positive and active collaborative role with movements. I call this model state-supported food sovereignty. In the second scenario, the state is regarded as an obstacle to the implementation of food sovereignty, so a model of governance is forwarded that does not require positive collaboration with the state. This model draws upon concepts and practices of indigenous nations and I call it indigenous sovereignty. I argue that these two versions actually conflict with one another but illustrate the complex context sensitivity of food sovereignty, which, in turn, promotes a productive tension among its advocates. The final section analyses a number of problems facing such advocates, especially class differences, gender inequality, and difficulties (and possibilities) around specifying just who is sovereign and the scope of the jurisdictions involved.

"This Is Sovereignty": History and Concepts

"Virtually all of the earth's land is parceled by lines, invisible lines that we call borders. Within these borders, supreme political authority typically lies in a single source – a liberal constitution, a military dictatorship, a theocracy, a communist regime. This is sovereignty" (Philpott 2001, 3). Sovereignty is a defining concept of modern philosophy and political practice.[6] Not only it is essential to our understanding of the interstate system (the sovereign state) and liberalism (the sovereign individual), crucial concepts (God, personhood, agency, autonomy, property), distinctions (nature / culture, public / private), and disciplines (economics) depend upon it. In the political sphere, a major impetus for the rise of the sovereign state and its system of territorial governance was the religious wars that scarred much of Europe in the sixteenth and seventeenth centuries. These wars were driven largely by fights over *who* should choose a territory's official religion. The feudal period was defined by multiple figures of authority – popes, emperors, kings, bishops, and nobles – jousting for power. These conflicts led to staggering human loss as well as economic – and ecological – ruin as marauding armies exhausted financial resources and depleted natural resources to fuel multiple war machines (Philpott 2001, 97–149). In response to the carnage caused by such political fragmentation, the Treaty of Westphalia was signed, and from the sixteenth to eighteenth centuries, this dynamic of dispersed and polyvocal authority was replaced by univocal state administration mechanisms defined by a single sovereign (king, parliament). As Ruggie observes, "The chief characteristics of the modern system of territorial rule is the consolidation of all parcelized and personalized authority into one public realm" (1993, 151). The state came to have the final say on religion, law-making, enforcement, punishment, taxation, and so on. As Held puts it, "The core of the idea of the modern state is an impersonal and privileged legal or constitutional order, delimiting a common structure of authority, which specifies the nature and reform of control and administration over a given community" (1995, 38).

Although the Treaty of Westphalia did not discuss sovereignty explicitly, it laid the foundation for the basic principles of the interstate system: the fundamental right of political self-determination; legal equality among states; and the principle of non-intervention of one state in the internal affairs (religious or otherwise) of another state (Philpott 2001, 32). Operationally, and conceptually, sovereignty involves a notion of what constitutes legitimate power; the specification of the proper scope of this power both within and outside the state; and rules describing the process by which an entity can become sovereign (Philpott 2001, 12, 15–21). In the modern Westphalian context, it is states (rather than cities or churches) that are sovereign (Sassen 2006, 31–73).

This conception of sovereignty leads to a very particular production of space. One need only compare a world map of states with one of climate types or eco-regions. In the latter, geographic areas may contain very different ecological types: jungles amidst mountains, or pockets of wetlands within an arid steppe. It may even be very difficult to distinguish one feature from another because of a mixing of types, or because the features are so temporally variable that they are spatially fluid. For example, many deserts are defined not by the absence of rainfall but by its irregularity. When the rain does come, patches of sparse vegetation can become lush, old riverbeds run vital, and the desert seems now a very mixed up type, with different ecological logics layered on top of each other (Bailey 1998, 85–103).

The world map of states, while it too has changed considerably over time, is structured by quite different dynamics. The scope of a state's sovereignty is coextensive with its territory and is mutually exclusive from other states. And because a (legitimate, non-"rogue") state requires internal and external legitimacy (the territorialized people must in some way consent, and other states must recognize this), there is to be no mixing or sharing of jurisdictions. In this regard, state space is akin to the space of a person, which, in liberalism at least, is very closely connected to the notion of private property and all that it "entails in terms of exclusive use, disposition, and control" (Ward 1998, 79). Mill is perhaps the most well-known and eloquent proponent of this view: as Elshtain describes his famous stance, "The sovereign self is the sole judge of his or her own good" (2008, 182). And this goes for the "self" in self-determination, whether as state or person.

With respect to relations *among* states, sovereignty has two key aspects: negative sovereignty, or the principle of non-interference, and positive sovereignty, the right to enter into voluntary relations with other states (e.g., treaty-making). "Nature" is divided up in accordance with the dictates of (state-based) political communities (rather than ecological dynamics) and is thus reduced to geographic space and becomes the property of either the state or persons.[7] More specifically, nature becomes "resources" to be managed in accordance with the national interest of the state in which it resides (Kamieniecki and Scully Granzeier 1998, 257).

In sum, sovereignty "expresses internally the supremacy of the governmental institutions and externally the supremacy of the state as a legal person" (Kamieniecki and Scully Granzeier 1998, 258). Internally, sovereignty shapes the boundaries of and relationships among the social, political and economic spheres, the rights of citizens in general, and definitions of property in particular, all in accordance with the idea that the state is the supreme figure of authority. American presidents have colourfully captured this notion with phrases such as "The buck stops here" and "I am the decider" (Bush" 2006). In the international arena, this supremacy is evident when states justify their actions in terms of appeal to notions of "national interest" and / or "national security."

In the section below we shall see how food sovereignty redefines self-determination and territory with major implications for customary notions of autonomy and non-interference and the distinctions between nature / culture and public / private.

Food Sovereignty: Self-determination, Agro-ecology, Social Reproduction, Territory

The concept of food sovereignty came about largely because of the inadequacy of the "food security" framework to defend the interests of peasants, small farmers, and rural communities, particularly in Latin America. Food security – formulated in 1974 by the Food and Agriculture Organization in response to the world food crisis of 1972 – "exists when all people, at all times, have access to sufficient, safe and nutritious food to meet their dietary needs and food preferences for an active and healthy life" (FAO 1996, as cited in Fairbairn 2010, 21–31). As a goal, food security seems admirable, but its lack of a specification of the means has caused hardships for farmers and consumers throughout the world. For example, food security permits and even encourages below-market-price agricultural goods "dumping," genetically modified seeds, and other expensive inputs. All undermine the economic position of small farmers, and the endorsement and promulgation of GMOs threatens biodiversity and undermines consumer choice. Indeed, because multinational corporations and states are deemed to be critical to the success of the food security program, the stark inequalities and power differentials within the food system are actually reinforced. At the international level, "food security" has in no way made food production or even the debate about it more democratic, nor has it seriously taken into account social and environmental concerns (Desmarais 2003, 134–76; Wittman, Desmarais, and Wiebe, 2010b, 2–3). In contrast, food sovereignty tackles such inequalities head on, as it requires the democratization of policy formation, production, distribution, and consumption. This is clear from Vía Campesina's very first formulation: "Food is a basic human right. This right can only be realized in a system where food sovereignty is guaranteed. Food sovereignty is the right of each nation to maintain and develop its own capacity to produce its basic foods respecting cultural and productive diversity. We have *the right to produce* our own food in our own territory. Food sovereignty is a precondition to genuine food security" (Via Campesina 1996; my *emphasis*).

Food sovereignty shifts the focus from the right to access food to the right to produce it. First declared in 1996 in Rome, food sovereignty is founded on the right of farmers and their communities to self-determination in agriculture. Like food security, food sovereignty too aims to eliminate the "globalization of hunger," but, in contrast to food security, it demands the reorganization of national and global food trade. Food sovereignty also stresses not just the "right to food," but the right to be "free from violence" and the achievement of "social peace" (La Vía Campesina 1996).

Over the last two decades, the food sovereignty framework, as developed by La Vía Campesina and its allies, has been modified. In each redefinition, the themes named above have remained, although points of emphasis have shifted. For example, in the earlier declarations, anti-dumping was an emphasized theme, while in more recent meetings such as the Nyéléni conference, violence against women was deemed central,[8] and as the global economic crisis has set in since 2008, opposition to "land grabs" has received much more attention (Borras and Franco 2010, 117).

Throughout these formulations, food sovereignty is frequently justified through appeals to human rights law. Indeed, Windfuhr and Jonsén point out that La Vía Campesina changed the notion of food sovereignty to better fit international human rights law. In the 1996 declaration, food sovereignty referred to the right of "peoples, communities and countries." At the International Planning Committee of Food Sovereignty meeting in 2004, the document was amended to include the right of "*individuals*, communities, peoples and countries" (Windfuhr and

Jonsén 2005, 12; my emphasis). This enabled food sovereignty to be more easily justified in the international arena as part of the right to food. The right to food then is a tool that food sovereignty advocates can use to pressure states to enact policies that will enable food security. In this vantage, advocates argue that food sovereignty is the best means to obtain food security and make sure the most vulnerable will have access to food. Put another way, food sovereignty is the medium by which food security can best guarantee the right to food. Yet others argue that the multidimensionality of the food sovereignty project is too ambitious, too demanding, and too controversial, and it distracts from the ultimate goal of feeding people. This argument has played out repeatedly in debates at the FAO (Wittman, Desmarais, and Wiebe 2010b, 2–3).

The meaning and practice of food sovereignty hinges upon the redefinition of self-determination and territory. Indeed, what constitutes autonomy, and thus "interference," can be understood only via these more basic political notions. I define self-determination as "maximal democracy" and territory as the space of eco-social reproduction (Menser 2008). As I have previously argued, food sovereignty aims to instantiate all four main tenets of maximal democracy: it constructs mechanisms and institutions for the instantiation of self-determination, develops the capabilities required for such practices, meets real material needs, and avoids temptations towards isolationism or autarky by interconnecting organizations and struggles that share these norms (Menser 2008). More specifically, food sovereignty as maximal democracy emphasizes the right and ability of farmers and their communities to assert control over agricultural production and meet the needs of local communities, workers, and local and non-local consumers. As Farvar and Pimbert assert, these movements are "challenging liberal views of citizenship as a set of rights and responsibilities granted by the state. Instead, in the context of locally-determined food systems, *citizenship is claimed and rights are realized through people's own actions*" (2006, viii; my emphasis). Food sovereignty is then a political program that advocates for a mode of production constructed and controlled by non-state subjects (farmers, farming communities) framed by specific norms (self-determination, human rights, sustainability) but inclusive of other groups and institutions at a variety of levels (including states).

Like sovereignty, self-determination is a defining concept in the Western liberal tradition. And, like sovereignty, it is closely connected to the notion of autonomy. Traditionally, *self-determination* means "to be the cause or author of one's action."[9] Relatedly, in the case of La Vía

Campesina and food sovereignty, the goal of self-determination is not the maximization of happiness or capital accumulation but dignity. Political scientist Vergara-Camus reports a common view among members of stalwart Movimento Sem Terra of Brazil (MST): "The MST land struggle is not only for the right to work the land, nor is it only against unemployment and marginalization from Brazilian society. It is also for the right to work autonomously, for the right to control one's own work, and the product of one's labour. In many discussions I had with Sem Terra, the sense of being at the mercy of someone else's will, of being treated as an object and not as a person, was emphasized again and again" (Vergara-Camus 2009, 384).

At first glance, this sentiment may seem to resonate strongly with the notion of self-determination in the liberal tradition from Locke and Mill to Nussbaum. But the passage highlights an important difference, which is that autonomy and dignity are not just political notions, they implicate the economic and ecological.

In contrast to the liberal tradition, in food sovereignty, the concept of labour is, as in the Marxist tradition, ineluctably social. Farmers are not construed as individual proprietors or entrepreneurs selling on the global market. Instead, they are community members territorially located; La Vía Campesina was formed by groups of producers, "peasants" (Desmarais 2008, 140). As peasants, the focus is not simply on maximizing production, it is on the preservation of the community and local ecology, or eco-social reproduction.[10] For example, in the southern Sahara borderlands, an effective means to meet social need is also the best way to address ecological instability and climate change. The answer there has not been GMO crops but communities of fate, kin networks, and voluntary associations: land networks have enabled people to borrow land when their own needs to be left fallow; women's natal networks have ensured that families and villages get seeds that are ecologically appropriate; and cattle networks help redistribute both meat and manure to those who need it so as to prevent overgrazing and soil infertility (Ching 2002, 4–5). As Ching argues, "High local population densities, far from being a liability are actually essential for providing the necessary labour to work the land, dig terraces and collect water in ponds for irrigation, and to control weds, tend fields, feed animals and spread manure" (2002, 4).

Social reproduction, not production, is at the centre of the food sovereignty project. Here, social reproduction comprises those practices that preserve and cultivate the ecological conditions necessary for the generational continuance (reproduction) of cultural practices that enable livelihoods that are meaningful, dignified, and economically adequate relative to the norms of the community. The values assigned to those ecological processes cannot be reduced to biological function or ecological role. For example, for the Iroquois, squash, maize, and beans are not just the basis of healthy diet and a method of planting (intercropping) that maintains soil fertility, they are the community's kin, the "three sisters" (Mann 2004, 13–14). Furthermore, the knowledge that makes these modes of (re)production possible has been accumulated over many generations. Seeds are potent examples of this historical-collective notion of labour, since they are themselves encapsulations of qualities accumulated over successive generations. The same is true for many types of agricultural practices from terracing to the utilization of "natural" pesticides and intercropping (Gliessman 2007, 18; Altieri 1995, 169–78).

It therefore follows that the political project of food sovereignty requires a mode of agricultural production that focuses not on maximizing output for sale on the global market but on meeting social need. Yet "social" need is multidimensional and includes the ecological as well as the economic and cultural. This alternative agricultural model is called "agro-ecology." In stark contrast to the rationalization of production found in industrial agronomy, the application of ecological principles to agricultural production, or agro-ecology, has since 2002 been designated an essential dimension of food sovereignty (Windfuhr and Jonsén 2005, 11). Agro-ecology is a mode of agricultural production that aims to maintain or increase productive capacity, ecological integrity, cultural integrity, and health in a geographically bounded community.[11]

The agro-ecological model of production, then, is also a model of territorially rooted social *reproduction*. In accordance with this approach, economic practices must not undermine the social or ecological conditions necessary for the continuance of the sociocultural practices and their reproduction. The space in which these dimensions interact and support one another is what I call "territory."[12] For agro-ecologists, not only must the farming practices be productive, they must be able to continue for generations in order to promote cultural integrity. As in the example from the southern Sahara borderlands above, maintaining the relevant cultural community can also enable ecological preservation.[13]

For agro-ecology, increasing "output" is not an end in itself, nor is it automatically good. It may or may not be desirable, given various factors and the overall state of the system. If increasing output decreases potable water availability, then it may not be desirable. Or if decreasing maize output enables forest regrowth, it may be deemed desirable for biodiversity preservation. Similarly, if application of a pesticide pollutes the water supply or has negative effects on worker health, then some crop loss may well be worth it from the ecological, biodiversity, and / or human health standpoint. However, if maize is crucial for cultural reasons and is already in short supply, then other pest-management practices could be sought out. But these practices must take into account the size and skills of the local labour supply.

It is should now be clear how the notion of food sovereignty is at odds with the usual notion of state sovereignty and the spatiality of the interstate system. In the liberal tradition, the fundamental unit is the individual citizen / private property, the fundamental polity is the state, and the spatiality of the interstate system is produced by a logic that is of an order different from natural or ecological space. While the interstate system depends upon and reinforces splits between individual / social, nature / culture, and public / private, in food sovereignty, the sovereign subject is not an individual citizen but a territorialized group of producers, and that group depends upon its particular ecological circumstances for its own reproduction both in economic resources and cultural needs. Crucially, food sovereignty does not eliminate any of the binaries, but it does alter their meaning, function, and significance.

One way to understand this conceptual reorganization is through the commons and social regulation. Generally speaking, private property is possessed by individuals who have extensive rights over who can use it and how. Markets are usually understood as the proper way to regulate and assign values to such pieces of property, but individual owners are the final authorities (sovereigns) over its use. Examples of private property range from land to labour to toothbrushes to one's own body. *Public* property is regulated and assigned a value by the state and is managed by an administrative agency authorized by the state and for the public benefit. Examples include parks, mineral resources, and the airwaves. In contrast, commons are owned not by individuals but by groups. These groups are not part of the state apparatus, although they may have some relationship to a state. Traditionally, commons were often "natural resources" such as bodies of water, forests, or pastures managed by a collective who created rules for extraction and use. The goal of such management is to meet the needs of all the users, however differently positioned, in a way that preserves or reproduces the resource in question over a long or indefinite period of time.[14] Even though commons are usually much more inclusive in terms of use than private property, they are still regulated; however, the logic of regulation is very different from that identified with private property (the maximization of profit) or with public property ("national interest").

Seeds are an almost archetypal case of the commons (for reasons discussed above), and that is why the emergence and proliferation of genetically modified seeds (which are patented and thus treated as private property and enforced as such by states) are so vigorously opposed by food sovereignty advocates (Wittman 2010, 99–101). Other examples of commons include the "digital commons" of file sharing (e.g., peer-to-peer programs) and software writing (Linux) (Kloppenburg 2010, 157–9). There are also many examples of resources managed as commons by non-territorial associations or municipalities with definite jurisdictions, particularly in the case of water management. And here, just as there are "public-private partnerships," there are "social-public" or even "social-public-private" associations that aim to fulfil social need and ecological preservation but deploy public institutions or market mechanisms towards that end – the commons (Ostrom 1990). And it is to this local-regional-national-international matrix that we now turn.

State-Supported Food Sovereignty in Cuba

It began with stockpiles of unshipped sugar, and once the millions of litres of oil arrived, Cuban agriculture entered a new era. In 1961 the USSR and its satellites imported the sugar and exported oil to Cuba, not only for domestic use but also for refining and shipment to other Latin American locales. With the plantations formerly owned and operated by U.S. multinationals now nationalized, in addition to the income accrued from oil (re)sales, Cuba was able to purchase or manufacture the usual array of industrial agricultural inputs: nitrogen-, phosphorus- and potassium-based fertilizers, pesticides, and mechanized equipment for plowing, harvesting, and transporting. It then built a state-owned and -managed monoculture-oriented global export model focused on the capital and technology-intensive production of a few crops (sugarcane, tobacco). During this period of "modernization," the size of Cuba's agricultural sector grew tremendously, rivalling present-day California. But in 1989, the Berlin Wall came down and the proverbial plug was pulled. Between 1989 and 1993, Cuban GNP fell from $19.3 billion to $10 billion. Between 1991 and 1994, Cubans lost on average thirteen kilograms each as oil and grain imports plummeted by 50 per cent.

The shock to the Cuban system was so pronounced that the government declared a "Special Period" akin to a wartime austerity program (Alvarez et al. 2006, 225–30).

Without Soviet financial support, importing industrial inputs and food became too costly. So in 1993, Cuba set out to transform its food system to meet the social needs of its domestic population within the restrictions of the new economic circumstances. The transformation hinged upon seven features:

1 Decentralization of the state farm sector through new organizational forms and production structures
2 Land redistribution to encourage production of different crops in various regions of the country
3 Reduction of specialization in agricultural production
4 Production of biological pest controls and biofertilizers
5 Renewed use of animals as traction in place of machinery
6 Promotion of urban family and community gardening movements
7 Opening of farmers' markets under supply-and-demand conditions
(Alvarez et al. 2006, 227–31)

With these changes, the government transferred some power to farmers, the market, and other non-state-managed associations and communities – especially in the agricultural production process, land management, and the distribution and sale of products.

Key to this transition was the development of non-industrial, locally produced inputs such as bio-pesticides and the cultivation of seed stocks and planting patterns appropriate for local growing conditions and the dietary needs of proximate communities. In other words, largely for reasons of economic necessity, Cuba switched to agro-ecology. Again, from the epistemological and managerial perspectives, this was a stark departure from the previous monocultural model where "a single technician can manage several thousand hectares on a recipe basis by simply writing out instructions for a particular formula or pesticide to be applied to the entire area by machinery" (Alvarez et al. 2006, 226). For example, before 1991, state officials did not permit farmers to grow sweet potatoes and maize together, although it was widely known that it was more efficient from the standpoint of resource use and output (242–4).

In contrast, in the agro-ecological model, farmers must become intimately familiar with the ecological particularities of each patch of soil to determine where organic matter needs to be added, and ascertain pest and natural enemy refuges and entry points. Largely for these kinds of reasons, the state shifted managerial control from state bureaucrats to farmers in the neighbourhoods. To facilitate this shift, farmers received the land rent-free (through leases) but property rights remained with the state. The state set quotas, but farmers essentially determined what they grew (Alvarez et al. 2006, 227).

What is especially intriguing from the perspective of food sovereignty and the sovereignty discussions above is the flexibility of the Cuban system on ownership, management, production, distribution, and research. Because of differences in population density, degree of urbanization, varying topography, and the range of food products required, a number of different organizational forms were mobilized. There are state-owned and -managed pig and poultry farms, small-scale worker-managed vegetable cooperatives, and individually owned farms – the last of which utilize 55 per cent of the agricultural land area. Foreign firms are permitted, but only in partnership with the state sector – not with co-ops or private farms. The corporate conglomerates grow citrus fruit, rice, and tomatoes (Alvarez et al. 2006, 234–9). But among these different modes, Alvarez et al. see the worker cooperatives as the most crucial for economic, political, ecological and sociocultural reasons: "The cooperative sector as a whole has flexibility, heterogeneity, the ability to combine diverse crops and technologies, a qualified labour force, and an unquestionable capacity to form groups with common interest (economy, ideology, community, and even family interests). These factors in combination with large acreage, sheer number of members, and social responsibility, make it the most important part of the new social structure of Cuban agriculture" (238). The cooperatives also cultivated social solidarity during a period of crisis that not only helped to meet domestic needs but mitigated social conflict by promoting economic inclusion and equity.

The Cuban people and their government effectively articulated all major aspects of food sovereignty as defined above: the ecological and economic are interlinked but in the terrain of the social, where groups manage agricultural production in a manner consistent with the norms of the commons, and so place a higher value on participation, social need, and ecological integrity. However, both the state and market, and public and private property have roles in this system. This pluralism of forms, I believe, illustrates a commitment to democratic participation and ecological integrity and shows that food sovereignty rejects a "one size fits all model" (Beauregard and Gottlieb 2009, 24). If this pluralism were not permitted, one could hardly speak of genuine democratic self-determination, since the model would be state-imposed. Yet, amidst the pluralism, some privileging occurs consistent with the demands of food sovereignty norms. Worker co-ops form the backbone of the Cuban model, fostering the social and cultural solidarity required to make the system work in a participatory manner to meet the goals of capability development and social need. Also crucial to the agro-ecological success of the transformation has been a Cuban member of La Vía Campesina. Founded in 1961 to facilitate the transfer of agricultural knowledge from "farmer to farmer," the role of the National Association of Small Farmers grew considerably during and after the Special Period as the importance of agro-ecology increased. Its growth was inextricably intertwined with the managerial transformations that gave more powers to farmers and their communities (Alvarez et al. 2006: 242–8). Indeed, the state has transferred control over land use to farmers for almost 70 per cent of the sector (242–4).

Unlike right-to-food advocates (Narula 2006, 750–1, 757–8), proponents of food sovereignty generally do not believe that large TNCs can play a play a positive role (Menser 2008, 34–5; Martínez-Torres and Rosset 2010, 167). Hence, the Cuban government's contracting with multinational corporations should be regarded with critical suspicion since they are likely to violate the norms of agro-ecology and democratic self-determination. However, despite the state's partnership with corporations, many Cuban administrative agencies actively support food sovereignty. In addition to programs for land distribution, agro-ecological research, and price regulations, a range of non-food-oriented government programs benefit farmers and consumers. These include government-funded health care and education, insurance, and access to credit, all of which reduce the need for an individual farmer's income to meet all social needs (Alvarez et al. 2006, 235, 244–5). But there have been problems: "In some cases, the relationships between the new cooperatives and the former state enterprises have been marked by an excess of tutelage, subordination, and dependence, remnants or legacies of an enterprise management structure that has not yet fully given way to a more appropriate and participatory planning process among the actors" (237).

Yet the presence of this difficulty is an expression of the success of the small-scale farming movement, which is now seen as a critical transformative agent in its own right, combined with the desire of the state to be an active partner in securing food sovereignty for Cuba. The decentralization forwarded by the state in conjunction with the National Association of Small Farmers and the cooperatives shows that food sovereignty is not just about non-interference, it is also about the promotion of democratic and social self-determination oriented to eco-social reproduction. From the perspective of Alvarez et al., agro-ecology required a shift in the approach of the state such that power was transferred to farming communities and associations; they became the privileged agents, and the state took on a more supportive and protective role. I call this model state-*supported* food sovereignty, since the assets of the cooperatives are owned by the state but managed by the workers. Because the goal of this hybrid model (worker-run, state-owned) is social need, I would argue that the land *functions* as a commons, even if it is legally held by the state.

Given Cuba's unique political history and present, is it relevant? Venezuela thinks so and has adopted some similar institutional mechanisms and policies. By 2005, the Venezuelan state had redistributed 3 million hectares of land and helped to launch 30,000 agricultural cooperatives (Beauregard and Gottlieb 2009, 32). The state had also provided technical assistance and equipment, founded a School of Agroecology, provided subsidies and credit to small farmers, and set up supply chains to get food to those who need it most through subsidized supermarkets and neighbourhood food pantries (37). Problems such as food hoarding have arisen, but, consistent with the food sovereignty frame, the institution addressing this difficulty is not the state or ruling political party but community councils, which are nodes of popular participation and democracy at the local level (34). Mali, Ecuador, and Bolivia are examples of other states that have integrated principles of food sovereignty into their constitutions and / or enacted them through legislation, but none have achieved successes on the level of Cuba (Beauregard and Gottlieb 2009).

Indigenous Sovereignty

While the case of Cuba demonstrates that the state can play a positive role in promoting food sovereignty, most states stand as overt obstacles. Yet the implementation of food sovereignty does not require positive collaboration from states, as robust movements in Mexico, Brazil, Indonesia, and Thailand have shown. Food sovereignty was not originated by states, but by movements justifying and organizing themselves against and despite states. Perhaps the most developed vision of sovereignty without states comes from indigenous peoples.

Like food sovereignty, the indigenous conception of sovereignty – which predates food sovereignty – is grounded in a conception of self-determination that "must take into account multiple patterns of human associations and interdependency" and integrates the political, economic, ecological, and sociocultural (Corntassel 2008, 116). But indigenous sovereignty differs from food sovereignty in a number of ways.[15] Most obviously, first, it is not formulated in terms of agriculture or food, but includes all cultural practices, from language and medicine to goods production and forms of worship (Carino 2006; Stavenhagen 2006, 211). Second, it is less worker-oriented and associationist and more communitarian.[16] Third, indigenous sovereignty is driven by an animist cosmological vision that regards specific non-humans not just as significant *ecological* beings but *cultural* beings (kin or community members) (Wilmer 1998, 55–6, 63–5; Kamieniecki and Scully Granzeier 1998, 264–8).

Indigenous sovereignty aims to develop capabilities and assign responsibilities to the different groupings, institutions, or associations within the cultural polity, including (where applicable) families, clans, communities, societies, homelands, and the natural world (Corntassel 2008, 118). Geographic places are not merely ecosystem components or locations of past events like sites on some historical register, they are eco-cultural territories, sites of social reproduction defined by the continued presence of cultural ancestors both human and non-human (Colchester 2000, 1365; Woodley et al. 2009, 5). Corntassel writes, "It is one's individual and shared responsibilities to the natural world that form the basis for indigenous governance and relationships to family, community, and homelands. These are the foundational natural laws and powers of indigenous communities since time immemorial" (2008, 121–2). This is why demands for reparations and the restoration of lands is crucial for the pursuit of indigenous sovereignty but less so for non-indigenous food sovereignty.

Indigenous attempts to be recognized as sovereign on the national and international stages have met with limited success. This failure is due in part to the difficulties that arise when trying to justify and articulate self-determination in the context of the human rights–interstate system framework. This is not surprising, given the ontological presuppositions of the liberal democratic state with its focus on individuals as the fundamental social unit and private property possession as the cornerstone of both individual (personal) freedom, and state's (political) freedom in the interstate setting as discussed above. Corntassel writes, "Unfortunately, in the contemporary rights discourse, 'Indigeneity' is legitimized and negotiated only as a set of state-derived individual rights aggregated into a community social context – a very different concept than that of collective rights pre-existing and independent of the state" (2008, 115). In contrast to the representation and interest-oriented focus of liberal states with their focus on rights protection, service delivery, and legal conflict resolution, indigenous sovereignty focuses on community responsibility to place and the development of powers and capabilities required to meet those obligations. Thus "Indigenous peoples have the right to maintain and develop their political, economic, and social systems or institutions, to be secure in the enjoyment of their own means of subsistence and development, and to engage freely in all their traditional and other economic activities" (122).[17] The best way states can aid in this project is not through positive collaboration (provision of loans, ownership-management partnerships, infrastructure development) but through active withdrawal. This withdrawal would likely involve the legal recognition of indigenous sovereignty, land transfers and / or title transfers, and the stopping of practices that encroach upon the sovereignty of those territories (from active resource extraction to more passive but deadly forms of pollution like the dumping of radioactive toxins proximate to watersheds, the siting of incinerators, overdrawing water tables, or damming rivers).

This is not to say that each indigenous community is seeking autarchy. On the contrary, some of the most politically potent transnational associations of the last two decades have involved indigenous communities (Hawken 2007, 71–114; Mander and Tauli-Corpuz 2006). Corntassel argues that the mark of a community that has achieved a real degree of "sustainable self-determination" is that it enters treaties with other indigenous nations (2008, 122).[18] On this point, Corntassel parallels the traditional understanding of state sovereignty, which of course not only emphasizes "the right of a state to determine its own domestic affairs but also its right to freely link with other sovereign states" (2008, 124). However, on the indigenous model, consistent with the maximal democracy approach, indigenous nations would link not with states but with other indigenous nations that share its normative framework. Intriguingly, Phillips argues that because the area of international economic law is so "ill-defined," indigenous communities could create trade agreements with their own normative structure and obtain formal legal recognition for these agreements at both the transnational and international levels (2006, 524). If this were to occur, the North American indigenous communities that signed these indigenous treaties, for example, would then not be bound by other trade agreements such as the North American Free Trade Agreement. This would mean that the dominant global political economic powers represented by the WTO and free trade agreements could be banned from operating in those areas. Many of these areas are rich with oil, gas, coal, plutonium, and other resources critical for the unsustainable global economy. Taking these resources out of the global mix could put further pressure on the dominant international system to become more sustainable, or, intriguingly, it could send the system into collapse.[19]

Problems and Prospects: Class War, Gender Inequality, Home Rule

As one would expect, the state-supported model articulated in Cuba shares much with that of indigenous sovereignty. Both seek to democratize socio-economic forms in a manner that promotes territorial eco-social sustainability through the model of agro-ecological production. This approach acts both at odds with the liberal version of state sovereignty and its distinctions between nature and culture, the right and the good, and public and private. Both also deploy critiques of the human rights paradigm but utilize it for instrumental reasons in the international arena and within their home states.

Yet there are major differences. Most significant for the considerations of this chapter is indigenous sovereignty's "nation" component. Food sovereignty permits a wide variety of social forms, from associations such as producer co-ops, farmworkers' unions, and women's groups, to communities, either cultural or geographic. It also includes indigenous nations. But most food sovereignty social groupings are not nations. There are three major implications of this divergence. First, food sovereignty obviously allows for the participation of a much wider array of social actors. Second, because of the differences between indigenous sovereignty and the interstate system in self-determination and territory, there is little chance for positive collaboration between the two, and many will see this as a drawback. Even if few other states have implemented changes that point in the food sovereignty direction, many advocates, including La Vía Campesina, argue that states could do more, and they can have a positive role to play through subsidies, loans, research, price controls, taxes, tariffs, and land reform.

For indigenous nations, the state form described above is antithetical to their desired mode of governance. But, like state-supported food sovereignty advocates, indigenous nations are not calling for the elimination of the state and the interstate system (at least not at UN meetings). The difference between the two is that indigenous nations see little chance for true collaboration, only a kind of cautious coexistence that can arise through state withdrawal. Relatedly, while La Vía Campesina continues to utilize the rights framework to support food sovereignty, even if in a confusing manner (both in terms of right to food and right to self-determination) (Windfuhr and Jonsén 2005, 34), indigenous nations are less optimistic (Corntassel 2008; Phillips 2006). However, even if one considers corporations incapable of being reformed, might the state form itself be altered in ways to support indigenous sovereignty? Bolivia and Ecuador, for instance, have modified their constitutions in order to grant rights to non-humans, thereby enlarging the polity in ways congruent with indigenous models. And if states changed their model of development from capital-intensive GDP-increasing projects to agro-ecological programs focused on social need *and* they adopted the long-term perspective of the precautionary principle oriented around social reproduction rather than capital accumulation *and* they changed their conception of territory, *then* state-supported food sovereignty would indeed move closer and closer to indigenous sovereignty.[20] Differences between the two would remain (such as the role of the spiritual-religious, and the conception of territory), but one could at least imagine the state playing a positive role in both frames. Of course, one might ask, if states did in fact make all those changes, would they still be states? The interstate system would certainly look quite different because states would actively withdraw from numerous territories across the globe and have to permit a new set of non-state sovereigns, but this is true for both food sovereignty and indigenous sovereignty.

Given the number of conjunctions in the conditional above, indigenous sovereignty may seem more difficult to obtain than food sovereignty, even if one favours a state-inclusive model. But the indigenous approach does have some advantages. A major difficulty for food sovereignty advocates is determining the border of the sovereign units. If the state is no longer the sole sovereign, and farming communities are, then the number of sovereigns threatens to get unwieldy. How many sovereigns would there be within each state or across state boundaries? In sizeable member states such as Brazil, India, and Thailand, the problem seems especially pronounced, but even in smaller ones (both geographically and in population), critical jurisdiction problems would arise. Although agro-ecology tends towards demarcations that are more ecological – as in bio-regions or eco-types – still, depending on the region, there are likely to be many different communities within such regions or that cut across such regions. If a state did transfer management powers to farming communities, then these kinds of problems would be bound to proliferate and debates over minimum size and how to adjudicate among communities within the same eco-region would become pronounced.

Indigenous nations may have an advantage over food sovereignty advocates in this regard, because their communities have degrees of cohesion that warrant the designation "nation" and their territories are already delineated, if not honoured within the interstate system (Stavenhagen 2006, 210). In the case of food sovereignty advocates, in most situations the farming communities are not nations. Often they are not even communities but associations – of workers, women, religious groups, etc. For example, the Brazilian Movimento Sem Terra explored by Massicotte in this volume is one of the most successful members of La Vía Campesina. I argued that they possess a very strong conception of territory as the space of social reproduction. However, that is not equivalent to the indigenous sovereignty notion of territory as homeland; for the Movimento Sem Terra (MST), the geographic or ecological particularity is not a crucial source of collective identity. Indeed, many MST members have travelled to unfamiliar parts of Brazil to gain land. "In contrast, indigenous peoples' movements do not demand just any land but, rather, what they consider to be their land and territories" (208). Both conceptions of land are welcome under food sovereignty, because both fulfil the tenets of maximal democracy and agro-ecology, but they differ on the role of territory in identity formation, and this affects the kind of sovereignty sought.

The inclusive pluralism of food sovereignty advocates such as La Vía Campesina enables the movement to be both vibrant and large, but it also makes it difficult to determine the composition and location of these sovereigns who are diverse in type and dispersed in place. In this volume, the two chapters by Ayres and Bosia, and by Zerbe in particular, explore the tensions derived from commodity imperatives within local food movements embracing a food sovereignty frame. Furthermore, this inclusiveness brings together groups who themselves have serious differences. Some, for example, are Marxist, drawn to the anti-capitalist character of food sovereignty, but "loathe ... the neopopulist dream of small family farming that dominates the movement's vision" (Borras 2010, 783). And even amongst those who do share the family or small farm ideal, class differences arise. For instance, in India, the La Vía Campesina stalwart Karnataka State Farmers' Association has been instrumental in fighting GMOs through lobbying and direct action, protesting against the WTO, and implementing agro-ecological programs.

They also give a vocal and visible Asian presence to what was in its early stages a Latin American–dominated movement. However, the Karnataka State Farmers' Association is made up of middle-class and "rich farmers" who do not embrace calls for land reform (Borras 2010, 783; Borras, Edelman, and Kay 2008, 275–6). La Vía Campesina co-founder Saturnino Borras emphasizes the importance of class analysis and notes differences among food sovereignty advocates that lead to conflict: "Rich farmers could be the oppressors of farmworkers, land reform is an issue to be resisted by rich farmers, high price for food products is a good policy for food-surplus-producing farmers, bad news for food-deficit rural households, credit facilities and trade issues may not be a critical issue for landless subsistence rural workers who do not have significant farm surplus to sell anyway, wages are not fa-voured issues by middle and rich farmers but a fundamental issue to rural workers, and so on" (2008, 276).

Another notable La Vía Campesina and food sovereignty proponent, Raj Patel, emphasizes the food sovereignty slogan adopted at the 2008 Maputo, Mozambique, meeting: "Food sovereignty is about an end to all forms of violence against women" (2010a, 124). Patel sees gender op-pression as the fundamental impediment to the realization of food sov-ereignty, agro-ecology, and what we have called self-determination and eco-social reproduction, an insight shared by McMahon and Massicotte, who bring feminist perspectives to their work in this volume on local food movements and women. La Vía Campesina has created a women's assembly and implemented quotas to address the issue of representa-tion among delegates to the regional and global assemblies, but this is hardly enough to resolve the deep inequalities in the agricultural sector, especially in ownership rates between men and women. Land owner-ship is also a potential sticking point between indigenous and non-indigenous groups within La Vía Campesina; since many of the former, as was discussed above, understand the relationships between humans and land such that individual ownership of land, by men or women, is anathema. Borras claims that the tension between the indigenous and peasants in La Vía Campesina is "likely to remain one of the most diffi-cult challenges within the global movement" (2010, 791).

One difference that probably is not so significant is that food sover-eignty polities are seeking sovereignty "only" in food, but indigenous sovereignty encompasses all of social (and economic) life. Food sover-eignty is highly multidimensional, not only because food itself connects the economy to medicine and health and to work and to gender, but because of agriculture's position in the global economy and its inter-connections with the energy sector, transportation, manufacturing, and so forth. Pursuing food sovereignty then can and should have an im-pact on energy production, hence the recent debates about biofuels at La Vía Campesina meetings. Put another way, efforts to establish sover-eignty literally have to start *somewhere*, since any claim to sovereignty is essentially territorial. Starting with the food sector gives a kind of tan-gibility to what otherwise would be the rather overwhelming project, as has been the case with indigenous peoples. In the United States, the food sovereignty rubric has taken root in a variety of locales (including sectors of Detroit and New York City) and proliferated remarkably in the last couple years, due in part to the 2010 U.S. Social Forum. But when one contemplates the territorial frame for such movements, per-haps the most compelling examples are from the anti-corporate "home-rule" movement (Patel 2010a, 166–8).

A number of U.S. counties and municipalities have banned corpora-tions from operating within their jurisdictions or have reasserted a mode of popular sovereignty that gives citizens within that jurisdiction control over specific land or resources (Patel 2010a). There are many things to like about these "home-rule" efforts from the food sovereign-ty perspective. First and foremost they involve well-defined jurisdic-tions with mechanisms for democratic participation (most often city councils), thus addressing one of the more difficult problems for food sovereignty advocates noted above. Second, they shift the balance of power within the jurisdiction, because corporations are stripped of their legal personhood. Third, some of the jurisdictions have granted rights to nature. Fourth, the assertion of sovereignty has been "partial." The first few cases were limited to agriculture (Pennsylvania, California, or Vermont, as explored by Ayres and Bosia in this volume), but explicit assertions in the current round focus on water.[21] One could imagine resolutions that banned not just corporate agriculture but also super-markets or fast food restaurants, thereby enabling locally owned food cooperatives and restaurants to more easily take root and serve as ven-ues for the locally sourced products.[22]

Conclusion

The two conceptions of food sovereignty forwarded in this chapter attempt to go beyond the more generic models that dominate the literature and to think more concretely about the challenges and implications for social movements aiming to democratize sectors of the economy. As Massicotte and Wright show in their case studies of Vía Campesina members in Brazil and the Philippines, respectively (this volume), when framed by the food sovereignty paradigm, agroecology, as a system of production, can contribute to the formation of an alternative economy that mixes capitalist, non-capitalist, and even anti-capitalist elements in a manner that reduces inequality, empowers individuals and communities, and is more socially and ecologically sustainable. While it is also crucial to chart the ways in which food sovereignty can be co-opted (see Martin and Andrée, and Bosia and Ayres, in this volume), I have argued that food sovereignty challenges the standard conception of sovereignty and the interstate system in three ways. First, from the perspective of Philpott's framework, the "who" is dramatically widened: both state-supported food sovereignty and indigenous sovereignty advocates are claiming to be sovereign, but not as states. Second, as Massicotte, Wright, Martin and Andrée, and Zerbe also argue in different contexts, the notion of territory as the space of (agro-ecological) social reproduction poses a challenge to the existing spatiality of the interstate system and the global economy in its current neoliberal form. It also brings forth spaces and structures and nurtures the subjects needed for an alternative political economy framed by the norms of participatory democracy, dignity, solidarity, and sustainability. Third, some may claim that the understandings of self-determination and territory at work in these movements push the concept of sovereignty so far as constitute a post-sovereignty politics.[23] However, the subjects pushing for food sovereignty in its state-supported and indigenous modalities are gaining numbers and ground by retaining and remaking the distinction so central to this rubric: the division between "us" and "them." From this perspective, food sovereignty is class war re-territorialized for the twenty-first century.

NOTES

1 Thanks to Thor Ritz, Justin Myers, David Spataro, Steve Mcfarland, Marc Edelman, and Nicole Rudolph for criticisms, comments, and edits, and the Brooklyn Food Coalition for efforts both bold and inventive.
2 For La Via Campesina, the crucial international and transnational pacts and organizations are NAFTA (1994) and the World Trade Organization (1995).

3 While many currents within La Via Campesina are explicitly anti-capitalist, much of the consensus links activists who are opposed more specifically to a neoliberal model that empowers transnational corporations in agriculture and the agro-industrial model of commodified food.

4 For a recent overview of the commercial, cultural, social, and political dimensions of the global food system, see Patel (2008). For a scientific literature review of the ecological effects, see Tilman et al. (2008).

5 See also International Planning Committee for Food Sovereignty, http://www.foodsovereignty.org.

6 The term is first coined, however, in the thirteenth century and gains currency in the medieval period in debates concerning the nature of the Christian God, law, and the power of kings (Elshtain 2008, 1–2, 29–55).

7 Most of the Earth's surface is not part of state space, however, so the "society of states" must also orient itself to such "open access" spaces such as the "high seas," ocean floor, and, more recently, the atmosphere (Ward 1998, 90–102).

8 The latest widely circulated version of food sovereignty was formulated in 2007 and is called the "Nyeleni Declaration." It is worth quoting at length because it shows the ever-expanding list of demands and subjects pushing for them: "Food sovereignty is the right of peoples to healthy and culturally appropriate food produced through ecologically sound and sustainable methods, and their right to define their own food and agriculture systems. It puts those who produce, distribute and consume food at the heart of food systems and policies rather than the demands of markets and corporations. It defends the interests and inclusion of the next generation. It offers a strategy to resist and dismantle the current corporate trade and food regime, and directions for food, farming, pastoral and fisheries systems determined by local producers. Food sovereignty prioritises local and national economies and markets and empowers peasant and family farmer–driven agriculture, artisanal fishing, pastoralist-led grazing, and food production, distribution and consumption based on environmental, social and economic sustainability. Food sovereignty promotes transparent trade that guarantees just income to all peoples and the rights of consumers to control their food and nutrition. It ensures that the rights to use and manage our lands, territories, waters, seeds, livestock and biodiversity are in the hands of those of us who produce food. Food sovereignty implies new social relations free of oppression and inequality between men and women, peoples, racial groups, social classes and generations" (Via Campesina 2007, 1; Patel 2010b, 190).

9   This is frequently thought to require the capacity to form intentions, reflect, and plan, but beings with such capacities are autonomous only if other beings do not interfere with the formation or exercise of the relevant capacities. For these reasons, coercion and preference deformation can undermine a being's autonomy or ability to be self-determined (Nussbaum 1998, 136–53).

10   For a historical and conceptual overview of these issues, see Mies and Shiva (1993, 1–23, 277–96).

11   This four-part scheme is a reconstructed version of Lacey (2003) but is consistent with the approaches of Altieri (1995), Cohn et al. (2006), Gliessman (2007), and Delgado (2008).

12   I am building upon Albro's usage of the term (2006, 394).

13   See Colchester (2000) and the case studies in Oglethorpe (2002), especially Gonzalez on the Philippines (2002, 16).

14   A frequent misunderstanding of commons is that they are spaces or resources that anyone can use in any way. Such unrestricted spaces are better thought of as "open access" spaces (Ostrom 1990, 1–28). See also note 5.

15   Following Wilmer (1998, 56), usage of the term *indigenous sovereignty* is not meant to imply that all indigenous societies have the same political or cultural forms, but there is a general epistemological and cultural framework that can be used to distinguish indigenous and non-indigenous peoples. See also Barker (2005).

16   For more on the differences between associationism and communitarianism, see Warren (2001, 21–3).

17   For Corntassel, examples of indigenous sovereignty include the Confederation of Indigenous Nationalities of Ecuador (CONAIE), the White Earth Land Recovery Project in the United States, the Native Federation of Madre Dios in Peru, and a variety of organizations in Oaxaca, Mexico (2008, 120–1). For more examples, see Carino (2006) and Gonzalez (2006).

18   For a list of markers that would indicate indigenous sovereignty is robustly instantiated see Woodley et al. (2009).

19   A more food-sovereignty-influenced version of the Bolivarian Alliance of Our Americas trade pact could constitute a realistic basis for such a project, especially because it has attached to it a lending agency, the Bank of the South, and several countries in the Americas are participating with Venezuela and Bolivia in the main leadership roles. See the reports of the Democracy Center for more information: "A Latin American Presidents Summit Comes to Cochabamba," 20 October 2009. http://www .democracyctr.org / blog / 2009 / 10 / latin-american-presidents-summit-

comes.html. Some "social" or "solidarity" economy trade proposals are
also useful on this note (Hines 2000).

20 Robyn Eckersley (2004) considers such an evolution a possibility, although
she does not use the food sovereignty framework but a closely related approach, which she calls the "green state."

21 Recent efforts and victories have come in Pennsylvania in opposition to
energy companies attempting to extract gas through the hydraulic fracturing of rock or "gas fracking." The results and residues generated by these
efforts have caused serious water-table and stream degradation (Margil
and Price 2010).

22 For example, in 2010 San Francisco's Board of Supervisors "voted to forbid
restaurants from giving away toys with meals that have high levels of
calories, sugar and fat" (Bernstein 2010).

23 See, for example, the work of Hardt and Negri, especially 2009.

REFERENCES

Albro, Robert. 2006. "Democracy and Bolivia's Indigenous Movements."
    Critique of Anthropology 26 (4): 387–410. http://dx.doi.org/10.1177/030827
    5X06070122.
Altieri, Miguel A. 1995. *Agroecology: The Science of Sustainable Agriculture.*
    Boulder, CO: Westview.
Alvarez, Mavis, Martin Bourque, Fernando Funes, Lucy Martin, Armando
    Nova, and Peter Rosset. 2006. "Surviving Crisis in Cuba: the Second
    Agrarian Reform and Sustainable Agriculture." In Rosset, Patel, and
    Courville 2006, 225–48.
Bailey, Robert. 1998. *Ecoregions: The Ecosystem Geography of the Oceans and
    Continents.* New York: Springer.
Barker, Joanne. 2005. "For Whom Sovereignty Matters." In *Sovereignty
    Matters: Locations of Contestation and Possibility in Indigenous Struggles for
    Self-Determination*, edited by Joanne Barker, 1–32. Lincoln: University of
    Nebraska Press.
Beauregard, Sadie, and Robert Gottlieb. 2009. *Food Policy for People:
    Incorporating Food Sovereignty Principles into State Governance.* http://www
    .oxy.edu/sites/default/files/assets/UEP/Comps/2009/Beauregard%20
    Food%20Policy%20for%20People.pdf.
Bernstein, Sharon. 2010. "San Francisco Bans Happy Meals," *Los Angeles
    Times*, 2 November.

Borras, Saturnino. 2010. "The Politics of Transnational Agrarian Movements." *Development and Change* 41 (5): 771–803.

Borras, Saturnino Jr., and Jennifer Franco. 2010. "Food Sovereignty and Redistributive Land Policies." In Wittman, Desmarais, and Wiebe 2010a, 106–19.

Borras, S. Jr, M. Edelman, and C. Kay. 2008. "Transnational Agrarian Movements: Origins and Politics, Campaigns and Impact." *Journal of Agrarian Change* 8 (2–3): 169–204. http://dx.doi.org/10.1111/j.1471-0366.2008.00167.x.

"Bush: 'I'm the Decider' on Rumsfeld." 2006. CNN, 18 April. http://www.cnn.com/2006/POLITICS/04/18/rumsfeld/.

Carino, Jill K. 2006. "Ancestral Land, Food Sovereignty and the Right to Self-Determination: Indigenous Peoples' Perspectives on Agrarian Reform." Contribution to the Civil Society Issue paper "Land, Territory, Dignity" for the International Conference on Agrarian Reform and Rural Development (ICARRD), Porto Alegre, Brazil, 7–10 March.

Ching, Lim Li. 2002. "Sustainable Agriculture Pushing Back the Desert," Institute for Science in Society.

Cohn, Avery, John Cook, Margarita Fernandez, Rebecca Reider, and Corinna Steward, eds. 2006. *Agroecology and the Struggle for Food Sovereignty in the Americas*. New Haven, CT: Co-published by Yale School of Forestry and Environmental Studies.

Colchester, Marcus. 2000. "Self-determination or Environmental Determinism for Indigenous Peoples in Tropical Forest Conservation." *Conservation Biology* 14 (5): 1365–7. http://dx.doi.org/10.1046/j.1523-1739.2000.00129.x.

Corntassel, Jeff. 2008. "Rethinking the Contemporary Indigenous-Rights Discourse." *Alternatives* 33 (1): 105–32. http://dx.doi.org/10.1177/030437540803300106.

Delgado, Ana. 2008. "Opening Up for Participation in Agro-Biodiversity Conservation. The Expert-Lay Interplay in a Brazilian Social Movement." *Journal of Agricultural & Environmental Ethics* 21 (6): 559–77. http://link.springer.com/article/10.1007%2Fs10806-008-9117-6.

Desmarais, Annette Aurelie. 2003. "The Vía Campesina: Peasants Resisting Globalization." PhD diss., University of Calgary.

– 2008. "The Power of Peasants: Reflections on the Meanings of La Vía Campesina." *Journal of Rural Studies* 24 (2): 138–49. http://dx.doi.org/10.1016/j.jrurstud.2007.12.002.

Eckersley, Robyn. 2004. *The Green State: Rethinking Democracy and Sovereignty*. Cambridge, MA: MIT Press.

Elshtain, Jean Bethe. 2008. *Sovereignty: God, State and Self.* New York: Basic Books.

Fairbairn, Madeleine. 2010. "Framing Resistance: International Food Regimes and the Roots of Food Sovereignty." In Wittman, Desmarais, and Wiebe 2010b.

Gliessman, Stephen R. 2007. *Agroecology: The Ecology of Sustainable Food Systems.* New York: CRC.

Gonzalez, Rhodora M. 2002. "GIS-Assisted Joint Learning: A Strategy in Adaptive Management of Natural Resources." In Oglethorpe 2002.

Hardt, Michael, and Antonio Negri. 2009. *Commonwealth.* Cambridge, MA: Harvard University Press.

Hawken, Paul. 2007. *Blessed Unrest.* New York: Viking.

Held, David. 1995. *Democracy and the Global Order: From the Modern State to Cosmopolitan Governance.* Stanford, CA: Stanford University Press.

Hines, Colin. 2000. *Localization: A Global Manifesto.* London: Earthscan.

Kamieniecki, Sheldon, and Margaret Scully Granzoion 1990. "Eco-Cultural Security and Indigenous Self-Determination: Moving toward a New Conception of Sovereignty." In Litfin 1998.

Kloppenburg, Jack. 2010. "Seed Sovereignty: The Promise of Open Source Biology." In Wittman, Desmarais, and Wiebe 2010b.

Lacey, Hugh. 2003. "Seeds and Their Socio-cultural Nexus." In *Science and Other Cultures: Issues in Philosophies of Science and Technology,* edited by Robert Figueroa and Sandra Harding, 91–105. New York: Routledge.

Litfin, Karen, ed. 1998. *The Greening of Sovereignty in World Politics.* Cambridge, MA: MIT Press.

Mander, Jerry, and Victoria Tauli-Corpuz. 2006. *Paradigm Wars: Indigenous Peoples' Resistance to Globalization.* San Francisco: Sierra Club Books.

Mann, Barbara Alice. 2004. *Iroquoian Women: The Gantowisas.* New York: Peter Lang.

Margil, Mari, and Ben Price. 2010. "Pittsburgh Bans Natural Gas Drilling." *YES Magazine,* 16 November. http://www.yesmagazine.org/people-power/pittsburg-bans-natural-gas-drilling.

Martínez-Torres, María Elena, and Peter Rosset. 2010. "La Vía Campesina: The Birth and Evolution of a Transnational Social Movement." *Journal of Peasant Studies* 37 (1): 149–75. http://dx.doi.org/10.1080/03066150903498804.

Menser, Michael. 2008. "Transnational Participatory Democracy in Action: The Case of La Vía Campesina." *Journal of Social Philosophy* 39 (1): 20–41. http://dx.doi.org/10.1111/j.1467-9833.2007.00409.x.

Mies, Maria, and Vandana Shiva. 1993. *Ecofeminism.* New York: Palgrave.

Narula, Smita. 2006. "The Right to Food: Holding Global Actors Accountable under International Law." *Columbia Journal of Transnational Law* 44:691–800.

Nussbaum, Martha. 1998. *Sex and Social Justice*. Oxford: Oxford University Press.

Oglethorpe, James, ed. 2002. *Adaptive Management: From Theory to Practice*. Gland, Switzerland: IUCN.

Ostrom, Elinor. 1990. *Governing the Commons: The Evolution of Institutions for Collective Action*. Cambridge: Cambridge University Press.

Patel, Raj. 2008. *Stuffed and Starved: The Hidden Battle for the World Food System*. New York: Melville House.

– 2010a. *The Value of Nothing*. New York: Picador.

– 2010b. "What Does Food Sovereignty Look Like?" In Wittman, Desmarais, and Wiebe 2010b, 186–96.

Phillips, Valerie J. 2006. "Parallel Worlds: A Sideways Approach to Promoting Indigenous-Nonindigenous Trade and Sustainable Development." *Michigan State Journal of International Law* 14:521–40.

Philpott, Daniel. 2001. *Revolutions in Sovereignty: How Ideas Shaped Modern International Relations*. Princeton, NJ: Princeton University Press.

Rosset, Peter, Raj Patel, and Michael Courville. 2006. *Promised Land: Competing Visions of Agrarian Reform*. Oakland, CA: Food First Books.

Ruggie, John Gerard. 1993. "Territoriality and Beyond: Problematizing Modernity in International Relations." *International Organization* 47 (1): 139–74. http://dx.doi.org/10.1017/S0020818300004732.

Sassen, Saskia. 2006. *Territory, Authority, Rights: From Medieval to Global Assemblages*. Princeton: Princeton University Press.

Stavenhagen, Rodolpho. 2006. "Indigenous Peoples: Land, Territory, Autonomy, and Self-Determination." In Rosset, Patel, and Courville 2006, 208–17.

Tilman, David, Kenneth G. Cassman, Pamela A. Matson, Rosamond Naylor, and Stephen Polasky. 2002. "Agricultural Sustainability and Intensive Production Practices." *Nature*, 8 August, 671–7. http://dx.doi.org/10.1038/nature01014.http://www.ncbi.nlm.nih.gov/entrez/query.fcgi?cmd=Retrieve&db=PubMed&list_uids=12167873&dopt=Abstract.

Vergara-Camus, Leandro. 2009. "The MST and ELZN Struggle for Land: New Forms of Peasant Rebellions." *Journal of Agrarian Change* 9 (3): 365–91. http://dx.doi.org/10.1111/j.1471-0366.2009.00216.x.

Via Campesina. 1996. "The Right to Produce and Access to Land."

– 2007. Declaration of Nyéléni. http://www.nyeleni.org/spip.php?article290.

Ward, Veronica. 1998. "Sovereignty and Ecosystem Management: Clash of Concepts and Boundaries?" In Litfin 1998.

Warren, Mark. 2001. *Democracy and Association*. Princeton: Princeton University Press.

Wilmer, Franke. 1998. "Taking Indigenous Critiques Seriously: The Enemy 'R' Us." In Litfin 1998, 55–78.

Windfuhr, M., and J. Jonsén. 2005. *Food Sovereignty: Towards Democracy in Localized Food Systems*. Warwickshire: ITDG Publishing. http://www.ukabc .org/foodsovpaper.htm.

Wittman, Hannah. 2010. "Reconnecting Agriculture and the Environment: Food Sovereignty and the Agrarian Basis of Citizenship." In Wittman, Desmarais, and Wiebe 2010a, 91–105.

Wittman, Hannah, Annette Desmarais, and Nettie Wiebe, eds. 2010a. *Food Sovereignty: Reconnecting Food, Nature and Community*. Halifax: Fernwood Publishing.

– 2010b. "The Origins and Potential of Food Sovereignty." In Wittman, Desmarais, and Wiebe 2010a, 1–14.

Woodley, Ellen, Eve Crowley Jennie Doy de Pryck, and Andrea Carmen. 2009. Cultural Indicators of Indigenous Peoples' Food and Agro-Ecological Systems." UN Food and Agricultural Organization (FAO). http://www.fao .org/sard/common/ecg/3045/en/cultural_indicators_paperapril2008.pdf.

3 Exploring the Limits of Fair Trade: The Local Food Movement in the Context of Late Capitalism

NOAH ZERBE

For many people, eating particular foods serves not only as a fulfilling experience, but also as a liberating one – an added way of making some kind of declaration. Consumption, then, is at the same time a form of self-declaration and of communication.

– Sidney Mintz, *Tasting Food, Tasting Freedom*

Introduction

As outlined in the introduction to this volume, recent years have witnessed increasing calls for rethinking the global food system. These calls, driven largely by perceived breakdowns in the global food system, have encouraged people to rethink the way in which the food they consume is produced. In this context, a growing number of alternative food networks have been proposed, which range from fair trade and organic production to community-supported agriculture and farmers' markets, from school and community gardens to projects addressing the challenges posed by urban food deserts. These alternatives are diverse, but they share a common focus on seeking to lay bare the social, political, and economic implications of our daily food choices. Because it is built on a relationship mediated by the market, the contemporary mainstream global food system is incapable of sustainable production and results in the alienation of producers and consumers. It is often argued that alternative food networks represent a symbolic alternative to the logic of neoliberal globalization. Despite their diversity, alternative food networks share a focus on the re-embedding of agricultural production into the broader social context, seeking to link more directly the sites of production and consumption, and rekindling E.P. Thompson's "moral economy of provision" that emphasized the collective well-being of society and placed limits on the operation of the market. Thompson's classic analysis of eighteenth-century food riots in Britain contended that popular uprisings were a direct response to the increased marketization of society. Participants in the food riots of the day were acting under the belief that they were collectively defending traditional rights and customs against the incursion of the market, and that such actions were supported "the wider consensus of community" (Thompson 1971, 78). Although Thompson's analysis was confined to the socioeconomic relations of eighteenth-century Great Britain, his concept of the "moral economy" has since been used to understand a wide variety of issues, from peasant production and resistance in Southeast Asia (Scott 1976) to contemporary challenges faced by peasant producers in Africa (Lonsdale 1992; Cheru 1989), Latin America (Orlove 1997), and the Islamic world (Tripp 2006).

While sympathetic to the overarching goal of the alternative food networks project, I argue here that their transformative potential is ultimately limited by the globalized system of agricultural production within which these networks operate. Focusing on the fair trade and local food movements – arguably the two largest and most influential of the alternative agro-food networks – I argue that their transformative potential – their potential to re-establish a "moral economy of provision" in Thompson's terms – is circumscribed by the commodity form on which they rely. To be clear, I am not suggesting in this chapter that the conventional system of agricultural production – a system based on regimes of accumulation through dispossession[1] – is preferable. Rather, by drawing on David Harvey's critique of neoliberalism, Karl Polanyi's arguments around commodification and de-commodification, and Karl Marx's concept of fictitious commodities and alienation, I argue that proponents of fair trade and local food may be overstating the challenge posed by these alternatives to the broader global food system. Fair trade and community-supported agriculture in no way exhaust the concepts of food sovereignty or food democracy. In its Statement on Peoples' Food Sovereignty, La Via Campesina (2006, 126) offered the most widely cited definition of food sovereignty, defining it as "the right of peoples to define their own food and agriculture; to protect and regulate domestic agricultural production and trade in order to achieve sustainable development objectives; to determine the extent to which they want to be self-reliant; to restrict the dumping of products in their

markets; and to provide local fisheries-based communities the priority in managing the use of and the rights to aquatic resources." From
its perspective, the globalization of food markets undermines food
sovereignty by relegating access to food to the market. Consequently,
efforts to dis-embed food from broader (global) market relations, and
re-subsume food production to broader social and cultural demands,
including a human right to food, the need for sustainable production,
and other limits, represents a central component of food sovereignty
strategies.

However, a challenge thus emerges in market-based alternative
food systems. Food sovereignty does not necessarily obviate the need
for food markets. Rather, it promotes the development of policies and
practices that emphasize social rather than simply individual reproduction and reinforce the rights of peoples to secure safe, healthy, and
sustainable food sources (see Menser's chapter in this volume for a
more detailed consideration). While markets may play a role in the
provision of food, under a food sovereignty regime the role of markets would be conditioned on broader social structures that limit the
market's influence.

Nevertheless, processes of neoliberal globalization and commodification are resisted through efforts to reassert concepts of food democracy and food sovereignty, which collectively seek to dis-embed food
from the broader market relations of global capitalism. From this perspective, then, the push for food sovereignty and democracy, however
circumscribed, represent an important part of effort to de-commodify
our food.

I begin by briefly outlining the historical development of the global
food system, emphasizing in particular the transition from Fordist to
post-Fordist systems of production that occurred in global agricultural
production beginning in the 1970s and intensified with the expansion
of global neoliberalism in the 1980s. I then explore the rise of fair trade
and the local food movement as alternative (and / or oppositional) systems of agricultural production. I argue that the ideological focus on
the individual inherent to neoliberalism led to a transformation of the
fair trade movement, moving away from the politics of citizenship to
the politics of consumerism. With this shift, citizenship was recast not
as a relationship between the collective citizenry and the state, but as a
series of individual, private, and quasi-public practices frequently centred on productive (work) or consumptive (shopping) activities (Rose
1999; Scammell 2000). Consequently, the transformative potential of

fair trade was increasingly restrained in the 1980s, and its ability to articulate an alternative vision of food production that could overcome the twin problems of the commodity fiction – the degree with which all factors of production, including money, nature, and human beings, come to be treated as commodities and organized under markets – and alienation was increasingly circumscribed. In the context of the local food movement, there is a risk that a similar problem may arise.

While still contextualized (and thus in many respects limited) by the market, local systems of production, I argue, are articulated under a regime of food sovereignty that may nevertheless provide a better opportunity to overcome the problems of alienation and the commodity fiction by directly linking producers and consumers and reasserting local control over food choices. However, these alternatives remain limited by their grounding in broader market relations. In the end, I conclude that while fair trade and local food begin to address some of the shortcomings of the mainstream food system, both ultimately are limited by the neoliberal model of consumer sovereignty from which they implicitly draw. Thus they represent an (admittedly important) effort to introduce greater levels of equity into the global food system, but may fall short of establishing a new model of social justice their proponents often advance.

The Rise of Post-Fordist Agricultural Production

At the end of the Second World War, a new global food system based on the political and economic dominance of the United States was established. The British preference for a global food system based on the principle of free trade, symbolized most dramatically by the repeal of the Corn Laws in 1849, was replaced by a new system that privileged U.S. production (Winders and Scott 2009; Winders 2009). The global food system, which in many ways mirrored the Bretton Woods system of embedded liberalism, permitted extensive state intervention in agricultural production while attempting to encourage greater international trade (Ruggie 1982). The rules of the new food regime, articulated initially under the General Agreement on Trade and Tariffs, permitted price supports, production controls, export subsidies, and other mechanisms intended to protect domestic producers.

Outside of the agricultural sector, the system of embedded liberalism began to break down in the late 1960s, when the spectre of unemployment and inflation (which would come to be referred to as the stagnation crisis of the 1970s) began to increase. The shift from a system of global Keynesianism and embedded liberalism to neoliberalism – symbolized most clearly by the election of Margaret Thatcher in the United Kingdom and Ronald Reagan in the United States – marked a dramatic increase in the influence wielded by financial capital over public policy. Under the Fordist model of agriculture, governmental assistance in the form of price supports, direct producer payments, and extension services to farmers were conceptualized as part of the broader social contract between labour and capital and a central element of the developmental project. But as the Fordist system began to break down, government assistance programs to U.S. farmers, which had been (at least rhetorically) a reaction to the perceived vulnerability of small farmers to the free market, were restructured (Potter and Lobley 2004). The state, especially in the developing world, withdrew its supports, and farmers were forced to produce – and survive – on the basis of the imperatives of the market alone.

This shift from the compromise of embedded liberalism to neoliberalism occurred across all sectors of the economy, beginning in the late 1970s. Harvey (2006, 24) describes the process of neoliberalization as "the financialization of everything and the relocation of the power center of capital accumulation to owners and their financial institutions at the expense of other factions of capital" – a description intended to highlight the shift away from production to investment. Ideologically, neoliberalism committed itself to the elevation of the individual over the community – a principle highlighted most dramatically by Margaret Thatcher's assertion that "there is no society, only individuals" – free markets, and a highly circumscribed state.

Within the agricultural sector, processes of globalization and neoliberalization played out in specific ways. Agriculture has, in a sense, always been global. The spread of plant genetic resources from one society to another can be traced in the genetic record, illustrated by the fact that major sites of consumption are often distant from the location of genetic origin for plant varieties. For example, despite having its origins in the Americas, maize became the staple crop of Southern Africa after its introduction by Portuguese explorers in the sixteenth century (McCann 2005). The Columbian Exchange, arguably the most significant event in agriculture since the development of farming settlements in the Fertile Crescent some ten thousand years ago, similarly transformed global agriculture, resulting in the introduction of tomatoes to

Italy, potatoes to Ireland, coffee to Ethiopia, paprika to Hungary, hot peppers to India, oranges to Florida, horses to the Americas, and so on (Crosby [1972] 2003).

Similarly, the colonial project involved, to a greater or lesser degree, an attempt to influence or control the spread of plant resources. The Dutch East India Company, for example, jealously guarded access to the Maluku Islands (often referred to as the "Spice Islands") of the South Pacific, and the illegal export and trade of clove, nutmeg, and other spices was punishable by death. Even the United States Navy entered the fray, ordering ships to collect plants during their voyages. These plants were returned to breeders in the United States with the goal of improving domestic plant varieties (Klose 1950). However, the long-range shipment of foodstuffs (as opposed to the movement of individual plants for their genetic information) remained limited. While cities relied on the movement of grains from widespread locations, the vast majority of individuals relied on food produced on a relatively local scale.

The deployment of new technologies, such as mass transportation and refrigerated shipping, encouraged the lengthening of food production chains and reduced local seasonal dependence, beginning in the late nineteenth century (Hobsbawm 1975). It also encouraged the gradual concentration of food processing, as witnessed by the development of the feedlots and slaughterhouses of Chicago and Kansas City in the early twentieth century. Throughout the twentieth century, and particularly during the post–Second World War era, the site of production and consumption continued to expand, separating the acts of growing and eating food (Goodman, Sorj, and Wilkinson 1987). This separation, most clearly demonstrated by the shift from the small family farms producing primarily for household consumption to massive, industrialized farms producing commodities primarily for sale, was driven largely by the need for capital to overcome the natural limits on farm production (i.e., seasonality) and to increase the rate of capital accumulation. Foods became increasingly available in regions far from the site of production and well outside their normal harvest time. The production of winter strawberries, for example, could be outsourced to Mexico to ensure that American consumers had ready access to the fruit, regardless of the season or the crop's normal production cycle. The result of these processes was a globalized, marketized food system in which relations between producer and consumer were mediated almost exclusively by the price mechanism of the market.

In more recent years, the evolution of the agrarian sector has been marked by simultaneous differentiation and integration (Goodman, Sorj, and Wilkinson 1987; Watts 1994). On the one hand, production and distribution of agricultural inputs and outputs has become increasingly concentrated among a smaller and smaller number of global firms. Today, many commodity markets are oligopolies, with just a handful of firms dominating production. In a report prepared for the National Farmers' Union, Henrickson and Heffernan conclude that the levels of agricultural market concentration in the United States have increased significantly over the past twenty years. By 2007, the four largest firms controlled 83.5 per cent of the beef packing industry (up from 72 per cent in 1990), 66 per cent of the pork packing industry (up from 37 per cent in 1987), 58.5 per cent of broiler processing (up from 35 per cent in 1986), 55 per cent of turkey processing (up from 31 per cent in 1988), and 80 per cent of soybean crushing (up from 61 per cent in 1982) (Hendrickson and Heffernan 2007). The UN Food and Agriculture Organization observes similar trends in global markets, concluding, "Agricultural commodity chains, particularly those of high-value crops and processed products, are increasingly dominated by transnational trading, processing and distribution companies. On its way from farmer to consumer, for example, nearly 40 per cent of the world's coffee is traded by just four companies and 45 per cent is processed by just three coffee-roasting firms" (Hallam et al. 2004, 30).

Markets for agricultural inputs reflect a similar concentration. The six largest agrochemical suppliers, for example, controlled an estimated 77 per cent of global markets, while the three largest firms (Bayer, Syngenta, and BASF) accounted for nearly half the market. While slightly more diversified, global seed markets are also increasing concentrated. In 2004, the four largest seed companies (DuPont, Monsanto, Syngenta, and Lumagrain Groupe) accounted for 30 per cent of global seed sales (United Nations Conference on Trade and Development 2006). As a result, global agricultural production chains come to resemble a reversed hourglass, where a large number of farmers purchase their inputs and sell their outputs to a small number of firms, which, as a result of their size and the degree of market concentration, are frequently able to dictate prices and terms to the farmer.

At the same time, the global food system taken collectively has also increasingly differentiated niche markets. Reflecting a broader global trend towards flexible (just-in-time) production under the post-Fordist system, agricultural production has also become increasingly diversified. Coffee markets, for example, are now less concerned with the bulk price of coffee as an undifferentiated commodity. The price of coffee on any single market can vary from a baseline price (termed class 3, or "exchange grade coffee"), depending on its country of origin and broader production characteristics. Thus coffee from some countries might enjoy a premium while others may be sold at a discount.[2] Specialty coffee (organic, shade grown, and fair trade) is generally not sold on commodity markets but is delivered according to terms laid out in individual contracts, negotiated directly between the coffee retailer or supplier and individual coffee growers. The global coffee market, in other words, is better conceptualized as a series of interconnected markets differentiated by the coffee's quality, geographic origin, and conditions of production (e.g., organic, conventional, shade grown, fair trade, etc.) than as a single, unified global commodity market.

Importantly, the changing nature of food production occurred concomitantly with the introduction of new household technologies and changing gender dynamics within the household. The introduction of microwave ovens and freezers, for example, accompanied by the increasing employment of women outside the household, redistributed household labour and changed patterns of food consumption. People made fewer shopping trips and increased their consumption of pre-prepared meals. They also increased their consumption of food outside the household, and families began to eat apart.

Widely explored and documented in the literature, the implications and dynamics of these processes include lengthening of global food chains (Goodman, Sorj, and Wilkinson 1987), increasing concentration of capital within the agricultural sector (Heffernan 2000; Heffernan, Hendrickson and Gronski 1999), intensifying environmental degradation (Altieri 2000), and expanding commodity relations (Kloppenburg 1988; Mann 1990).

The development of integrated markets also led to a decline in regional food specificity. Regional diets increasingly gave way to more uniform tastes, perhaps signalled most clearly by the displacement of local and regional restaurants by national (and increasingly international) franchise restaurants offering uniform fare across the globe. This represented the displacement of space from the site of consumption and has been widely criticized under the label of "Americanization" and "McDonaldization" (Mathews 2000; Rappoport 2003; Ritzer 2008).

Towards a Market Society

As Polanyi famously observed, prior to the development of market society in the nineteenth century, all previous economic systems were firmly embedded in broader political and social orders in which non-economic principles such as reciprocity, redistribution, and social obligation played key organizing roles. But with the rise of market society, broader social obligations are displaced by purely economic relations, the commodity fiction comes to play a key organizing role, and social relations become embedded in the market rather than the historical reverse of embedding the market in broader social relations.

Similarly, in the context of food production and consumption, the production and distribution of food under market society differs dramatically from that of non-market societies. The political economy of food under non-market societies historically took a variety of forms, ranging from gift-based economies (such as the potlatch system practised by Native American peoples in the Pacific Northwest), to state distribution (as was the case under ancient Roman grain codes), to simple coercive appropriation (Sahlins 1972). The emergence of market society transformed systems of food production. Indeed, as Wood (2002, 96–7) observes, market society "gives the market an unprecedented role in capitalist societies, as not only a simple mechanism of exchange or distribution, but the principle determinant and regulator of social reproduction. The emergence of the market as the determinant of social reproduction presupposed its penetration into the production of life's most basic necessity: food."

From this perspective, the restructuring of the global food system that has occurred since the late 1970s may be said to represent the intensification of market society through its further penetration into the realm of food. Polanyi lamented the destructive impulse of such a system, famously concluding,

> To allow the market mechanism to be sole director of the fate of human beings and their natural environment, indeed, even of the amount and use of purchasing power, would result in the demolition of society... Robbed of the protective covering of cultural institutions, human beings would perish from the effects of social exposure; they would die as the victims of acute social dislocation through vice, perversion, crime, and starvation. Nature would be reduced to its elements, neighborhoods and landscapes defiled, rivers polluted, military safety jeopardized, the power

to produce food and raw materials destroyed ... No society could stand the effects of such a system of crude fictions even for the shortest stretch of time unless its human and natural substance as well as its business organization was protected against the ravages of this satanic mill. (Polanyi [1944] 2001, 73)

While the destructive impulse of a pure market society is clear, it should be remembered that Polanyi's market society represented a hypothetical ideal type. In reality, Polanyi recognized that *all* markets are socially embedded to a greater or lesser degree. The fundamental difference between capitalist and non-capitalist systems is not *whether* the market is socially embedded. Rather, the fundamental difference centres on the *degree* or *character* of that embeddedness. Andrée (this volume) emphasizes the way in which an oversimplified version of Polanyi's framework is sometimes used to argue that alternative food networks are embedded while global agriculture networks are not. Both traditional and alternative networks are embedded in broader social relations, subject to demands by agents at various levels. Calls to adopt a Polanyian framework in this context thus represent a reaction against the subjugation of relations of social reproduction to the imperatives of the market. Andrée's use of the term *neoliberalization* highlights the way in which the expansion of market-based regulation and dramatic cuts in the role of the state further affect the ongoing struggle between liberalization and calls for broader social protections expressed most clearly in Polanyi's double movement.

Polanyi's approach is further qualified by Block's (1990) introduction of the linked concepts of marketness and instrumentalism. The concept of "marketness" describes the degree to which price plays a determining role in economic transactions. Under conditions of high marketness, price dominates all other considerations. However, under low marketness, non-price considerations take on greater importance, and price becomes just one of any number of variables on which a specific transaction may be based.

The concept of "instrumentalism" complements this analysis by highlighting the individual motivations for economic activity. High instrumentalism means that individuals emphasize their own economic goals and preferences and engage in opportunistic behaviour in the pursuit of those goals and preferences. Low instrumentalism is associated with non-economic goals and concerns, such as friendship, family, morality, or spirituality (Hinrichs 2000).

Block's introduction of marketness and instrumentalism clarifies Polanyi's concept of the embedded market, emphasizing the continuum on which all markets and societies operate, thereby highlighting the central role of political and social agency in defining and redefining market–society relations (see table 3.1). In 1850, the U.S. economy was dominated by small-scale agricultural production, which accounted for approximately 80 per cent of all economic output (Block 1990, 56). The system and relations of agricultural production in 1850 also looked very different from today's. Farmers – like workers more generally – have always sought to insulate themselves from the most rapacious effects of the market. In the 1850s, farm production was insulated from the most immediate effects of the market. Farm labour generally drew from the household, in particular from the unpaid labour of women and children, rather than the paid help of formal farmhands. Farm production thus frequently centred in the coordination of family labour across a complex series of tasks intended to reproduce the household. Farmsteads exhibited a higher level of autonomy from the market, as homes frequently grew their own food, baked their own bread, and sewed their own clothing. The welfare of the community and the individual frequently depended on the development of reciprocal networks of social obligation between neighbours and community members. While foodstuffs produced on the farm may regularly be sold on spot markets, the instrumentality and marketness of production were severely limited by social obligations within and between households. Reflective of this fact, a large proportion of economic transactions took place within the household economy (57–8).

Contrasted with the globalized system of agricultural production and consumption today, U.S. farming in the 1850s highlights the changing degree of marketness and instrumentalism at play. Polanyi's purpose was to analyse the constant struggle between market regulation and state regulation – a struggle played out through the double movement. Ultimately, the solution to the problem of the commodity fiction centred on recognizing of the unique nature of fictitious commodities (land, labour, and money).

The Fair Trade Movement

Since its humble origin in the charity shops of Western Europe in the 1940s and 1950s, fair trade has blossomed into a significant global industry. Today, fair trade is perhaps the most developed of the

Table 3.1. Marketness and Instrumentalism

	High marketness	Low marketness
High instrumentalism	Economic transactions are dominated by the price mechanism, with self-interest playing a central role. This is the theoretical model of neoclassical economics.	Transactions are dominated by non-market concerns, but price plays a central role. The self-interest of individual actors plays a central role.
Low instrumentalism	Transactions are dominated by price but emphasize non-individualistic or non-economic goals.	Transactions are dominated by non-market concerns, regardless of price. This represents an economic system in which the market is fully embedded in (and is ultimately subservient to) broader social relations.

alternative agro-food networks. While still representing a small proportion of global trade, fair trade products nevertheless achieved an estimated €2.9 billion (approximately US$4 billion) in fair trade certified sales in 2008, and continue to grow at approximately 22 per cent per year (Fairtrade Foundation 2009a, 2009b). More than five hundred companies specialize in fair trade products, and more than 100,000 points of sale offer fair trade products to consumers (Krier 2008) (see table 3.2).

Advocates of fair trade caution that the success of the fair trade movement should not be based solely on expanding sales figures or volumes. Because the goal of fair trade is to connect, at least symbolically, producers and consumers, the success of the fair trade movement, they contend, should be measured in either the degree to which it results in an improvement in the livelihoods of producer families and their communities (Krier 2008) or in the articulation of an alternative system of food provision (Raynolds 2000). Fair trade, as defined by FINE,[3] is "a trading partnership, based on dialogue, transparency and respect, that seeks greater equity in international trade. It contributes to sustainable development by offering better trading conditions to, and securing the rights of, marginalized producers and workers – especially in the south. Fair trade organizations (backed by consumers) are actively engaged in supporting producers, in awareness raising and in campaigning for changes in the rules and practices of conventional international trade" (Krier 2008, 23). Under the fair trade model,

Table 3.2. Top Five Fair Trade Markets by Net Retail Value of Sales (Euros, 2007)

Country	Sales (2007) (in € millions)	Sales growth, 2005–7 (%)
France	210.0	92
Germany	141.7	100
Switzerland	158.1	10
United Kingdom	704.3	154
United States	730.8	112
Worldwide total	2,381.0	109

Source: Adapted from Krier (2008, 43).

consumers pay a social premium for the commodities they purchase. This premium permits fair trade importers to offer higher prices to the producer and to finance local development initiatives, such as building schools, in the producing communities.

According to its proponents, the fair trade model operates at once "within and against" the market (Brown 1993, 156). While operating through the market, it seeks to develop a notion of political consumerism that fundamentally transforms and ultimately overcomes the exploitative relationship of traditional trade channels, challenging the "abstract capitalist market principles" under which market exchange normally operates (Raynolds 2000, 206). This is accomplished through three key elements, embodied in FINE's definition of fair trade: (1) promoting sustainable development, (2) improving the livelihoods and empowering workers and producers, especially in the global South, and (3) seeking to transform conventional trade practices.

Although fair trade operates across a number of commodities, including cacao, tea, honey, bananas, sugar, orange juice, and coffee, the fair trade relationship generally involves an agreement between producers and retailers or certification agencies. Fair trade networks have demonstrated an ability to deliver social and economic benefits for Southern producers and communities. In their analysis of fair trade coffee production, Murray, Raynolds, and Taylor (2003) conclude that fair trade benefits individual producers (who receive higher, more predictable, and stable prices for their produce as well as improved access to credit), their families (through improved educational opportunities and greater family stability), and their communities (primarily as a result of the social premium paid to finance cooperative activities). Fridell,

Hudson, and Hudson (2008) reach a similar conclusion, noting that coffee growers engaged in fair trade production have benefited from higher incomes, greater price stability, greater diversification of production, and a higher level of political autonomy and empowerment than their non-fair trade counterparts, while simultaneously engaging in more sustainable and ecologically friendly production processes. Field studies confirm these general observations. In their analysis of fair-trade tea producers in South Africa, for example, Raynolds and Ngcwangu (2010) observe that fair-trade production provides economic opportunities for poor Blacks historically disadvantaged by the legacies of the apartheid system. Wilson (2010) similarly notes that fair-trade coffee producers in Nicaragua benefited from technical assistance, access to cooperative processing facilities, and credit markets.

Nelson and Pound's (2009) study provides perhaps the most compelling analysis of the potential benefits of fair trade systems. Their study, which compiled thirty-three separate case studies concentrated in Latin America and the Caribbean (twenty-six cases) and fair trade coffee (twenty-five cases) found that thirty-one of the thirty-three case studies demonstrated positive economic benefits resulting from the fair trade agreement. These benefits centred on the provision of more stable incomes (twenty-seven cases) and in improved access to credit and financing (eleven cases). It was noted, however, that fair trade producers do not necessarily enjoy higher household incomes than non-fair trade producers, as the cost of certification offset the fair trade premium offered to producers. Consequently, few studies demonstrate dramatic improvements in living standards for fair trade producers.

In more theoretical terms, fair trade seeks to address the twin problems of commodity fetishism and alienation inherent in global trade networks. By making the conditions of production transparent, fair trade seeks to link producers in the global south with consumers in the global north, thereby highlighting the social and environmental context of production. A fair trade label, in other words, is intended to reassure consumers that the products they are purchasing were produced in an environmentally and socially sustainable way and that the producer received a "fair" price for the commodity. The fair trade model might thus be described as a relationship that more directly connects producers and consumers in a way that avoids the tendency towards commodity fetishism, that brings the conditions of production squarely into the consumption process, and that highlights the social and ecological character of prediction and consumption (Hudson and Hudson

2003). In principle, fair trade's ability to lay bare the conditions of production provides a mechanism whereby individuals may overcome the commodity fiction, considering not just the final sale price of the commodity but the ways in which their choice to consume the commodity implicates them in broader networks of (in)justice and (in)equality.

But while the fair trade movement's proponents may represent it as a potential corrective to the logic of accumulation and alienation – making the relationship between the sites of food production and food consumption more transparent – the transformative potential of the fair trade movement is nevertheless limited by the degree to which it remains confined in the neoliberal framework, particularly its emphasis on individualism and consumer sovereignty. While offering consumers better information regarding the market decisions they make, fair trade nevertheless "accepts that the needs of poor Southern producers are ultimately subservient to the demands of Northern consumers" (Fridell 2007b, 266). From this perspective, fair trade represents the commodification of social justice rather than the assertion of social justice on a global scale. This limitation leads Fridell to conclude that "while fair trade does represent an important symbolic challenge to the principles of market exchanges under capitalism, it is unlikely to service as the basis for envisioning a project that moves beyond the symbolic toward a long-term, fundamental challenge to the core aspects of commodification" (80).

Thus while this system is certainly preferable to conventional marketing channels as the result of the higher wages and better working conditions it affords the worker, it can hardly be said to overcome the problem of alienation. As Marx notes, the alienation of labour consists in the fact that the worker "does not realize himself in his work, that he denies himself in it, that he does not feel at ease in it, but rather unhappy, that he does not develop any form of physical or mental energy, but rather mortifies his flesh and ruins his spirit. The worker, therefore, is only himself when he does not work ... His labor therefore is not voluntary but forced – forced labor. It is not the gratification of a need, but only a means to gratify needs outside itself. Its alien nature shows itself clearly by the fact that work is shunned like the plague as soon as no physical or other kind of coercion exists" (Marx [1844] 2000, 110–11).

Although offered a social premium for their products under the fair trade model, fair trade networks often deny Southern producers agency, alienating the workers both from the creative process of production and from the product of their labour. If they choose to participate in fair trade, producers are obligated to meet the requirements laid out by the

fair trade certification agency. The conditions within which they operate – although preferable to the conventional relations of production –
are outside their control.

The alienation of fair trade workers is a function primarily of the
technocratic management system at the heart of certification, a process
that undermines the moral imperative of the fair trade system, establishing a hierarchy of production in which the producers continue to
work under conditions dictated by certifying agencies based in the
global North. Workers remain alienated from the conditions and product of their labour. Dolan (2010), for example, observes that Kenyan fair
trade tea producers were often unaware they were producing under a
fair-trade system because, with the exception of the social premium
paid to the cooperatives to finance community development, there was
no real difference between conventional and fair trade production. The
same social and economic structures were at play in both systems. A
number of interviews with local leaders in the fair trade in Kenya reflected frustration with the lack of transparency, the top-down nature
of decision-making, and the strict regulation imposed on fair trade
producers. In his analysis of fair trade cotton production in Mali and
Burkina Faso, Bassett (2010) reaches a similar conclusion, noting that
fair trade does not address the fundamental inequalities and power relationships in global cotton markets.

From the perspective of the Northern consumer, the transformative
potential of fair trade similarly remains limited. Although consumers
are willing to offer a social premium for the products they are consuming, their relationship with the producer nevertheless remains mediated by the commodity. While the number of hands through which the
commodity passes is reduced, permitting the producer to receive a
greater portion of the final sale price, the geographic and social distance
remains great. Northern consumers are not really relating to the Kenyan
who grew their tea, the El Salvadoran who grew their bananas, or the
Ethiopian who grew their coffee. They are, at best, relating *to* the individual *through* the fair trade product. The social relations of production,
though improved, remained mediated through the market and continue to be expressed through the product. The central problematic of the
commodity form – defined by Marx ([1867] 1990, 164–5) as consisting
"simply in the fact that the commodity reflects the social characteristic
of men's own labor as objective characteristics of the products of labor
themselves, as the socio-natural properties of those things" – remains.

Further, the relations of production continue to be dominated by
the competition imperative. One defining feature of capitalism is the

way in which the dynamics of competition under capitalism force workers and owners to behave in particular ways. Indeed, as Wood (1999) notes, market imperatives and accumulation take precedence over social needs and ecological stability. "Once the market becomes an economic 'discipline' or 'regulator,' once economic actors become market-dependent, even workers who own the means of production, individually or collectively, will be forced to respond to the market's imperatives – to compete and accumulate, to exploit themselves, and to let so-called 'uncompetitive' enterprises and their workers go under" (Wood 1999, 23).

In this context, fair trade producers operating in competition with conventional marketing channels face similar pressures and imperatives. While fair trade production has grown rapidly in recent years, its growth has outpaced increase in consumer demand. Consequently, fair trade markets have become flooded, and fair trade products are increasingly sold through conventional marketing channels. In her analysis of fair trade coffee producers in Costa Rica and Guatemala, for example, Berndt (2007, 16) observes that fair trade producers are able to sell only about 20–25 per cent of their harvest to a fair trade buyer. The vast majority of their production is sold on conventional coffee markets at less than fair trade prices because of insufficient demand. Similar problems have been noted for other fair trade commodities, including bananas, cocoa, sugar, and tea (Torgerson 2010; Hallam et al. 2004).

Fair trade, in short, remains grounded in the same economic structures of global neoliberalism as more conventional forms of agricultural production. While guaranteeing farmers basic floor prices and higher rates of return may improve their status and social well-being, the fair trade model is nevertheless unable to fundamentally transform the social relations of production and consumption that separate Northern consumers and Southern producers. Social relations – fair trade or not – remain mediated by the market. Producers and consumers continue to relate to one another primarily through the consumption of commodities. Fair trade, in other words, is not an alternative to the market. At its best, fair trade represents an important reform of the market, but it remains fundamentally a part of it. It represents an effort to introduce protective strategies, indispensable under capitalism, but is not fundamentally transformative of it.[4] At worst, however, fair trade may represent, as Fridell (2007a) warns us, a depoliticized alternative to the logic of neoliberalism, shifting the locus of social protection from the state to the market while simultaneously entrenching a model of social ethics predicated on the principle of consumer sovereignty at the very heart of the neoliberal project.

Local Food Alternatives: Consumer Sovereignty or Moral Economy?

The rise of the local food movement beginning in the mid-1980s represents another attempt to address the limitations of the conventional food system. While taking a variety of forms including community kitchens, community-supported agriculture, urban and school gardens, and farmers' markets, the local food movement represents an effort to re-embed food production into broader social relations through a moral economy of provision. This relationship, which was prevalent in the food sector prior to the rise of the supermarket, is "not formal or contractual, but rather the fruit of familiarity, habit, and sentiment, seasoned by the perception of value on both sides" (Illmulchis 2000, 298).

Because of the unique, direct nature of the relationship between producer and consumer, community-supported agriculture (CSA) may represent the highest level of de-commodification of the current alternatives. In a CSA, individuals purchase "shares" in a farm for a set price at the beginning of the growing season. Each share gives them a portion of the total production of the farm, usually picked up by the consumer at a set weekly time. If the season is good, the consumer may enjoy a plentiful harvest. Conversely, in a poor season, the consumer may receive a much smaller weekly bounty. Indeed, perhaps the most transformative element of the CSA system is the way that it shifts the risk of farming, reshaping the relationship between producer and consumer, requiring that the consumer assume some of the risk of the farming normally borne by the farmer alone.

But for their proponents,[5] CSAs also have the potential to more fundamentally transform broader social relations as well. As Cone and Myhre (2000, 188) conclude, CSAs could "'re-embed' people in time and place through linking them to a specific piece of land and an awareness of the seasons." Food could be produced closer to the site of consumption and without the extensive reliance on chemical inputs characteristic of industrial production. Local social capital would be reinforced, as food producers and food consumers would be directly connected, nurturing a stronger sense of community.

But, as Fieldhouse (1996, 47) suggests, this may best be described as an effort to "soften" the market mechanism rather than overcome or replace it. Under the CSA system, relations between producer and consumer continue to be influenced (though perhaps not dominated) by price. For the majority of shareholders, CSAs provide a ready supply of quality produce at a pre-set price. Many shareholders never participate in the other, community-building activities offered by CSAs, such as farm days, educational opportunities, and seasonal festivals, the very social interactions that would serve to help construct a more powerful alternative. Consumers remain price-conscious, and farmers are aware that if the price of the share appears to be too high or if the value appears to be too low, their customers (the shareholders) will likely not renew their share next year, seeking greener pastures elsewhere. A study of shareholders at Redwood Roots Community Farm in Humboldt County, for example, found that the primary reasons individuals joined the CSA included buying fresh and organic produce (the two responses that received the most answers). Only 9.7 per cent of respondents indicated that they joined the farm because they supported the philosophy of CSAs. The two most frequent reasons given for not renewing farm shares were that it was inconvenient or the price was too high (Delello 2004). Cone and Myhre (2000) reach similar findings in their analysis of eight CSAs in Minnesota.

In more theoretical terms, the motivation for farmers' participation in local agriculture (in the form of both farmers' markets and CSAs) illustrates the tension between instrumentalism and marketness in the face of apparent efforts to re-embed markets. Hinrichs (2000), for example, cites several studies of farmers' motivations for participating in markets, most of which conclude that there are two main motivations for their participation: enjoying the market experience and maximizing their earnings. This is not surprising, given economic pressures on small farmers, but it also suggests that farmers' markets serve, at best, a dual purpose, and that the degree of social re-embedding occurring at farmers' markets is limited by a degree of instrumentalism. Consumers at farmers' markets are similarly driven by conflicting motives, simultaneously seeking out low prices (good value) for high-quality food while at the same time enjoying the direct contact with the producers of their food. Customers may be willing to pay a premium for the farmers' market experience, but they are not price-insensitive. Indeed, the movement towards localization of food, such as through farmers' markets, "can generate genuinely valued social ties, but the familiarity and trust between producer and consumer does not necessarily lead to a situation where price is irrelevant or where instrumental interests are completely set aside. Sometimes what producers are selling to consumers at farmers' markets is, in part, the aura of personal relations and social connections. Embeddedness itself then becomes some of the 'value added' in the farmers' market experience" (Hinrichs 2000, 299).

Despite its potential, the local food movement has not been able to reshape the discourse over community food security in the way that its proponents suggest. Like the fair trade movement, the local food movement presents an alternative to the conventional food system but falls short of being fundamentally oppositional.

The real challenge posed by local food is not so much in the act of consumption. That is, after all, an act still based in the market. The challenge, rather, derives from the opportunity to expand and reconnect with other members of the body politic, to form community, and to provide the foundation for other forms of social and collective action. As McMahon (this volume) observes, the "radically progressive possibilities" are opened by critically examining our social relations of production and consumption in ways that fundamentally challenge the local food movement's basis in the consumerist politics of middle-class urbanism. In this sense, while the local food movement may not represent a dramatic or transformative challenge to the dominant system of global food provision, it nevertheless may provide a foundation on which to articulate a vision of food sovereignty, relocating the site of access to food away from the global market. In fair trade, this opportunity is missing. That is the fundamental difference between the local food and the fair trade movements. That is also where the real, transformative potential of the local food movement rests.

Conclusion: Fair Trade and Local Food in the Context of Late Capitalism

Whatever its limits, the local food and fair trade movements do represent improvements over the conventional food system. By providing producers with higher prices and more stable streams of income, both address some of the central problems associated with the conventional food system. This struggle over social provision and for improving the terms and conditions of work is a common feature to worker movements under capitalism. This is no small feat and should rightly be celebrated. But, in their current forms, both movements are alternative rather than oppositional.

The risk is that focusing on the local obfuscates broader structural and global issues that condition (and perhaps limit) individual agency. As David Harvey (1996, 353) notes, "The contemporary emphasis on the local, while it enhances certain kinds of sensitivities, erases others and thereby truncates rather than emancipates the field of political engagement and action." Individual actions may make the individual feel better (as a consumer), but by itself, it does little to offer the kind of fundamental transformation necessary to address the global environmental crisis. Similarly, in the context of the global food system, buying and eating locally may make individual consumers feel better about their decisions, but alone it may not result in the kind of fundamental transformation of the global food system that its advocates propose.

Such challenges are, of course, not limited to the fair trade and local food movements. Consumer-based food movements, whether they be "buy local" campaigns, food-procurement policies at public institutions, or other similar programs must remain cognizant of the inherent limits of their approach. Using consumer action to improve the conditions of food production is an important first step in the shift towards a food sovereignty regime. However, any movement that ends with consumer-based political agency necessary leaves unchallenged the broader regime of accumulation and the systems of production on which it is founded.

The local food movement must therefore be accompanied by a broader push to rethink community food security and social justice. To take but one example, while a handful of CSAs are reaching out to local disadvantaged communities, most research suggests that CSAs generally remain the purview of white, upper-middle-class consumers. In this respect, the local food movement has much to learn from the environmental justice movement, which successfully addressed questions of privilege in the context of environmentalism. A similar food justice movement would take as its starting point the right to quality food into its consideration of local, organic production. Such a movement would necessarily be more oppositional and transformative, because it would integrate, in a fundamental way, questions of power and privilege in the context of food. Its emphasis on the moral economy of provision would represent a fundamental challenge to the conventional food system, where access is mediated exclusively by the price mechanism. It would also represent a more fundamental re-embedding of food production into broader social relations, reducing both the instrumentalism and the marketness of food production.

NOTES

1 Harvey defines accumulation by dispossession as "the continuation and
   proliferation of accumulation practices which Marx had treated of as
   'primitive' or 'original' during the rise of capitalism. These include the
   commodification and privatization of land and the forceful expulsion of
   peasant populations ... conversion of various forms of property rights
   (common, collective, state, etc.) into exclusive private property rights ...
   suppression of rights to the commons; commodification of labor power and
   the suppression of alternative (indigenous) forms of production and consumption; colonial, neocolonial, and imperial processes of appropriation
   of assets (including natural resources); monetization of exchange and taxation, particularly of land; the slave trade ... and usury, the national debt,
   and most devastating of all, the use of the credit system as a radical means
   of accumulation by dispossession" (Harvey 1995, 159). In this context,
   Harvey argues that accumulation by dispossession comprises four main
   features: (1) privatization and commodification, (2) financialization, (3) the
   management and manipulation of crises, and (4) state redistributions.
2 Commodity market pricing for coffee, for example, generally assumes
   class 3 (exchange grade coffee) delivered from par-based countries (Costa
   Rica, El Salvador, Guatemala, Kenya, Mexico, New Guinea, Nicaragua,
   Panama, Tanzania, and Uganda). Coffee quality can increase or decrease
   prices, with class 1 (specialty) and class 2 (premium grade) coffee demanding price premiums, and class 3 (below standard grade) and class 4
   (off-grade) being discounted. Colombian coffee receives a price bonus of
   two cents per pound, while other producers' coffee is sold at a discount
   (Honduras and Venezuela discount one cent per pound, Burundi, India,
   and Rwanda discount three cents per pound, and the Dominican Republic,
   Ecuador, and Peru deliver at a price discount of four cents per pound). For
   a more detailed discussion, see Coffee Research Institute (2006).
3 Created in 1998, FINE is an informal collective network of the four main
   fair trade organizations: Fairtrade Labeling Organizations International
   (FLO), the World Fair Trade Network (formerly the International Fair
   Trade Association), the Network of European Worldshops, and the
   European Fair Trade Association.
4 Echoing Karl Polanyi, Wood (1999, 15) observes that protective strategies
   "have been a necessary part of capitalism since the beginning. Capitalism,
   despite its material achievements, is by its very nature a disruptive and
   destructive way of organizing social life, because it subordinates all

human goals to the imperatives of accumulation, because it inevitably dispossesses huge multitudes of people, and so on."
  5 See, for example, Halweil (2004) and Blatt (2008), each of whom argues strongly in favour of more localized food systems.

REFERENCES

Altieri, M. 2000. "Ecological Impacts of Industrial Agriculture and the Possibilities for Truly Sustainable Farming." In *Hungry for Profit: The Agribusiness Threat to Farmers, Food, and the Environment*, edited by F. Magdoff, J.B. Foster, and F. Buttel, 77–92. New York: Monthly Review.
Bassett, T. 2010. "Slim Pickings: Fairtrade Cotton in West Africa." *Geoforum* 41 (1): 44–55. http://dx.doi.org/10.1016/j.geoforum.2009.03.002.
Berndt, C. 2007. *Does Fair Trade Coffee Help the Poor? Evidence from Costa Rica and Guatemala.* Mercatus Center Policy Series, Policy Comment No. 11. http://mercatus.org/sites/default/files/publication/Fair%20Trade%20Coffee.pdf.
Blatt, H. 2008. *America's Food: What You Don't Know about What You Eat.* Cambridge, MA: MIT Press.
Block, F. 1990. *Postindustrial Possibilities: A Critique of Economic Discourse.* Berkeley: University of California Press.
Brown, B. 1993. *Fair Trade: Reform and Realities in the International Trading System.* London: Zed.
Cheru, F. 1989. *The Silent Revolution in Africa: Debt, Development, and Democracy.* London: Zed.
Coffee Research Institute. 2006. "Coffee Trade: New York Coffee Exchange." http://www.coffeeresearch.org/market/coffeemarket.htm.
Cone, C.A., and A. Myhre. 2000. "Community Supported Agriculture: A Sustainable Alternative to Industrial Agriculture?" *Human Organization* 59 (2): 187–97.
Crosby, A.W. (1972) 2003. *The Columbian Exchange: Biological and Cultural Consequences of 1492.* Westport, CT: Praeger.
Delello, C. 2004. "Community Supported Agriculture: A Case Study in Humboldt County." MA thesis, Humboldt State University.
Dolan, C.S. 2010. "Virtual Moralities: The Mainstreaming of Fairtrade in Kenyan Tea Fields." *Geoforum* 41 (1): 33–43. http://dx.doi.org/10.1016/j.geoforum.2009.01.002.
Fairtrade Foundation. 2009. "Global Fair Trade Sales Increase by 22%." News release, 8 June. http://www.fairtrade.org.uk/press_office/

press_releases_and_statements/archive_2009/jun_2009/global_fairtrade_
sales_increase_by_22.aspx.

Fieldhouse, P. 1996. "Community Shared Agriculture." *Agriculture and Human Values* 13 (3): 43–7. http://dx.doi.org/10.1007/BF01538226.

Fridell, G. 2007a. "Fair Trade Coffee and Commodity Fetishism: The Limits of Market-Driven Social Justice." *Historical Materialism* 15 (4): 79–104. http://dx.doi.org/10.1163/156920607X245841.

– 2007b. *Fair Trade Coffee: The Prospects and Pitfalls of Market-Driven Social Justice*. Toronto: University of Toronto Press.

Fridell, M., I. Hudson, and M. Hudson. 2008. "With Friends Like These: The Corporate Response to Fair Trade." *Review of Radical Political Economics* 40 (8): 8–34.

Goodman, D., B. Sorj, and J. Wilkinson. 1987. *From Farming to Biotechnology: A Theory of Agro-Industrial Development*. New York: Blackwell.

Hallam, D., Pascal Liu, G. Lavers, P. Pilkauskas, G. Rapsomanikis, and J. Claro. 2004. *The Market for Non-Traditional Agricultural Exports*. Food and Agriculture Organization. http://www.fao.org/docrep/007/y5445e/y5445e00.htm.

Halweil, B. 2004. *Eat Here: Reclaiming Homegrown Pleasures in a Global Supermarket*. New York: W.W. Norton.

Harvey, D. 1995. *A Brief History of Neoliberalism*. New York: Oxford University Press.

– 1996. *Justice, Nature, and the Geography of Difference*. Malden, MA: Blackwell.

– 2006. *Spaces of Global Capitalism: Towards a Theory of Uneven Geographic Development*. London: Verso.

Heffernan, W. 2000. "Concentration of Ownership and Control in Agriculture." In *Hungry for Profit: The Agribusiness Threat to Farmers, Food, and the Environment*, edited by F. Magdoff, J.B. Foster, and F. Buttel, 61–75. New York: Monthly Review.

Heffernan, W., Hendrickson, M., and R. Gronski. 1999. *Consolidation in the Food and Agricultural System: Report Prepared for the National Farmers' Union*. Report for National Farmers Union. http://www.foodcircles.missouri.edu/whstudy.pdf.

Hendrickson, M., and W. Heffernan. 2007. "Concentration of Agricultural Markets." http://www.foodcircles.missouri.edu/07contable.pdf.

Hinrichs, C.C. 2000. "Embeddedness and Local Food Systems: Notes on Two Types of Direct Agricultural Market." *Journal of Rural Studies* 16 (3): 295–303. http://dx.doi.org/10.1016/S0743-0167(99)00063-7.

Hobsbawm, E. 1975. *The Age of Capital, 1848–1875*. London: Weidenfeld and Nicolson.

Hudson, I., and M. Hudson. 2003. "Removing the Veil? Commodity Fetishism, Fair Trade, and the Environment." *Organization & Environment* 16 (4): 413–30. http://oae.sagepub.com/content/16/4/413.

Kloppenburg, J. 1988. *First the Seed: The Political Economy of Plant Biotechnology, 1492–2000.* Madison: University of Wisconsin Press.

Klose, N. 1950. *America's Crop Heritage: The History of Foreign Plant Introduction by the Federal Government.* Aimes: University of Iowa Press.

Krier, J.-M. 2008. *Fair Trade 2007: New Facts and Figures from an Ongoing Success Story.* Culemborg: Dutch Association of Worldshops.

La Via Campesina and People's Food Sovereignty Network. 2006. "People's Food Sovereignty Statement." In *Food Is Different: Why We Must Get the WTO Out of Agriculture,* edited by Peter M. Rosset, 125–40. London: Zed Books.

Lonsdale, J. 1992. "The Moral Economy of the Mau Maui: Wealth, Poverty, and Civic Virtue." In *Unhappy Valley: Conflict in Kenya and Africa,* edited by B. Berman and J. Lonsdale, 315–504. London: James Currey.

Mann, S.A. 1990. *Agrarian Capitalism in Theory and Practice.* Chapel Hill: University of North Carolina Press.

Marx, K. (1844) 2000. *Economic and Philosophic Manuscripts of 1844.* http://www.marxists.org/archive/marx/works/1844/manuscripts/preface.htm.

– (1867) 1990. *Capital.* Vol. 1. New York: Penguin.

Mathews, G. 2000. *Global Culture/Individual Identity: Searching for Home in the Global Supermarket.* Oxford: Taylor and Francis.

McCann, J. 2005. *Maize and Grace: Africa's Encounter with a New World Crop, 1500–2000.* Cambridge, MA: Harvard University Press.

Mintz, S. 1996. *Tasting Food, Tasting Freedom: Excursions into Eating, Power, and the Past.* Boston: Beacon.

Murray, D., L. Raynolds, and P. Taylor. 2003. *One Cup at a Time: Poverty Alleviation and Fairtrade Coffee in Latin America.* http://www.fairtrade.net/uploads/media/Colorado_State_U_Study__Fairtrade_and_Poverty.pdf_05.pdf.

Nelson, V., and B. Pound. 2009. *A Review of the Impact of Fairtrade over the Last Ten Years.* London: Fairtrade Foundation. http://www.fairtrade.org.uk/resources/natural_resources_institute.aspx.

Orlove, B.S. 1997. "Meat and Strength: The Moral Economy of a Chilean Food Riot." *Cultural Anthropology* 12 (2): 234–268. http://dx.doi.org/10.1525/can.1997.12.2.234.

Polanyi, K. (1944) 2001. *The Great Transformation: The Political and Economic Origins of Our Time.* Boston: Beacon.

Potter, C., and M. Lobley. 2004. "Agricultural Restructuring and State Assistance: Competing or Complementary Rural Policy Paradigms?" *Journal of Environmental Policy and Planning* 7:34–50.

Rappoport, L. 2003. *How We Eat: Appetite, Culture, and the Psychology of Food*. Toronto: ECS.

Raynolds, L. 2000. "Re-embedding Global Agriculture: The International Organic and Fair Trade Movements." *Agriculture and Human Values* 17 (3): 297–309. http://dx.doi.org/10.1023/A:1007608805843

Raynolds, L., and S.U. Ngcwangu. 2010. "Fair Trade Rooibos Tea: Connecting South African Producers and American Consumer Markets." *Geoforum* 41 (1): 74–83. http://dx.doi.org/10.1016/j.geoforum.2009.02.004.

Ritzer, G. 2008. *The McDonaldization of Society*. Los Angeles: Pine Forge.

Rose, N. 1999. *Powers of Freedom*. New York: Cambridge University Press. http://dx.doi.org/10.1017/CBO9780511488856.

Ruggie, J.G. 1982. "International Regimes, Transactions, and Change: Embedded Liberalism in the Postwar Economic Order." *International Organization* 36 (2): 379–415. http://dx.doi.org/10.1017/S0020818300018993.

Sahlins, M. 1972. *Stone Age Economics*. Hawthorne, NY: Aldien de Gruyter.

Scammell, M. 2000. "The Internet and Civic Engagement: The Age of the Citizen Consumer." *Political Communication* 17 (4): 351–5. http://dx.doi.org/10.1080/10584600050178951.

Scott, J.C. 1976. *The Moral Economy of the Peasant*. New Haven, CT: Yale University Press.

Thompson, E. 1971. "The Moral Economy of the English Crowd in the Eighteenth Century." *Past & Present* 50 (1): 76–136. http://dx.doi.org/10.1093/past/50.1.76.

Torgerson, A.M. 2010. "Fair Trade Banana Production in the Windward Islands: Local Survival and Global Resistance." *Agriculture and Human Values* 27 (4): 475–87.

Tripp, C. 2006. *Islam and Moral Economy: The Challenge of Capitalism*. Cambridge, MA: Cambridge University Press. http://dx.doi.org/10.1017/CBO9780511617614.

United Nations Conference on Trade and Development. 2006. *Tracking the Trend towards Market Concentration: The Case of the Agricultural Input Industry*. New York: UNCTAD.

Watts, M. 1994. "What Difference Does Difference Make?" *Review of International Political Economy* 1 (3): 563–70. http://dx.doi.org/10.1080/09692299408434300.

Wilson, B.R. 2010. "Indebted to Fair Trade? Coffee and Crisis in Nicaragua." *Geoforum* 41 (1): 84–92. http://dx.doi.org/10.1016/j.geoforum.2009.06.008.

Winders, B. 2009. "The Vanishing Free Market: The Formation and Spread of the British and U.S. Food Regimes." *Journal of Agrarian Change* 9 (3): 315–44. http://dx.doi.org/10.1111/j.1471-0366.2009.00214.x.

Winders, B., and J.C. Scott. 2009. *The Politics of Food Supply: U.S. Agricultural Policy in the World Economy*. New Haven, CT: Yale University Press.

Wood, E.M. 1999. "The Politics of Capitalism." *Monthly Review (New York, N.Y.)* 51 (4): 12–26.

– 2002. *The Origins of Capitalism: A Longer View*. London: Verso.

4 Local Food: Food Sovereignty or Myth of Alternative Consumer Sovereignty?

MARTHA McMAHON

Introduction

In addition to my academic research, I own a small farm that depends on the local food movement, like many other small-scale farms in British Columbia (BC). But the local movement faces challenges that make the future of the movement and of our small, ecologically focused farms uncertain.[1] Despite its benefits, the turn to the local is not changing the underlying reasons why most small and midsize farms are struggling. Part of the reason for the limited efficacy of this movement lies with the ongoing hegemony of food security as an organizing concept. This hegemony continues, I argue, because those of us who are part of this movement have not yet developed an adequate food sovereignty framing of our complex problems, one that mitigates the harsher remedies associated with food security, as outlined in Menser's chapter.

This chapter starts with local troubles and local responses to them. More particularly, it starts with a difficult journey with sheep and concludes with an understanding that food sovereignty cannot be equated with either food security or food localization, important though each may be. Although I begin with my own experience, this is not intended as a biographical validity test of ideas but as a starting point for analysis, as food sovereignty should allow one to connect the individual and local to the institutional and political-economic.

While we BC farmers face problems, we also have opportunities. Over fifty years ago C.W. Mills coined the term *sociological imagination* as an incitement to connect "the personal troubles of milieu and the public issues of social structure" (Mills 1959, 8). Troubles, like those facing my farm and other small-scale farmers, are often experienced as individual-level problems. They feel like *our* problems. We are told by governments, consultants, and high-level think tank reports that we are not efficient enough, not adequately competitive for a global market place, too small, under-capitalized, don't have good enough marketing skills or business plans. Increasingly, we face barriers to marketing our food or processing our farm products because, we are told, we represent a biosecurity hazard, we lack adequate food safety infrastructure, or we don't comply with new regimes of agri-food governance. Sometimes we are offered grants to pay consultants to "fix us." But C.W. Mills, along with feminist sociologist Dorothy Smith (2005), teaches us to connect seemingly private experiences with public issues. Like the women's movement that long ago offered the key insight that the personal is also political, the introduction to this book explains how peasants, small-scale farmers, displaced rural and indigenous people, fishers, health workers, urban consumer and food justice activists are identifying the connections between the individual or local-level troubles and wider structural and institutional arrangements around food and agriculture. Food sovereignty offers that kind of connecting lens, bringing together what might be misunderstood as disconnected crises and troubles locally and globally.

Until one makes the analytical and empirical connections, for example, hunger appears to be essentially a matter of not enough food in some individuals' lives, women peasant farmers are (mis)understood to be poor because they lack market access and the right technologies, the rising rates of obesity and diabetes will appear to be the result of individuals making the wrong food choices, and the economic struggles of small-scale BC farmers is misrepresented as simple inefficiency. Food sovereignty and food democracy can be understood as initiatives, efforts, and networks to make connections between the daily experience of troubles and the political-economic and institutional levels. The intention in food sovereignty is not only to connect but to be able to coordinate effective responses. Making such connections may start in different places with different experiences, and may lead to different strategies, but it typically leads to an analysis of neoliberalization – a term that is shorthand for specific configurations of economic and political (including private governance) arrangements, described and analysed in other chapters of this collection. As the introductory chapters explain, these arrangements have been long in the making. If the concept of neoliberalization analytically connects the sources of such disparate troubles as food price crises, land grabs, diabetes and obesity levels, food scares, and the loss of small-scale farms, the concepts of food sovereignty and / or food democracy analytically and politically connect a variety of actors', networks', and individuals' responses and attempts at solutions.

This chapter approaches food sovereignty through the experience of farming on Southern Vancouver Island. It argues that food sovereignty offers a conceptually and politically enabling framework for respond-ing to local troubles in food and agriculture. It is conceptually enabling because as it is taken up locally it allows small-scale farmers to see be-yond the local to the wider political and economic arrangements that often almost invisibly organize their farming. It is politically enabling because it provides resources that potentially allow them to mobilize and coordinate action with other farmers, consumers (see Smythe, this volume), and food sovereignty activists located elsewhere.

At the same time, this chapter argues that the local food movements in the region where I farm will be unable to realize the political po-tential of food sovereignty if they remain tied to the concept of food security, understood as an individualist, consumer-focused, and ad-ministrative discourse of food redistribution and safety, even when conjoined with the more recent strategy of food localization. Although the language of food sovereignty is starting to be used more widely in the Canadian food movement, as Martin and Andrée explore in their contribution to this volume, its political insights regarding the power imbalances between food producers and consumers are not necessarily widely understood. As a result, localization is still conflated with the goal of the food movement, rather than one of many strategies that form part of a toolkit for making broad-based and equitable social change.

Some of the distinctive features of the region in which I farm are that the vast majority of farms are small, about half earn less than $10,000 a year; about 36 per cent of all farmers in BC are women, and most farm households rely on off-farm income. The supply-managed commodity sectors[2] such as milk and poultry are the most "economically viable" kinds of farms, and a small number of commodity farms produce most of the market dollar value of agri-food products, though some small organic farms are extraordinarily productive on a per acre basis. Of the small-scale ecological farms in the region where I farm, over half are worked by women. While farm incomes are low, the number of farms is declining, although until now somewhat more slowly than elsewhere in Canada. At the same time, there is an increase in the number of very small farms in a few peri-urban areas. Historically, BC farms did not hire a great deal of farm labour, but today migrant workers from Mexico (and elsewhere) are increasingly brought in on temporary work permits and are becoming the new face of farm labour.

For the last fifteen years I have been part of a network of largely women farmers who have worked to build new local food systems, enable landless people to get into farming, set up farmers' markets, organize farmer apprenticeships and mentorships, and develop new markets. There are also a wide variety of other overlapping local, regional, and national groups and networks organizing around food and agriculture. My contribution to these efforts is marginal compared to what many of my fellow farmers are doing.

Although there is much to encourage us locally and farmers' accomplishments are remarkable, scratch the surface and small-scale farming continues to have a precarious future. A single regulatory change that harmonized food safety regulations helped put nearly half the small-scale sheep farmers near me out of business a few years ago. New internationally standardized codes of "good agricultural practices" (GAP) could soon do the same to small-scale vegetable growers. Yet small-scale farmers, here as elsewhere, display enormous resilience and creativity, as several chapters in this text show. The excesses of the market (if a market in the economic sense really exists) can often produce imaginative social movements of resistance and powerful collective responses. Many consumer, activist, and farmer organizations have turned to the local as a way of responding to problems in the globalizing food system. Unfortunately, my experience, including a review of recent writings on these topics, leads me to the conclusion that the food localization agenda is simply not enough on its own.

A Local Journey and a Global Agenda

It was a warm summer evening. Myself and six lambs (as they would say it in Ireland, where I used to farm) found ourselves hurtling down the TransCanada Highway as darkness fell. On that recent July evening, cars sped by our slow farm truck. They cut in and out about us with silent indictments to "get out of my way" or even "get off the road." As my small truck, with wisps of hay sticking out from the back, moved along a highway full of fast-moving cars, some with tops down, I had to ask if we – the sheep and I – really did embody local efforts at food security, let alone food sovereignty. It seemed everything we encountered proclaimed the message that we should not be there, that there is no longer any place for the "likes of us."

We had come off an evening ferry from Pender Island, one of the Southern Gulf Islands between Vancouver Island and mainland BC. It has a population of about 2,500 permanent residents and about six small sheep farms. Our ferry was late. While waiting to board at the Pender Island terminal, tourists took pictures. These Rare Breeds Cotswold lambs are beautiful to those with what Haraway (2008, 42) might call "the good manners to know how to see." Like many of the older non-commercial breeds of farm animals, they face extinction. They have an obvious dignity in their bearing and intelligence in their actions, and their lustrous locks had made them the prized sheep of the pre-industrial British woollen trade, which, when it developed, became part of the basis for the globalizing impulses of an empire, on which, it was said, the sun never set. The lambs claim no nationality whatsoever, though even now at the start of the twenty-first century their lives are inextricably shaped by global social relationships and the seductive appeal to the local.

By the time the lambs and I got off the ferry, it was dusk. We had a legally mandated appointment next day with a representative of the provincial government of BC and federal government of Canada. We had to make the journey in the evening because the first morning ferry would make us late. We had an hour-and-a-half's journey ahead of us that evening. I was driving. The lambs were in the back. We were going to the abattoir.

We made that evening trip because recent legislation had closed down local on-inland abattoirs in an effort to transcontinentally harmonize meat production standards and to keep open the Canadian-U.S. border for trade in live cattle and beef. The fact that the lamb would be sold exclusively locally – would become local food – should not distract us from realizing that the relations that organize local food are often part of trans-local if not global institutional political economic and governance arrangements, impressing on us that the local by itself is not an antidote for neoliberalization.

Methodology

In this chapter I use the concept of local food networks to refer to a loose collection of associated civil society groups, initiatives, organizations, projects, and also individuals associated with local health and regional public authorities who are trying to address problems in the food system. Although these networks are diverse and fluid, a key strategy for accomplishing change is the promotion of local food.

Political economic factors such as corporate domination in the food system or international trade regimes are sometimes discursively implicated in the problems but more often appear as the stage settings or externally imposed pernicious props that backdrop the ethical efforts of individuals. Their connections to the consumer who is to act either as agent of change or is the object of protection are under-theorized and remain analytically mysterious. This is understandable because, as many I have talked to tell me, people feel there is little they can do about, for example, corporate concentration. Buying local is something they can imagine doing. Thus my work involves a critique of the weaknesses in local food movement political analysis and (what sociologists call) "subject positions" and is *not* a criticism of individuals.

I conceptualize local food networks as part of "movement for change" in civil society, rather than "a movement" (hooks 1989). Movement for change is seldom easily contained, conceptually or empirically. Movement may not fit within the boundaries of the organizations that claim to articulate its meaning, nor necessarily be led by such organizations. Thus organizations' or groups' policy statements, goals, listserve postings, etc., need to be read discursively rather than as texts that tell us about an external empirical world in any easy way. My use of the terms *local food networks* or *movement* is by necessity a contrivance. It can only point in the direction of tendencies and trends and cannot be fully adequate to capture the fluidity and diversity of social movement. The data for this chapter come from a variety of different sources: local food networks and municipal and health authority and related food security websites in BC, local environmental and conservancy websites and meetings, interviews with small-scale local farmers, my work as a farmer who sells locally, research on the impact of recent food safety legislation on small farmers and research on survival strategies of peri-urban farmers (Eagle, Tunnicliffe, McMahon, and van Kooten 2008) on Southern Vancouver Island, and reflection on fifteen years of participation in local meetings and events to do with local food and food security. My methodological position is a partial and situated perspective (Harding 1986, 1991; Haraway 1988), and my perspective is sociological.

The Turn to the Local

In matters of food, there has clearly been a turn to the local. Local food is now seen by many as bringing social, health, and environmental benefits. I am part of this turn to the local. In this section I critically reflect on the local food movement of which I am part, in order to suggest some ways out of its limitations, while not losing sight of the possibilities it opens. Local food movements are part of wider initiatives to address problems around food and agriculture. There are significant differences in what are understood to be the causes of these problems and, by implication, in the proposed solutions.

In BC the turn to the local does not appear to have improved the situation for the majority of small farmers. The number of farmers in the province fell from 21,835 in 1996 to 19,759 in 2006 (BC Ministry of Agriculture 2011). From a governance perspective this may not matter, because the actual number of hectares farmed has increased (from 2,529,060 in 1996 to 2,611,383 in 2010), as have gross farm receipts, invested farm capital, and farm wages paid. While gross receipts are up, in real terms net farm income in most cases has been falling. From a food security perspective, the loss of farmers may not matter either, if food is nutritious, safe, cheap, and plentiful enough even for low-income individuals and families to access it. From a food sovereignty perspective the loss of farmers, however, does matter, because farmers *themselves* and the social and ecological relationships that they embody, not just the food for sale that they produce, matter (Desmarais 2007; Patel, Balakrishnan, and Narayan 2007; Patel 2010: Wittman, Desmarais, and Wiebe 2010). If, following McMichael (2008, 2010), we think of food sovereignty as rooted in the agro-ecological relationships of peasant and small-scale farmers, one might appreciate that these socio-ecological relationships offer subject positions different from that of the consumer from which to start to engage the power relations that organize the agri-food system. It is not the only starting point but it is a critically important one.

The new regimes of bio-governance described below and through which the "rare breeds and local" sheep and I are moving into extinction seems far from the world envisioned by local food networks. The contemporary turn to the local offers to reconnect: to reconnect producers and consumers of food, people and place (Hinrichs 2000, 2003; Morgan, Marsden, and Murdoch 2006). It also offers to disconnect: that is, to disconnect the consumers who choose to do so from the "industrial food system." The language of connection and disconnection, however, is misleading. It conflates geographic proximity / distance with social relationship. Consumers and producers are already connected in the "industrial" food system. But they may feel connected in ways they don't want. The unwanted aspects of the connections range widely from cost to health (and health-care budgets), food-safety fears, ecological damage, poor-quality food, social injustice, or animal welfare, for example. Local food offers not reconnections as much as it offers alternative connections / disconnections. The local turn is often attributed to popular media like Michael Pollan's books *The Omnivore's Dilemma* (2006) and *Real Food* (2009), *Fast Food Nation* (Schlosser 2001), or documentaries like *Food Inc.* or *King Corn*. These and a series of food scares have left consumers feeling that they can no longer trust their food, or their governments' ability to ensure its safety (Blay-Palmer 2008).

As pointed out in the introduction to this volume, one way of reading the turn to the local is to see it as a response to increased neoliberal penetration of food and agricultural sectors. The accompanying increased globalization, deregulation, and corporate concentration, it can be argued, lowered standards of safety and the nutritional quality of food and increased the risks to consumers and the exploitation of both animals and workers in food and agriculture industries (Hatt and Hatt 2012). If globalization seems to embody in the food we eat the ills of market-produced space-time distanciation, then the local appears to be a form of civil society resistance providing social and ecological connections between people, place, and the food they eat. Local food represents non-market interpersonal relations of trust rather than reliance on universally codified measures of quality or goodness found in supermarket grades and standards (Busch 2000; Friedberg 2004). On a broader dimension, the turn to the local speaks to the rise of the reflexive consumer of late modernity (Beck, Giddens, and Lash 1994; Giddens 2006).

The concept of reflexive consumption captures the process by which individuals define themselves through active engagement with the attributes or qualities of the commodities they choose to purchase (whether social justice, fair trade, ecological qualities, or nutritional value). Miele's (2006) and Smithers and Joseph's (2010) work on farmers' markets, however, suggests that the reflexive food consumer is both partially and inconsistently reflexive. Their research shows that qualities attributed to food purchases are selectively and inconsistently attended to and are typically engaged only in particular sites of consumption, and around specific products. Similarly local farmers I have talked to report that there is "more talk than action." One can feel connected to the idea of eating locally even if one's purchase is sporadic, tenuous, and limited. Local organic greens or fair trade coffee can become iconic or totem items for seeing oneself as supporting local food or being an ethical consumer. Thus "wanting to eat locally" can be almost as effective as part of identity claims as the actuality. Food, including the refusal of certain kinds of food or of food generally (as in anorexia), is key to identity construction in late modernity (Giddens 2006).

Stoneman (2009) is cynical about the activist and academic faith in reflexive consumption. It implies, he argues, an "informational" model of the subjectivity of the consumer. He invokes the image of software the consumer can use to read an almost endless list of qualities, whether fair trade, low fat, bird friendly, nutritional contents, and so on, which the consumer can then choose. If consumers are informed about the ills of the global food system, the reasoning goes, they will adjust their consumption habits. While this faith in the educated consumer may express the liberal utopian fantasy that all social problems can be solved by the sound choices of informed individuals (Stoneman 2009), it may also point to emerging new post-industrial regimes of production and consumption that are being driven by a post-industrial creative class (Hines 2010, 2012) for whom reflexivity operates as a kind of positional good.

For Guthman (2007, 2008a, 2008b) alternative food movements are not truly alternative. Rather, she argues, they operate to reproduce neoliberalizing forms, spaces of governance, and mentalities at the same time they tend to romanticize the local farmer. This may be particularly the case locally, I would argue, where organizing around food is fuelled by anxieties about food security, safety, and broader qualities of "our food." The invocation of food security or appealing to the safety of the local may offer a psychological antidote to the food anxieties of our times: a promise of a future place of security (see below).

Lavin (2009) argues that local food politics such as that discussed by Michael Pollan has been so widely taken up in the United States precisely because it resonates with the subjective lived experience of neoliberalism. This is an experience in which political agency is all but unthinkable except in terms of consumerism. Food is the "quintessential consumable" and an intimate commodity, not only because it is ingested and sustains the body but also because food sustains the social self, builds sociability, and embodies social relationships. New meanings of food need to be understood as part of a wider turn to the body as a critical site of identity in late modernity. Attention paid to the sourcing, preparation, and consumption of food provides unique opportunities for identity construction, whether as an ethical, virtuous, informed, or health-conscious person. It also provides opportunities for the conspicuous displays of good taste and offers old and new sites for claiming and establishing social capital, gendered social identities, and other status claims. It is not surprising that food should be such an active site for social movement.

If consumption is so central to identity formation in late modernity in its neoliberalizing moment and in the creation of ever more sites for the deployment of consumption-based identities, why then should the subject of late modernity feel such food-related insecurity? Could it be that because food is the quintessential act of consumption the popular media exposures of the ills of the food system make it clear that the consumer is losing the illusion of sovereignty so promised by the market where, according to neo-classical economics, the consumer is (supposed to be) king?[3] If so, this would shatter a foundational myth of market-dominated societies.

Changing Public and Private Agri-Food Governance

The turn to local food coincides with and is connected to new meta-regulatory projects of public and private governance, most commonly in the context of discourses of food safety and biosafety. Animal bodies in particular (but soon to include all kinds of vegetable life-forms) are critical sites of interest and activity for new forms of governance and biosecurity regulation. As agri-food governance increasingly becomes private and globalized, nation states impose industry-based established practices as the legally required best or "good agricultural practices" for farmers of every size and scale. One of the spectres haunting the future of food for both the local and the global is the menacing association of other bodies and disease. This spectre is coming into direct conflict with many of the aspirations held for local food and for alternative futures for agriculture, whether agro-ecological, poverty reduction, or rural revitalization. New forms of governance driven by the dystopian side of modernity (Beck 1992) and consumer anxieties increasingly now frame local small farmers, global food corporations, consumers, public and private regulatory authorities, and of course the food we all eat, albeit in different ways. Food-related websites share horror stories of the newest case of contaminated eggs. Farmer magazines and government websites reveal policymakers' and regulatory authorities' preoccupation with food safety and disease control. My sheep will soon all wear legally required electronic tags to allow birth-to-death monitoring and surveillance in order to protect, I am told, Canadian global markets and the local consumer. How did these local and global corporate

interests become so intertwined, and can (or should) local food movements try to untangle them? This question is particularly significant
because in BC (and Canada more generally) the turn to local food is not
simply a civil society movement or even an alternative market moment.
It is also becoming an administrative, economic, and institutional turn.
It involves new patterns of governance (if not governmentalities), investment, and bio-politics. In the long run, food as a new moment if not
movement of administration and governmentality, will be far more determining for farmers (and my lambs) than the consumer politics of
local food movements (McMahon 2011).

Food Movements Are Not All Alike:
Food Security vs Food Sovereignty

We can think of food movements as embodying (not always clearly articulated) definitions of the problem and proposed solutions. In a recent
article, Holt Giménez and Shattuck (2011) offer an analytic framework
for understanding contemporary food movements. They distinguish
between neoliberal, reformist, progressive, and radical movement approaches. At risk of oversimplification, the differences between them
are captured in the following shorthands for their respective solutions
to crises in food and agriculture: food enterprise, food security, food
justice, and food sovereignty (Holt Giménez and Shattuck 2011). The
first two offer solutions to problems that are understood as (current or
projected) imbalances in the food supply and demand (e.g., too little
food being produced, the spectre of a growing population, growing demand for meat by increasingly affluent populations) or inefficiencies
in the system (e.g., blocked market access, trade barriers or outdated
technologies). While food enterprise solutions to problems in the agri-
food system will focus on freeing the market to work efficiently, reformist food security solutions will include initiatives such as those for a
green revolution in Africa or the work of the Bill and Melinda Gates
Foundation. These two kinds of solutions are compatible with the current neoliberalizing[4] food regime. The third kind of movement, food
justice, concerns itself with problems of access to food, including good
food, by low income sections of the population. Holt Giménez and
Shuttuck see these kinds of progressive food movements such as much
of the community food movement in Canada and the United States as
ambiguous vis-à-vis neoliberalization. That is, they argue that this kind
of movement could be absorbed into dominant agri-food movement as

opportunities for niche markets and redistributive food security initiatives. Or it could throw its lot in with the fourth kind of movement. They see the fourth, food sovereignty, as clearly transformative. Themes of all four are found interwoven in the discourses of the local food movement where I live. However, the tensions and contradictions of their political and institutional origins are seldom theorized. Thus the allegiances and implications of local food movements can get pretty confusing. Not surprisingly, therefore, academics like Julie Guthman (2007, 2008a, 2008b) repeatedly expose the neoliberal tendencies of local food politics in the United States and find local food movements in support of small-scale farmers to be in tension with food justice, which they see as a progressive food movement tendency (Guthman, Morris, and Allen 2006). This leads such critics to be somewhat dismissive of farmer movements and agrarian politics in the United States. Critics like Guthman, however, tend to work with a distributional notion of justice that is not conceptually aligned with the more radical understanding of food sovereignty held in some local food movements outside of the California context in which she is situated (2008b).

Canadian civil society food movements often invoke the goal of food security. However, the concept of food security comes with baggage. It incorporates legacies from its institutional origins in concerns about the food supply. Sometimes redefined as community food security, food security has recently incorporated a progressive social justice turn in its meaning (see Martin and Andrée, this volume), which may or may not be counter-hegemonic (Fairbairn 2012). Thus the discourse of food security conceals several different registers of meaning.

Mooney and Hunt (2009) argue that the assumed consensus on the term *food security* conceals at least three very distinct collective action frames: food security as freedom from hunger or adequate food supply; food security as part of community development; and food security as minimizing risks in the industrial food system's vulnerability to normal accidents (such as microbial contamination) as well as intentional actions such as bioterrorism. Each frame, they explain, can be read in a different key. These keys express power differentials in the endorsement or critique of dominant institutional practices in food and agriculture. Like Holt Giménez and Shattuck (2011), they argue that some keys of meaning of food security may challenge institutionalized relations in the agri-food system; others reproduce them.

Early modern framings of food security (the term wasn't necessarily used) as a concern with hunger, food, and political unrest often derived from Malthusian assumptions about populations outstripping the food supply. When the spectre of hundreds of thousands dying of starvation (as in the colonies of Ireland and India) came into conflict with new notions of good government, and later in the dislocations and threats of political upheaval after the Second World War, food security developed into a governing managerial trope of feeding the hungry, typically organized around security concepts of national or global food supplies. Thus food security may often contain less of a social justice agenda than an administrative one. It may involve the distribution of food but it does not necessarily involve the redistribution of income and wealth, recognition, or political participation against which models of social justice can be assessed (Fraser 2005, 2009). The discourse of food security as hunger alleviation is a powerfully persuasive one. It is used to justify interventions such as the Gates Rockefeller Alliance for a Green Revolution in Africa (AGRA) and its working partnerships with Monsanto and other major agri-industry corporations. A focus on food safety is also often found within conservative meanings of food security. The creation of food safety protocols or legislation thus becomes a food security issue. Food security as food safety is increasingly becoming a significant regulatory and economic discourse and, despite the impression of technical neutrality, is creating an almost insurmountable barrier to small-scale farming (DeLind and Howard 2008; McMahon 2011), as our experience with new slaughter regulations in BC attests to (McMahon 2011).

The language of food security can be found in the four movement tendencies identified by Holt Giménez and Shattuck. There are notable efforts to shift the agenda of Canadian local and national civil society food movements from a discourse of food security towards food sovereignty (Kneen 2010; Martin and Andrée, this volume). Even in its progressive register, however, food security focuses on relations of distribution and access but not on the social and biosocial relations through which food is provisioned or produced. Food sovereignty looks beyond distributional understandings of food security and social justice to invoke far more radically democratic and ecological registers of food politics in which people's material, symbolic, and ethical relationship with their natural worlds, their rights to control their food systems, concern for biodiversity, livelihood for rural dwellers, local sustainability, gendered equality, and resistance to neo-liberalization, for examples, are central (Patel 2010; Patel, Balakrishnan, and Narayan 2007; see also McMichael, Massicotte, Wright, and other chapters in this volume).

How does any of this help me understand my experience as a farmer? From food sovereignty emerges a not yet fully formulated concept of agrarian citizenship (Wittman 2010), offering me (as a farmer) a political counter to the neoliberal consumer of local food in whom Guthman and other academics have so little faith. My working relationship with (non-human) nature and the co-production of the social and the natural, self and environments, become central here. Although my farm depends economically on local consumers, food sovereignty offers me, and them, an alternative to simply reproducing neoliberal food relations, a deficiency constantly identified by social justice critics of the local food movements (Guthman 2008a, 2008b; Lavin 2009; Stoneman, 2009). The notion of agrarian citizen also challenges the concept of farmer as *food entrepreneur* so central to neoliberal and reformist solutions to agri-food and agrarian problems, and on which the economic viability of local farms (as meeting niche markets) is being encouraged to rely in new (public and private) agricultural policy recommendations. Sarah Wright's account in this book of a farmer-led food sovereignty movement in the Philippines is very encouraging, because it shows that tendencies that threaten to depoliticize food movements can be resisted and that alternatives are possible. Thus, despite the considerable pressures to depoliticize local food initiatives where I live, local food does not have to be reduced to a niche market for the alternative, quality- or ethically concerned neoliberal consumer. But such a depoliticization can too easily happen. Food sovereignty helps us recognize the difference between niche markets and food democracy that might not be clear otherwise.

Beyond Food Security and Localization:
Taking Agrarian Citizens Seriously

A major challenge facing the local food movement comes from the ways in which it has absorbed an individual, consumer-focused, administrative-orientated and hence problematic discourse of food security from the wider neoliberal context from which it has emerged. The wider local context, as Guthman's (2008a, 2008b) work on food movements in California shows, can foreclose the progressive political possibilities opened by the turn to the local. The dominant discourse in local food networks where I live is that of food security. The dominant strategy or solution to food- and agriculture-related problems is local food. But these are borrowed discourses and strategies with multiple origins in, as Holt Giménez and Shattuck (2011) and Mooney and Hunt (2009) show, very different institutional and political projects, from neoliberal, to neoliberal reformist, to social justice, even to food sovereignty. It is not just a matter of semantics. Different framings of the problem lead to very different kinds of solutions. The unreflective use of the discourse of food security in the neoliberal context of the conflation of consumption-politics and citizenship means that local food movements cannot easily escape the neoliberalizing tendencies that Guthman (2008a, 2008b) and others find so problematic. Similarly, the strategy of local food glosses over political differences: local food can be resistance to corporate-driven neoliberal agri-food regimes. But it is not necessarily so.

We locally have not developed our own political analysis. Our discourses are full of tensions and contradictions that confuse the issues and allow us to gloss over the hard, potentially divisive questions. We tend to challenge poverty, but not privilege. This political-economic analytic fuzziness stands in contrast, for example, to the farmer-led food sovereignty movements we learn about in other chapters in this book that look at how some agri-food activists are redefining the politics of place and scale in ways that challenge rather than parochialize social constructions of the local.

Yes, in the short run, the consumer-focused turn to the local helps me sell my farm produce and feed my wonderful sheep. Yes, as a small-scale farmer, this feels like a good thing. In the longer run, however, the current turn to the local is not changing the underlying reasons why most small and midsize farms are struggling or why economic concentration in the agri-food sector continues despite growing ideological commitment to the local.

There is a lot written and said about local food, its possibilities and limitations as a means of social change. The issue, however, is not just what is said, but who gets to speak at all and what frames of reference are allowed into the conversation to shape policies and actions. Typically farmers are spoken for, or spoken about: they are represented as being helped, saved, encouraged, or as being in need of becoming better ecological citizens. Sometimes a local celebratory farmer is showcased or quoted. Among those I talk with, some worry that the new public and policy interest in agriculture is overly urban-driven by people who have little understanding of farming. Many fear the new policy and public interest will continue to leave most small- and mid-size farmers without a voice (Country Life in BC 2010, 5). Yet many smaller farmers near big cities also think that urban consumers are their hope for the future and see direct marketing as their best survival strategy (Tunnicliffe 2011). But not all farmers are on the same page. Agriculture is diverse, as are farmers. Some have followed years of government and policy-advisor advice and have gotten bigger to survive and be able to compete globally. Others, especially but not only smaller farmers, have turned to the local as a survival strategy and / or because it offers more ecological options.

Does it matter that farmers' voices (though not pictures of them or their farms) are relatively marginal in local food movements? Even on a very local, immediate, and practical level, it matters. For example, the absence of farmers' voices means that consumer demand for "safer food" can unintentionally legitimate corporate-designed agri-food governance that is driving small farmers out of business. It makes it easier for consumers to confuse niche marketing with food democracy, even when only a minority of entrepreneurial farmers is engaged. Whereas some elements of redistributional food justice may be possible without farmers' political participation, food sovereignty is not.

My point here is that local farmers can contribute more than good food to "good" food politics. But providing food, it appears, is the role they are most expected to play. The political potential of agrarian-based citizenship (Wittman 2010) is seldom seriously engaged by city-based local food networks (or many academics), although it may be discursively deployed. The concept of agrarian citizenship invokes social as well as ecological bases of citizenship in which the ideological separation of nature and society (mirrored in the separation of rural and urban), so foundational to modernity, is overcome (Wittman 2010). It connects food, agriculture, society, and environment through systems of mutual co-production, interdependence, and obligation in which resilience, not maximum efficiency, is an organizing principle (91). Against this alternative and in the context of climate change and coming ecological challenges, the progressive food security movements' focus on redistributional justice in the absence of resilient food systems seems superficial. It may do little but redistribute misery.

To suggest that local food networks are too urban (as I do) is not to essentialize a geographic location. It is to raise questions about socio-spatial-ecological relations. Neither is it to argue that farmers embody a privileged access to some truth, as romanticized in the cliché "the answer lies in the soil." It is to argue that local food movements need to seriously engage what Wittman (2010) calls the "rights of nature" and the materiality of the bio-social co-production of food embodied (including symbolically) in the lives of those who work in agriculture, whether as farmers, or farm labourers, including migrant labour. Erik Nicholson (2010), national vice-president of the United Farm Workers of America, stresses that the belief that local food will automatically lead to fair wages or good work conditions for farm workers or small farmers is an ethically irresponsible myth.[5] Sarah Wright's chapter in this volume lends weight to the argument here that farmers' political engagement is a precondition for building genuine alternatives in alternative food movements. It should also be remembered, however, as Martin and Andrée's chapter points out, that issues taken up under the framing of food sovereignty in the global North may not be the same as those in the global South. They suggest that in Canada, for example, such struggles are not as clearly located in the fields of peasants but as struggles for greater food democracy in cities where NGOs rather than peasant farmers are creating new sites of food governance. This may indeed be so, but I am suggesting that you can't have a food sovereignty movement without farmers (globally and locally) being central.[6]

Commitments to food democracy and food justice force us to think deeply about who are constituted as subjects. Feminist analysis can help expand our "geographies of political and ethical responsibility" (Jackson, Ward, and Russell 2009; Massey 2004; Young 2003). Massicotte's chapter in this volume also highlights the importance of feminist analysis for thinking about agri-food. Iris Marion Young (2003) offered political responsibility and solidarity as alternatives to guilt and liability as ways of thinking about how producers and consumers are connected, not by being close (the focus of local food movements), but institutionally connected often across distance in a food system that produces injustice and harm. This means that the politics of alternative food need to be organized by relationships rather than geography, building a new form of agrarian citizenship that strengthens communities on the basis of solidarity and respect for nature's own needs and cycles. This process, it seems to me, contributes to building food sovereignty; it requires going beyond the local and linking rural and urban citizens.

The privileged beneficiaries *as well as the victims* of harmful institutional arrangements, Young argues, have the political responsibility to change such institutions and create new, justice-producing ones. I argue that the projects of local food, food security, and sustainability need to be reconceptualized through democratic political alliances with and between consumers and farmers locally, and relationships of solidarity with peasant farmers' and landless people's movements globally.

Buying local or ethical food is not a substitute for political alliance. Although my focus here is on farmers, partly because of my local BC context, such alliances would include the other usual political constituents of La Via Campesina, such as farm labour, indigenous peoples, and particularly important in BC, First Nations fishers. Without such a move, local food movements will find it hard to avoid becoming simply an alternative consumer sovereignty movement for the relatively privileged with some welfare provisions for the local urban poor and niche marketing opportunities for some peri-urban farmers.

A radically democratic engagement between local food movements and farmers could help to start to transform local farmers *and* these movements. That is, without politically engaging farmers, local food networks will be colonized by the social relations they intend to change. And farmers where I live seeking change need local food urban networks for many reasons (many more than we / they yet realize), if they and local farmer organizations are to develop politics that are adequate to the new political economic realities in which they farm and become part of an emergent food sovereignty movement in the urbanized Canadian context. In these political engagements, all the actors will be changed. The multiple identities of farmer or consumer or activist forged in the context of a neoliberalized agri-food regime will be very different from identities that need to be forged in the context of food sovereignty. Again, lessons learned from feminism caution against social movements simply valorizing existing identities or subjectivities that are produced in the context of inequality. The point is to dismantle oppressive relations rather than simply valorize the identities of the oppressed or the marginalized.

Is a Revolution Happening?

There is much to arrest the mind and focus the emotions in taking animals to slaughter, even if the food is to be local. Why do I not feel like joining in the celebration of what the Canadian journal *Alternatives* (July 2010) characterized as "The People's Food Revolution"? And are movements for food security and food sovereignty as interchangeable as *Alternatives* suggests in its call for papers?

I have drawn on my experience in local food networks to suggest that the use of the term *food security* in food movements is dangerously under-theorized and carries concealed tensions. It is historically connected to colonial legacies and is currently often closely and paradoxically

associated with a neoliberalization of agriculture that proposes remedies to problems in the food system that are very different from those
envisioned by many in the Canadian food movement. All this makes the
concept of food security a risky concept to take up for those advocating
emancipatory change. The concept and language lend themselves too
easily to established institutionalized ways of organizing food and agriculture and to powerful interests. Certainly there are strong impulses
towards transformative change within the Canadian food security movement, such as efforts in Food Secure Canada to shift the focus from food
security to food sovereignty (Kneen 2010; Martin and Andrée, this volume). And I am not denying the importance and value of many of the
urban agriculture initiatives, community kitchens, and community food
security projects among marginalized groups. It is particularly noteworthy that the First Nations near where I live self-consciously describe
their initiatives in terms of food sovereignty rather than food security,
and that these efforts are conceived as the undoing of many of the harmful consequences of colonization and the reclaiming of relationships to
traditional lands and cultural food heritages (Morrison 2011). All of this
affirms that the naive adoption of the discourse of local food security
rather than a political engagement with the project of local / global food
sovereignty will reduce what could have been a progressive social
movement to being what DeLind (2011) calls a tool of the status quo.

In response to *Alternative*'s call for papers then, I am not alone in my
ambivalence. The debates about food seem to be increasing in both academic and popular literature. Some see local food as a radically new and
different kind of food system and others see local food as niche phenomena dedicated to the lifestyle choices of particular (usually affluent middle-class urban) social categories. And of course there are other readings
of local food too. Where does this leave me and my sheep?

Harris (2009) and Kleiman (2009) conclude that we can appreciate
but do not have to fully adopt those academic critiques that see the
turn to the local as unreflective neoliberalization or defensive localism
(Dupuis and Goodman 2005). They remind us that this local turn creates new space for alternatives, as it does for so many of the local small-
scale women farmers I know (and know of) in BC. Taken on their own,
critical analyses of the dangers of neoliberalization in local city-based
food movements do not have enough to offer farmers or local food
movements in developing concrete alternatives. They offer little political guidance to action. In the meantime, sheep have to be fed, the tractor must be paid for, the fences aren't keeping the sheep at home, a dog

has killed seven of my neighbour's sheep, there is no money to hire help, and there is no local abattoir. It all feels like such a long haul. On practical as well as analytic grounds, I feel little reason to celebrate.

Perhaps I can't celebrate because I am not convinced it is a revolution and feel it will not bring significant social change. My loyalties are torn between feeling I should celebrate the local food movement and all its accomplishments and being honest that so many farmers I know are not doing well. DeLind (2011) wonders if the local food movement in the United States is not going in the wrong direction when she compares it to Dalhberg's notion of a regenerative food system with its deeper commitment to equity, citizenship, place-building, and sustainability. Could it be that local food movements are too focused on the Northern-consumer, too city-based, too out of touch with the realities of most farmers' lives, too lacking in strategies for changing macroeconomic and institutional arrangements, and too ready to confuse real food security with token bits of distributive food justice to be truly transformative? Fraser's (2005, 2009) feminist analysis of social justice distinguishes between affirmative and transformative remedies. Drawing on lessons from feminist social organizing from which we learned that simply celebrating or validating women and "womanly ways" was an inadequate social justice strategy, we can see that celebrating local food and small farmers, or simply affirming people's (the poor in particular) right to adequate, safe, nutritionally or culturally appropriate food is also inadequate. The subject-positions of both farmers and consumers (including the poor's) are left untransformed: subjectivities are forged under conditions of inequality, privilege, or oppression and limited in their opportunities for full citizenship by those histories and institutionalized arrangements. Ironically privilege and power, and not just poverty, are barriers to full citizenship. Virtuous consumption on its own will not transform the conditions and social relations that produce problems in the agri-food sector. It may merely provide alternative consumer options – new kinds of illusions of sovereignty for alternative consumers.

Truly transformative change in the food system will require engaging with food sovereignty movements globally and engaging in genuinely democratic partnerships with farmers locally, nationally, and transnationally. It will change our understandings of publics and question older boundaries and borders (Brem-Wilson 2011). Speaking for, on behalf of, or about small farmers is not politically adequate: indeed it is dangerous. Extending boundaries of political responsibility would involve co-transformation of city-based food movements *and* of farmers and farmer organizations, not least in gendered relations. Food sovereignty is not an identity politics for farmers. It would involve co-producing the meaning and shape of what food sovereignty movements would be like locally and regionally. As several chapters in this book point out, there is still little concrete information on what food sovereignty would mean in practices in the North. The NFU in Canada is already engaged in such a project, and some city-based groups are starting to take the project up. Food sovereignty does not imply the adoption of a given political ideology but a project to be engaged and produced.

The factors that are driving mid- and small-scale Canadian farmers off the land and imprison those who stay farming in an increasingly tighter price-cost squeeze are precisely the ones that the food sovereignty movement is engaging. And it is these that the local food movement needs to far more seriously resist.[7] These factors include corporate concentration, global dumping of food, and industry-driven regulatory regimes and global trade regimes that have historically turned the terms of trade against smaller agricultural producers and commodity production, especially in the global South.[8] Thus while academic analysis helps us theorize the subject position of the neoliberal consumer, and local community activism encourages a turn to the local, the economic location of many farmers in the global South and increasingly in the North, particularly small and mid-sized farmers, is bringing them into deeper material contradiction with power in the global agri-food system. Changing the contemporary corporate food regime will require new kinds of alliance between progressive (usually urban) food security and food sovereignty movements (Holt Giménez and Shattuck 2011), not just the strategy of buying local food.

The stage is set for new kinds of political analysis, new agricultural imaginaries, and the possibility of strategic alliances between Northern consumer-focused food movements and farmer organizations. If either social justice goals or agro-ecological ones are to be realized, power relations in the agri-food system must be dismantled, not reproduced, as they often are. Both global philanthropic organizations and international food retail conglomerates or companies (including Walmart) also now invoke sustainability, fair trade, food security, or concern for small farmers, as they offer to enter partnerships with agricultural sectors in the global South and sell "good" food to consumers in the North. Such projects offer to reconstruct the small farmer as the food entrepreneur within neoliberalization rather than the agrarian citizen of food sovereignty. Perhaps it is time to imagine new global and trans-local strategic alliances in which the subject positions of both food consumers and of farmers are progressively transformed as the relationship between nature and society is also transformed. Moreover, this would require new public imaginaries or imaginaries of the public, new kinds of collectivities, and new publics (Brem-Wilson 2011).

Surrogate Pilgrims

But what of the lambs in the back of my pickup truck on the way to the abattoir? If I and the other farmers I know remain imprisoned by the terms that frame the academic debates or the local food movement's political imaginaries, we, lambs included, may be left doing little more than feeding the neoliberal processes of subjectification (Guthman 2007, 2008a, 2008b; Lavin 2009). Perhaps the entire lexicon of the debate is flawed (McWilliams 2010). The accepted dichotomies – conventional / organic, small / industrial, free range / confined, local / global, and so on – McWilliams writes, make sense only at the extremes. Food miles are unreliable indicators of environmental impact, labels may offer *reliable* coding of narrow qualities of fair trade or bird friendliness but may lack validity. In empirical terms they may not lead to either social justice or ecological sustainability. Similarly, feminist analysis suggests that we need to expand our geographies of responsibility and our potential for political participation by thinking in terms of *relationship of co-production* instead of identities and spatial boundaries. The political limitations of the subject position of neoliberal consumer and of farmer as food entrepreneur can be opened to more radically progressive possibilities by looking at who we are in the relationships in time and place in which we are embodied, embedded, and which co-produce us. I do not mean in the biographical sense, but the embodied, biosocial and eco-political sense.

What if we read local food networks for the politics of the possible, open to emergent forms of politics informed by food sovereignty movements (Brem-Wilson, 2011; Martin and Andrée, this volume), reading for difference, not the reproduction of dominance, asks Edmund Harris (2009). Such a new imagining might require not only recognizing the global in the local and the local in the global, but dissolving the boundaries that rigidly associate the good with the small and local. It would open space for agrarian citizenship, like Peter Andree's farmer-citizen, the role of "agriculture of the middle,"[9] diversity in scales of farming and in the reconnection of food, nature, and community through political projects such as food sovereignty. The sovereignty invoked in such an imaginary is not the Westphalian sovereignty of the nation state but new forms of citizenship yet to be forged.

The lights turn red and I gear down, trying not to brake too fast, because it would throw the lambs off balance. If you have travelled in the back of a pickup, you know what that feels like. What if there was a publicly funded infrastructure for local agro-ecological agriculture, or small-scale abattoirs that gave expression to the recognition of food as a public good and respect as an animal's entitlement? What if the "politics of the possible" (Guthman 2008b) engaged the public imaginary around new infrastructural arrangements for food, prefigurative institutions, and new, more just, and respectful terms of exchange between consumers and farmers locally and globally, and between them and the companion and other species who feed them? These socio-political imaginaries cannot be found in the marketplace. They cannot be bought by even the best-intentioned consumer. Without them it is hard not to conclude that, on that recent summer evening, the lambs and I were simply travelling relics, and our journey a pilgrimage more than part of social movement for food sovereignty. Perhaps we were surrogate pilgrims in politically ineffectual gestures of atonement by the privileged for an unjust food system. But such despair is politically conservatizing and does little to make the lambs' lives and deaths better. As the chapters in this collection concretely and vividly remind me, food sovereignty is not about feel-good politics for farmers, or about recapturing a lost past through a turn to the local. It is about confronting globally interconnected relations of power in the present, opening space for new (and old) agro-ecological practices and new, just forms of agri-food governance. The chapters in this book inspire hope and determination for such a project.

NOTES

1 The author is a part-time farmer and full-time academic.
2 Nationally mandated system established in the 1960s to protect farmers from the vagaries of the market. These systems restrict imports and require farmers to own "quota" for the right to produce for domestic markets. See Winson (1992) for a history of the establishment of supply management in Canada.
3 From a sociological point of view it was never true that the consumer was king. From an economic point of view, it is or should be true. From a social constructionist point of view one can see that it is a kind of collective fantasy most dramatically embodied by a consuming public in those places

that Ritzer calls cathedrals of consumption, or for everyday folk at Walmart or Canadian Superstores.

4 Martin and Andrée (this volume) suggest using the term *neoliberalizing* to capture this process as a dynamic and open-ended pattern of market-oriented regulatory restructuring that is far from uniform (see also Guthman 2008b).

5 It is significant that the issue of the work conditions of migrant labour was raised at the BC Food Systems Network (BCFSN) annual meeting in 2010, which then continued online, organizing for improved health services for these workers. Associated with fooddemocracy.org, and the indigenous food sovereignty project, this is a dynamic and changing network actively shaped by activists from both rural and urban regions, and is increasingly engaging food sovereignty.

6 Mine is a call to start creating political alliances of the kind being developed by the National Farmers Union (NFU). Not all Canadian farmers would agree with me, of course. But even the Canadian Federation of Agriculture, Canada's largest farmer organization, has adopted the term *food sovereignty*, albeit its use is far from counter-hegemonic (see Martin and Andrée, this volume).

7 Some local and Canadian farmer organizations do engage such issues, but many do not. It depends, for example, on how their constituency is located in the market, the source of funding, or advisory (client) relationship with provincial and federal governments. Canada's agriculture is not fully neoliberalized (Skogstad 2008). There are still marketing boards and supply management in some areas, although these are under threat. In personal conversation I find many local farmers often have a populist politics in which government, corporations, and big financial institutions are identified as the problem. The federal and provincial governments may be keen to have farmers speak with a (falsely) unifying voice, but one can expect the political divisions within Canadian farming to increase.

8 The terms of trade that need to be renegotiated are not just those between countries or North and South, but the very basic assumptions of neoliberal economics that invoke the market (operationalized as price) as the legitimate determiner of value but deny the power relations that frame such economic exchange.

9 See Agriculture of the Middle. http://www.agofthemiddle.org/.

REFERENCES

BC Ministry of Agriculture. 2011. *Census of Agriculture*. http://www.agf.gov
.bc.ca/stats/Census/2011AgriCensusBCHighlights.pdf.

Beck, Ulrich. 1992. *Risk Society: Towards a New Modernity*. New Delhi: Sage.

Beck, Ulrich, Anthony Giddens, and Christopher Lash. 1994. *Reflexive Modernization: Politics, Tradition and Aesthetics in the Modern Social Order*. Palo Alto, CA: Stanford University Press.

Blay-Palmer, Alison. 2008. *Food Fears from Industrial to Sustainable Food Systems*. Aldershot, Hampshire: Ashgate Publishing.

Brem-Wilson. Josh. 2011. "La Via Campesina and the Committee on World Food Security: A Nascent Transnational Public Sphere?" Paper prepared for the International Studies Association Annual Conference, Montreal, March. http://www.allacademic.com/meta/p_mla_apa_research_citation/ 5/0/2/6/3/p502639_index.html.

Busch, Lawrence. 2000. "The Moral Economy of Grades and Standards." *Journal of Rural Studies* 16 (3): 273–83. http://dx.doi.org/10.1016/S0743-0167(99)00061-3.

DeLind, Laura B. 2011. "Are Local Food and the Local Food Movement Taking Us Where We Want to Go? Or Are We Hitching Our Wagons to the Wrong Stars?" *Agriculture and Human Values* 28 (2): 273–83.

DeLind, Laura, and Phillip Howard. 2008. "Safe at Any Scale: Food Scares, Food Regulation and Scaled Alternatives." *Agriculture and Human Values* 25 (3): 301–17. http://dx.doi.org/10.1007/s10460-007-9112-y.

Desmarais, Annette. 2007. *La Via Campesina: Globalization and the Power of Peasants*. Halifax: Fernwood Publishing.

DuPuis, E. Melanie, and David Goodman. 2005. "Should We Go 'Home' to Eat?: Towards a Reflexive Politics of Localism." *Journal of Rural Studies* 21 (3): 359–71. http://dx.doi.org/10.1016/j.jrurstud.2005.05.011.

Eagle, A.J., R. Tunnicliffe, M. McMahon, and G.C. van Kooten. *Farming on the Urban Fringe: The Economic Impacts of Niche and Direct Marketing Strategies*. University of Victoria working paper, 2009.

Fairbairn, Madeleine. 2012. "Framing Transformation: The Counter-Hegemonic Potential of Food Sovereignty in the US context." *Agriculture and Human Values* 29 (2): 217–30.

Fraser, Nancy. 2005. "Reframing Justice in a Globalizing World." *New Left Review* 36:69–88.

– 2009. "Who Counts? Dilemmas of Justice in a Post-Westphalian World." *Antipode* 41 (1): 281–97.

Friedberg, Susanne. 2004. *French Bean and Food Scares: Culture and Commerce in an Anxious Age*. New York: Oxford University Press.

Giddens, Anthony. 2006. *Sociology*. 5th ed. Cambridge: Polity.

Guthman, Julie. 2007. "The Polanyian Way? Voluntary Food Labels as Neoliberal Governance." *Antipode* 39 (3): 456–78. http://dx.doi.org/10.1111/ j.1467-8330.2007.00535.x.

– 2008a. "Bringing Good Food to Others: Investigating the Subjects of Alternative Food Practice." *Cultural Geographies* 15 (4): 431–47. http://dx.doi.org/10.1177/1474474008094315.

– 2008b. "Neoliberalism and the Making of Good Food Politics in California." *Geoforum* 39 (3): 1171–83. http://dx.doi.org/10.1016/j.geoforum.2006.09.002.

Guthman, Julie, Amy Morris, and Patricia Allen. 2006. "Squaring Farm Security and Food Security in Two Types of Alternative Food Institutions." *Rural Sociology* 71 (4): 662–84.

Haraway, Donna. 1988. "Situated Knowledges: The Science Question in Feminism and the Privilege of Partial Perspective." *Feminist Studies* 14 (3): 575–99. http://dx.doi.org/10.2307/3178066.

– 2008. *When Species Meet*. Minneapolis: University of Minnesota Press.

Harding, Sandra. 1986. *The Science Question in Feminism*. New York: Cornell University Press.

– 1991. *Whose Science? Whose Knowledge?* New York: Cornell University Press.

Harris, Edmund. 2009. "Neoliberal Subjectivities or a Politics of the Possible? Reading for Difference in Alternative Food Networks." *Area* 41 (1): 55–63. http://dx.doi.org/10.1111/j.1475-4762.2008.00848.x.

Hatt, Ken, and Kierstin Hatt. 2012. "Neoliberalizing Food Safety and the 2008 Canadian Listeriosis Outbreak." *Agriculture and Human Values* 29 (1): 17–28.

Hines, J. Dwight. 2010. "In Pursuit of Experience: The Post-Industrial Middle-Class Colonization of the Rural American West." *Ethnography* 11 (2): 285–308.

– 2012. "The Post-Industrial Regime of Production/Consumption and the Rural Gentrification of the New West Archipelago." *Antipode* 44 (1): 74–97.

Hinrichs, C. Clare. 2000. "Embeddedness and Local Food Systems: Notes on Two Types of Direct Agricultural Markets." *Journal of Rural Studies* 16 (3): 295–303. http://dx.doi.org/10.1016/S0743-0167(99)00063-7.

– 2003. "The Practice and Politics of Food System Localization." *Journal of Rural Studies* 19 (1): 33–45. http://dx.doi.org/10.1016/S0743-0167(02)00040-2.

Holt Giménez, Eric, and Annie Shattuck. 2011. "Food Crises, Food Regimes and Food Movements: Rumblings of Reform or Tides of Transformation?" *Journal of Peasant Studies* 38 (1): 109–44. http://dx.doi.org/10.1080/03066150.2010.538578.

hooks, bell. 1989. *Talking Back: Thinking Feminist: Thinking Black*. Cambridge: South End.

Jackson, Peter, Neil Ward, and Polly Russell. 2009. "Moral Economics of Food and Geographies of Responsibility." *Transactions of the Institute of British Geographers* 34 (1): 12–24. http://dx.doi.org/10.1111/j.1475-5661.2008.00330.x.

Kleiman, J. 2009. "Local Food and the Problem of Public Authority." *Technology and Culture* 50 (2): 399–417. http://dx.doi.org/10.1353/tech.0.0273.http://www.ncbi.nlm.nih.gov/entrez/query.fcgi?cmd=Retrieve&db=PubMed&list_uids=19831224&dopt=Abstract.

Kneen, Cathleen. 2010. "Mobilisation and Convergences in a Wealthy Northern Country." *Journal of Peasant Studies* 37 (1): 229–35.

Lavin, Chad. 2009. "Pollanated Politics, or, the Neoliberal's Dilemma." *Politics and Culture* 9:57–67.

Massey, Diane. 2004. "Geographies of responsibility." *Geografiska Annaler* 86 (1): 5–18. http://dx.doi.org/10.1111/j.0435-3684.2004.00150.x.

McMahon, Martha. 2011. "Standard Fare or Fairer Standards: Feminist Reflections on Agri-food Governance." *Agriculture and Human Values* 28 (3): 401–12. http://dx.doi.org/10.1007/s10460-009-9249-y.

McMichael, Phillip. 2008. "Peasants Make Their Own History, but Not Just as They Please." *Journal of Agrarian Change* 8 (2–3): 205–28. http://dx.doi.org/10.1111/j.1471-0366.2008.00168.x.

– 2010. "Food Sovereignty in Movement: Addressing the Triple Crisis." In Wittman, Desmarais, and Wiebe 2010, 186–96.

McWilliams, James. 2010. "Why Can't We All Just Sit Down and Eat Nicely Together?" *Grist Talks: Food Fights*. http://grist.org/article/food-fight-do-locavores-really-need-math-lessons/1/#mcwilliams.

Miele, M. 2006. "Consumption Culture: The Case of Food." In *Handbook of Rural Studies*, edited by P. Cloke, T. Marsden, and P. Mooney, 344–54. London: Sage. http://dx.doi.org/10.4135/9781848608016.n24.

Mills, C. Wright. 1959. *The Sociological Imagination*. Oxford: Oxford University Press.

Mooney, Patrick, and Scott Hunt. 2009. "Food Security: The Elaboration of Contested Claims to a Consensus Frame." *Rural Sociology* 74 (4): 469–97.

Morgan, Kevin, Terry Marsden, and Jonathan Murdoch. 2006. *Worlds of Food: Place, Power, and Provenance in the Food Chain*. Oxford: Oxford University Press.

Morrison, Dawn. 2011. "Indigenous Food Sovereignty." In Wittman, Desmarais, and Wiebe 2010, 97–113.

Nicholson, Erik. 2010. "Improving Food Worker Livelihoods: An Interview with UFWA's Erik Nicholson." Worldwatch Institute. http://www.worldwatch.org/node/6485.

Patel, Rajeev. 2010. "What Does Food Sovereignty Look Like?" In Wittman, Desmarais, and Wiebe 2010, 186–96.

Patel, Rajeev, Radhika Balakrishnan, and Uma Narayan. 2007. "Transgressing Rights: La Via Campesina's Call for Food Sovereignty." *Feminist Economics* 13 (1): 87–116. http://dx.doi.org/10.1080/13545700601086838.

Pollan, Michael. 2006. *The Omnivore's Dilemma: A Natural History of Four Meals*. New York: Penguin.

– 2009. *In Defense of Food: An Eater's Manifesto*. New York: Penguin.

Schlosser, Eric. 2001. *Fast Food Nation: The Dark Side of the All-American Meal*. New York: Houghton Mifflin.

Skogstad, Grace. 2008. *Internationalization and Canadian Agriculture: Policy and Governing Paradigms*. Toronto: University of Toronto Press.

Smith, Dorothy E. 2005. *Institutional Ethnography: Sociology for the People*. Oxford: AltaMira.

Smithers, John, and Alun E. Joseph. 2010. "The Trouble with Authenticity: Separating Ideology from Practice at the Farmers' Market." *Agriculture and Human Values* 27 (2): 239–47. http://dx.doi.org/10.1007/s10460-009-9250-5.

Stoneman, Scott. 2009. "Learning to Learn from the Food Crisis: Consumer Sovereignty and the Restructuring of Subjectivity." *Politics and Culture* 2. http://www.politicsandculture.org/2009/11/03/scott-stoneman-learning-to-learn-from-the-food-crisis-consumer-sovereignty-and-the-restructuring-of-subjectivity/.

Tunnicliffe, Robin. 2011. "Making It Work." MA thesis, University of Victoria.

Winson, Anthony. 1992. *The Intimate Commodity*. Toronto: Garamond.

Wittman, Hannah. 2010. "Reconnecting Agriculture and the Environment: Food Sovereignty and the Agrarian Base of Ecological Citizenship." In Wittman, Desmarais, and Wiebe 2010, 91–104.

Wittman, Hannah, Annette Desmarais, and Nettie Wiebe, eds. 2010. *Food Sovereignty: Reconnecting Food, Nature and Community*. Halifax: Fernwood Publishing.

Young, Iris Marion. 2003. "From Guilt to Solidarity: Sweatshops and Political Responsibility." *Dissent* (Spring): 39–45.

PART TWO

Food Sovereignty in Comparative
Perspective

5 Citizen-Farmers: The Possibilities and the Limits of Australia's Emerging Alternative Food Networks

PETER ANDRÉE

Can the new local and organic food networks popping up across the industrialized world counter the environmental and social degradation caused by conventional agriculture and food supply chains? This chapter bites off just a piece of this question by looking at the experience of emerging alternative food networks in Australia, a country with one of the world's most liberalized agricultural sectors based in cheap mass production for export markets (Dibden and Cocklin 2005). It draws together research on a range of emerging production and distribution models, including organic farming, permaculture, and forms of localized marketing such as farmers' markets and community-supported agriculture (CSAs), arguing that the recent growth in these initiatives is both a reaction to and a manifestation of neoliberal trends in Australia. This growth is a response to the downward pressure neoliberal trends have placed on commodity prices paid to farmers, but it is also a manifestation of these trends, in that the proliferation of niche markets, governed by voluntary rules of conduct, is considered by some (e.g., Parkins 2009) as a common expression of neoliberal re-regulation. A number of recent studies have commented on the trend towards food localism and related, consumer-driven, initiatives "as embedded in and reinforcing of neoliberal forms of governance" (Blue 2009). Rather than simply repeat this refrain, my goal here is to understand the potential implications of these initiatives – what Guthman (2008a, 1181) calls the "politics of the possible [that] lies in the indeterminacy of neoliberalism" – through an examination of the practices of the farmers who participate in them, and of the consequences of those practices on the agri-food landscape.

This book examines the new politics of food surfacing in response to food systems dominated by massive corporations, primarily as expressed through citizen actions and social movements working to realize social justice and environmental sustainability. While not all alternative food network activities should be understood as overtly political, some of them do exemplify an emerging "ecological" citizenship. According to Dobson (2003), ecological citizenship is a non-territorial and highly participatory understanding of citizenship that manifests in, among other ways, private actions that benefit the public good. Ecological citizenship values are clearly evident when farmers and consumers choose to support or practise specific forms of production or distribution because they are believed to be better for the earth or its people, especially when those activities entail extra personal efforts or cost. As a result, even though the Australian initiatives studied here were never actually described as being rooted in the goals of "food sovereignty" by those interviewed,[1] these initiatives can be linked to more explicit expressions of food sovereignty and food democracy seen in Canada (Martin and Andrée, McMahon, both this volume), the United States (Bosia and Ayres, this volume), and elsewhere. Indeed, one of the defining characteristics of any sovereignty claim – and this appears to be especially true for food sovereignty – is that it is embodied in the material practices of living in a specific place. Sovereignty is also about taking personal and collective responsibility for the land and the people who rely on it. The practices of a growing number of those whom I refer to as Australia's new "citizen-farmers" can thus be understood as nascent expressions of food sovereignty – perhaps less in terms of rights-based claims over land, as some advocates of food sovereignty emphasize (Menser, this volume), but more as expressions of responsibility, care, and a willingness to act to protect specific places and people in the face of forces that would do them harm. At this point in time, the actions of the citizen-farmers described herein are largely individualist practices tied to specific locales, but those actions can also be linked to collective goals and forms of governance with the potential for wider societal impact.

This chapter explicitly furthers two of the four lines of inquiry introduced in chapter 1. First, it presents a nuanced reading of the impact of neoliberal globalization on agriculture, showing how the phenomenon of neoliberalization[2] shapes food systems in both positive and negative ways (in relation to social justice and sustainability goals). Second, it furthers the discussion of the relevance of Polanyi's idea of embedded markets to the analysis of contemporary food politics, at first theoretically, and then through the lens of my case study.

One of Polanyi's key contributions to political economic thought is to point us towards the subjective dimensions of market relations. In this chapter, particular attention is paid to the subjective experiences of farmers – situated as they are amidst conflicting consumer demands, state inducements, and their own values and economic interests. This analysis is based on twenty-nine interviews with farmers or sets of farm-partners and six interviews with farm-product processors or distributors from the State of Victoria, in southeast Australia, undertaken between September and December 2006. Interview questions focused on what farmers produce, how they market that product, and choices they made related to the environmental, economic, and social sustainability of their farms. My analysis of those interviews is organized around three sets of issues relevant to our Polanyian framing: the possibilities and limits of market-based alternative food initiatives in relation to social and ecological protection, the role of individual vs collective agency in achieving that protection, and the role of the state in relation to the food networks in question.

The argument developed in this chapter is multilayered. To begin, I argue that the category "alternative food networks" actually encompasses a range of initiatives, some of which counter the destructive tendencies of corporate-led globalization, while others are the direct result of the model's application in Australia and remain compatible with it. The next section then argues for the need to understand these food networks in Polanyian terms at the intersection between government policies, markets, and individual as well as collective behaviour. With regards to the impacts of these alternative food networks in the context of the neoliberalization of Australia's agri-food system, to which the chapter then turns, the research results reveal both opportunities and challenges. On the one hand, I argue that the current structure of these networks, especially in their strongly individualistic and market-oriented character, suggest that they may not serve as loci of the type of resistance to corporate neoliberalization that we see in the global South (e.g., Massicotte, Wright, both this volume) as well as among some farmers in the global North (e.g., the orientation of Canada's National Farmers' Union as discussed by Martin and Andrée, or the alter-globalization ideologies of the French farmers presented by Bosia and Ayres, this volume). On the other hand, these food networks do entail a range of positive ecological and socio-economic impacts, by helping to sustain and reinvigorate rural communities, lower transportation distances, build bridges between producers and consumers, and sometimes even change the values and practices of more conventional farmers. Finally, I argue that the long-term success of these networks will depend ultimately on collective action, suggesting that even the individualized initiatives discussed herein may have the potential to be the first step towards broader collective governance mechanisms.

Alternative Food Networks

Also termed alternative agri-food initiatives (Goodman 2003), short food supply chains (Renting, Marsden, and Banks 2003), alternative food supply chains (Ilbery and Maye 2005), or alternative agri-food networks (Goodman 2004; Andrée, Dibden, Higgins, and Cocklin 2011), alternative food networks are distinguished from conventional supply chains by their turn away from standardized and industrial systems of food provisioning, in terms of farming practices, distribution, or both, towards a focus on notions of "quality," "place," and "nature" (Goodman 2003, 2004). Most attention in the rural sociology and geography literature on this topic is focused on the "re-localization" of food, through CSAs, on-farm shops, farmers' markets, and other forms of face-to-face or spatially proximate sales (e.g., DuPuis and Goodman 2005; Hinrichs 2000; Holloway and Kneafsey 2000; Kirwan 2004, 2006; Marsden and Sonnino 2005; Sage 2003). Alternative food networks are not *necessarily* defined as locally oriented, however. Spatially "extended" alternative supply chains, such as global networks for fair trade or regional specialty products are also designed to provide consumers with value-laden information aimed at re-socializing and re-spatializing market relations (Renting, Marsden, and Banks 2003; Fonte and Papdopoulos 2010). It is also important to recognize that some "alternative" food networks have even more qualities in common with the conventional food systems they are often characterized in opposition to. The large-scale organics industry in California with its 8,000-hectare intensive farms, long-distance distribution, and poor labour practices, as described by Guthman (2004), is the paradigmatic example.

In this chapter, the emphasis is on those alternative networks that are seen (or intended) to provide "environmental" benefits, with this concept understood holistically to include a variety of potentially beneficial outcomes for both natural and social environments. Perceived benefits are either associated with how products are produced (e.g., organic, biodynamic, or permaculture production, the adoption of on-farm environmental management systems, free-range and grass-fed livestock production, wild-crafted "bush" foods), or with the smaller carbon footprint resultant from proximity between producer and consumer (e.g., the products are distributed through farmers' markets, community-supported agriculture schemes, and on-farm shops). In fact, products sold through many of these initiatives are deliberately marketed to consumers in ways that highlight their environmental virtues.[3] These alternative food networks are a fairly recent phenomenon in Australia, but their number is growing rapidly. Some farmers participate in them as a form of resistance to the dominant food system, which they may see as not supporting their aims around ecological sustainability, allowing for the production of high-quality food, or respecting animal welfare. Others participate simply because these networks present new economic opportunities at a time when they have been squeezed out of traditional commodity production through intense competition (Andrée et al. 2010). Each of these reasons, including the search for greater economic autonomy, can be seen as a form of resistance to key elements of the conventional food system (Douwe van der Ploeg 2007), and the alternative food networks that these farmers turn towards thus can be understood as examples of voluntary, market-based, agri-environmental governance, even if the "environment" is not always at the forefront of a farmer's choices to embark in this direction.

Entrepreneurialism, self-governance, market-based environmental outcomes, and value-added production: these concepts all figure centrally in these networks. Significantly, these particular concepts are also key goals (albeit far from an exhaustive list – and this point becomes an important point as my argument progresses) of the neoliberalization processes that have restructured food systems around the world in recent decades in favour of large-scale agriculture and the growing power of a limited number of food processing and distribution companies. To help us make sense of the fact that alternative food networks appear to be both a reaction to the competition associated with the neoliberalization of Australia's agri-food system in recent decades and a manifestation of "roll out" neoliberalization (Peck and Tickell 2002) intent on achieving positive environmental outcomes, this chapter now turns to the theoretical insights of Karl Polanyi and others who have extended his insights to the present era.

A Polanyian Analysis

Recent interest in alternative food networks has been accompanied by reinvigorated interest in the works of Karl Polanyi and his notion of "embeddedness" (e.g., Sonnino and Marsden 2006; Guthman 2007, 2008b; Raynolds 2000; Murdoch et al., 2000). Polanyi argues that the liberal economists' emphasis on market "self-regulation" is ultimately misguided – a utopian fantasy. For all of human history, markets have been "embedded" in a wider context of forms of redistribution determined by kinship or religious or political relations (1968). As a result, state efforts to "dis-embed" markets from these social and ecological relations (in order to harness the efficiencies generated when supply and demand dictate prices) are likely to lead to social and ecological destruction, to dangerous political-economic stalemates as new costs are imposed on specific groups in society, and / or to societal responses designed to prevent that destruction through efforts to recreate a more embedded economy (Polanyi [1944] 2001). Rather than leading to a reduced role for the state, attempts to dis-embed markets from society are thus likely to entail "greater state efforts to assure that ... groups will bear these increased costs without engaging in disruptive political action" (Block 2001, xxv). Alternatively, these groups are likely to respond through spontaneous counter-movements to build protective structures to re-embed markets, whether this eventually takes the form of new environmental regulations or the provision of social services such as health care and unemployment insurance instituted by the state, or other forms of regulation governed in the first instance through society itself (such as shift in social norms that eventually led to the legal abolishment of slavery).[4]

Unfortunately, his renewed notoriety has meant that Polanyi's ideas are sometimes oversimplified. In particular, "embeddedness" is often reduced to referring only to the social relations of trust and reciprocity that underpin certain forms of economic activity. This has led to claims that farmers' markets, for example, which clearly rely on relations of trust and regard between consumers and producers (Kirwan 2004; Sage 2003), are embedded, while more anonymous supply chains are not. This reading of Polanyi can be traced back to the Granovettor (1985) paper that reintroduced this concept to economic sociology. Notably, however, Granovettor decided to focus primarily on the personal relations (or the "proximate" level of causal analysis) within which market relations are embedded, because he felt that structural sociologists of a more substantivist bent had paid insufficient attention to this level (506). In other words, his focus on trust and reciprocity should not detract from an analysis of broader structural factors, such as government policy and supply chain dynamics, within which food networks are also embedded.

This point relates to a second issue raised by some recent invocations of this concept, namely that it is "embeddedness" that distinguishes alternative food networks from conventional commodity chains (e.g., Raynolds 2002; Murdoch, Marsden, and Banks 2000). Winter (2003) and Sonnino (2007) show why this reading of Polanyi is ultimately untenable. As Winter notes, "In truth, all market relations are socially embedded, and in a range of contrasting ways... We cannot equate "alternativeness" with embeddedness in a deterministic manner" (2003, 25). For example, local organic supply chains may be embedded in particular places, values, and institutions, but supermarket supply chains are also embedded in (albeit very different) conventions of product quality. Soninno concurs: "In reality, recent literature shows that embeddedness is not an inherent and fixed characteristic of some (i.e. local) food systems" (2006, 64). For Soninno and Marsden, food network analysts' attention should focus on *how* supply chains of all types are embedded in terms of specific social and ecological norms, practices, and relationships, and what the implications of those dynamics are (2006). These authors then differentiate between the horizontal dimensions of embeddedness – the immediate conditions and strategies that enable the development of food networks – and the vertical dimensions – the multi-level governance system in which supply chains are linked to the broader society, economy, and polity. Zerbe (this volume) seeks to transcend this oversimplification by qualifying different forms (or "degrees") of embeddedness with the added concepts of high and low "marketness" and high and low "instrumentalism," noting that economic transactions that are embedded in social relations in the way emphasized by Kirwan, Raynolds, and others tend to be less determined by the price mechanism or the self-interest of the individuals involved in the transaction.

With these nuances as background, I suggest that we bring the following three elements to a Polanyian analysis of alternative food networks: First, markets are inevitably constructed and enabled by both the state (defined narrowly as the official arms of national, sub-national, and local governments) and ideology. In Polanyi's language, they are "opened ... by an enormous increase in continuous, centrally organized and controlled interventionism" (Polanyi [1944] 2001, 140–1). As a result, even an analysis of alternative food networks – networks that appear to have developed with little active encouragement from the state in most countries (outside of Western Europe) – needs to consider how these networks emerge in relation to wider political-economic trends promoted by the state and dominant ideologies. Second, the liberal "free-market" project will never be fully realized, because this path inevitably leads to social and ecological problems – which will elicit a response: social forces will emerge, in one form or another, to protect land and labour. In alternative food networks we see evidence of one form of this resistance to the environmental and social problems of the food system through efforts to establish autonomy from dominant supply chains (Douwe van der Ploeg 2007), even if they still harness market forces to support that autonomy. Third, Polanyi highlighted the importance of the subjective experience of participants in these market–society relations. This was evident in his work on pre-capitalist social relations, though it is equally relevant (as Granovetter [1985] shows) to all economic transactions.

To these three elements of a Polanyian analysis we need to add some points about the specificities of various re-embedding efforts in the post-1970s era.[5] In environmental policy, the process of neoliberalization is often summed up by concepts such as deregulation, commodification, privatization, devolution, and self-regulation (McCarthy and Prudham 2004; Guthman 2008b). As Polanyi would expect, deregulation and privatization has led to contradictions and crises, and resulted in re-regulation of one sort or another. Neoliberalized re-regulation often involves a shift out of government to industry (or individual) self-regulation, or to voluntary organizations, citizen coalitions, and public-private partnerships, etc. (Guthman 2008b). In the context of agri-environmental governance, the Polanyian counter-movements that have arisen to deal with the environmental and social problems of the agri-food system are increasingly associated with voluntary, extra-state, regulatory measures. These tend to take one of two forms. The first are top-down, multinational-corporation-driven environmental governance systems such as the "EurepGAP" agricultural production standards imposed by European supermarket chains on their supply chains around the world, beginning in the 1990s (Campbell 2005). The second form is better characterized as "bottom-up," NGO- and producer-driven initiatives such as organic farming standards and fair trade networks (Raynolds 2000; Guthman 2007) – with the caveat that sometimes these also become top-down. The state's role in either context is often as a facilitator of "best practices," and as a purveyor of seed funding to support these "market-based initiatives" designed to solve some of the problems caused by the conventional agricultural model.

Given the state's limited role in these new forms of agri-food governance, it appears all the more important to follow Polanyi in examining the subjective experience of their participants, such as the farmers discussed below, in order to understand implications. Guthman (2008b, 1243) reinforces this point by characterizing the "mentalities of rule" (a term closely related to Foucault's (1991) "governmentality")[6] of the neoliberal era: "Material neoliberalizations are inextricably bound with the production of neoliberal mentalities of rule – specifically attempts to enforce market logics, to create conditions in which competition can flourish, to shift caring responsibilities from the public sphere (welfare) to personal spaces (self-help) and to depoliticize (or render futile) various social struggles over resources and rights."

Building on these theoretical insights, the remainder of this chapter discusses the implications of alternative food networks as responsive forms of social and environmental protection. I pay particular attention to their relation to broader neoliberalization trends in Australia, both material and ideational.

Australia's Agri-Food Landscape

The primary focus of Australian agriculture is on the supply of bulk commodities to export markets. This is a context where productivism has taken one of its starkest neoliberal forms among industrialized countries. Since the 1970s, and with greater enthusiasm since the mid-1990s, Australian governments have pursued a commitment to free trade and open competition on the world market, expressed through the elimination of tariffs, import restrictions, and production subsidies. As a result, OECD statistics from 2005 show that, on average, only 5 per cent of the income received by Australian farmers is in the form of government support, compared with 32 per cent in the European Union and 16 per cent in the United States (OECD 2006). The limited support for farmers in Australia largely takes the form of short-term adjustment assistance, drought relief, and agri-environmental payments. Whereas the European literature tends to equate productivism with state-supported (and often heavily subsidized) production (e.g., Lowe, Murdoch, Marsden, Munton, and Flynn 1993) – even in countries such as the

United Kingdom that have espoused neoliberal modes of governance – the outcome of the liberalization of Australian agriculture has been a form of hyper-productivism or "competitive productivism" (Dibden and Cocklin 2005). This competitive productivist orientation has placed enormous pressures on farmers to increase efficiencies in order to survive in a global market distorted by subsidies and tariff barriers, and characterized by unstable and until recently low commodity prices.

Those farmers who sell their products domestically – a market that still accounts for over two-thirds of all sales for vegetables, fruit, poultry, eggs, pig meat, and rice, despite Australia's strong export orientation (based on figures from DAFF 2005) – face additional pressures due to limited tariff protection and progressively concentrated domestic food processing, distribution, and retail sectors. The largest two supermarket chains (Coles and Woolworths) account for between 51 and 76 per cent of total retail food sales (Delforce, Dickson, and Hogan 2005).[7] The supermarkets thus represent the locus of power in the domestic supply chain. In recent years they have used their power to vertically integrate supply chains through exclusive supply arrangements with some farmers and processors. They have also followed the trend seen elsewhere in the world in the establishment of "private labels" owned by, or produced for, the retailer. These products are designed to offer consumers a quality alternative to proprietary branded foods while providing the retailer with increased margins of profit (Delforce, Dickson, and Hogan 2005).

What does all of this mean for farmers and the environment in Australia? Economically, the majority of Australian farmers remains caught in the cost-price squeeze, as costs for inputs and farm machinery rise while the price producers are paid decreases. In 2003, for example, pea producers received only 12 per cent of the price paid for frozen peas in grocery stores, and this was down from 16 per cent ten years earlier. In dairy, price declines have been even more dramatic due to industry deregulation: from 1997 to 2003 the percentage of retail price received by farmers dropped from 40 per cent to 25 per cent (DAFF 2005). On average, farm share of the retail price of food has dropped from about 30 per cent in the 1980s to 15–20 per cent in 2003 (George, Broadley, and Nissen 2005). These economic realities have contributed further to the longtime trend in declining farm numbers in Australia, a trend that has had devastating impacts on the viability of rural communities. For example, the number of potato farmers in the Fassifern Valley of Queensland fell from about 480 to 50 between 1999 and 2004, though total production remained the same (ibid.).

In terms of environmental sustainability, productivist agricultural practices in Australia, as in Europe and North America, tend to be intensive, input-dependent, often monocultural, and aimed at maximizing production and gaining economies of scale through farm consolidation, which involve a range of practices widely recognized as environmentally damaging and probably unsustainable in the long term (Clark and Lowe 1992; Potter 1998). Globally, agriculture and the transportation of food account for 10–20 per cent of greenhouse gas (GHG) emissions. Unfortunately, Australian farmers are also likely to face the brunt of climate change caused by GHG emissions, as witnessed in the serious droughts that affected the country in the late 2000s.

Increasing recognition of the environmental consequences of Western-style agriculture for Australia's fragile environment (Cocklin 2005) has resulted in two major trends. On the one hand, the state is increasingly acknowledging these problems and trying to respond with environmental management strategies designed to minimally affect the competitiveness and productivity of agriculture. This has resulted in a set of policy objectives emphasizing environmental protection and remediation and imposing additional pressures on farmers (Dibden and Cocklin 2005, 2009), although with minimal new economic supports to respond to those pressures. A second set of responses, though less common, takes the form of alternative food networks.

From the point of view of consumption, the main factors driving alternative food networks in industrialized countries appear to be growing demand for diversity and distinctiveness in food, increased public concern over issues such as health, ecology, and animal welfare, and a series of food scares that have undermined public confidence in conventional production (Bell and Valentine 1997; Ilbery and Maye 2005; Renting, Marsden, and Banks 2003; see also the introduction to this volume). For farmers, under continuous pressure to reduce costs, identify new revenue streams, or capture added value, alternative food networks represent possible routes towards continued viability.

There is insufficient space here to present the full range of emerging food networks identified in Australia, and there are few quantitative data collected relevant to these networks. The exceptions are for organic production and farmers' markets. The first Australian farms were certified as organic in the mid-1980s, and national organic and biodynamic standards were developed in 1992. By the 2000–1 season, the farm gate value of certified organic produce was estimated to be AUS$89 million, or 0.3 per cent of the total farm gate value for all food and fisheries production (although 4 per cent of horticulture) (Wynen 2003). Three years later, estimates put the total value of the organic industry at AUS$140.7 million (DAFF 2004). In 2003, there were 1700 certified organic farmers in Australia, along with 300 organic processors or distributors (ABARE 2003). Australia actually has the largest amount of certified organic land of any country in the world, at ten million hectares, though much of this is grazing land in the outback and not very productive. The first farmers' market in Australia (in recent memory) began in 1999 in Koonwarra, Victoria (interview 26), inspired by similar markets in the United States (Erlich, Riddell, and Wahlqvist 2005). In 2004, it was estimated that seventy farmers' markets across Australia generated AUS$40 million directly for vendors (Coster and Kennon 2005). By 2010, there were seventy-five markets established throughout Victoria, most of them operating on a monthly basis and run by the vendors themselves (White Hat 2010). The markets provide a variety of new opportunities to farmers and micro-food processors to sell raw or value-added products.

The next three sections are structured around three broad themes most relevant to a Polanyian analysis of alternative food networks to emerge from my interviews with Victorian farmers. These are the possibilities and limits of market-based environmental and social protection as currently embodied in these networks, the role of individual versus collective action in addressing the social and environmental problems of the dominant food system, and the role of the state in supporting protection measures led essentially by civil society.

Market-Based Environmental Protection?

Is ecological and social "protection" possible by relying on market-based initiatives? Alternative food networks established with limited government intervention appear to assume that this is possible to a large extent, though empirical analysis presents a more nuanced picture. Evidence that supports an affirmative answer to the question includes the fact that some market mechanisms allow farmers with strong ecological and social values to practise farming as an expression of their politics and to get paid a premium for doing so by similarly committed consumers. These "citizen farmers" are discussed here first. Another positive sign is the fact that these markets may draw in farmers who, for other reasons, are attracted to alternative food networks, thus leading them to also adopt more environmentally and socially beneficial production and food distribution practices. Finally, market-based models do have wider spin-off effects, both in inducing the spread of environmentally friendly technologies across the countryside and in reducing the costs of these products for consumers.

The term *citizen-farmer* is not a new one, though it is given a new definition here. Thomas Jefferson saw the citizen-farmer as the foundation of true democracy in the United States. He believed that effective democracy demanded connection to a particular place (Curtin 2002).[8] In Jefferson's republican vision, the land-owning farmer was thus the ideal citizen. In contemporary agri-environmental politics, the concept of citizen-farmer might be most easily understood in relation to the related concept of citizen-consumer, which is defined as the political economic actor who identifies not with consumerism but political change, and who uses his or her own consumer behaviour to promote change (Slocum 2004). In a study highlighting the underlying contradictions of this hybrid, Johnston (2008) notes that the citizen-consumer acts by "voting with their dollar" to satisfy both the ideologies of consumerism (an idea rooted in individual self-interest) and citizenship (an ideal rooted in collective responsibility to a social and ecological commons).[9] Similarly, in the case of agriculture, citizen-farmers make economic choices about how to organize their farms in relation to their own social perceptions of what "good" or "responsible" agriculture entails. This ecological citizenship results in the development of farm operations that attempt to satisfy a range of public goods beyond immediate profitability, often including worker and animal welfare, environmental sustainability, the preservation of traditional skills, the (re)building of rural communities, etc. My conception of the citizen-farmer is closely allied with the notion of civic agriculture, defined by Lyson as the trend towards locally oriented agriculture and food systems intended to rebuild communities in the face of the social and environmental destruction wrought by industrialized agricultural systems (Lyson 2004). Further, while there are many similarities, it is the individualism of the citizen-farmer that appears to set the concept apart from the more collectivist, and historically- and culturally-rooted, concept of agrarian citizenship developed by Wittman (2010). While the term food sovereignty never came up in interviews, the citizen farmers of Australia can still be seen to be implementing several of the central pillars of a food sovereignty agenda (see Martin and Andrée, this volume) in their daily practices, including taking control of their own production practices, trying to farm and distribute food in an environmentally and socially responsible way, and maintaining skill sets that are otherwise rapidly being lost.

Typical of these citizen-farmers was one who practises permaculture (which includes year-round cover crops and many permanent plantations of tree species such as strawberry eucalyptus). He explained to me, "I think that the structure, the industrial linkage between land use and food consumption, is skewing land use so dramatically that it must change if we've got to get carbon back into balance ... We are sequestering carbon like crazy, our soils are so stable now, where the carbon build-up has been fantastic, where next door [a conventional farm] I reckon there must be so much carbon loss, which has its own environmental problems, where you can only feel that we have got this equation right ... I wish that all farmers would take on year-long-green farming as a model" (interview 26).

Another typical perspective is from an organic vegetable producer. She and her husband farm fifty hectares of land and employ twelve people directly. She went on a trip to the United States and Europe to explore alternative distribution models and came back with a new vision of how she wants to do business, shifting her farm's orientation from international markets to local markets:

> We're envisaging ... sustainable growth because it has sound environmental and ecological basis behind not shipping the food further ... [In the United States] I saw all these CSA [community supported agriculture] examples which were so much more aligned with the philosophy and yet still provided great financial rewards for people, so I was fascinated by those examples ... I came home and I said, "Well, I believe that farmers' markets and local food will be a big growth area in the future and I want to be part of that." It's not where the market's at today, but if I want my market ... if I want my business to have 50 per cent local sales in five years' time, then I have to start doing something today to move towards that ... So I thought, well, OK, to do that we need to build our brand. (Interview 14)

In 2004, this particular farm had no local sales, with all of production exported to Japan. By 2006, 20 per cent of their sales were through farmers' markets, direct sales to local restaurants, farm-gate sales, and a twenty-subscription CSA. For the 2006–7 season they were selling 100 subscriptions for thirty weeks of produce baskets, based on models from Oregon and Denmark. From her quote, it is also immediately evident how this citizen-farmer's environmental values are conjoined with entrepreneurial subjectivity – the branding of the farm's product for local markets. The entrepreneurialism associated with alternative food networks is a recurrent theme. These farmers are trying to create markets for more environmentally friendly production and distribution practices where none have existed for some time, and this takes vision, long hours, and hard work.

Advocates of a shift to carbon sequestration and local markets are actually a minority, even among producers who participate in these networks. In fact, this was only the third of the three common reasons for choosing to participate garnered from the farmers interviewed. More important were the search for economic viability and control over production in the face of increasingly demanding, and lower-paying, mainstream markets.

The first of these reasons was clearly described by a farmer who ran an orchard on the outskirts of Melbourne, selling into the wholesale markets until the late 1980s. She noted that in the late 1980s Footscary, the fruit market in Melbourne, "was set up as a growers' market, and all the growers used to go in with their trucks, and people used to come round and ... buy off the backs of trucks. But with these big supermarkets, they've got rid of that ... [T]he market has nearly died, and a lot of the agents buy direct from farms anyway, like Safeway [one of the two major supermarket chains] ... That made us really look at where we were going" (interview 1).

This couple chose to move to a farm far away from the city, in a tourism region, where they can sell fruit directly to the public from their orchards. This story is representative of many interviewees, for whom participation in an alternative food network was forced to a large extent by the foreclosure of other options through the increasing power of supermarkets in the supply chain. The other political-economic dynamic that has eliminated options for farmers, thereby pushing many into "alternative" directions, is the issue of land prices. This is particularly true in those parts of rural Victoria that are seeing migration from urban centres by early retirees and others seeking a new life in the country. This migration has raised prices for land well above their value for agricultural purposes in half the state (Barr 2005). Under these circumstances, an increasing number of mid-sized farmers are turning to alternative food networks, wholly or in part, as a way to increase profits on the same land base.

The second main goal for farmer participation in these networks is to be able to make decisions that farmers would like to make about the quality of food they produce. And once again, the political-economic context matters, since these producers are choosing to pursue what they deem to be quality, rather than the dictates of higher links in conventional supply chains such as the supermarkets.

Notably, however, even though not all are citizen farmers, by participating in these new networks many of the producers under study are also adopting practices and distribution methods that have a lower environmental impact. Some of these producers don't even completely agree with the agendas that drive citizen-consumers to purchase their product. This outcome was revealed most clearly by a poster that one potato farmer has at his market stand. This poster reads: "In the interests of offering you the best potatoes [we] utilise equal opportunity stock selection, trauma free memory recall, non confrontational potato relations, culturally aware growth policies, group therapy, socially non violent awareness raising and no electric prodders. You could almost say ... no potato is forced to get in the box" (interview 16). One thing striking about this poster, aside from its jab at consumers looking for happy potatoes, is a byline that advertises (quite seriously) "genetically unmodified stock, environmentally considered cultivation, hand picked quality" (interview 16). When asked about this line, the producer admitted that while the statement was indeed true, whether such practices were any better or worse than conventional practices was all "rubbish" to him anyway. This reveals just how much changing consumer perceptions and expectations about food are affecting the countryside and the choices made by some farmers who wish to cater to them, even if they may disagree! While the goal of this research was not to quantify the scale of these impacts, it is clear that shifting consumer values are changing the Australian countryside and what happens there.

One question this raises is whether the more discerning consumer palate will necessarily support more environmentally sustainable approaches. Even if these alternative farmers have social and environmental values associated with their production and distribution practices, it is taste that keeps the customers returning. For some, this is not a daunting challenge, given the way that the conventional food system has selected for tasteless products that have a long shelf-life: "We've taken fruit to these farmers' markets, apricots are a classic example, with little spots all over them ... and the customers look at them and they say to us, 'They look rough but they taste really good.' Nobody ever questions that ... And this business about the supermarkets saying they have to look really pretty and every one's got to look exactly the same ... people don't care about that. What they want is something that actually tastes good" (interview 20). This farmer does keep catering to the palate to ensure he is successful in his operation, and close contact with his customers helps.

In a second example, when asked why her consumers buy from her, a free-range, rare-breed, pork producer noted, "The rare breed and the free-range is the two points that are pushed" (interview 9). When asked which of those two are most appealing to consumers, she stated: "Look, I'd say they probably run on par with each other because your rare breed gives you your basic genetic start and your free-ranging then gives it that dimension of flavour, so by the time it gets on to their plate, it's the combination of those two, and I don't think you could say one's more than the other, yes" (interview 9).

Notably, this conversation also quickly turned from the moral values of the production practices to flavour. A similar conversation took place with a farmer who sells free-range eggs. He noted that the customers first come because of animal welfare concerns and they want free range. They also like to know where their food comes from, buying directly from the producer. But then "our customers just say they're so ... I couldn't really say they're ... they just say they're so fresh and I guess that relates to the taste, yes. They just come back for them" (interview 12).

That flavour and socio-ecological values appear to stand on a par with consumers in these food networks relationships is revealing, for what happens if and when the more socially and ecologically preferable option is not the one that tastes better? And in the more extreme case, what if the more environmentally destructive food option is actually the one that tastes better? For example, in recent years there has been a trend towards corn-fed feedlot beef in Australia, which is promoted as the better-tasting beef (because it has more marbling of fat), but it is ultimately more environmentally destructive than the grass-fed alternative. Then there is the question of what happens when you can't sell your ecological advantage. One group of producers in Victoria studied by Higgins, Dibden, and Cocklin (2008) faced exactly this situation. With encouragement and financial support from the federal government, they adopted environmental management systems on their farms. They then branded their product as *Enviro-meat* to sell through local butchers' shops. Unfortunately, they had difficulty commanding a premium for this product, because it was not actually labelled organic, which many health-conscious consumers were willing to pay more for.

Another limitation of the environmental protections represented by some of these alternative food networks is that they may never produce a product accessible to all consumers. Are these new food networks all about pricey niche products that allow well-off consumers to feel good about themselves and only some farmers to reap the benefits? The interviews conducted for this research illustrate that the answer to this is indeed often yes. Some of these products are more expensive because of the high capital costs of setting up a farmhouse cheese operation that yields relatively little product (interview 3), the high costs of delivery associated with a small quantity of goods (interviews 6 and 16), or the high costs of agricultural land near urban areas. As an example of the last, one farmhouse cheese producer noted, "In another area, land might be $4,000 or $5,000 an acre, or thereabouts, and we've got $20,000 an acre, so you've got that money sunk in and you need to get a return on it" (interview 15). These factors lead to high-priced products. These factors mean that some alternative food networks will always remain expensive and exclusive, and this represents a limit to their having a wider impact.

On the other hand, markets continue to do what they do best, even these markets embedded in alternative sets of priorities. Competition is reducing prices and making their products more widely available too. This dynamic was revealed by a couple of specialty potato growers who have together increased the diversity of potatoes grown in Australia many times over. They note that they had to start selling into the "better-off areas" fifteen years ago to make the operation viable. They sold to "people that will buy things where price doesn't come into a decision … People want quality, and if you can provide quality, you can charge for it." However, over time, as the market grew and other producers adopted the new varieties as well, prices have come down: "If you go to the wholesale market you probably see a few of the varieties we do … They're commonly available" (interview 16). In order to keep pace and maintain their own niche, these innovators have moved on to new varieties, and still maintain their high prices: "Every year we've discussed putting prices up, and invariably when we do, we seem to be busier." This example demonstrates that prices for some specialty products do come down over time while simultaneously increasing the biodiversity of food-producing crops in Australia as a whole.

There are also unexpected spinoff benefits of adopting new farming practices. One couple exemplifies organic farmers selling into conventional supply chains both domestically and internationally. By Australian standards, they operate a mid-sized farm of seventy hectares, employing from ten to thirty labourers (mostly Australian nationals), depending on the time of year. Sixty per cent of the farm's crop is asparagus and onions, with other vegetables representing the remainder. After over twenty years of running a conventional farm with his father, they switched to organic production when they took over the helm nine years ago. This was an act of resistance against productivist norms, which include the use of synthetic pesticides and fertilizers. He sums up their reasons succinctly: "I just wanted to try something more natural" (interview 33). This couple's decision to grow organically and market into organic channels had positive ecological impacts. The most obvious is a reduction in pesticide use, which has benefits for farm workers, farm owners, the environment, and the health of customers. Another beneficiary of this change is the soil on the farm, which receives considerably more organic material in the form of composted manure and is thus more resistant to drought and produces healthier plants than would an operation reliant on chemical fertilizers. A third, perhaps less obvious, implication is in increased on-farm biodiversity. At one time this farm was focused solely on asparagus production, as many of its neighbours still are. The decision to produce organically led to a wider mix of crops for two reasons: organic farming depends on crop rotations to reduce weed and insect pressures, and the domestic market for organic asparagus was simply not large enough at the time of conversion, so they decided to diversify their product line (interview 33).

What is most interesting about this story is the synergies between the farm's practices and the increasing ecological sustainability of the conventional practices of neighbouring farms. Across developed countries, vegetable producers have significantly reduced their use of pesticides in recent decades. This has been possible, in part, through the adoption of integrated pest management (IPM) practices. In IPM, entomologists are contracted to visit farms, track pest problems, and recommend a variety of mechanical, biological, and chemical solutions. For conventional vegetable operations in Australia, IPM is expected to allow for a 20 per cent reduction in chemical use, and a 50 per cent reduction in offsite impacts (DEWR 2001). With the growth of IPM across the horticultural sector, this organic farm now has access to local expertise on biological insect control that did not exist before (interview 33). Through their shared IPM technician, neighbours have also learned about what is possible using organic growing techniques, and at least two have recently decided to convert to organics. This example shows how the emergence of "alternative" food networks may lead to deeper socio-environmental impacts across the sector. It also shows just how intertwined "conventional" and "alternative" food networks actually are, due to the fact that they are both embedded in evolving social norms – in this case, regarding agrichemical usage.

Individual versus Collective Action

Individual entrepreneurial responses clearly play a significant role in the development of alternative food networks. This fact raises the possibility that these initiatives over-emphasize *individualized* solutions, thereby delaying a broader *socialized* effort, whether organized through the state or a mass effort marshalled by civil society, to address the problem. The evidence found in Victoria, however, suggests that individual initiatives may also be the first step to collective projects.

A poor fit between social challenges and individual responses was revealed most clearly by livestock producers who now sell their meat directly to consumers. The challenges these particular producers faced were multiple, from finding ways to sell all parts of a carcass rather than just favourite cuts, to developing the appropriate types of networks (and access to infrastructure) in order to slaughter, cool, cut, package, and then distribute their animals' meat: "There's a huge infrastructure for selling meat at a farmer's market ... so it's not something that the average person would even consider taking on" (interview 9). Many of the farmers who have moved in this direction have been similarly overwhelmed by the details (interviews 16, 34, 19), and at least one eventually gave up on the endeavour, despite strong customer support (interview 34). Because of the food safety laws in the State of Victoria, which require all fresh meat to be killed and butchered in accredited facilities, those who succeeded essentially had to buy their own abattoir (interview 21), set up their own butcher shop (interview 25), or develop a business partnership with a butcher (interviews 29 and 9). Each of these steps involves complicated contractual arrangements and the development of entirely new skill sets. These individuals also took on significant new financial risks in order to make these business relationships possible. Is this the way forward for agriculture to start dealing with the environmental and social costs associated with the long-distance transport of food? If it is, few of today's farmers will be able make the transition without broader supportive structures.

Notably, the challenge is not just in acquiring marketing skills and setting up new businesses. In Victoria, food producers are facing these challenges because of the state's neoliberalized food markets, which assume that all animals will be killed in large, centralized facilities, and then moved through conventional channels to customers. Such facilities require onerous regulatory standards to ensure the safety of the products, especially since a small mistake (e.g., an E-coli contamination)

can have widespread consequences. Such standards may not be as suit-
ed to smaller, more localized scales of production and distribution, but
this is not currently considered in the policy realm. As a result, farmers
who don't want to work within the conventional distribution model
still have to meet the same regulatory standards. A similar situation
faces farmhouse-cheese producers.

One outcome of the challenges for livestock producers selling directly
to the public is to form, in the majority of cases, co-operative relationships and new partnerships with other farmers to make this possible
(interviews 5, 9, 19, 25, and 29). This emerging response is important,
because it reveals how neoliberalization is *necessitating* collective responses and the formation of collective identities, despite its *emphasis*
on the individual entrepreneur.

Notably, for some of the citizen-farmers interviewed, a collective
identity comes quite naturally as a reaction against the norms of the
system they face, and the fact that it appears to be built of such tight
relationships between industry and government. This solidarity was
clearly seen among some of the organic farmers interviewed, who work
hard to support one another. As one informant stated, "I think because
there's such lack of support from everywhere, especially government,
that you've got to help each other out, you've got to share the knowledge to be able to just keep it going … Fight the good fight and all that
sort of stuff, you know, against the big companies" (interview 3). There
were multiple examples of the kind of collective action in Victoria: the
establishment of new joint marketing initiatives (interviews 13 and 29),
regional producer groups (interview 6), "local" labelling regimes (interviews 26 and 37), farmers' markets controlled by the farmers themselves (interview 24), and "food and wine trails" (interviews 1, 11, and
17), among others.

One quotation illustrates the way that farmers see these efforts: "Our
aim on that [food and wine] trail is to support each other, but primarily
for total excellence. Everyone on that trail is sincere about total excellence of product and experience … The integrity of that has flowed
through to the dollar" (interview 1). Noteworthy in this statement is the
emphasis on collective action, on the pride of these producers in what
they have achieved, but also how this activity is strongly connected to
neoliberal norms of achieving financial success through excellence and
exclusivity.

Guthman (2007) criticizes precisely this dimension of many alternative food networks defined by niche labelling regimes, because they are

not actually challenging the structural problems of the neoliberal food system. Instead, while these networks purport to redistribute money to farmers to support more environmentally or socially friendly production practices of one sort or another, they are ultimately analogues to the very things they are designed to resist: "property rights that allow these accredited commodities to be traded in global markets" (456). She argues that in order to ensure that higher levels of profit go to those on the inside, labels are designed to exclude. In their practices of exclusion, different networks ultimately have different distributional effects, from the redistribution from consumers to producers, characteristic of fair trade networks, to the more competitive dynamics that occur in the post-transition organic sector – dynamics that ultimately tend to push down prices. "So while labels might be good for some (Pollyannian?), they are hardly good for everybody (Polanyian). Furthermore, the degree to which that they produce competition and reproduce inequality – themselves benchmarks of neoliberalism – suggests a more fundamental imperative to examine these as a form of neoliberal governance" (464).

This is a fair critique. However, I would argue that these labels are really trying to level the playing field of competition in the marketplace through giving consumers the information needed to make choices to support production or distribution practices they would like to support, rather than those practices remaining hidden and thus implicitly deemed irrelevant. Starting to equalize opportunity in this way may still not be a fundamental challenge to all limitations of neoliberalization, but it may be a step towards the Polyanian re-embedding that Guthman seeks. This alternative analysis can be confirmed by the fact that many of the collective identities emerging are perceived by the producers themselves as a step towards state- or nation-wide standards.

For example, new associations are forming, and national standards are being established for a range of initiatives: organics, farmers' markets, free-range egg production (interviews 12 and 23), and wild-harvested bush foods (interviews 19 and 26), among others. The kinds of issues these associations are dealing with are fairly minor at this stage. For example, the emerging Victorian farmers' market association is dealing with the fact that under the Victoria Food Act, farmers' market vendors need to get a permit in each council (regional jurisdiction) where they do business, which could be quite a number for some producers (interview 14). For their part, free-range egg producers are organizing among themselves to ensure that national standards do not allow for the debeaking[10] of "free-range" birds (interview 23), though this is not a unanimous sentiment in this group (interview 12).

These collective initiatives, even if state- or country-wide, may not be challenging the underlying structures of the dominant food system yet, but in the environmental sector it has long been recognized that the first step towards mandatory regulation is sound voluntary standards. When enough producers get on board, the push can then come to make the voluntary rules mandatory (Bernstein and Cashore 2000). In the end, I do concur with Guthman, that "the best hope for these labels ... is that they would produce more collectivist political subjects who in time would develop forms of governance more commensurate to the socialized problems before us" (2007, 474). Fortunately, the story in Victoria suggests that collectivist identities founded in shared values around more responsible farming practices are emerging.

The Role of the State

On the surface, many of these initiatives occur without the active involvement of any level of government at all. The organics industry, for example, has emerged of its own accord. And when the state does get involved in these networks it may even go against the network's needs. The food safety laws associated with meat processing are a case in point. Another example is the engagement of higher levels of government with food trails, with governments apparently ambivalent to the economic and rural development potential of farm-gate sales. This lack of interest was exemplified by proposed farm zoning legislation in Victoria in 2006, which would allow farmers to sell fresh produce like strawberries from the farm gate, but not to sell product that was processed off-farm like strawberry jam, even if made with the farm's own ingredients. Notably, the state government *was* cognizant of the concerns of smaller wineries, which it proposed to exempt from the legislation. In another example that actually pits winery tourism against food tourism, the group of producers who have spent twenty years in establishing the Milawa Gourmet Region, named for the Central Victorian community that lies at its hub, are now seeing their efforts pushed to the sidelines by state efforts to promote tourism in the King Valley Wine Region – a wider area that includes Milawa (interview 10). New government promotional materials highlight "local produce in the King Valley," but the brand by which the heart of the region has become known is completely absent (anonymous 2007).

It is important to note that the multiple arms of the state – understood as the aggregate of multiple levels of government – are not all on the same page. These same regional food trails tend to get some support

from the local council governments for training and business development, and even from the state-level government for road signage (interview 1). We also see vestiges of earlier (pre-neoliberal) governmental
norms and practices affecting these networks. The potato innovators
discussed above have, until quite recently, been receiving active support from a governmental potato research station to introduce new tu-
ber varieties in Victoria. Recent action from farmer groups of the type
described above (interviews 14, 26, and 29) has also led the government
of Victoria to more actively support regional farmers' markets and a
nascent farmers' market association (Bracks et al. 2006).

Nonetheless, a big part of the problem when governments generally
adhere to a neoliberal vision, as we have seen in Australia in recent
decades, is that this vision is a very powerful force. For example, the
neoliberal push to develop export markets was identified by Andrée,
Dibden, Higgins, and Cocklin (2010) as a key characteristic of how governments in Australia interact with alternative food networks, and it is
particularly evident in the organic sector. In recent years, the Australian
government has undertaken at least two studies of this area, looking
mainly at export market growth and the potential of the domestic industry to meet that demand (DAFF 2004; McKinna 2006). Then, in 2007
and again in 2009, the Victorian government, in cooperation with the
Australian Federation of Agriculture, released two directories certified
organic producers, processors, and distributors in the state. Designed
to "boost domestic and overseas demand for all our certified organic
products including fibre, nutracueticals and agricultural inputs" over
one hundred of the businesses in each directory are tagged with the
phrase "export ready," whether this is their modus operandi or not
(State of Victoria 2009, 1).

Such state initiatives can also be tied to the neoliberal mentalities of
rule identified among these farmers. This was brought to life through
the case of a farmhouse-cheese manufacturer who was offered support
from the federal government for export. This cheese-maker had to go to
France to buy a $100,000 piece of equipment. He learned that the fed-
eral government had travel grants to support that kind of initiative. In
the end, his grant application was approved, but only after he had
made the actual trip, and the letter stated that the funding could not be
used for trips already taken. This left him very bitter:

> In the end I just don't think governments really understand businesses.
> I don't think governments really should be in that, but I think if an

investment is worth making, it's worth making, you know. And if an investment isn't worth making, what the hell is the government doing propping it up? I just don't … I can't get my head around the concept quite frankly … Obviously international trade, there are big issues in international trade and there's obviously a role for government there. The infrastructure is very important, you know, and … infrastructure, and just in terms of, I'd have to say, things like tax levels … but tax makes a big difference when you're talking about what to invest in and what not to invest in. And the amount of tax you have to pay makes a big difference to those investment decisions. So the best thing the government can do is reduce tax, actually. But I can't believe I'm saying things, but anyway, that is true. That is true. (Interview 15)

This farmer's quote exemplifies a neoliberalization of perspective that I observed more broadly in the sample of farmers interviewed. He is not challenging the logic of land markets that lead to all of the best land around Melbourne being valued for wineries (or urban development) rather than the kind of food production he is engaged in, nor does he directly challenge the way that two supermarkets are able to "eat him alive," although this dynamic was mentioned earlier in the interview (interview 15). Instead, he wishes to see tax relief in order to have the capital to invest in his business. This echoes Guthman's (2008b, 1251) point about how neoliberal mentalities push aside social struggles over resources and rights: "The politics of the possible are not only narrowed by the political economy of neoliberalism, but by its governmentalities."

Conclusions

Are these alternative food networks the first step towards the wider adoption of ecological agriculture and food distribution practices in Australia? I suggest that they represent a small first step down that road. The strongly individualist and market-disciplined perspectives of these farmers show just how big a challenge it will be to change the larger structures. As Peck, Theodore, and Brenner (2009) state, "The short- and medium-term prospects for such forms of alternative politics will surely be structured (and to some extent constrained) by the neoliberalized terrains on which they must be prosecuted."

Guthman (2007) notes the troubling rationalities that label-based food networks produce. We can make a similar list for the initiatives studied here. Most disconcerting from the point of view of advancing a food sovereignty agenda grounded in socialized action are the assumptions implicit in these networks that the state has a limited role in solving the environmental issues associated with food systems; that individual initiative of producers and consumers can solve these problems primarily through the market; and that the environmental values implicit in many of these networks (e.g., organic foods) are commensurate with an export-oriented economy, regardless of the specific environmental costs and benefits of the product in question. The fact that the politics of labour practices were not even mentioned in any of the interviews, and that issues of how markets for land constrain the future of agriculture were raised only twice, suggest another set of problematic assumptions that beg further research of these types of "alternatives."

On the other hand, these examples show that just because alternative food networks are market-driven does not mean public goods are not being realized through them. In fact, many of these networks are designed to achieve environmental and social benefits – in terms of having food eaten closer to where it is produced, for example. While imbued with certain neoliberal norms, these activities are also building inroads into, or re-colonizing, neoliberal spaces by newly embedding them in what are ultimately *social* values. They support the innovations of what I have termed Australia's new "citizen-farmers" and are causing positive spillover in the countryside. The zeal of these farmers is also making their networks very appealing to other entrepreneurial farmers seeking a way out of the cost-prize squeeze. Finally, this research shows that the long-term success of these networks may depend on collective action, suggesting that individualized initiatives have the potential to be the first step towards governance mechanisms (whether state-, industry-, or civil society-based) with a wider impact both on the ground and on the mindsets of their farmer participants. These are the potential outcomes associated with the growth of alternative food networks in Australia that analysts with an interest in the institutionalization of food sovereignty will want to follow closely.

NOTES

1 Interviews were framed in terms of production and distribution choices made by the farmers, rather than in terms of ideological motivation.

2 The term *neoliberalization* is favoured over *neoliberalism* because it better captures the dynamic and open-ended nature of this prevailing pattern of market-oriented regulatory restructuring (Guthman 2008a; Peck, Theodore, and Brenner 2009).

3 While shopping "locally" or from farms that adopt specific ecological practices can be associated with a range of social, environmental, economic, and cultural benefits, this is not *necessarily* the case (see Andrée 2006). There are also different effects from different kinds of alternative food networks, both for the environment and for society more broadly (Guthman 2007, 457). However, these issues lie beyond the scope of this chapter.

4 In an important reassessment of how Polanyi is interpreted in the political economy literature, Lacher (1999) argues that Polanyi never actually supported the protectionist regulatory initiatives of the post–Second World War Period that has become widely known as "embedded liberalism" (Ruggie 1982), and was in fact in favour of deeper forms of democratic socialism that would take land and labour out of markets entirely.

5 In agriculture, neoliberalization has been highly uneven. Many industrialized countries continue to maintain high levels of production subsidies (e.g., Japan, the EU, and the United States), while others have high tariff barriers to protect certain groups of domestic producers (e.g., Canada). Australia and New Zealand are actually the only two industrialized countries to (fairly) consistently pursue the neoliberal agenda of deregulation, tariff barrier reduction, subsidy reduction (or elimination), coupled with an export orientation intended to build on their comparative advantages.

6 For an explanation of "governmentality," see Martin and Andrée, this volume.

7 This is one of the most highly concentrated food systems in the world. Among other OECD countries, similar market share (50–70 per cent) is usually reached only when the sales of the five largest firms are aggregated. The five largest retailers in France, for example, account for 80 per cent of sales, while in the United Kingdom they account for 64 per cent of sales and in the United States only 32 per cent (Soler 2005).

8 Jefferson rejected the possibility that Native Americans who continued to live traditional lifestyles had a connection to place because of their nomadic tendencies, so his view of citizenship must be seen as closely connected with a colonizing understanding of "civilization" (Curtin 2002).

9 This is only one of two readings of the citizen-consumer in the neoliberal era. Other authors frame the citizen-consumer in terms of what is seen as another core shift within neoliberalism: the reinvention of citizens *as* consumers (Clarke 2007).

10 Debeaking involves clipping a young chick's beak to prevent it from being able to harm other chickens as it matures. It is a controversial practice associated with larger-scale poultry production.

REFERENCES

Andrée, P. 2006. "And Miles to Go before I Eat … Local Limitations." *Alternatives Journal* 32 (3): 15–16.

Andrée, P., J. Dibden, V. Higgins, and C. Cocklin. 2010. "Competitive Productivism and Australia's Emerging 'Alternative' Agri-food Networks: Producing for Farmers' Markets in Victoria and Beyond." *Australian Geographer* 41 (3): 307–22. http://dx.doi.org/10.1080/00049182.2010.498038.

Australian Government Department of Agriculture (ABARE). 2003. *Australian Food Statistics*. Department of Agriculture, Fisheries and Forestry. http://www.daff.gov.au/__data/assets/pdf_file/0003/182622/austfoodsstats2003.pdf.

Barr, N. 2005. "Understanding Rural Victoria." Department of Primary Industries, State of Victoria.

Bell, D., and G. Valentine. 1997. *Consuming Geographies: We Are Where We Eat.* London: Routledge.

Bernstein, S., and B. Cashore. 2000. *Global Business Regulation*. London: Cambridge University Press.

Blue, Gwen. 2009. "On the Politics and Possibilities of Locavores: Situating Food Sovereignty in the Turn from Government to Governance." *Politics and Culture* 2. http://www.politicsandculture.org/2010/10/27/on-the-politics-and-possibilities-of-locavores-situating-food-sovereignty-in-the-turn-from-government-to-governance/.

Bracks, S., J. Brumby, B. Cameron, and T. Theophanous. 2006. *Provincial Victoria: Moving Forward – Not Back; Policy for the 2006 Victorian Election.* Melbourne: Australian Labor Party.

Campbell, Hugh. 2005. "The Rise and Rise of EurepGAP European (Re) Invention of Colonial Food Relations?" *International Journal of Sociology of Food and Agriculture* 13 (2): 1–19.

Clark, J., and P. Lowe. 1992. "Cleaning Up Agriculture: Environment, Technology and Social Science." *Sociologia Ruralis* 32 (1): 11–29.

Clarke, John. 2007. "Citizen-Consumers and Public Service Reform: At the Limits of Neoliberalism?" *Policy Futures in Education* 5 (2): 239–48. http://dx.doi.org/10.2304/pfie.2007.5.2.239.

Cocklin, C. 2005. "Natural Capital and the Sustainability of Rural Communities." In *Sustainability and Change in Rural Australia*, edited by C. Cocklin and J. Dibden, 171–91. Sydney: UNSW.

Coster, M., and N. Kennon. 2005, *"New Generation" Farmers' Markets in Rural Communities*. Barton: Rural Industries Research and Development Corporation.

Curtin, Deane. 2002. *Ecological Citizenship*, edited by F. Engin and Bryan S. Turner. Handbook of Citizenship Studies. London: Sage.

Delforce, R., A. Dickson, and J. Hogan. 2005. *Australia's Food Industry: Recent Changes and Challenges*. Vol. 2. Canberra: ABARE.

Department of Agriculture, Fisheries and Forestry (DAFF). 2004. *The Australian Organic Industry: A Summary*. Canberra: Food Policy and Communications Section: Australian Government Department of Agriculture, Fisheries and Forestry Canberra.

– 2005. *Australian Agriculture and Food Sector Stocktake*. Canberra: DAFF.

Department of the Environment and Water Resources (DEWR). 2001. *State of the Environment Australia*. Land Theme Report. Canberra: DEWR.

Dibden, J., and C. Cocklin. 2005. "Sustainability and Agri-Environmental Governance." In *Agricultural Governance: Globalization and the New Politics of Regulation*, edited by V. Higgins and G. Lawrence, 135–52. Abingdon: Routledge.

– 2009. "'Multifunctionality': Trade Protectionism or a New Way Forward?" *Environment and Planning* 41 (1): 163–82.

Dobson, Andrew. 2003. *Citizenship and the Environment*. Oxford: Oxford University Press. http://dx.doi.org/10.1093/0199258449.001.0001.

Douwe van der Ploeg, Jan. 2007. "Resistance of the Third Kind and the Construction of Sustainability." Paper presented to the ESRS conference, Wageningen, 23 August. http://www,jandouwevanderploeg.com/EN/publications/articles/resistance-of-the-third-kind/.

Dupuis, M., and D. Goodman. 2005. "Should We Go Home to Eat? Toward a Reflexive Politics of Localism." *Journal of Rural Studies* 21: 359–71.

Erlich, R., R. Riddell, and M. Wahlqvist. 2005. *Regional Foods: Australia's Health and Wealth*. Rural Industries Research and Development Corporation. Australian Government: Barton, ACT.

Foucault, Michel. 1991. "On Governmentality." In *The Foucault Effect*, edited by G. Burchell, C. Gordon, and P. Miller, 87–104. Chicago: University of Chicago Press.

George, A., R.H. Broadley, and R.J. Nissen. 2005. "Can Australian Horticulture Survive and Meet the Global Challenge?" *Acta Horticulturae* 694:289–94.

Goodman, D. 2003. "The Quality 'Turn' and Alternative Food Practices: Reflections and Agenda." *Journal of Rural Studies* 19 (1): 1–7. http://dx.doi .org/10.1016/S0743-0167(02)00043-8.

– 2004. "Rural Europe Redux: Reflections on Alternative Agro-Food Networks and Paradigm Change." *Sociologia Ruralis* 44 (1): 3–16. http:// dx.doi.org/10.1111/j.1467-9523.2004.00258.x.

Granovetter, Mark. 1985. "Economic Action and Social Structures: The Problem of Embeddedness." *American Journal of Sociology* 91 (3): 481–510. http://dx.doi.org/10.1086/228311.

Guthman, Julie. 2004. *Agrarian Dreams*. Santa Cruz: University of California Press.

– 2007. "The Polanyian Way? Voluntary Food Labels as Neoliberal Governance." *Antipode* 39 (3): 457–78.

– 2008a. "Neoliberalism and the Making of Food Politics in California." *Geoforum* 39 (3): 1171–83. http://dx.doi.org/10.1016/j.geoforum.2006.09.002.

– 2008b. "Thinking Inside the Neoliberal Box: The Micro-Politics of Agro-Food Philanthropy." *Geoforum* 39 (3): 1241–53. http://dx.doi.org/10.1016/j .geoforum.2006.09.001.

Higgins, V., D. Dibden, and C. Cocklin. 2008. "Neoliberalism and Natural Resource Management: Agri-Environmental Standards and the Governing of Farming Practices." *Geoforum* 39 (5): 1776–85. http://dx.doi.org/10.1016/j .geoforum.2008.05.004.

Hinrichs, C. 2000. "Embeddedness and Local Food Systems: Notes on Two Types of Direct Agricultural Market." *Journal of Rural Studies* 16:295–303.

Holloway, L., and M. Kneafsey. 2000. "Reading the Space of the Farmers' Market: A Preliminary Investigation from the UK." *Sociologia Ruralis* 40:285–99.

Ilbery, B., and D. Maye. 2005. "Alternative (Shorter) Food Supply Chains and Specialist Livestock Products in the Scottish-English Borders." *Environment & Planning* 37 (5): 823–44. http://dx.doi.org/10.1068/a3717.

Johnston, Josée. 2008. "The Citizen-Consumer Hybrid: Ideological Tensions and the Case of Whole Foods Market." *Theory and Society* 37 (3): 229–70. http://dx.doi.org/10.1007/s11186-007-9058-5.

Kirwan, J. 2004. "Alternative Strategies in the UK Agro-Food System: Interrogating the Alterity of Farmers' Markets." *Sociologia Ruralis* 44 (4): 395–415. http://dx.doi.org/10.1111/j.1467-9523.2004.00283.x.

– 2006. "The Interpersonal World of Direct Marketing: Examining Conventions of Quality at UK Farmers' Markets." *Journal of Rural Studies* 22:301–12.

Lacher, Hannes. 1999. "Embedded Liberalism, Disembedded Markets: Conceptualising the Pax Americana." *New Political Economy* 4 (3): 343–60. http://dx.doi.org/10.1080/13563469908406408.

Lowe, P., J. Murdoch, T. Marsden, R. Munton, and A. Flynn. 1993. "Regulating the New Rural Spaces: The Uneven Development of Land." *Journal of Rural Studies* 9 (3): 205–22. http://dx.doi.org/10.1016/0743-0167(93)90067-T.

Lyson, Thomas. 2004. *Civic Agriculture*. Medford, MA: Tufts University Press.

Marsden, T., and R. Sonnino. 2005. "Rural Development and Agri-Food Governance in Europe: Tracing the Development of Alternatives." In *Agricultural Governance: Globalization and the New Politics of Regulation*, edited by V. Higgins and G. Lawrence, 50–68. Abingdon: Routledge.

McCarthy, J., and S. Prudham. 2004. "Neoliberal Nature and the Nature of Neoliberalism." *Geoforum* 35 (3): 275–83. http://dx.doi.org/10.1016/j.geoforum.2003.07.003.

McKinna, D. 2006. *Export Potential for Organics: Opportunities and Barriers*. Canberra: Rural Industries Research and Development Corporation.

Murdoch, J., T. Marsden, and J. Banks. 2000. "Quality, Nature & Embeddedness: Some Theoretical Considerations in the Context of the Food Sector." *Economic Geography* 76:107–25.

Organisation for Economic Cooperation and Development (OECD). 2006. *Agricultural Policies in OECD Countries: At a Glance – 2006 Edition*. Brussels: OECD Agriculture and Food.

Parkins, John R. 2009. "Managing Conflict in Alberta: The Case of Forest Certification and Citizen Committees." In *Environmental Conflict and Democracy in Canada*, edited by Laurie E. Adkin, 174–90. Vancouver: UBC Press.

Peck, J., and A. Tickell. 2002. "Neoliberalizing Space." *Antipode* 34 (3): 380–404. http://dx.doi.org/10.1111/1467-8330.00247.

Peck, J., N. Theodore, and N. Brenner. 2009. "Postneoliberalism and Its Malcontents." Paper presented at the Canadian Political Sciences Association meeting, Ottawa, 28 May.

Polanyi, Karl. (1944) 2001. *The Great Transformation*. Boston: Beacon.

– 1968. *Primitive, Archaic and Modern Economies*. Boston: Beacon.

Potter, C. 1998. *Against the Grain: Agri-Environmental Reform in the United States and the European Union*. Wallingford: CAB International.

Raynolds, Laura T. 2000. "Re-embedding Global Agriculture: The International Organic and Fair Trade Movements." *Agriculture and Human Values* 17 (3): 297–309. http://dx.doi.org/10.1023/A:1007608805843.

Renting, H., T.K. Marsden, and J. Banks. 2003. "Understanding Alternative Food Networks: Exploring the Role of Short Food Supply Chains in Rural

Development." *Environment & Planning* 35 (3): 393–411. http://dx.doi
.org/10.1068/a3510.

Ruggie, John Gerard. 1982. "International Regimes, Transactions, and Change:
Embedded Liberalism in the Postwar Economic Order." *International
Organization* 36 (2): 379–415. http://dx.doi.org/10.1017/S0020818300018993.

Sage, C. 2003. "Social Embeddedness and Relations of Regard: Alternative
'Good Food' Networks in South-West Ireland." *Journal of Rural Studies* 19
(1): 47–60. http://dx.doi.org/10.1016/S0743-0167(02)00044-X.

Slocum, Rachel. 2004. "Consumer Citizens and the Cities for Climate
Protection Campaign." *Environment & Planning* 36 (5): 763–82. http://dx.doi
.org/10.1068/a36139.

Soler, L. 2005. "Retailer Strategies in the Food Marketing Chain." *Journal of
Agricultural and Food Industrial Organization* 3 (1).

Sonnino, Roberta. 2007. "Embeddedness in Action: Saffron and the Making of
the Local in Southern Tuscany." *Agriculture and Human Values* 24 (1): 61–74.
http://dx.doi.org/10.1007/s10460-006-9036-y.

State of Victoria. 2009. *Victorian Organic Products Directory*. Melbourne. http://
www.ofa.org.au/papers/Victorian-Organic-Products-Directory-2009.pdf.

White Hat. 2010. "The White Hat Guide to Farmers' & Growers' Markets in
Victoria." White Hat. http://www.whitehat.com.au/victoria/Markets/
Farmers.asp.

Winter, M. 2003. "Embeddedness, the New Food Economy and Defensive
Localism." *Journal of Rural Studies* 19 (1): 23–32.

Wittman, H. 2010. "Reconnecting Agriculture and Environment: Food
Sovereignty and the Agrarian Basis of Ecological Citizenship." In *Food
Sovereignty: Reconnecting Food, Nature & Community*, edited by
H. Wittman, A.A. Desmarais, and N. Wiebe. Halifax: Fernwood.

Wynen, E. 2003. *Organic Agriculture in Australia: Levies and Expenditure – A
Report for the Rural Industries Research and Development Corporation*. RIRDC
Publication no. 03/002. Canberra: RIRDC.

6 From Food Security to Food Sovereignty in Canada: Resistance and Authority in the Context of Neoliberalism

SARAH J. MARTIN AND PETER ANDRÉE

In Canada, the concept of food sovereignty is being adopted by civil society organizations in resistance to neoliberal food governance and in order to frame alternatives. At the forefront of this movement is the People's Food Policy Project (PFPP), an initiative that brings together left-leaning farm organizations, international solidarity non-governmental organizations (NGOs), and community food security NGOs to, in their own words, "creat[e] a food policy based on the principles of food sovereignty" (PFPP 2010, 1). These activists' efforts are taking place, arguably, in the heart of the neoliberal global food system described in the introductory chapters to this volume. Canada has been a strong advocate for trade liberalization, and it practises what it preaches: it is the world's fourth-largest exporter and fourth-largest importer of agricultural products (Agriculture and Agri-Food Canada 2009).

The discourse of food sovereignty was initially produced in *resistance* to the neoliberal food system embraced by Canada. In the mid-1990s the transnational coalition of peasant and farmers organizations, La Vía Campesina, emerged to fight the inclusion of agriculture in World Trade Organization (WTO) from the margins of the neoliberal food system, and some Canadian farmer organizations were there from the beginning (Desmarais 2007). Given that much of the literature on the food sovereignty movement is concentrated on the global South, and is thus focused primarily on agrarian and peasant setting,[1] the decision of the PFPP to unite under the banner of food sovereignty offers an opportunity to examine what food sovereignty means "in a wealthy Northern country," to borrow a phrase from Cathleen Kneen (Holt-Giménez et al. 2010, 229). What does the shift from the discourse of food *security* to food *sovereignty* tell us about Canadian food movements and how they are working in the context of neoliberalization?

In keeping with others writing on this subject (Desmarais 2003; Holt-Giménez et al. 2010; McMichael 2006), including McMahon's chapter in this volume on her experiences as a farmer in British Columbia, we believe that the adoption of food sovereignty in Canada should be understood as a form of resistance. This resistance reveals commonalities between the experiences of peasants and small farmers in the global South and the global North. In fact, we trace the adoption of food sovereignty among Canadian farm organizations below. However, our primary goal in this chapter is to emphasize another trend – a trend that suggests that neoliberal food governance is not solely a site of resistance for those who have adopted the discourse of food sovereignty.

This chapter makes a contentious claim – at least for those who understand neoliberalism only in terms of marginalization and disempowerment. We argue that the endorsement of food sovereignty by some activists, especially NGOs focused on ensuring equitable access to healthy food for all, signifies an increasing authority, capacity, and legitimacy in the governance of food. This increasing authority is possible only by leveraging some of the practices that exemplify neoliberal governance. Governance, for us, is broadly defined. It includes state institutions and policies, but also includes industry self-governance mechanisms (including the fair trade structures described by Zerbe in this volume), the contributions of churches and other civil society organizations to the social safety net, as well as the webs of norms that tie structures together. We trace the increasing authority of urban food security organizations, as we call them,[2] from the early 1980s as an example within this broader definition of governance of food. Urban food security NGOs have developed programs that target communities for development, and individuals for skill- and capacity-building, in areas that are largely abandoned by the state. They are supported by a wide net of partnerships with various levels of government, foundations, and the private sector. The larger of these organizations have developed considerable capacity and expertise in food governance; they wield a form of knowledge / power with its own ways of framing and solving food-production and food-distribution issues. In the era of neoliberal globalization, this knowledge is an important counterweight to the knowledges of the state and its corporate partners, as discussed in chapter 1.

The fact that representatives of these urban food security organizations are now using the food sovereignty framework developed by La Vía Campesina and its partners as a way to "problematize the food system" (interview by Sarah Martin, 25 January 2010) and as a "lens for decision making" (interview by Sarah Martin, 30 November 2009) around which projects they will or will not devote their energies to is consistent with a larger pattern. This chapter argues that urban food security NGOs are increasingly practising a form of sovereignty in the realm of food governance. Their adoption (tentative as it may be, as we discuss below) of the discourse of food sovereignty fits with this reality and opens space for further claims of authority in new sites of food governance. The urban food security NGO picture presented here is a way of approaching "food sovereignty" that is very different from the discourse of resistance enacted by farm-based groups in Canada, yet both of these paths are now converging in the Canadian food movement through initiatives exemplified by the PFPP.

The next section introduces our theoretical framework, rooted in critical political economy and the concept of governmentality. This is followed by an overview of the PFPP. We then turn to situating our argument in relation to tensions others have noted within the food sovereignty movement at the international level. Next, we show how Canadian NGOs adopted the discourse of "food security" in the 1980s and 1990s to frame their work and is illustrates an increasing authority in food governance. The migration of "food sovereignty" from transnational forums to Canadian civil society, and new sites of food governance, is illustrated by activists involved with the PFPP. Along the way we illustrate how food sovereignty is also being co-opted by mainstream farming organizations in Canada with various agendas, adding a further layer to the analysis. Our conclusion draws together the threads of our argument. Food sovereignty must be understood as being about more than the "agrarian citizenship" (McMichael 2006, 48) documented by McMahon, Wright, and Massicotte (all this volume). The discourse of food sovereignty, we argue, is also producing and is being produced in new sites of governance within the social safety net where many urban food security NGOs play a central role. What brings these urban food security NGOs and farm groups aligned with La Vía Campesina together, and what ultimately separates their perspectives from those of the other Canadian agricultural groups, is a more radical analysis of the ills of the food system in relation to neoliberalization and neoliberal food governance.

Theory

This chapter examines shifts in discourse. How we structure our understanding of the world through language helps to define what can or
cannot happen next (Fairbairn 2010). In Foucauldian terms, discourse is
both productive and disciplinary (Andrée 2007). The widespread adoption of a discourse reveals the forces at work at that historical moment
that give rise to specific ways of thinking, talking, and being, and it is
these deeper forces and their effects that we also seek to expose. Given
this orientation towards discourse as both constituted within, and con-
stitutive of, power relations, this chapter does not present prescriptive
definitions of food sovereignty or of food security. Rather, we are starting with the assumption that shifts in the meaning of food security, and
then the growing adoption of the language of food sovereignty, reveal
important insights about how food issues are understood and acted
upon by specific constituencies over time.

Our theoretical frame combines the lenses of critical political economy
and governmentality. Most critical political economists who examine
food politics are sociologists: one school examines agrarian political
economy (Borras 2009; Buttel 2001; Goodman 1981); another is the school
of international political economists (IPE) that builds on Wallerstein's
world system theory and the French historian Braudel's work to develop
food regimes to explain the structural changes in the global food system
(Friedmann 1992; Friedmann and McMichael 1989; McMichael 2004;
Wittman 2009). In Canada, some political economists studying agriculture and food take a more pragmatic approach and address policy and
civil society engagement (Koc, MacRae, Desjardins, and Roberts 2008;
MacRae, Henning, and Hill 1993). Political scientists also write about
food politics from within the frame of IPE, drawing on theorists such as
Gramsci (Andrée 2007) and South American thinkers such as Escobar
(Massicotte 2010) in order to examine civil society responses.

One element to unite critical political economists is their emphasis on
neoliberalism as a target of analysis. We use the term *neoliberalization*
following on Peck and Tickell's (2002) discussion of neoliberalism as a
process (see Andrée this volume). Since the 1970s, the state in industrialized countries was *rolled back* and withdrew from the provision of social services. The state began to prescribe a free market tonic for social
and economic maladies, thereby *rolling out* regulations that facilitated
and normalized trade liberalization and other market-based "solutions." Social projects were localized and the market was universalized.

This localization of social projects contributed to the rise of urban food security NGOs and their provision of services. The universalized market and its main disciplinary vehicle, the WTO, contributed to the emergence of the transnational food sovereignty movement, as farmers and peasants began to resist the neoliberalization of agriculture. Thus neoliberalization helps to explain these broad shifts. However, a critical political economy lens is less helpful in explaining why food bank workers in Toronto or community development workers in New Brunswick are increasingly using the language of food sovereignty, a term rooted in farmer and peasant struggles, to describe their work (Martin 2010).

Whereas a critical political economy highlights the practices and power relations between the state, the market, and civil society, theorists of discourse and governmentality seek to explain the operation of power by "mak[ing] explicit the forms of political reason and ethical assumptions" exposed through "problems of rule" (Walters and Haahr 2005, 290). That is, relations of power are clarified, focusing on how problems of governance are posed and how they are "solved." This approach includes how one is governed by the state, and how one governs oneself. "Governmentality is in this sense a complex in which the exercise of political power gets thought and organized in terms of the government of social and economic processes" (298).

How does the concept of governmentality help us study the emergence of food sovereignty in Canada? Through this lens, calls for food sovereignty can be seen as claims of authority being made over community and local sites of governance that are not unlike claims made by nation states with regards to national sovereignty, as described by Menser (this volume). These claims draw their authority from an individual's "right to choose" (Guthman 2007), or the "right to know" the provenance of food (Smythe, this volume). In other cases, food sovereignty claims are rooted in the authority of a farmer's or peasant's experience, and the depth of their knowledge over what might be "right" for their land and subsistence (Massicotte and Wright, both this volume). In contrast, we highlight the authority that is found in the day-to-day practice of food provisioning within one's community, as prescribed and practised by many urban food security NGOs.

Definitions of food security have shifted over time, and we agree that these changes have political, economic, and material outcomes in particular places (Jarosz 2011). But these shifts are not only about a "top-down" entrenchment of neoliberalization. In the face of shifting sites of governance, we have observed how urban food security NGOs have been able to frame and forward their own "bottom-up" agendas. These two frames, a critical political economy frame and attention to the discourses and practices of governmentality, together reveal a complex story about food sovereignty in Canada.

The People's Food Policy Project

To tell the story of how Canadian activists are adopting the language of food sovereignty in their work, this chapter draws on the authors' experiences in the Canadian food movement as community organizers around sustainable agriculture and community food security (Andrée), as well as one of the author's (Martin) experiences undertaking interviews as part of her MA research in collaboration with organizers of the People's Food Policy Project in 2009 and 2010.[3] The PFPP – in their own words – was a pan-Canadian network of citizens and organizations creating Canada's first comprehensive food sovereignty policy by mobilizing people in their own communities. The aim, according to one key leader, was "to radically re-align the food system in Canada" (Holt-Giménez et al. 2010, 235; 2011). The PFPP was primarily volunteer-driven, with coordination provided by a full-time staff person hired with funding from Heifer International.[4] Over three thousand people contributed to the policy through "kitchen table" meetings held in rural and urban, marginalized and wealthy communities from coast to coast to coast, and through online submissions. The meetings were facilitated by dozens of community-based animators and culminated with the publication of *Resetting the Table: A People's Food Policy for Canada* (PFPP 2011).

Before their engagement with the PFPP process, many of the individuals and organizations who participated were more comfortable with the terms *food security* or *community food security* (both concepts are unpacked below) to characterize their work. To reframe their efforts from the perspective of food sovereignty, as the PFPP leadership actively encouraged, was a challenge. Some remained uncomfortable with the language, as food sovereignty is considered radical in comparison to food security (Holt-Giménez and Shattuck 2011). For example, one PFPP animator described food sovereignty as "too academic and radical" to use in her day-to-day work (Sarah Martin, interview, 30 October 2009).

By deploying food sovereignty, the leadership of the PFPP was engaging in contentious politics and opening up political space for debates that appeared to be settled. Indigenous claims notwithstanding, there is little debate about who has sovereignty over resources, private property, or land redistribution in Canada. And while it may be safe for a Torontonian to call for more community gardens, the financing of land grabs on the Prairies is generally left untroubled and relegated to the business pages. From the perspective of food sovereignty, and their own associations with La Vía Campesina and its radical vision, the PFPP leadership was pushing its participants to think through, and take positions on, these larger structural issues related to food, its production, and its distribution in Canada, including broad questions of trade, aid, science and technology, and sustainable fisheries, among others.

Food Sovereignty at the International Level: Scope and Tensions

A review of the literature reveals that food sovereignty is framed in multiple ways. In general, food sovereignty is understood as a resistance discourse (or what McMichael [2004, 57] calls a "counter movement" non-state concept) and is posed as a solution and tool to use against the negative effects of a dominant food regime or global food system. Food sovereignty is increasingly gaining the attention of scholars in a variety of empirical realms, from rural development (Patel 2009), and international political economy (McMichael 2008), to social movements (Teubal 2009).[5] These are areas that all intersect with neoliberal governance and its "deep inequalities of power" (Patel 2009, 663), whether in unfair trade practices (Desmarais 2002; 2003), hunger and environmental degradation (Cohn and Yale 2006), or the 2007–8 food crisis (Bello 2008; Nicholson and Delforge 2008; Rosset 2009). By targeting neoliberalism (Patel and McMichael 2004) or globalization (Shiva 2003), a universalized discourse of struggle, rebellion, and emancipation rooted in agro-ecological relations is produced. The discussion focuses on ways to resist, reclaim, and fight the negative effects of neoliberalization. That said, over the last two decades food sovereignty discourse has not remained static.

As noted by Menser (this volume), La Vía Campesina defined food sovereignty in 1996 as "the right of each nation to maintain and develop its own capacity to produce its basic foods, respecting cultural and productive diversity" (Desmarais 2007, 34). In 2000, this definition was expanded to include the "right of peoples to define their agricultural and food policy" (Desmarais 2007, 2).[6] Food sovereignty thus has its origins in resisting neoliberalization primarily at the national and international scale. After ten years of engagement, the definition was expanded once again at Nyéléni, Mali, at the Forum for Food Sovereignty organized by La Vía Campesina and its partner organizations from around the world. The declaration of that conference is summarized in the six "pillars" of food sovereignty (which in turn formed the basis for PFPP discussions): food for people, values food providers, localizes food systems, encourages local control, builds knowledge and skills, and works with nature. The six pillars reflect a complex set of relations. "Sovereign" action is no longer solely the state or nation. Rather the focus is on communities and localized control. Thus new sites of governance and politics are imagined and enacted. However, as these "pillars" land in specific sites and are put into practice, tensions arise.

Some of these tensions are not new. For example, Desmarais (2007) identifies a division in the early days of the establishment of La Vía Campesina between the (largely international) NGOs, which sought to speak for the emerging global farmers' movement, and the farm organizations themselves. Holt-Giménez identifies a schism at the level of practice, between NGOs who support sustainable agricultural practices and the farm organizations themselves, as represented by La Vía Campesina, with their more radical call for policy changes (Holt-Giménez et al. 2010).[7]

There are similar tensions arising within the Canadian food movement. Who is going to be the voice for food sovereignty? Those who are marginalized by lack of equitable food access (and rollback neoliberalization), or farmers who are marginalized by unfair and universalized markets (and roll-out neoliberalization)? In discursive terms, where is authority drawn on, who will draw on it, and to what end? For the PFPP, the act of mobilizing a unified voice to produce policies for the federal government means working through these tensions. One way to begin to understand these tensions is to consider how the predecessors of some of today's civil-society organizations were solving the problems of food access. How did urban food security NGOs negotiate the rollback of services and begin to gain authority?

The Discourse of Food Security in Canada

Food security remains the touchstone discourse for many activists in Canada. *Food insecurity* is often used interchangeably with *hunger*

(Jarosz 2011), so we can look to how hunger and food security began to be used by NGOs in Canada. This section describes how food security discourse first emerged at the international level in 1974 at a forum where Canadian NGOs had a new role. Food security began at the international and national scale and shifted to a focus upon households and gendered individuals (Jarosz 2011). This shift resulted in the opening up of new sites of governance for urban food security NGOs.

Prior to the 1970s, the problem of hunger was framed not as a political issue but as a technical issue to be resolved by experts, and one that occurred outside of Canada's borders. After the Second World War, states such as Canada used food aid to support their farmers by disposing of surplus grain and extended their technical expertise to "needy" areas of the world (Cavell 1952). Fairbairn refers to this period as discursively grounded in the "right to food" and "freedom from hunger" guaranteed by technological advancements and free markets (Fairbairn 2010, 19).

With the onset of a food crisis in the early 1970s and the convening of the 1974 World Food Conference in Rome, the adoption of this new international discourse of "food security" placed the onus on states to intervene. Nonetheless, hunger continued to be seen as a problem that occurred *outside* of Canada's borders. Articles and speeches from that time illustrate how the food security discourse was still underpinned by the technical "problem" of agricultural production (Brown 1975). In turn, the solution to hunger was to export surplus crops and productivist agricultural technologies that had served countries such as Canada so well. Among the assumptions of "food security," as reviewed by Fairbairn (2010), is that it gave the state the right to intervene in markets in order to help stabilize prices, and that it encouraged the (somewhat contradictory) goals of the industrialization of agriculture in the global South and food aid delivered by the North. While food security discourse was initially presented as a state project, the concept also brought with it some new openings for NGO engagement.

The 1974 Rome Conference marked a shift in the participation of Canadian NGOs. With funding from the Canadian government, a number of those involved in international advocacy attended the conference. The Canadian NGO delegation was characterized by Van Rooy as "part of a new activist community, largely in opposition to their governments ... [who] diagnosed the world food crisis as a political problem, based in the structure of North–South relations, while their governments interpreted the crisis largely as a problem of technical production, exacerbated by difficult weather" (Van Rooy 1997, 94–5). The participation of the Canadian delegation represented a shift from the strictly state-to-state negotiations of past international stages and pointed to the increased authority of NGOs, particularly in the field of international development. In some ways, this was the first recognition that states no longer held a monopoly on providing solutions to food security or hunger. This recognition of NGO expertise and intervention would become central to the developments that followed in Canada.

In the 1980s the problem of hunger was viewed increasingly as a Canadian issue (Davis and Tarasuk 1994; Riches and CCSD 1986), and food security was useful to describe this new domestic issue when hunger was "discovered" in Canada. As the state began to roll back social services, NGOs became the main service providers, and they used food security to frame their work. The first civil-society interventions included the establishment of emergency food banks to support those who were affected by the rollback of social welfare programs as part of the neoliberalization of Canadian government services. In response to increasing unemployment and poverty,[8] food banks were set up by charitable organizations (including churches) and organized labour (Riches and CCSD 1986). Civil society organizations could leverage resources, at least in the short term, to combat hunger and food insecurity. By 1992, food banks in Canada outnumbered McDonald's franchises three to one (Koc et al. 2008).

It was during the 1990s that the phrase *food security* came to be used as a central organizing concept for the work of civil-society organizations active in food issues in Canada. For example, in 1991 the Dieticians of Canada published an official position paper entitled *Hunger and Food Security in Canada* (Canadian Dietetic Association 1994). The first mention of domestic "food security" issues in a Canadian newspaper occurred in 1992, when a *Toronto Star* article referred to a study in North York, which found "there is hunger around us" (Josey 1992, 1). The downloading of government services and the problem of hunger had begun to reshape how Canadian NGOs operated.

How was food security understood and acted upon from the 1970s to the 1990s? First, the food security problem meant that individuals and households were now the site of intervention.[9] Programs were framed in terms of "food insecure" individuals, households, and communities. Food banks, and later NGO projects, such as cooperative buying clubs, collective kitchens, and community gardens (in the late 1980s) shifted

from emergency services to improving longer-term capacities of households to achieve their *own* food security. Thus individuals and local
communities began to emerge as new sites of food governance. Further,
these individuals needed to provision for themselves and not simply
receive charity.

For example, the Nanaimo FoodShare Society's Lunch Munch Program focused "on building long-term food security through self-help
and skill-building programs" (Barron 2002). Similarly, the Salvation
Army's Good Food Box and the Food Bank's Community Outreach
programs "help[ed] build capacity for food security by supporting self-
help programs such as community gardens, community kitchens,
gleaning projects" ("High Cost of Eating" 2004). This shift from emergency services, or "free food" programs as they are sometimes referred
to by practitioners, to capacity building and self-help illustrates how
food security discourse was increasingly concerned with the governing
of individuals' conduct, and specifically what Foucault (2007) would
call their "self-conduct." In keeping with neoliberal ideology, social
welfare had shifted from a state duty to personal responsibility. This
focus did not mean that these programs produced only individualistic
outcomes. Levkoe chronicles how beyond offering tools to develop individual knowledge and skills, participation in these programs may
also radicalize participants, thereby affecting their political decisions
(Levkoe 2006). Still, the solutions were generally framed as self-help
and knowledge acquisition, where the individuals were ultimately responsible for their own "food security" (Guthman 2007).

Second, food security was increasingly within the purview of a wide
range of actors. Unique civil-society–local government partnerships
were created with municipal, regional, and provincial governments.
This was made possible by Canadian political structures that grant a
high degree of autonomy to provinces and even municipalities to intervene in public welfare (Koc et al. 2008). Since national social welfare
programs were being rolled back by the federal government, policies
and programs emerged from municipalities and communities. Munici-
pally sponsored food policy councils, such as the Edmonton Food Policy
Council (established in 1988) and the Toronto Food Policy Council (established in 1990), had a more radical analysis of the root causes of
food insecurity in poverty, trade agreements, and federal agricultural
policy. These councils supported the work of food security organizations through declarative food charters that linked social justice claims
to policy and new programming possibilities. For example, the Toronto

Food Charter states, "Food security is ... not just a set of problems. It creates opportunities" (Toronto Food Policy Council 1998). By the 1990s, such diffuse networks of food governance led to partnerships that were unimaginable when food banks were first introduced as stop-gap measures. For example, the Edmonton Food Policy Council conducted surveys on food security in order to support the work of food banks with funds from the federal Department of Health and Welfare (Faulder 1991). In addition, the Canada Prenatal Nutrition Program was developed in the mid-1990s with help from organizations such as the Stop 103 Foodbank in Toronto and with funds from the Department of Health and Welfare. The site of intervention was not universalized programs but rather located in specific communities. Consequently, food security problems were administered by small disaggregated NGOs, often cobbling together funding from disparate sources. On the one hand, this is certainly a result of rollback neoliberalization and the downloading of services. On the other hand this downloading has fostered the expertise and capacity of food security NGOs.

Third, some of the organizations that emerged to play the role of a safety net, such as FoodShare and the Toronto Food Policy Council, took it upon themselves to look for deeper structural (political and economic) causes of food insecurity, albeit one that remained rooted within what can be called a social welfare problematic. While a range of contributing causes to food insecurity came under scrutiny, the focus remained on programs that had previously been the purview of federal government policy, such as market intervention and full employment. For example, a survey by the Scarborough Hunger Coalition reported that the most important factors that would "help them achieve food security" were "lower food costs, employment and affordable housing" (Infantry 1997), all of which are typically seen as Canadian provincial and federal government projects, rather than community projects. Toronto's FoodShare, established in 1985 by the mayor of Toronto, Art Eggleton, and others concerned about the growth of hunger and food banks, is an example of an organization that sought to implement a wider array of strategies for dealing with food insecurity (Moffett and Morgan 1999). In 1993, a newspaper article described FoodShare as planning "to change the political and economic situation as it affects 'food security,' with the aim of overhauling the food distribution system in this city" (Kane 1993). In this way, food security was used to frame local solutions to political and economic problems. These NGOs sometimes framed issues in ways that would require the intervention of macro-economic policy levers or higher levels of government, but they had limited access to those levers themselves.

By the end of the 1990s the food security movement gained another face. Through the work of FoodShare and the Toronto Food Policy Council in Canada, along with similarly oriented organizations across North America, the equitable "food access" community was increasingly interacting with the "sustainable food production" advocates through initiatives like community gardens, Good Food Boxes, and community-supported agriculture. These movements came together through the larger concept of "community food security." Community food security was defined as "a condition in which all community residents obtain a safe, culturally acceptable, nutritionally adequate diet through a sustainable food system that maximizes community self-reliance and social justice" (Bellows and Hamm 2003, 37). This framework emphasizes the use of community-based institutions and sectors, from agriculture to community development to public health and government assistance, all working to achieve food security for all households in a given area or region (CFSC 2009). Community food security represents the vision of a decentralized, smaller-scale food system, and yet claims solidarity with global coalitions (Levkoe 2006). Notably, this is another shift in scale. Food security was initially adopted at the global scale and later reconfigured down to the individual and household scale. The community-food security movement had now set its sights on the "local" or "community" scale, perhaps reflecting the movement actors' increased authority and institutional capacity at that level.

What does this story of shifts in the food security discourse tell us about authority, and how is it constructed? As a "developed" nation, Canada was part of the world food security "solution" with its model of productivist agriculture after the Second World War and into the 1970s and 1980s. However, the "discovery" of hungry Canadians in the 1980s was discordant with this narrative. Food security could not be understood as a domestic issue for an agricultural exporter. To gain authority as a discourse, it had to be translated to individuals, families, and communities. Concomitantly, through roll-out neoliberalization, NGOs began to intervene in the space formally occupied by national programs. Food security discourse provided the authority needed by these organizations to intervene with programs directed at individuals, households, and communities. Food banks were initially a response to a "welfare crisis" (Riches and CCSD 1986) as the interventions became institutionalized (Riches 2002) and "non-emergency" (Johnston and

Baker 2005, 313), the welfare crisis was set aside, and a focus on food security emerged. At the same time, the establishment of food policy councils and formal adoption of food charters by municipalities, health boards, and provinces – "citizen-based vehicles to engage their public institutions" (Koc et al. 2008, 132) – created a new source of authority to draw on as programs grew in size and scope.

Urban food security NGOs were advocating for the marginalized as well as providing programs of support under the rubric of community food security, but this constrained their impact nationally. This changed in 1996, when a national voice was sought by the Canadian government to participate in the World Food Summit. A similar call was made for the World Food Summit of 2002, in each case echoing the initial participation of these groups in 1974 at the World Food Conference in Rome. The activity of organizing for these international conferences eventually led to the formation of Food Secure Canada / Sécurité alimentaire Canada (FSC-SAC) in 2005, now the national "voice of the food movement" in Canada (PFPP 2011, 25). Food Secure Canada is focused on three interlocking commitments: zero hunger, a sustainable food system, and healthy and safe food (FSC 2012). According to Koc et al. (2008), "the … challenge for FSC-SAC is how to make an impact within the increasingly reregulated policy decision system." Significantly, some key activists within FSC-SAC launched the People's Food Policy Project in 2008 framed through the lens of food sovereignty.

The Discourse of Food Sovereignty in Canada

While new sites of governance were being created in the cities, farmers and farm organizations were negotiating the neoliberalization of agriculture, thus setting the stage for the current confluence of these two sets of actors in the PFPP. When social welfare programs were being rolled back by the federal government, Canadian agriculture experienced the *roll-out* of neoliberalization at the federal government level through a series of free trade agreements and new regulations aimed to facilitate trade.

At the outset, food sovereignty discourse was rooted in the interests of farmers and peasants, or in McMichael's words "farmer-driven agriculture" (McMichael 2004, 58), and that included Canadian farmers and their allies. However, in marked contrast to the urban NGO experience described above, farmer and peasant organizations involved in this movement explicitly rejected the framework of "food security" as being of value internationally to address their concerns as producers on issues like land reform, food "dumping," corporate concentration, and more (Wittman, Desmarais, and Wiebe 2010). Their rejection of the administrative discourse of food security was rooted in an effort to (re) politicize food and agricultural issues.

The participation of some Canadian farm organizations in La Vía Campesina led to the radicalization of their agendas. The prime example can be found in the experience of the National Farmers Union (NFU). Nettie Wiebe, past NFU president, notes, "La Vía Campesina organizations are far more radical in their analysis than the NFU … It took these peasant movements to say unequivocally that the WTO is a malicious agenda against small farmers everywhere, and that we want agriculture right out of the WTO. It took the La Vía Campesina to say this in order to strengthen the NFU position here at home in terms of our critique of the WTO. I don't think we would have ever dared in our context to take such a position on our own. We would have been laughed right out of the room; it would have been such a marginal unlikely position here in Canada" (Desmarais 2007, 143).

The NFU argued that the WTO and free trade agreements not only failed Canadian farmers but were destructive to farmers worldwide. The NFU referenced La Vía Campesina's statements on the loss of national food sovereignty in order to illustrate the effects of neoliberalization on farmers and nations (NFU 1999). For the NFU, food sovereignty means highlighting and rejecting the federal government's active role in the neoliberalization of agriculture in Canada, especially where this involves abandoning domestic policies that protect farmers or the environment. Terry Boehm, national director of the NFU, described food sovereignty in this way: "It's the ability of the community – whether it's a nation-state, a province, a local community, or even a small organization of farmers – to determine what is appropriate in terms of food production and in terms of social and economic justice that flows from growing food. This power includes the autonomy to determine what's appropriate in both those areas and also in terms of the broader economic and ecological context" (Beingessner 2010, 48).

Other farm organizations have adopted a similar reading of food sovereignty. For example, in Quebec La Vía Campesina's member the Union paysanne represents smaller independent farmers and their non-farmer sympathizers. Union paysanne has emerged within the last ten years to take a deliberate stance in favour of small-scale and ecologically oriented "peasant" agriculture – an unusual term in the context of the global North – and against the industrial agri-food model, including genetically modified organisms, and the use of growth hormones as well as non-therapeutic antibiotics in raising farm animals (Union paysanne 2010).

Significantly, agricultural organizations that represent large producers have also adopted the terminology of food sovereignty in recent years, although with a decidedly different intent that may be inconsistent with La Vía Campesina's view. For example, the Union des producteurs agricoles (UPA), an organization that primarily represents large commodity producers in Quebec, has called on the federal government to promote food sovereignty. In anticipation of a WTO meeting, Laurent Pellerin, president of the UPA, stated, "We produce for [the] domestic market ... We don't bother with international rules" (CP Newswire 2005). The UPA calls for food sovereignty in order to ensure "food security" through practices like supply management and other forms of collective marketing (UPA 2010). This position, which reaffirms distinctive domestic policies that protect Canada's dairy and poultry producers (by limiting imports and guaranteeing farmers fair prices) that are not consistent with neoliberal ideologies, is highly compatible with La Vía Campesina positions. However, it is notable that the UPA does not support the entire agenda of La Vía Campesina – for example, agro-ecology. The UPA is thus using the language of "food sovereignty" (as well as "food security," for that matter) strategically, perhaps because of the terminology's growing national and international currency.

Similarly, the Canadian Federation of Agriculture (CFA) also began to use the language of food sovereignty in 2008. The CFA is a national umbrella organization representing provincial farm organizations and national commodity groups. At first glance the adoption of food sovereignty looks to align with the UPA. However, the CFA's Farm and Food Sovereignty and Security Declaration emphasizes "the importance of both domestic and export markets for Canadian agriculture producers" and reaffirms a farming approach that "includes but is not necessarily limited to intensive modern livestock production methods, biotechnology and pest management products" (CFA 2008). Thus the CFA's definition of food sovereignty includes the right to export food produced in Canada and to employ technologies such as genetically modified organisms. This is in stark contrast to Union paysanne, NFU, and La Vía Campesina positions. For instance, both the Union paysanne and the NFU promoted a Canadian campaign in support of Bill C-474, which, should it have been accepted by Canada's Parliament, would have amended the Seeds Regulations to restrict the sale of new genetically engineered seed, pending social and economic impact studies (NFU 2010; Union paysanne 2010). Farmers are not a homogeneous group, and it is no surprise that there are divergent views, some more closely aligned with the agri-food industry. However, activists associated with the NFU reject these more anaemic references to food sovereignty. Hilary Moore of the NFU states, "I believe so wholeheartedly in food sovereignty and the complexity and radicalness of it that I fret it's getting manipulated into something less complicated and less radical" (as quoted in Beingessner 2010, 44).

While those with a more radical perspective on food sovereignty might not like it, this divergence of views on what food sovereignty means to various actors is being taken into consideration by analysts, resulting in the circulation of less politicized visions in attempts to be inclusive. For example, the definition of food sovereignty by Blouin, Lemay, Ashraf, Imai, and Konforti (2009, 4–5) "avoids references to peasant agriculture and avoids anti-capitalist rhetoric (neither of which are suitable to the Canadian context where peasant agriculture contributes about one eighth of total food production) while re-affirming sustainable development as the number one priority for food policy. The language used in the definition, particularly terms like 'sustainable development' and 'decent working conditions and incomes,' is also inclusive enough to unite productivist as well as alterglobalist organizations."

In addition to the farm organization perspectives documented here, 2008 and 2009 saw food policy tours conducted separately by two federal members of Parliament, Alex Atamanenko (NDP) and Carolyn Bennett (Liberal), both referencing food sovereignty in their literature. In 2008 the NDP also adopted the People's Statement on Food Sovereignty as a general principle. Finally, in 2010 the federal Minister of State Gary Goodyear announced funding for the Manitoba Alternative Food Research Alliance totalling one million dollars. This research program is based at the University of Manitoba and references food sovereignty in its mandate (University of Manitoba 2010). These developments show that the language of food sovereignty is now being adopted by Canada's mainstream political parties, organizations representing some of the largest commodity producers, and by large-scale federally funded research projects. To put it most simply, this has moved from being a discourse of the marginalized to being associated with organizations that are not marginal at all. Along the way, we can see the contours of an emergent debate about what food sovereignty should mean in practice for Canada, and how radical its interventions should be.

The PFPP stepped into the fray in 2007 and began to define a shared food sovereignty platform among multiple actors in the Canadian food system with an emphasis on those marginalized by the neoliberalization, including indigenous people, small farmers, and individuals facing income-related food insecurity. The PFPP's ambit included farm organizations like the NFU and Union paysanne, as well as advocacy groups such as Beyond Factory Farming. Also included were the urban food security NGOs discussed at length above, who formed the bulk of the FSC membership. Finally, NGOs doing international solidarity and development work in the agricultural sector, including USC Canada and InterPares, as well as Aboriginal organizations, were also involved in the process (though we haven't focused on their perspectives in this chapter). Through their work together and the resultant policy positions, this heterogeneous group of individuals and organizations have adopted a discourse of food sovereignty largely consistent with the La Vía Campesina view (and in contradistinction to positions by the CFA and UPA) in reaction to struggles for farmer protection, Aboriginal rights, and the fight against hunger.

The outcomes of the PFPP policy process released in 2011 include concrete policy positions on localizing food systems and making them more ecological, on eliminating poverty, on a national healthy food strategy that includes school meal programs, gardens, and food literacy programs, and on the need to respect indigenous food sovereignty as a starting point (PFPP 2011). What is notable, beyond the content of the *Resetting the Table* policy statement, is *how* these positions were arrived at, which was through a deep and broad process of grassroots consensus-building among participating organizations and individuals, including the creation of an Indigenous Circle. The PFPP process illustrates the idea, as stressed by Menser, Massicotte, Wright, and others in this volume, that the true promise of food sovereignty lies in policymaking structures rooted in the principles of deliberative democracy and inclusion.

Notwithstanding the PFPP's formal policy outcomes, framed as they are through the discourse of food sovereignty, it is important to recognize that the uptake of this language is still tentative among some of the PFPP constituency, especially among "food security" activists. For example, several of the animators interviewed by Martin spoke to the idea that they prefer to work "within food security and not use radical language" (Sarah Martin, interview, 30 October 2009). Levkoe argues that urban food security initiatives can produce a radical subject (2006). Our analysis suggests that this may not be occurring evenly and perhaps not for everyone involved.

Interviews with activists also reveal the complexity of the confluence between the food security and food sovereignty agendas. A community development director, who works in the Maritimes for a national NGO that focuses on "leveraging partnerships," stated, "We have found new possibilities for programs and community development." As she sums up her perspective, "We could not have been behind this project without food security and food sovereignty" (interview by Sarah Martin, 24 January 2010). This statement indicates the growing confidence and active authority over community food distribution that we identified in our discussion of food security work in this country. These NGOs are now active participants in the process (alongside neoliberal state rollbacks) of creating space for new programs and new administrative interventions. Furthermore, this particular NGO representative presents food security and food sovereignty as compatible, while organizations La Vía Campesina are much more cautious on how and when they see these terms fitting together, given the different assumptions that underpin each concept.

Conclusion

It is no surprise that organizations such as the NFU and Union paysanne use food sovereignty to frame their work and political aims because these organizations are aligned with La Vía Campesina and are not necessarily linked to the productivist practices that characterize most of Canadian agriculture. In relation to neoliberalization, then, these farmers increasingly share the experience of peasants in the global South. And it is perhaps no surprise that the emergence and apparent elasticity of the term *food sovereignty* opens up space for co-option by large commodity producers and others. However, the tentative adoption of food sovereignty by urban food activists associated with the PFPP makes sense only when framed in relation to food security and the growing role of urban food security organizations in the actual daily governance of food. Through self-help and community gardens, skills workshops such as canning, Good Food Boxes, and more, a different set of power relations are revealed – one in which a new kind of "sovereignty" has been produced and claimed.

Authority for urban food security NGOs is drawn from sites of gover-nance that have been abandoned by the state. The state is only one of many "partners" from which resources are drawn, therefore sovereign-ty is reconfigured to these new sites of food governance. As a result, we believe that food sovereignty discourse accurately describes and indeed legitimizes these urban food activists and their work in particular ways and illuminates an understanding of authority and power relations. Sovereignty is no longer the exclusive domain of the state for those who employ food sovereignty discourse in both rural and urban contexts.

As a result, the "solution" we see emerging in urban Canada is not just a counter-movement that confronts neoliberalization under the rubric of "agrarian citizenship" (McMichael 2006, 408), but also individual capac-ity-building and community development. This clarifies what Levkoe says about community and collective endeavours: "We are working to help to revive respect for these skills, and to make them available as tools to promote individual and community growth" (FoodShare 2010). This comment illustrates how the site of sovereignty and authority is an indi-vidualized actor whose growth is tied to the community rather than as a citizen tied to a sovereign state. How this view of food sovereignty can ultimately fit together, or not, with that produced by farmer organiza-tions like the NFU in processes like that begun by the PFPP becomes an intriguing question for future research to address. Will these new sites of governance be transformative, or colonized by the relationships they in-tend to change (McMahon, this volume)?

The People's Food Policy Project is working to build bridges among farm organizations, NGOs and indigenous peoples, among others, but different understandings and experiences of what *sovereignty* may actu-ally mean in daily practice with food in Canada suggest that the process will be challenging. One important starting point for the actors now en-gaged in this dialogue, we believe, is for them to think carefully about how their positionality and the history of their movements shapes how they understand a seemingly simple statement such as "food sover-eignty now!" Only then can a truly shared agenda emerge from their discussions, as is the hope for the PFPP leaders and La Vía Campesina too (Patel and Kerr 2011).

It is important to recognize that the new sites of governance described in this chapter have been produced within the complex processes of neo-liberalization. Wayne Roberts, former head of the Toronto Food Policy Council, when commenting on food safety regulations and street food stated, "Neoliberalism is rampant in the food movement, in other words get off our fucking backs!" (Roberts 2010). This statement reaffirms the point made by Guthman (2008), when she argues that food activism in California has a dialectical relationship with neoliberalism, both responding to the negative impacts of neoliberalization, but often also reinforcing neoliberal subjectivities through the politics of consumption, entrepreneurialism, and self-help. We take this analysis one step further, noting that since the problematic of neoliberalism is partially solved by the continued administrative interventions of food security NGOs, neoliberalism has actually helped to create the conditions, in both resistance *and* empowerment, for some of the food sovereignty claims that are now being forwarded in a wealthy Northern country like Canada.

NOTES

1 A notable exception is Wittman, Desmarais, and Wiebe (2011), which also has a Canadian focus.
2 We recognize that many of these organizations also address rural poverty, but the majority focus on urban issues of poverty and food access.
3 This chapter does not describe the PFPP process in detail (for that, see Kneen's contribution in Holt-Giménez et al. [2010], as well as Andrée, Cobb, Moussa, and Norgang [2011]). Nor does it present the results of Martin's interviews in detail. That will be the subject of future publications. Our goal here is to provide a more contextual analysis of the discursive shifts seen in the Canadian food movement.
4 Heifer International is a multi-denominational Christian charity with farm roots based in the United States. While the PFPP has funding from Heifer International, it also has in-kind support from USC Canada and Inter Pares and is partnered with a wide variety of community and farm organizations across Canada.
5 A survey of Google Scholar, targeting *food sovereignty* and limiting searches to social sciences, shows the growth as follows: 2000 – 8 articles; 2001 – 15; 2002 – 20, 2003 – 62; 2004 – 64; 2005 – 86; 2006 –121; 2007 –137; 2008 – 147; 2009 – 205; 2010 – 416; 2011 – 464.
6 La Via Campesina's definition of food sovereignty has evolved in more ways than we can elucidate upon here. See Menser (this volume) as well as various chapters in Wittman, Desmarais, and Wiebe (2011), especially Appendix 1, which presents the seven principles of food sovereignty adopted by *La Via Campensina* in 1996.
7 Both Menser (this volume) and Massicotte (this volume) illustrate how ultimately food sovereignty and the agroecological paradigm promoted by these NGOs are highly commensurable.

8 The first food bank was established in 1981 in Edmonton (Koc, MacRae,
   Desjardins, and Roberts 2008).
9 Fairbairn identifies this same shift in the understandings of food security
   presented at the international level in the early 1980s.

REFERENCES

Agriculture and Agri-Food Canada. 2009. "Overview of the Canadian
    Agriculture and Agri-Food System 2009." http://www4.agr.gc.ca/AAFC-
    AAC/display-afficher.do?id=1261159658146&lang=eng#a2.
Andrée, P. 2007. *Genetically Modified Diplomacy: The Global Politics of
    Agricultural Biotechnology and the Environment*. Vancouver: UBC Press.
Andrée, P., M. Cobb, L. Moussa, and E. Norgang. 2011. "Building Unlikely
    Alliances around Food Sovereignty in Canada." *Studies in Political Economy*
    88:133–62.
Barron, R. 2002. "Foodshare Society to Serve 8,000 Meals to Kids in Summer."
    Nanaimo Daily News, 19 July.
Beingessner, N. 2010. "Getting to Food Sovereignty: Grassroots Perspectives
    from the National Farmers Union. Interview with Terry Boehm and Hilary
    Moore." In *Food Sovereignty: Reconnecting Food, Nature & Community*, edited
    by H. Wittman, A.A. Desmarais, and N. Wiebe, 23–58. Halifax: Fernwood
    Publishing.
Bello, W. 2008. "How to Manufacture a Global Food Crisis." *Development*
    51 (4): 450–5. http://dx.doi.org/10.1057/dev.2008.60.
Bellows, A.C., and M.W. Hamm. 2003. "International Effects on and Inspiration
    for Community Food Security Policies and Practices in the USA." *Critical
    Public Health* 13 (2): 107–23. http://dx.doi.org/10.1080/0958159031000097652.
Blouin, C., J.-F. Lemay, K. Ashraf, J. Imai, and L. Konforti. 2009. *Local Food
    Systems and Public Policy: A Review of the Literature*. Ottawa: Équiterre and
    the Centre for Trade Policy and Law, Carleton University.
Borras, S.M. Jr. 2009. "Agrarian Change and Peasant Studies: Changes,
    Continuities and Challenges – An Introduction." *Journal of Peasant Studies*
    36 (1): 5–31. http://dx.doi.org/10.1080/03066150902820297.
Brown, L.R. 1975. "The World Food Prospect." *Science* 190 (4219): 1053–9.
Buttel, F.H. 2001. "Some Reflections on Late Twentieth Century Agrarian
    Political Economy." *Sociologia Ruralis* 41 (2): 165–81. http://dx.doi.org/
    10.1111/1467-9523.00176.
Cavell, N. 1952. "Canada and the Colombo Plan." Speech to the Empire Club
    (Toronto), Empire Club of Canada, 4 December.

CP Newswire. 2005. "Quebec Farmers Want Canada to Promote 'Food Sovereignty' at WTO Meeting." *Canadian Press NewsWire*, 29 November.

Davis, B., and V. Tarasuk. 1994. "Hunger in Canada." *Agriculture and Human Values* 11 (4): 50–7. http://dx.doi.org/10.1007/BF01530416.

Desmarais, A.-A. 2002. "Peasants Speak – The Via Campesina: Consolidating an International Peasant and Farm Movement." *Journal of Peasant Studies* 29 (2): 91–124. http://dx.doi.org/10.1080/714003943.

– 2003. "The Via Campesina: Peasant Women on the Frontiers of Food Sovereignty." *Canadian Women's Studies* 23:140–5.

– 2007. *La Via Campesina: Globalization and the Power of Peasants*. Halifax: Fernwood Publications.

Fairbairn, M. 2010. "Framing Resistance: International Food Regimes and the Roots of Food Sovereignty." In *Food Sovereignty: Reconnecting Food, Nature & Community*, edited by H. Wittman, A.A. Desmarais, and N. Wiebe, 15–31. Halifax: Fernwood Publishing.

Faulder, L. 1991. "Finding Ways to Put Food on the Table." *Edmonton Journal*, 21 January.

Food Secure Canada (FSC). 2012. "About Us." http://foodsecurecanada.org/about-us.

FoodShare. 2010. "Homepage." http://www.foodshare.net/.

Foucault, M. 2007. *Security, Territory, Population: Lectures at the Collège de France, 1977–1978*. Houndmills, Basingstoke, Hampshire: Palgrave Macmillan. http://dx.doi.org/10.1057/9780230245075.

Friedmann, H. 1992. "Distance and Durability: Shaky Foundations of the World Food Economy." *Third World Quarterly* 13 (2): 371–83. http://dx.doi.org/10.1080/01436599208420282.

Friedmann, H., and P. McMichael. 1989. "Agriculture and the State System: The Rise and Decline of National Agricultures, 1870 to the Present." *Sociologia Ruralis* 29 (2): 93–117. http://dx.doi.org/10.1111/j.1467-9523.1989.tb00360.x.

Goodman, D. 1981. *From Peasant to Proletarian: Capitalist Developments and Agrarian Transitions*. Oxford: B. Blackwell.

Guthman, J. 2007. "The Polanyian Way? Voluntary Food Labels as Neoliberal Governance." *Antipode* 39 (3): 456–78. http://dx.doi.org/10.1111/j.1467-8330.2007.00535.x.

– 2008. "Neoliberalism and the Making of Food Politics in California." *Geoforum* 39 (3): 1171–83.

"High Cost of Eating." 2004. *Kamloops This Week*, Kamloops, BC, 19 October.

Holt-Giménez, E., Roland Bunch, Jorge Irán Vasquez, John Wilson, Michel P. Pimbert, Bary Boukary, and Cathleen Kneen. 2010. "Linking Farmers'

Movements for Advocacy and Practice." *Journal of Peasant Studies* 37 (1): 203–36. http://dx.doi.org/10.1080/03066150903499943.

Holt-Giménez, E., and A. Shattuck. 2011. "Food Crises, Food Regimes and Food Movements: Rumblings of Reform or Tides of Transformation?" *Journal of Peasant Studies* 38 (1): 109–44. http://dx.doi.org/10.1080/03066150 .2010.538578.

Infantry, A. 1997. "Poor Families Often Hungry, Survey Shows Coalition Wants Food Insecurity Addressed by All Governments." *Toronto Star*, 29 May.

Jarosz, L. 2011. "Defining World Hunger: Scale and Neoliberal Ideology in International Food Security Policy Discourse." *Food, Culture and Society* 14 (1): 117–39. http://dx.doi.org/10.2752/175174411X12810842291308.

Johnston, J., and L. Baker. 2005. "Eating outside the Box: FoodShare's Good Food Box and the Challenge of Scale." *Agriculture and Human Values* 22 (3): 313–25. http://dx.doi.org/10.1007/s10460-005-6048-y.

Josey, S. 1992. "Health Study Paints Stark Portrait of Hunger Food Bank Clientele Rising, 20 per cent of Users Hold Jobs." *Toronto Star*, 5 March.

Kane, M. 1993. "Groups Try New Ways to Share the Fare." *Toronto Star*, 7 July.

Kneen, C. 2011. "Food Secure Canada: Where Agriculture, Environment, Health, Food, and Justice Intersect." In Wittman, Desmarais, and Wiebe 2011.

Koc, M., R. MacRae, E. Desjardins, and W. Roberts. 2008. "Getting Civil about Food: The Interactions between Civil Society and the State to Advance Sustainable Food Systems in Canada." *Journal of Hunger & Environmental Nutrition* 3 (2): 122–44. http://dx.doi.org/10.1080/19320240802243175.

Levkoe, C.Z. 2006. "Learning Democracy through Food Justice Movements." *Agriculture and Human Values* 23 (1): 89–98. http://dx.doi.org/10.1007/ s10460-005-5871-5.

Macrae, R.J., J. Henning, and S.B. Hill. 1993. "Strategies to Overcome Barriers to the Development of Sustainable Agriculture in Canada: The Role of Agribusiness." *Journal of Agricultural & Environmental Ethics* 6 (1): 21–51. http://dx.doi.org/10.1007/BF01965613.

Martin, S.J. 2010. "Farming the Margins of Neoliberalism: Food Sovereignty in Canada." MA thesis, Carleton University.

Massicotte, M.-J. 2010. "La Via Campesina, Brazilian Peasants, and the Agribusiness Model of Agriculture: Towards an Alternative Model of Agrarian Democratic Governance." *Studies in Political Economy* 85:69–98.

McMichael, P. 2004. "Global Development and the Corporate Food Regime." Presented at the XI World Congress of Rural Sociology, Trondheim.

– 2006. "Peasant Prospects in the Neoliberal Age." *New Political Economy* 11 (3): 407–18. http://dx.doi.org/10.1080/13563460600841041.

– 2008. "Peasants Make Their Own History, But Not Just as They Please."
Journal of Agrarian Change 8 (2–3): 205–28. http://dx.doi.org/10.1111/j.1471-0366.2008.00168.x.

Moffett, D., and M.L. Morgan. 1999. "Women as Organizers: Building
Confidence and Community through Food." In *Women Working the NAFTA
Food Chain: Women, Food and Globalization*, edited by D. Barndt, 222–36.
Toronto: Second Story.

National Farmers Union (NFU). 1999. "NFU Submission to the Standing
Committee on Foreign Affairs and International Trade on the Effects of
Export-Oriented Agriculture on Canadian Families, Canadian Consumers
and Farmers around the World." Winnipeg, Manitoba.

– 2010. "Bill C-474 Ag: Hearings Cancelled, Farmers-Markets at Risk!"
Press release, 28 October. http://www.nfu.ca/story/archived-press-releases.

Nicholson, P., and I. Delforge. 2008. "Via Campesina: Responding to Global
Systemic Crisis." *Development* 51 (4): 456–9. http://dx.doi.org/10.1057/
dev.2008.51.

Patel, R. 2009. "Food Sovereignty." *Journal of Peasant Studies* 36 (3): 663–706.
http://dx.doi.org/10.1080/03066150903143079.

Patel, R., and R.B. Kerr. 2011. "The New Harvest: Agricultural Innovation in
Africa." *Journal of Peasant Studies* 38 (3): 657–60. http://dx.doi.org/10.1080/
03066150.2011.583813.

Patel, R., and P. McMichael. 2004. "Third Worldism and the Lineages of Global
Fascism: The Regrouping of the Global South in the Neoliberal Era." *Third
World Quarterly* 25 (1): 231–54. http://dx.doi.org/10.1080/014365904200018
5426.

Peck, J., and A. Tickell. 2002. "Neoliberalizing Space." *Antipode* 34 (3): 380–404.
http://dx.doi.org/10.1111/1467-8330.00247.

People's Food Policy Project (PFPP). 2010. "History of the PFPP." http://
peoplesfoodpolicy.ca/history.

– 2011. "Resetting the Table: A People's Food Policy for Canada." http://
peoplesfoodpolicy.ca/policy/resetting-table-peoples-food-policy-canada.

Riches, G. 2002. "Food Banks and Food Security: Welfare Reform, Human
Rights and Social Policy; Lessons from Canada?" *Social Policy and
Administration* 36 (6): 648–63. http://dx.doi.org/10.1111/1467-9515.00309.

Riches, G., and CCSD. 1986. *Food Banks and the Welfare Crisis*. Toronto: James
Lorimer.

Roberts, W. 2010. "Food Policy and Sustainability." Presented at the
Environmental Studies Association of Canada, Montreal, 31 May.

Rosset, P. 2009. "Agrofuels, Food Sovereignty, and the Contemporary Food
Crisis." *Bulletin of Science* 29 (3): 189–93.

Shiva, V. 2003. "The Future of Food: Countering Globalisation and Recolonisation of Indian Agriculture." *Futures* 36 (6–7): 715–32.

Teubal, M. 2009. "Agrarian Reform and Social Movements in the Age of Globalization: Latin America at the Dawn of the Twenty-First Century." *Latin American Perspectives* 36 (4): 9–20. http://dx.doi.org/10.1177/0094582X09338607.

Toronto Food Policy Council. 1998. "Toronto's Food Charter." http://www.toronto.ca/food_hunger/pdf/food_charter.pdf.

Union paysanne. 2010. "Déclaration de principe de l'Union Paysanne." http://www.unionpaysanne.com/index.php?option=com_content&view=article&id=12&Itemid=256.

L'Union des producteurs agricoles (UPA). 2010. "Food Sovereignty." http://www.upa.qc.ca/en/Agriculture_and_society/Food_sovereignty.html.

University of Manitoba. 2010. "Alternative Food Research Receives $1 Million Boost." 4 February. http://myuminfo.umanitoba.ca/index.asp?sec=2&too=100&dat=2/4/2010&sta=2&wee=1&eve=8&npa=21635.

Van Rooy, A. 1997. "The Frontiers of Influence: NGO Lobbying at the 1974 World Food Conference, the 1992 Earth Summit and Beyond." *World Development* 25 (1): 93–114. http://dx.doi.org/10.1016/S0305-750X(96)00092-7.

Walters, W., and J.H. Haahr. 2005. "Governmentality and Political Studies." *European Political Science* 4 (3): 288–300. http://dx.doi.org/10.1057/palgrave.eps.2210038.

Wittman, H. 2009. "Reworking the Metabolic Rift: La Vía Campesina, Agrarian Citizenship, and Food Sovereignty." *Journal of Peasant Studies* 36 (4): 805–26. http://dx.doi.org/10.1080/03066150903353991.

Wittman, H., A.A. Desmarais, and N. Wiebe, eds. 2010. *Food Sovereignty: Reconnecting Food, Nature & Community*. Halifax: Fernwood Publishing.

– 2011. *Food Sovereignty in Canada: Creating Just and Sustainable Food Systems*. Halifax: Fernwood Publishing.

7 Food Sovereignty in Practice: A Study of Farmer-Led Sustainable Agriculture in the Philippines

SARAH WRIGHT

Introduction

Farmers' movements in Asia have long been saving, exchanging and improving seeds and animal breeds, doing farmer-led research, continuously struggling for genuine agrarian reform, aspiring towards food sovereignty and autonomy of communities – and are intensifying these efforts and strengthening their movements. These are farmers' rights in practice, upheld by rural communities in situ.

> Concept paper of the conference Farmers Rights and Food Sovereignty,
> Bandung, Indonesia, 2006

The myth that there is no alternative to the current system of industrial export agriculture is a powerful one. Much discussion of food and food production, whether within academia, in mainstream media discourse, or in critical accounts, for example, focuses on the overwhelmingly negative impacts of an encroaching and all-consuming capitalist system. Certainly, as the introduction to this volume elaborates, the pressures associated with a neoliberal approach to agriculture are profound and the need for alternatives is pressing. While these analyses are important, even vital, what they *can* do, however, is contribute to a debilitating and disempowering construction of a world within which alternatives are marginalized and scripted as close to impossible (Community Economies Collective 2001; Gibson-Graham 2006).

Yet attention to the activities of social movements such as those associated with food sovereignty reveals a different story. Rather than a story of lack and hopelessness, this is a story of abundance and possibility

(Gibson-Graham 2006; Wright 2008b). It is important to recognize that alternatives can and do exist, and that the tyrannies and exclusions of the capitalist system represent but part of the picture. So while it is crucial to continue building critiques that focus on the imbalances, exclusions, and oppressive effects of a globalized neoliberal system of food, it is also important to recognize the important work that *is* being done, to pay attention to the ways that farmers, social movements, indeed all kinds of people in all kinds of ways, create and defend alternatives. This means acknowledging the important knowledges that come from the margins and taking a social movement approach that foregrounds the voices of peasants and social movements often marginalized in debates over food (Andrée et al., this volume).

In this chapter, I look to food sovereignty as a framework that works explicitly against the debilitating mantra that "there is no alternative" (TINA). Food sovereignty highlights both that there are already a large number of so-called alternatives, and that they represent the realities of life for billions. In particular, I focus on the work of one social movement from the Philippines called Magsasaka at Siyentipiko para sa Pag-unlad ng Agrikultura (Farmer-Scientist Partnership for Agricultural Development), or MASIPAG. MASIPAG is a word that means "industrious" in Tagalog, the national language of the Philippines. The group is a Filipino network of small farmers with a membership of over 35,000 farming families that emerged in 1985–6. The network builds upon the concepts of food sovereignty and farmers' rights to improve the quality of life of resource-poor farmers through a farmer-led sustainable agriculture approach. The members of MASIPAG are committed to organic production and are either in conversion or fully organic. While organic production is an important part of the MASIPAG approach, however, farmer-led sustainable agriculture goes beyond organic to encompass a bottom-up approach to development within which actions are imagined, initiated, and led by small-scale farmers. For MASIPAG, the environmental, economic, and social aspects of a farmer-led approach are fundamentally intertwined.

In looking to the work of MASIPAG, I aim to contribute to literature on diverse economies and on food sovereignty in two major ways. First, I will build on work in the social sciences that stresses the importance of recognizing alternatives beyond and beneath the capitalist system (Cameron and Gibson 2005; Gibson-Graham 2006, 2008; Lawson 2005). Such work insists that the economy is not a monolith that encompasses and enfolds everything, but is characterized by diversity and multiplicity (Community Economies Collective 2001; Gibson-Graham 1996, 2006; Lee 2000, 2006; Leyshon, Lee, and Williams 2003). It is underpinned by economic relationships and values very different from the dictates of formal capitalism (Leyshon and Lee 2003). My discussion of MASIPAG will help build a picture of the diverse economy, drawing particularly on the work of social movements in the global South. While exciting work has helped reveal vibrant worlds outside and beyond formal capitalist economies, little has drawn on the experiences of those living and working in the majority world (Carmody 2005; Hughes 2005; see also Pollard and Samers 2007). Here my intent is first to help build a picture of the role of social movements in creating and living alternatives, and to understand the ways that different kinds of knowledges can and should be empowered to bring about different kinds of futures.

My second contribution is to build on literature on food sovereignty by expanding understandings of just what food sovereignty means in practice. Here too I am adding to a detailed analysis of social movements and the ways that they actually *do* food sovereignty. While food sovereignty has provided an important conceptual and organizing tool, much remains to be done in building a rich understanding of social movements' approaches, visions, and practices as they go about the very real work of constructing alternatives (but see Desmarais 2007; McMichael 2008; Massicotte, this volume). Here knowledges from the margins are not dismissed as somehow inadequate or trivial but are valued for their transformative potential (Wright 2005). Similarly, while there is much information extolling the benefits of food sovereignty (see, for example, Desmarais 2007; Godrej 2007; Mousseau and Mittal 2006), there has been a lack of specific studies that actually measure the impacts on small farmers. Put simply, my aim is to contribute some evidence that can cut through much of the rhetoric surrounding food and agriculture.

To accomplish this, I will present the results of a study conducted in 2007–9 that investigated the impacts of farmer-led sustainable agriculture in the Philippines as practised by the MASIPAG network (Bachmann, Cruzada, and Wright 2009). The study, which incorporated 840 small-scale rice farmers, is one of the largest undertaken on sustainable agriculture and the largest ever focused primarily on organic production in rice-based small-scale farming systems.

The study had very positive outcomes. Both the full and in-conversion MASIPAG farmers eat a more diverse, nutritious, and secure diet than their counterparts practising conventional agriculture, they have considerably higher on-farm diversity, better soil fertility, and better farm management skills. The group also tended to experience increasing incomes in contrast to stagnant or declining incomes for the reference group. It is clear that the small-scale farmers and farmers' organizations in the network continue to build vibrant and viable agro-economic systems with positive environmental, economic, and social outcomes. The activities of the network, and their emphasis on successfully defending and creating spaces outside the mainstream economy, help build a picture of an economy that is both diverse and full of alternatives.

The group's focus on food sovereignty and farmers' rights rather than simply organic agriculture or alternate economies is telling. Although the approach taken by the network is both organic and alternative, the idea of sovereignty, of farmers in control of their own destinies, underpins its work. This emphasis distinguishes it from the work of many other social movements and mainstream development agencies. For MASIPAG, agriculture must be farmer-led and be both designed and implemented by the small-scale farmers in the network. Rather than producing first for the market, production is diversified with an emphasis on food provision for the family and the community. Eliminating the need to purchase chemical inputs, the farmers are tied neither to the dictates of agrochemical companies nor to moneylenders. Through their work in farmers' organizations they can practise *bayanihan* (communal labour), teach other farmers, support each other through difficult times, and approach the market at least partially on their own terms. The organization facilitates empowerment among the farmers who are more involved in their communities and who are more positive about and in greater control of their lives. This approach not only makes knowledges marginalized by mainstream approaches to agriculture visible, but centres these knowledges as valid, important, and cutting edge. Here is a way to generate a sense of control and autonomy in a world increasingly dominated by a neoliberal approach to agriculture.

What emerges is a picture of an economy thoroughly place-based and social, embedded both in its local community and the very soil of the farms. It is an economy underpinned by norms very different from those promulgated by conventional industrial agriculture. These are norms of reciprocity and communality, of health for families and the land, of self-sufficiency and autonomy. Food-sovereignty, as practised by the MASIPAG network, links people with each other and with place in ways that change the geographies of food production and consumption and the very meaning of economic practice.

On the Question of Alternatives

The importance of displacing capitalo-centric accounts of the economy, and of food and agricultural systems more specifically, is increasingly recognized within the social sciences (see, for example, Community Economies Collective 2001; Gibson-Graham 1996, 2006; Leyshon, Lee, and Williams 2003). In economic geography, for example, the work of J.K. Gibson-Graham (1996, 2005, 2006, 2008) and others (Hughes 2005; Lee 2006; Leyshon, Lee, and Williams 2003) points out that far from being homogeneous and all-encompassing, the economy is in fact a diverse space. This is a space full of alternatives and of people and organizations that have carved out spaces of non-capitalism, underpinned by different kinds of values and supported by different forms of exchange.

Common constructions of the economy as a singular and homogeneous entity are called into question. Rather than working with "The Economy," work on diverse or alternate economies looks to delink our understanding of economic practice from formal capitalism. Instead, attention is brought to the diverse, unstable, and complex economic practices, both formal and informal, paid and unpaid, that make up our economic lives. Lee (2006, 414), for example, maintains that the economy is "an integral part of everyday life, full of the contradictions, ethical dilemmas and multiple values that inform the quotidian business of making a living. In short, it is ordinary."

The economy, then, is not inherently capitalistic while capitalism is not the hegemonic, all-encompassing system often portrayed (Gibson-Graham 2006, 198). Rather, capitalism is understood in its most minimalist sense as a set of specific practices that occur in specific places. Economies are characterized by proliferation (Leyshon and Lee 2003) and diversity (Community Economies Collective 2001). Any discourse to the contrary disempowers the alternatives and the myriad practices of economic life. We become blind to the presences and complicit in reinforcing a discourse of capitalism-as-hegemony. Such presences include labour arrangements (paid, alternative paid, and unpaid labour), diverse forms of enterprises (capitalist, alternative capitalist, and non-capitalist), and diverse markets (capitalist markets, alternative markets, and non-market systems) all underpinned by different ways of generating and distributing surplus and different ways of understanding value (Community Economies Collective 2001; Gibson-Graham 2006).

Supporting work on diverse economies is a commitment to working from an "ontology of proliferation." This means that in place of lack, absence, and deficit, the world is viewed as a place of bounty, presence, and surplus. The economy, indeed the world, is understood as a site of limitless potential. Such an ontological shift encourages different readings and calls for the acknowledgment of different ways of being, acting, and valuing the world. Indeed, J.K. Gibson-Graham calls for social scientists to both recognize and enact alternatives to capitalism. As McCarthy (2006b, 804) states, "The recognition of and search for alterity is a vital political act."

Work on diverse economies has thus focused its attention on tangible examples of alternate economic practice. Researchers have looked to the use of credit unions (Fuller and Jonas 2003), local exchange trading systems (LETS) (see, for example, Amin, Cameron, and Hudson 2003; Lee et al. 2004; Seyfang 2001a, 2001b; Williams, Aldridge, and Tooke 2003), fair trade commodities (Mutersbaugh et al., 2005), second-hand retailers (Crewe, Gregson, and Brooks 2003), and cooperatives (Gibson-Graham, 2006).

Food and agriculture have also constituted a significant focus with work in rural studies and on agro-food networks increasingly recognizing the importance of documenting and animating alternatives. This is a search for what Krueger and Agyeman call "actually existing sustainabilities" (2005). Work in forestry, for example, has focused on the use of subsistence activities in forests in the United States, documenting the ways that forest use does not adhere to assumptions of resource use in advanced capitalist countries (Emery and Pierce 2005). Others have looked to community forestry (Kitchen, Marsden, and Milbourne 2006; Wilson and Memon 2005), certified timber (Klooster 2005; Taylor 2005), short food supply chains (Renting, Marsden, and Banks 2003), non-capitalist norms in the fishing industry (St Martin 2007), and fair trade (Sage 2003; Seyfang 2006; Zerbe, this volume).

There are common concerns, however, about the transformative potential of an alternative economic focus. Some authors, for example, are uneasy about the viability of these systems, and their ability to meet social justice concerns (e.g., if organic or "quality" produce is available only to middle- and upper-class consumers) (see, for example, Andrée et al., this volume, for an elaboration of tensions between the concepts of food democracy and food sovereignty; Aguilar 2005; Hughes 2005; Smith and Stenning 2006, for a discussion of power imbalances in alternative systems in general, or Bryant and Goodman 2004, for a discussion of limits of "alternatives" in agriculture in particular). Work on fair trade as well as on community forestry and certification of timber products is concerned that agendas associated with the description and policing of "fairness" are very much driven by Northern consumers (Bryant and Goodman 2004; Freidberg 2003b; Gonzalez and Nigh 2005; Hughes 2005; Klooster 2005; Lyons and Burch 2007; McCarthy 2006a; Mutersbaugh et al. 2005; Renard 2005). Guthman (2004) is worried that the issue of rents on premium and marked "alternative" goods will drive down prices, eventually excluding smaller operators. These dynamics mean that organic agriculture along with other "alternative" economic practices exhibit many of the features of mainstream processes, making it difficult, or impossible, for it to maintain its "alternativeness" (see also Bryant and Goodman 2004; Raynolds 2004; Zerbe, this volume).

While these are important concerns, they do tend to reflect the orientation of much of the research towards case studies from the global North (Carmody 2005; Hughes 2005; Wright 2010). Indeed, Lockie and Halpin (2005) criticize the focus of the discussion on organic agriculture as particularly Californian and call for a more aggregated approach attentive to place-based specificities. Where studies, such as those associated with fair trade, do explicitly take a perspective from the global South, they tend to be focused on the question of trade. These are farmers and fisherfolk attempting to engage with the global agro-food system on slightly different terms (Lyons and Burch 2007). There are, unsurprisingly, limits on the extent to which they achieve this. Yet food sovereignty comes from a very different perspective and, as such, provides an important counter-perspective. Concerns of "conventionalization," mainstreaming, and commodity fetishism, for example, do not resonate when looking to the experiences of farmers practising farmer-led sustainable agriculture oriented towards their own consumption, the needs of the village, and only then for the (local) market. Indeed, food sovereignty itself has emerged in part from the limitations of attempting to engage with the global market on its own terms.

Food Sovereignty

It is within this context that I turn to the question of food sovereignty and to MASIPAG. Certainly as a movement, a framework for understanding sustainable agricultural systems, and as a platform for action, food sovereignty has much to offer. Food sovereignty calls for new geographies of food production and consumption that are centred on small-scale, locally based food networks underpinned by principles of autonomy and farmers' rights (Desmarais 2007; McMichael 2008). In calling for food sovereignty, social movements are calling for a re-spatialization of food systems and a reconfiguring of power relations associated with the production, consumption, and distribution of food (McMichael 2006).

While approaches to food sovereignty are varied (for a thorough discussion, see Menser, this volume), MASIPAG's approach to food sovereignty is based both on the notion of farmers' rights and beyond-capitalist production (Wright 2008a). For MASIPAG, a food sovereignty approach means producing food primarily for personal consumption and for local networks. Although it is not anti-trade, it is against the idea of global trade as the prime motivation for production. Trade, where it occurs, should happen on terms set by farmers and communities. Rather than market-oriented production decisions, made far from farmers' fields, that promote export and international trade at any cost, MASIPAG's approach to food sovereignty supports the knowledges of farmers themselves.

Unlike many platforms associated with alternative agricultural networks, food sovereignty as advocated by MASIPAG is premised on neither a defensive localism nor a middle-class concern for "quality" produce. These are small-scale, often subsistence farmers who, while they do prioritize place-based agricultural systems, are also highly concerned with networks and exchange. The building of international networks through international conferences and forums centred on food sovereignty such as the one in Selingue, Mali, in 2007, and on Farmers' Rights and Food Sovereignty in Bandung, Indonesia, in 2006, show that food sovereignty is foremost about reimagining networks and about creating a different kind of networked space at once grounded in the most place based soils of any farm, and at the same time differently global.

At its core, food sovereignty, both for MASIPAG and for its other practitioners and advocates, is rooted in practice. A detailed understanding of the practices associated with food sovereignty, however, is an area that is relatively thin in terms of the current work (for exceptions see Altieri 2009; McMahon, Andrée, Massicotte, all this volume). While the concept has been driven by farmers' organizations with a vast and diverse array of experiences and practices, the literature has yet to detail these practices and experiences in depth. This means there is a need to elaborate further on how social movements actually do food sovereignty. It also reveals a need for greater documentation of the actual impacts of a food sovereignty approach on small farmers. In line with this focus, I turn now to MASIPAG and the Philippines.

Food Sovereignty in Practice

In this section, I will focus on the work of the MASIPAG network and the results of a 2007–9 study that detailed the impacts of the organization's farmer-led sustainable agriculture approach (Bachmann, Cruzada and Wright 2009). MASIPAG emerged following a 1985 conference focused on the problems associated with the so-called Green Revolution in agriculture. The conference brought together farmers with NGOs, peoples' organizations, and scientists who concluded that farmers were becoming increasingly indebted, their farms polluted, and agro-diversity dangerously eroded as a result of high-input, capitalist agriculture. Furthermore, the conference concluded, the knowledges and skill of Filipino farmers were in danger of being lost.

Farmer representatives at the conference donated forty-seven rice varieties that became the basis of the MASIPAG seed collection. MASIPAG formally started the following year with a farm dedicated to the conservation and improvement of rice varieties. Farmers and scientists worked together to develop a rice-breeding program and to support sustainable and culturally appropriate agricultural techniques. Essential to the vision of the group was the need to address environmental, social, and economic issues simultaneously in a way that recognized them as inherently interwoven. From the onset, the group adopted organic approaches, placing a commitment to chemical-free, sustainable agriculture within a broader framework of farmer empowerment and economic independence. Today, MASIPAG is a nationwide organization with offices in the three main regions of the Philippines: Luzon, the Visayas, and Mindanao. MASIPAG works in forty-five of the seventy-nine provinces, with twenty provincial coordinating bodies and a total of 672 people's organizations (POs) that reach approximately 35,000 farming families. MASIPAG cooperates with sixty NGOs and fifteen scientists from various universities in the country and has forty regular staff. The network has three national backup farms that act as in situ agricultural seed banks, ten regional community seed banks, and 272 trial farms in forty provinces that hold more than two thousand local varieties and farmer-bred lines (Bachmann, Cruzada and Wright 2009).

Central to the organization's original critique of the Green Revolution and industrial agriculture was the idea that these forms of agriculture constituted a "colonization of the mind" where solutions were seen as coming from external "experts." The farmers themselves were designated a passive role of consumers of technologies. As a result, MASIPAG has a focus on farmer-led agriculture, which means farmers themselves lead the network, train other farmers and develop new rice strains (and to a limited extent varieties of corn, vegetables and poultry). The network insists the work and knowledges of farmers be recognized, and that their efforts in breeding seeds, developing appropriate, ecologically friendly agricultural systems, creating and sustaining communities, and in providing healthy, organic food be acknowledged and supported. Farming families are encouraged to learn and work together in groups. These groups, or people's organizations, form the basis of the MASIPAG structure and are the level through which most work gets done, training is conducted, and decisions are made. Technological change, environmental protection, and social change are all prioritized. Combined, the three aspects lead to tangible benefits, ownership and control of resources, a more ecologically sound approach to agriculture, and social empowerment. As one MASIPAG farmer (personal interview, 23 October 2008) explained, "Even if one is practising a full organic system with MASIPAG seeds, if he has no concern for other farmers and society, then he cannot be considered a true MASIPAG farmer."

A commitment to self-sufficiency on a local level underpins the network's approach to development. MASIPAG prioritizes people's food needs over issues of income or profit. In an increasingly globalized world with volatile food and input prices, this emphasis provides better food and livelihood security than strategies focused purely on increased incomes. The food security implications of a farmer-led sustainable agriculture approach are thus profound. As one MASIPAG farmer, Eddie Panes (personal interview, 24 October 2008), explains, "Now we ensure food security of the household. Food first, before selling in the market. The family first, before money. We prioritize diversity, because that is our source of food for every day, instead of planting the whole farm to a single cash crop such as rice. Before MASIPAG, we used to prioritize cash, for paying debts. Now we prioritize food."

Methodology of the Study

The study surveyed 840 small farmer households in the Philippines. Of the 840 farmers, 280 were full MASIPAG farmers using farmer-led, sustainable agriculture, 280 were new MASIPAG members in the process of converting to a sustainable approach (referred to as "in conversion"), and 280 used conventional, chemical agriculture of predominantly small-scale, mono-cropped rice. Computerized pure random sampling was used for the full and in-conversion MASIPAG farmers. Simplified random sampling was used to select participants for the reference group. The average household of those who engaged in the survey was 5.2 people with an average farm size of 1.5 hectares. The average age of interviewees was forty-nine years with ages ranging from twenty-one to eighty-one. Rice was the primary crop on all farms, with 70–96 per cent of the major plots dedicated to rice production.

The work was conducted using three separate surveys. The concept was designed and tested in a first survey in the Visayas region in 2007 and then replicated with minor adjustments in Luzon and Mindanao in 2008. In total, the three studies, covering the three areas of the Philippines, give a national result. Surveys focused on questions of food security and food sovereignty, income, yield, environmental outcomes, and farmer knowledge and empowerment. Interviews with farming households lasted from 2.5 to 3.5 hours. The results of each regional study were then presented to farmer groups of the region for two-day validation workshops. The national data compilation was discussed and validated on a final three-day workshop with MASIPAG farmer leaders, MASIPAG staff, NGO representatives, and collaborating scientists in 2008. To complement the huge volume of quantitative data, eighteen qualitative farmer interviews were conducted during the final national workshop.[1]

Food Security and Food Sovereignty

In this section, I will discuss the results of the study with particular attention to food sovereignty. The results focus on a variety of measurements that encapsulate the different aspects of food security and food sovereignty: accessibility of food, quality of food (nutrition, diversity, and safety); freedom from vulnerability (reliability of food sources, minimized risk), and control over production (autonomy and self-reliance). The aim here is to give a richer understanding both of how the network practises food sovereignty and of the impacts of a food sovereignty, or farmer-led sustainable agriculture, approach on small farming households.

First, and perhaps most importantly, those farmers using sustainable agriculture were found to be much more food secure than those using conventional farming techniques. This reveals both the strengths of a food sovereignty approach and the weaknesses of conventional agriculture. Indeed, the food security of MASIPAG farmers has dramatically improved over the last seven years, showing the positive impact of sustainable agriculture on food security. A full 88 per cent of those farmers practising farmer-led sustainable agriculture found their food security better or much better than in 2000. On the other hand, many conventional farmers, 18 per cent, found themselves increasingly food insecure. This contrasts with the MASIPAG farmers, only 2 per cent of whom found themselves in this situation (see table 7.1).

Conventional farming has clearly failed most farming communities. The results show that, far from helping farmers generate income and end hunger, a focus on high-input monoculture farming leads to decreasing food security for many farmers. Producing primarily or, in the case of many farmers, solely for the market means that families are reliant on income to buy food. If debts are high, yields are unexpectedly low, prices are low, or simply the benefits do not sufficiently outweigh costs, farming families must cut corners on food or go without. For MASIPAG farmers, on the other hand, the majority of the food comes from the farm. A food sovereignty approach means greater autonomy and security in farm production leading to multiple benefits. As Gabriel Diaz, a farmer and trainer from Mindanao, explains, "There is a big difference between the MASIPAG and non-MASIPAG farmers. In MASIPAG, the farmer holds the decisions. For farmer-led agriculture, the farmer is not dependent on the inputs or seeds from other people. He has control over the inputs and can reduce them. The inputs we use come from the farm. The focus is the security of the family. We don't get hungry. The first thing we think of in our farm is our family having enough to eat. This is before going to market" (personal interview, 23 October 2008).

Importantly, the results were positive both for the quantity and quality of food intake. The results show that MASIPAG farmers eat a more balanced diet than the conventional farmers. This is a reflection of the diversity of the produce grown on the farm, a more stable net income, an orientation towards food grown for personal consumption rather than for the market, and changing food preferences and knowledge about nutrition. As one farmer (personal interview, 25 October 2008) stated, "Compared to 2000, we can see that the full organic are eating a more balanced diet because of their understanding and awareness through the MASIPAG programs and their practice in their lives." An emphasis on increased crop diversity is a strength of a food sovereignty approach and one that has important ramifications for farming

Table 7.1. Perceived Changes in Food Security

Food security is:	MASIPAG (%)	Conversion farmers (%)	Conventional farmers (%)
Much better	43	20	3
Better	45	51	36
Same	11	22	43
Worse	2	7	18

families. A diversified farm means that the risk of crop loss due to pests, diseases, and calamity is minimized. Different crops have different levels of resilience to pest and disease outbreaks and to extreme climatic events. They also are harvestable throughout the year, spreading income and food sources through different seasons. In addition, with more food grown on the farm, farming families are more self-reliant.

Total productivity of the farms was significantly higher for those working within a food sovereignty framework. The research focused on 107 crops and tree species in six categories: food crops, cash crops, vegetables, fruits, agroforestry, and herbal plants (see table 7.2). The findings show a very sharp divergence between farmers using conventional agriculture and those participating in the farmer-led sustainable agriculture program. Depending on the region, the MASIPAG group cultivated fourteen to sixteen (which is 50 per cent on average) more crops than the conventional farmers. These differences are highly statistically significant. The MASIPAG program has thus achieved an outstanding result in increasing biodiversity on farms. In times of rapid global decline of biodiversity, this impact needs to be valued even higher.

The trend associated with diet is also positive. From 2000, the MASIPAG farmers have had an increasingly diverse diet (see table 7.3). The farmers practising farmer-led sustainable agriculture eat 68 per cent more vegetables, 56 per cent more fruit, 55 per cent more protein-rich staples, and 40 per cent more meat than in 2000. While there are some increases for conventional farmers, increases are much smaller than for the MASIPAG farmers. The rates of increase for MASIPAG farmers are double those for conventional farmers for vegetables, 3.7 times higher for protein-rich staples and 2.5 times higher for meat. This suggests that farmer-led sustainable agriculture is able to work against the broader trend of increasing malnutrition to supply an increasingly diverse and healthy diet to farming families.

Table 7.2. Top Five Most Common Crops Grown in Each Category

Staples and cash crops	Fruit	Vegetables	Agroforestry	Herbal plants
Banana	Jackfruit	Malunggay (moringa)	Kakawati	Lemongrass
Rice	Guava	Eggplant	Leucaena	Kalawag
Coconut	Mango	String beans	Bamboo	Sambong
Taro	Papaya	Okra ·	Mahogany	Oregano
Cassava	Avocado	Kang kong (water spinach)	Labnog	Lagundi

Table 7.3. Families Reporting Increased Consumption of Diverse Food Products

Households report an increase in the consumption of:	MASIPAG farmers (%)	Conversion farmers (%)	Conventional farmers (%)
Vegetables	68	60	34
Herbal medicines	60	44	22
Fruits	55	46	40
Protein-rich staples	55	40	15
Fish	45	39	26
Eggs	42	34	17
Meat	40	30	16

Elpidio Paglumotan, or Jojo, told of his experience moving away from a situation of chronic food insecurity as a farm worker, to one of being able to meet his family's food needs and generating a surplus to sell. His story tells both of the importance of land redistribution and of the success of a farmer-led sustainable agriculture approach:

Originally, we were labourers in the hacienda. We went through the process of getting a small portion of land. We established our organization, registered it, and in 1995–6 we took over the land. At first we farmed the land using chemical practice, but in 1997 we had an orientation and training in MASIPAG and established a trial farm. After verification trials, we had our first MASIPAG crop in the second cropping season in 1997. We saw visible differences with the yields and especially when we computed the inputs and income. We saw that we had higher net income with the organization. We now have a diverse system with many crops. We now have rice, vegetables, livestock, fruit trees, and herbal medicines. When we were still farm workers, there would be a period of three to four months per year where there would be no work. We would have no money and nothing for food. When we had the land but were in chemical farming, we wouldn't have enough yield left over for ourselves as all would go to the traders as payment for the loans. Now we are MASIPAG farmers. We have more harvest, we can stock, we can store. We can have food. We even have enough vegetables to eat with rice and we have enough to last the full year. We have not only enough for food; we have a surplus for income. We can sell vegetables and root crops. There is a very big difference between being farm workers and farmers, and between being conventional farmers and organic. In organic farming, you have control over the farming system which gives you food security. (E. Paglumotan, personal interview, 25 October 2008)

Jojo Paglumotan clearly demonstrates how the principles of food sovereignty translate into concrete practices and impacts for small farmers who choose to focus on production for personal consumption. Food production is seen as resting directly in the hands of the farming family. Combined with impressive increases in on-farm diversity, this means farmers practising farmer-led sustainable agriculture are able not only to generate a diverse diet for themselves, but also to generate surplus for sale to the market. Decreased exposure to risks is combined with greater control and self-reliance. In using inputs from the farm itself, such as compost and green manures as well as seed selection and breeding, farmers are exposed neither to increases in the cost of inputs nor fluctuations in the sale of produce.

The issue of quality of food consumption is also important. While some literature on organic farming and sustainable agriculture sometimes criticizes a desire for healthy, organic food as a middle-class concern associated with commodity fetishism (see, for example, Bryant and Goodman 2004; Freidberg 2003a; Goodman 2004; Guthman 2002), the small farmers of the MASIPAG network (earning on average fifty-two pesos or approximately US$1.14 per day from an average farm size of 1.5 hectares) rate this as an important feature for all, regardless of income. Here the food sovereignty approach taken by the network is premised on the right to healthy organic food, pointing out that this has health implications for both producers and consumers. The quality of food grown by the farmers practising farmer-led sustainable agriculture was valued as healthy and pesticide free, while growing without pesticides is a vitally important health benefit. In households practising conventional chemical agriculture, the spraying of pesticides is often undertaken by children without safety equipment, as it is lighter work than other agricultural tasks.

This study investigated any change in the health status of household members. In the group of farmers practising farmer-led sustainable agriculture, 85 per cent rated their health today better or much better than in 2000. In the reference group of conventional farmers, only 32 per cent rated it positively, while 56 per cent saw no change or even 13 per cent stated worse health. Marcelino dela Rosa from Luzon explains, "My decision to become a MASIPAG farmer was greatly influenced by my desire to provide quality organic food for my family mainly for health reasons. It is also an expression of my commitment for the welfare of small farmers" (personal interview, 23 October 2008).

Income

The ability to maintain a steady income is a major challenge for any farmer worldwide. This has been a particular criticism of the neoliberal approach to agriculture that has compounded the inherent insecurities of farming, driving prices down and the cost of inputs up (Ong'Wen and Wright 2007). Income is also an issue raised by recent studies of fair trade (Bryant and Goodman 2004; Gonzalez and Nigh 2005; Klooster 2005; Mutersbaugh et al. 2005; Taylor 2005) that question the ability of farmers to change their engagement with a capitalist system of agriculture. The experiences of the farmers of the MASIPAG network, however, do point to the importance of the diverse economy and alternative agriculture if it is placed firmly within a food sovereignty, rather than merely an organic, approach. An investigation of the net income per hectare for the different farmer groups indicates that farmers using a food sovereignty approach are the most successful. They had a net income per hectare of 23,599 pesos, the conversion group, 17,457 pesos, and the conventional farmers, 15,643 pesos. This means the full MASIPAG farmers have a net income per hectare one and a half times that of the reference group of conventional, chemical farmers.

These results are directly contrary to the official line promoted by many aid and development agencies as well as national governments.

Indeed, the push for export-led agriculture and production for markets has been the defining feature of agricultural outreach since the Green Revolution beginning in the 1940s. Yet this study ironically shows that those farmers producing first for themselves and their communities using a food sovereignty approach rather than taking a primarily market orientation actually do better in an economic sense than those farmers practising market-oriented agriculture. In a large part, this is due to eliminating the need to purchase agrochemical inputs. Agricultural inputs – chemical pesticides, fertilizers and seeds – are the single most important production cost for conventional, high-input farmers. Production costs for full organic farmers were half that of conventional farmers. These differences are highly statistically significant.

While the net income figure is revealing, the benefits of a food sovereignty approach are even clearer when considering the total income balance of a farming household (see table 7.4). The amount of food grown on the farm and consumed by the household is an important part of income calculations often overlooked in conventional economic analyses. While conventional farmers need to purchase food from the market, the farmers involved in sustainable agriculture are able to cut costs and increase food security by consuming the diverse produce grown. The food consumed has an important economic value. For the small-scale farmers involved in the study, outlaying money for food is often a burden. The study reveals the economic contribution of personal consumption of produce. While MASIPAG farmers consumed 33,842 pesos of their own farm produce, conventional farmers consumed 24,096 (see table 7.5). These results are highly statistically significant.

When the value of farm products is incorporated into income calculations, a better picture of farmer livelihoods emerges. This gives us the figure for net income plus subsistence, a figure that reveals the full extent of the benefits that accrue to those involved in farmer-led sustainable agriculture. Net income plus subsistence is calculated as the gross income minus all production costs plus the value of food eaten by the farm family based on farm-gate prices. Nationally, the income of MASIPAG farmers per hectare when subsistence is taken into account was 51,488 pesos per annum. For the farmers in conversion it was 38,734 pesos, and for the conventional farmers it was 32,062 pesos. This means the income of farmers practising farmer-led sustainable agriculture was 1.6 times that of the conventional farmers. The differences are highly significant statistically.

Table 7.4. Net Income and Net Income Plus Subsistence

	MASIPAG farmers	Conversion farmers	Conventional farmers
Net agricultural income per hectare (cultivated)			
National average	23,599***	17,457***	15,643***
Net agricultural income plus subsistence			
National average	69,935***	68,361***	54,915***
Net agricultural income plus subsistence per hectare			
National average	51,488***	38,734***	32,062***

*** Highly statistically significant

Table 7.5. Value in Pesos of Own Farm Products Consumed in the Past Year[2]

Products consumed	MASIPAG farmers	Conversion farmers	Conventional farmers
Rice	14,506	13,073	12,222
Seeds	1,221	1,403	662
Fruits	1,158	875	439
Vegetables	5,218	5,625	3,638
Livestock	1,572	1,584	1,261
Poultry	2,095	1,501	1,502
Feeds	2,372	1,618	1,395
Processed products	515	312	203
Corn	1,338	1,239	458
Herbal	325	183	88
Firewood	3,836	3,962	3,079
Organic fertilizer	1,402	872	58
Others	405	735	258
Total	33,842 pesos***	31,145 pesos***	24,096 pesos***

*** Highly statistically significant

The impact on the poorest farmers is particularly striking. This is highlighted by looking at results for the poorest quarter of participants. For the poorest quarter of respondents, net income for those involved in fully converted sustainable agriculture was 1.5 times that of the conventional farmers. The poorest quarter of MASIPAG farmers had an average net income plus subsistence per hectare of 12,610 pesos while conventional farmers averaged only 8,590 pesos per hectare per annum. Comparing farmers of equal educational status also shows the profound benefits of farmer-led sustainable agriculture to the most marginalized. MASIPAG farmers with an elementary level of education had a mean net income of 19,434 pesos compared to 10,127 pesos for conventional farmers. This means the income of those MASIPAG farmers with less formal education was nearly twice that of their conventional counterparts.

A food sovereignty approach has thus managed to significantly increase the incomes of the poorest and least formally educated members. Many development efforts that aim to generate income struggle to increase incomes for the most needy. Average incomes may be improved, but it is often only the medium- and higher-income groups that benefit while the poorest remain behind. Ultimately, this increases inequality. Reversing this trend is precisely what practising a food sovereignty approach has achieved.

Social and Environmental Outcomes

For the farmers of the MASIPAG network, a food sovereignty approach means farming organically. This provides important environmental benefits through the elimination of chemical fertilizers and pesticides, increased biodiversity, better soil fertility management, and other sustainable farming techniques. The agriculture practised by the MASIPAG farmers in this study, however, is not simply organic agriculture.

The farmer-led approach used in this study supports the development of diverse local agricultural systems based on a range of place-based farmer knowledges. This has both social and environmental outcomes. For example, the focus on local markets has environmental benefits beyond the direct impact on the farm through the elimination of greenhouse gases. The integrated nature of benefits is underscored by a comment from a farmer at the Mindanao workshop: "MASIPAG farmers are different from other farmers because they are free to choose their technologies and are able to implement these in their farms, from the choice of seeds, enriching soil fertility, to managing pests and diseases of their crops and livestock. In the MASIPAG farmers is the desire to discover and find other methods for the farm and to gradually restore the culture of cooperation" (personal interview, 25 October 2008).

The importance of autonomy or sovereignty over production decisions is a recurring theme. Farmers point to the issue of control as absolutely central to the network's success. Many forms of organic agriculture are done in ways that locate farming expertise, seed breeding and technological development, and ultimate control *away* from the farmers themselves, a criticism that is highlighted widely in the literature (Kaviraj 1997; Marglin 1996; Wright 2005). The key to the kind of farmer-led sustainable agriculture practised by the farmers in this study, on the other hand, is its bottom-up approach with an emphasis on autonomy for farmers.

MASIPAG farmers take key roles in the organization, including through the breeding of rice. This has flow-on effects that see the MASIPAG farmers as more positive and involved in a wide range of leadership in their community. Farmer-to-farmer education, the use of farmer leaders as trainers, and cross-farm visits between farmers are also valued as effective methods of training that prioritize the knowledge and leadership qualities of farmers. In the community, more communal activities, such as shared communal work (*bayanihan*) and producer cooperatives are found among the MASIPAG farmers. These have important flow-on effects in income, security, and social outcomes.

MASIPAG, as a farmer-led network, places strong emphasis on the work of people's organizations (POs). People's organizations are membership-based, grass roots community groups. In the case of MASIPAG, these are groups of farmers who get together to organize activities, trainings, and other events. The survey results show that many of the farmers practising farmer-led sustainable agriculture take active leadership within their local organizations. Among the MASIPAG members, every second is a PO-leader, every third is a farmer trainer or committee member, every tenth a rice breeder, every twenty-fifth a maize breeder, and one in hundred a chicken gene pool caretaker.

A sense of empowerment means farmers feel they can make a positive difference in their lives and communities. The MASIPAG farmers in the survey report a sense of positivity and the potential for positive change. The conventional farmers, on the other hand, struggle to feel empowered and positive. Marcelino dela Rosa, a MASIPAG farmer,

farmer trainer, farmer rice breeder, and main caretaker of the Provincial Back-up Farm in Nueva Ecija, Luzon, described his involvement:

> After more than five years of organic farming now, I found fulfilment in what I do. I am a DIFS [diversified integrated farming system] practitioner and at the same time a rice breeder. I am contented and happy in the knowledge that the food that I provide my family is safe and chemical-free food. All the things that I grow are organic, including those that I sell in the market. So I produce food – rice, mangoes, vegetables – that actually heals sick people. As rice breeder I can give rice seeds to other farmers, which can actually free them from bondage to debt, help them farm without harming the environment, and likewise provide healthy food for their family. (Personal interview, 23 October 2008)

Collective action and the formation of groups have an important part to play. They form the basis of the network farmer-to-farmer training approach, provide support for new members, and facilitate the communal labour of *bayanihan* that allows for a group level of empowerment as well as bringing social and economic benefits for those involved. Another way that farmers' groups bring significant change is through the formation of marketing or producer cooperatives. Many of the MASIPAG farmers create organizations that aim to facilitate better terms of access to markets. In particular, the high rates of interest and low prices for goods can be circumvented through eliminating the middleman in transactions. Between 6 and 16 per cent of both full and transition MASIPAG groups surveyed sold via marketing groups, while only 1 per cent of conventional farmers did so. A comparison of the farmers with group marketing versus all other farmers shows a marked influence on household incomes. Crop income, livestock income, and total income were about 45 per cent higher for the farmers in the marketing groups. Clearly, in terms of income, marketing through cooperatives is a significant factor regardless of other production decisions (see table 7.6).

Eddie Panes talks of the many benefits of a marketing group:

> There is a very big change. In the past, when we were still on conventional, we could not make decisions. Now on our marketing group, we are able to make decisions – like determining prices for different varieties and eating qualities – because we are the ones now selling our products.

Table 7.6. Impact of a Marketing Group on Income

Income in pesos	Marketing group	Non-marketing group
Total income	134,775	91,270
Crop income	63,631	43,293
Livestock income	14,336	9,831
Sample size	67	755

We are in control; we now make the decisions according to our wishes. We also earn much more, unlike before – because we are now doing the selling … That is why we gain much from MASIPAG – we are able to decide on our wishes. But of course this goes through the group process – the majority decision is always followed. Collective ideas – so when it fails, all of us share the blame. We have an advantage: our group is united because of this process. (Personal interview, 24 October 2008)

Conclusions: "To determine and develop our futures"

The words of the farmers as they describe the successes and strengths of the MASIPAG program are redolent with allusions to the need for autonomy, independence, and self-reliance. They repeatedly stress the importance of wresting control back from corporations, money-lenders, and government "experts." Eddie Panes talks of being able to "decide on our wishes" and Marcelino dela Rosa of being "free from bondage." Gabriel Diaz says of MASIPAG, "The farmer is not dependent … he has control," while Jojo Paglumotan says, "You have control over the farming system." The organization itself states that it works in farmer-led agriculture "to determine and develop our futures."

It is on this question of sovereignty, on the ability to determine and develop their own future, that the farmers of the network possibly have the most to contribute to literature on agro-food systems and on diverse economies. Drawing from the experiences of these farmers reveals the limits of focusing on alternative economies that are fundamentally market-oriented. While the critiques of fair trade, certification programs, and initiatives in the global North are important, the experiences of the MASIPAG farmers reveal a different way of doing economy and a different way of doing "alternative" agriculture. The network goes beyond simply practising organic agriculture or working with "diverse economies," developing instead a system based on more fundamental change. Their approach is an example of a diverse economy, they do practise organic agriculture, but they do so in a way that places the question of sovereignty, farmer empowerment, and farmer control at the centre of their work.

Farmer groups underpin the network, providing a basis for social as well as economic and environmental change. As Eddie Panes eloquently explained, marketing groups shift decision-making power away from middlemen, away from the market, and away from the whims of Northern consumers back to the farmers themselves. Before, he said, they "could not make decisions." Now, "We are in control." For MASIPAG, the farmers' organization helps facilitate the development of a true farmer-led approach.

The work of MASIPAG also reveals the social, environmental, and economic as thoroughly intertwined. Farmer-led sustainable agriculture is not only a contribution to livelihood security, health, food security, the local environment, or climate change; it is all of those things. Many criticisms and concerns of alternative agriculture systems come from approaches that attempt to separate environmental from social elements, economic from social or environmental, and so on. This is what leads to conventionalization and Northern dominance. Yet the food sovereignty approach pursued by MASIPAG, and pursued so successfully, is integrated and holistic. Healthy organic food is not seen as the domain of the privileged but as a right for all, from the subsistence farmer to the fellow-villager purchasing food in the marketplace. Chemical inputs are eschewed for health reasons, environmental reasons, reasons of farmer empowerment, and economic viability. There is no separating the tangled strands of social, cultural, economic, and environmental cause and effect.

There is a mirror of the success of a food sovereignty approach, a doppelgänger that lurks behind the success story of this chapter, in the failure of conventional agriculture. While this is a story of increasing incomes, better health outcomes, and social empowerment, there is also a bleaker story told by the data about farmers practising conventional agriculture. Here, despite a market orientation in which goods are produced primarily for sale, farmers actually earn *less* than those producing in a food sovereignty approach. The poorest farmers, in particular, see their incomes eroded and indebtedness increase. This is a story not only of decreasing incomes, but of worsening health, less viable ecosystems, and a sense of futility. The Philippines government has opened up the national agricultural market completely since 1998 and promoted high-input agriculture since the 1960s. Indeed, national governments and mainstream aid agencies throughout the world have promoted this approach for decades. It is clear that a complete over-haul of policies is required.

There is much to learn from taking seriously the work done by social movements in the global South. In the context of a failed approach to mainstream development and the declining incomes and increasing vulnerabilities of conventional agriculture, there *are* solutions. As MASIPAG insists, far from helpless and thoroughly colonized by capitalism, the farmers of the network do incredible work in enacting alternative futures. Here, there is a chance to learn from the practices of food sovereignty and the ways that alternative economies can and do transform the lives of many. This is evident only when we recognize the long-term social, economic, and ecological contributions of farming communities.

Internationally, there are many instances of farmers and farmer movements carving out different kinds of spaces, different forms of agriculture underpinned by different kinds of values. And in doing so successfully – in terms of food security outcomes, increasing viability of local economic systems, and increasing agro-diversity. Food sovereignty means recognizing the work that has been and is being done, and acknowledging farmer agency and farmer knowledges as farming communities continue to create hard-won, viable, and vital alternative agricultural and economic systems.

ACKNOWLEDGMENTS

I would like to acknowledge the inspirational work of the MASIPAG network as well as its fantastically friendly and helpful staff and members. This article is based on a study written by Elizabeth Cruzada, Lorenz Bachmann and myself. I'd like to thank them both for letting me use the results here. The study was funded by MISEREOR and was carried out by the staff, farmers and member scientists of the MASIPAG network.

NOTES

1 The core research team was composed of Ms Bess Cruzada, MASIPAG coordinator, Organizational Management and Development; Ms Camela Ong Vano, MASIPAG data specialist; Prof. Nelita Lalican, of the Agricultural Systems Cluster of the University of the Philippines in Los Banos; and the team leader, Dr Lorenz Bachmann, an agronomist from

Germany. During the first survey, the team was complemented by Prof. Romeo Teruel, Department of Economics, and Prof. Virgilio Aguilar, Department of Social Sciences, both from the University of St La Salle in Negros Occidental, Philippines.

2 Farmers were asked to compare their current situation to that of the "past year." The study itself was conducted over three survey waves from 2007 to 2009 so the year described by famers ranged from 2006 to 2008.

REFERENCES

Aguilar, F. 2005. "Excess Possibilities? Ethics, Populism and Community Economy: A Commentary on J.K. Gibson-Graham's 'Surplus Possibilities: Postdevelopment and Community Economies.'" *Singapore Journal of Tropical Geography* 26 (1): 27–31. http://dx.doi.org/10.1111/j.0129-7619.2005.00199.x.

Altieri, M. 2009. "Agroecology, Small Farms and Food Sovereignty." *Monthly Review* 61 (3): 102–13.

Amin, A., A. Cameron, and R. Hudson. 2003. "The Alterity of the Social Economy." In Leyshon, Lee, and Williams, *Alternative Economic Spaces*, 27–54. http://dx.doi.org/10.4135/9781446220825.n2.

Bachmann, L., B. Cruzada, and S. Wright. 2009. *Food Security and Farmer Empowerment: A Study on the Impacts of Farmer-Led Sustainable Agriculture in the Philippines.* Baños, Philippines: MASIPAG.

Bryant, R.L., and M.K. Goodman. 2004. "Consuming Narratives: The Political Ecology of 'Alternative' Consumption." *Transactions of the Institute of British Geographers* 29 (3): 344–66. http://dx.doi.org/10.1111/j.0020-2754 .2004.00333.x.

Cameron, J., and K. Gibson. 2005. "Alternative Pathways to Community and Economic Development: The Latrobe Valley Community Partnering Project." *Geographical Research* 43 (3): 274–85. http://dx.doi.org/10.1111/j.1745-5871.2005.00327.x.

Carmody, P. 2005. "Review of *Alternative Economic Spaces*, by A. Leyshon, R. Lee, and C.C. Williams." *Annals of the Association of American Geographers* 95 (4): 897–9. http://dx.doi.org/10.1111/j.1467-8306.2005.00492_6.x.

Community Economies Collective. 2001. "Imagining and Enacting Noncapitalist Futures." *Socialist Review* 28:93–135.

Crewe, L., N. Gregson, and K. Brooks. 2003. "Alternative Retail Spaces." In Leyshon, Lee, and Williams, *Alternative Economic Spaces*, 74–106. http:// dx.doi.org/10.4135/9781446220825.n4.

Desmarais, A. 2007. *La Via Campesina: Globalization and the Power of Peasants.* London: Pluto.

Emery, M., and A. Pierce. 2005. "Interrupting the Telos: Locating Subsistence in Contemporary US Forests." *Environment & Planning* 37 (6): 981–93. http://dx.doi.org/10.1068/a36263.

Freidberg, S. 2003a. "Cleaning Up Down South: Supermarkets, Ethical Trade and African Horticulture." *Social & Cultural Geography* 4 (1): 27–43. http://dx.doi.org/10.1080/1464936032000049298.

– 2003b. "Culture, Conventions and Colonial Constructs of Rurality in South–North Horticultural Trades." *Journal of Rural Studies* 19 (1): 97–109. http://dx.doi.org/10.1016/S0743-0167(02)00037-2.

Fuller, D., and A. Jonas. 2003. "Alternative Financial Spaces." In Leyshon, Lee, and Williams, *Alternative Economic Spaces*, 55–73. http://dx.doi.org/10.4135/9781446220825.n3.

Gibson-Graham, J.K. 1996. *The End of Capitalism (as We Knew It)*. Oxford: Blackwell.

– 2005. "Surplus Possibilities: Postdevelopment and Community Economies." *Singapore Journal of Tropical Geography* 26 (1): 4–26. http://dx.doi.org/10.1111/j.0129-7619.2005.00198.x.

– 2006. *A Postcapitalist Politics*. Minneapolis: University of Minnesota Press.

– 2008. "Diverse Economies: Performative Practices for 'Other Worlds.'" *Progress in Human Geography* 32 (5): 613–32. http://dx.doi.org/10.1177/0309132508090821.

Godrej, D. 2007. "Daring to Dream." *New Internationalist* 400:4–6. http://newint.org/features/2007/05/01/keynote/.

González, A.A., and R. Nigh. 2005. "Smallholder Participation and Certification of Organic Farm Products in Mexico." *Journal of Rural Studies* 21 (4): 449–60. http://dx.doi.org/10.1016/j.jrurstud.2005.08.004.

Goodman, D. 2004. "Rural Europe Redux? Reflections on Alternative Agro-Food Networks and Paradigm Change." *Sociologia Ruralis* 44 (1): 3–16. http://dx.doi.org/10.1111/j.1467-9523.2004.00258.x.

Guthman, J. 2002. "Commodified Meanings and Meaningful Commodities: Re-thinking Production-Consumption Links through the Organic System of Provision." *Sociologia Ruralis* 42 (4): 295–311. http://dx.doi.org/10.1111/1467-9523.00218.

– 2004. "Back to the Land: The Paradox of Organic Food Standards." *Environment & Planning* 36 (3): 511–28. http://dx.doi.org/10.1068/a36104.

Hughes, A. 2005. "Geographies of Exchange and Circulation: Alternative Trading Spaces." *Progress in Human Geography* 29 (4): 496–504. http://dx.doi.org/10.1191/0309132505ph563pr.

Kaviraj, S. 1997. "A Critique of the Passive Revolution." *Economic and Political Weekly* 23:45–7.

Kitchen, L., T. Marsden, and P. Milbourne. 2006. "Community Forests and Regeneration in Post Industrial Landscapes." *Geoforum* 37 (5): 831–43. http://dx.doi.org/10.1016/j.geoforum.2005.09.008.

Klooster, D. 2005. "Environmental Certification of Forests: The Evolution of Environmental Governance in a Commodity Network." *Journal of Rural Studies* 21 (4): 403–17. http://dx.doi.org/10.1016/j.jrurstud.2005.08.005.

Krueger, R., and J. Agyeman. 2005. "Sustainability Schizophrenia or 'Actually Existing Sustainabilities?' Toward a Broader Understanding of the Politics and Promise of Local Sustainability in the US." *Geoforum* 36 (4): 410–7. http://dx.doi.org/10.1016/j.geoforum.2004.07.005.

Lawson, V. 2005. "Hopeful Geographies: Imaging Ethical Alternatives. A Commentary on J. K. Gibson-Graham's 'Surplus Possibilities: Postdevelopment and Community Economies.'" *Singapore Journal of Tropical Geography* 26 (1): 36–8. http://dx.doi.org/10.1111/j.0129-7619.2005.00201.x.

Lee, R. 2000. "Shelter from the Storm? Geographies of Regard in the Worlds of Horticultural Consumption and Production." *Geoforum* 31 (2): 137–57. http://dx.doi.org/10.1016/S0016-7185(99)00036 6.

– 2006. "The Ordinary Economy: Tangled Up in Values and Geography." *Transactions of the Institute of British Geographers* 31 (4): 413–32. http://dx.doi .org/10.1111/j.1475-5661.2006.00223.x.

Lee, R., A. Leyshon, T. Aldridge, J. Tooke, C. Williams, and N. Thrift. 2004. "Making Geographies and Histories? Constructing Local Circuits of Value." *Environment and Planning D: Society and Space* 22 (4): 595–617. http://dx.doi .org/10.1068/d50j.

Leyshon, A., and R. Lee. 2003. "Introduction: Alternative Economic Geographies." In Leyshon, Lee, and Williams, *Alternative Economic Spaces*, 1–26. http://dx.doi.org/10.4135/9781446220825.n1.

Leyshon, A., R. Lee, and C. Williams, eds. 2003. *Alternative Economic Spaces*. London: Sage.

Lockie, S., and D. Halpin. 2005. "The 'Conventionalization' Thesis Reconsidered: Structural and Ideological Transformation of Australian Organic Agriculture." *Sociologia Ruralis* 45 (4): 284–307. http://dx.doi.org/10.1111/ j.1467-9523.2005.00306.x.

Lyons, K., and D. Burch. 2007. *Socio-Economic Impacts of Organic Agriculture in Africa*. Bonn: International Federation of Organic Agriculture Movements.

Marglin, S. 1996. "Farmers, Seedsmen, and Scientists: Systems of Agriculture and Systems of Knowledge." In *Decolonizing Knowledge: From Development to Dialogue*, edited by F. Apffel-Marglin and S. Marglin, 185–247. Oxford: Oxford University Press. http://dx.doi.org/10.1093/acprof:oso/ 9780198288848.003.0006.

McCarthy, J. 2006a. "Neoliberalism and the Politics of Alternatives: Community Forestry in British Columbia and the United States." *Annals of the Association of American Geographers* 96 (1): 84–104. http://dx.doi .org/10.1111/j.1467-8306.2006.00500.x.

– 2006b. "Rural Geography: Alternative Rural Economies – The Search for Alterity in Forests, Fisheries, Food, and Fair Trade." *Progress in Human Geography* 30 (6): 803–11. http://dx.doi.org/10.1177/0309132506071530.

McMichael, P. 2006. "Food Sovereignty vs the Corporate Food Regime." Conference Papers, International Studies Association, San Diego, CA, 22 March.

– 2008. "Peasants Make Their Own History, But Not Just as They Please." *Journal of Agrarian Change* 8 (2–3): 205–28. http://dx.doi.org/10.1111/j.1471-0366.2008.00168.x.

Mousseau, F., and A. Mittal. 2006. "Food Sovereignty: Ending World Hunger in Our Time." *Humanist* 66 (2): 24–6.

Mutersbaugh, T., D. Klooster, M.-C. Renard, and P. Taylor. 2005. "Certifying Rural Spaces: Quality-Certified Products and Rural Governance." *Journal of Rural Studies* 21 (4): 381–8. http://dx.doi.org/10.1016/j.jrurstud.2005.10.003.

Ong'Wen, O., and S. Wright. 2007. *Small Farmers and the Future of Sustainable Agriculture*. Berlin: Heinrich Boll Foundation.

Pollard, J., and M. Samers. 2007. "Islamic Banking and Finance: Postcolonial Political Economy and the Decentring of Economic Geography." *Transactions of the Institute of British Geographers* 32 (3): 313–30. http://dx.doi.org/ 10.1111/j.1475-5661.2007.00255.x.

Raynolds, L.T. 2004. "The Globalization of Organic Agro-Food Networks." *World Development* 32 (5): 725–43. http://dx.doi.org/10.1016/j.worlddev .2003.11.008.

Renard, M. 2005. "Quality Certification, Regulation and Power in Fair Trade." *Journal of Rural Studies* 21 (4): 419–31. http://dx.doi.org/10.1016/j.jrurstud .2005.09.002.

Renting, H., T. Marsden, and J. Banks. 2003. "Understanding Alternative Food Networks: Exploring the Role of Short Food Supply Chains in Rural Development." *Environment & Planning* 35 (3): 393–411. http://dx.doi .org/10.1068/a3510.

Sage, C. 2003. "Social Embeddedness and Relations of Regard: Alternative 'Good Food' Networks in South-West Ireland." *Journal of Rural Studies* 19 (1): 47–60. http://dx.doi.org/10.1016/S0743-0167(02)00044-X.

Seyfang, G. 2001a. "Community Currencies: Small Change for a Green Economy." *Environment & Planning* 33 (6): 975–96. http://dx.doi.org/10 .1068/a33216.

– 2001b. "Money That Makes a Change: Community Currencies, North and South." *Gender and Development* 9 (1): 60–9. http://dx.doi.org/10.1080/13552070127737.

– 2006. "Ecological Citizenship and Sustainable Consumption: Examining Local Organic Food Networks." *Journal of Rural Studies* 22 (4): 383–95. http://dx.doi.org/10.1016/j.jrurstud.2006.01.003.

Smith, A., and A. Stenning. 2006. "Beyond Household Economies: Articulations and Spaces of Economic Practice in Postsocialism." *Progress in Human Geography* 30 (2): 190–213. http://dx.doi.org/10.1191/0309132506ph601oa.

St Martin, K. 2007. "The Difference That Class Makes: Neoliberalization and Non-Capitalism in the Fishing Industry of New England." *Antipode* 39 (3): 527–49. http://dx.doi.org/10.1111/j.1467-8330.2007.00538.x.

Taylor, P.L. 2005. "A Fair Trade Approach to Community Forest Certification? A Framework for Discussion." *Journal of Rural Studies* 21 (4): 433–47. http://dx.doi.org/10.1016/j.jrurstud.2005.08.002.

Williams, C.C., T. Aldridge, and J. Tooke. 2003. "Alternative Exchange Spaces." In Leyshon, Lee, and Williams, *Alternative Economic Spaces*, 151–67. http://dx.doi.org/10.4135/9781446220825.n7.

Wilson, G.A., and P.A. Memon. 2005. "Indigenous Forest Management in 21st-Century New Zealand: Towards a 'Postproductivist' Indigenous Forest–Farmland Interface?" *Environment & Planning* 37 (8): 1493–517. http://dx.doi.org/10.1068/a37144.

Wright, S. 2005. "Knowing Scale: Intellectual Property Rights, Knowledge Spaces and the Production of the Global." *Social & Cultural Geography* 6 (6): 903–21. http://dx.doi.org/10.1080/14649360500353350.

– 2008a. "Locating a Politics of Knowledge: Struggles over Intellectual Property in the Philippines." *Australian Geographer* 39 (4): 409–26. http://dx.doi.org/10.1080/00049180802419104.

– 2008b. "Practising Hope: Learning from Social Movement Strategies in the Philippines." In *Fear: Critical Geopolitics and Everyday Life*, edited by R. Pain, S. Smith, and S. Graham, 223–34. Aldershot, UK: Ashgate.

– 2010. "Cultivating Beyond-Capitalist Economies." *Journal of Economic Geography* 86:297–318.

8 Free Markets for All: Transition Economies and the European Union's Common Agricultural Policy

IRENA KNEZEVIC

A swallow swoops into Helena's barn and perches itself on one of the beams in the roof. Jadwiga smiles because it's really not supposed to be there, "They are helping the farmer because they are eating a lot of flies. But the EU regulation is not allowing them to keep swallow nests in the barn, so the farmers were asked to destroy them. But all Poles [believe] that swallows [bring] happiness so no-one will destroy them. When there is no swallows, you have to hang plastic, special plastic, full of chemicals that the flies will stick to. So, what is better, chemical or swallow?"

Saroja Coelho (2007)

Following the collapse of socialist regimes in Eastern and Central Europe (ECE) in the late 1980s and early 1990s, political and economic reforms that would soon take place there came under a common name of *transition*. The European Union (EU), through its enlargement policy bent on expanding its already 500 million consumer market, embraced the opportunity to groom prospective new member states by facilitating their transition. Its promise of "butter mountains and wine lakes" has led to *transition* and *EU accession* being used interchangeably in the European context. The transition has succeeded to varying degrees throughout the region, but has generally failed to deliver the promised benefits to all. Despite the EU's image of being the harbinger of democracy and human rights, its agenda has proven to be primarily neoliberal, with expanding free markets and international trade as a priority. Within this framework, no room has been made for food security concerns, and minimal opportunities have been given for democratic citizen participation in policy creation. The results of EU-assisted transition in ECE reveal that the process has effectively facilitated the success of global capital, but at the same time clashed with the cultures it attempts to absorb.

The process of reform, and particularly harmonization with the EU's Common Agricultural Policy, have reshaped the food economy of ECE and also upset the social and cultural fabric around food and foodways. Change in diet, interruption of local economies, and pressure on producers to be "competitive" have been but the most intimate ways in which ECE citizens are experiencing the effects of EU accession. The following discussion draws on the research conducted between 2007 and 2009 that involved numerous policy documents and conversations with countless officials in Brussels and in the western Balkans region in ECE. I grew up in the western Balkans, so my fluency in the local dialects and culture prompted me to explore policy changes in this understudied region and allow my research to be guided by informal conversations with local residents. Originally conceptualized as straightforward policy analysis, that study soon came to encompass a range of general observations and a substantial turn to the role of informal economy in the region's foodways.

The foodscape (Winson 2004)[1] of three of the hopeful future EU members in the western Balkans[2] (Bosnia and Herzegovina, Croatia, and Serbia, which were once all part of the former Yugoslavia) illustrates some of the failures of transition and belies the contradictions of the neoliberal project. The changes that have taken place there over the last two decades were paradoxically expected to bring democracy and freedom, but have instead resulted in growing social inequality and little or no room for public debate. The lack of formal channels for achieving food security and food sovereignty, however, has inadvertently contributed to a subversive food economy that escapes formal control of transnational capital. Interrogating that subtle resistance in the form of an informal food economy provides a fascinating glimpse of what food sovereignty can mean in everyday practice and not just theory – how it can manifest itself even where the term *food sovereignty* is absent. Moreover, such an investigation offers an insight into the diversity of resistances to the neoliberal global food regime, and trade-focused global politics. As several authors in this volume illustrate, much that resistance is taking shape in what are formally recognized as social movements. This study explores a more subtle form of food sovereignty and at the same considers how that form fits into the larger issues of political and economic sovereignty.

In the post-socialist ECE, the imposition of the Western ideal of free-market "democracy" has introduced new internal inequalities while at the same time eating away at state power. Critics observe that the EU is not only suffering from a democracy deficit (Just 2007) but is also greatly contributing to "erosion of state sovereignty," as policy areas no longer fall under state control only (Sutcliffe 2010, 73). The loss of state decision-making power is accompanied by citizens' inability to influence policy, and this is arguably not a case of failed democracy in transition states; instead, it is a failure *of* democracy – failure of a particularly designed form of market democracy to deliver political agency in the context of international agreements and unfettered trade. As a result, ECE citizens are reclaiming this agency by making sovereign decisions over their food through participation in informal markets, individually and collectively.

Transition

In the contemporary economic and political literature, *transition economy* is a category associated with a very specific transition – that of socialist, centralized economy into a free market state. The category covers most of ECE and consists of nation states once ruled by some sort of communist government. While diverse, the ECE experiences have much in common with one another, including some general political timelines. The socialist governments led by the Communist Party came to the helm of ECE countries following the Second World War. Most of them, with the notable exception of Yugoslavia, belonged to the Eastern Bloc, a geopolitical alliance that stood in opposition to the capitalist forces united under the North Atlantic Treaty Organization. Characterized by state- rather than market-controlled economies and a single-party political system, ECE countries and the capitalist West were each other's economic and ideological threat for decades. Their political tensions lasted well into the late 1980s when a series of diplomatic efforts finally ended this Cold War. While the end of the Cold War promised peace and cooperation, it also signalled the weakening of socialist ideology, and the socialist regimes in ECE soon fell one by one, with the crowning fall of the Soviet Union in 1991. Yugoslavia's dismembering started that same year, setting into motion a series of events that included civil wars and created the conditions for what is described below.

Privatization has been at the core of transition, with formerly social enterprises finding their way quickly into the private hands of those already wielding much political power and material wealth. While at the heart of free market economy (which the EU inextricably links to democracy and improved quality of life), and treated generally as an economic issue, the shifting of the economy into private hands has had wide-reaching social consequences. Growing inequalities and abuse of political power are but the aftermath of the privatization that often took place in haphazard and questionable ways laden with corruption and favouritism. In the western Balkans the messy process of privatization mostly took place before any effective regulatory body was capable of overseeing the process and ensuring its legitimacy. Bribery and social capital (connections and perceived power) guided much of the process. Hence, the foundations of new capitalism, in that region at least, are questionable at best and criminal at worst.[3] Nevertheless, privatization was internationally encouraged in unison, and, as Harrison Schwartz (2006) points out, economic reform in ECE has universally been treated in terms of *how* and not *whether* to privatize.

In agriculture, privatization has meant sudden disappearance of state enterprises as well as subsidies, which affected agricultural input without adjusting agricultural practices. The disappearance of subsidies took place across ECE, despite the fact that the United States, Canada, and the EU members, all models of capitalism, heavily subsidize their agriculture. The result, Macours and Swinnen (2000) found, was a drop in output across the post-socialist world, and they estimated that privatization was directly responsible for 39 per cent of the decrease in production. A 2002 study by Liefert and Swinnen also acknowledges the overall drop in agricultural output, as well as the ultimate neoliberal measurement of progress – the gross domestic product across post-socialist countries. They add that "the contraction and commodity restructuring of transition agriculture has therefore been an inevitable part of market reform" (5)[4] and note that "reform has threatened food security in Russia and other transition economies because of problems involving *access* to food for segments of the population and certain regions within countries" (19, emphasis in original). This assessment of reform success presents the question of who indeed is meant to benefit from transition. If drop in output and increase in disparities are indicative of successful reform, then the entire purpose of transition is unclear.

In the broader political and economic context Warner (2009) argues that while economists and public administrators link privatization with democracy and consider that market approach to governance maximizes public services though cost-saving management of budgets (competitive public market), "empirical evidence is mounting that privatization has failed to deliver the promised cost savings" (133). Warner adds that privatization and institutional changes required by the global free trade regimes can actually undermine the civic foundation on which good governance depends. While a fundamental element of the capitalist system, privatization appears to have benefited only a few, and to have had overall negative effects on the transition economies.

As a result of this rapid economic and political transformation, the social milieu has also been altered in this part of the world. The most poignant side effects of this often haphazard reform have been increased crime and corruption, and organized crime's involvement in politics. This has particularly been the case in the western Balkans, where the series of 1990s civil wars made the area especially vulnerable to both crime and international influence. Yet instead of seeing such issues as a priority, the international community seems to push market liberalization as the solution for all ills. Many international projects (including EU initiatives) are selling free markets *as* development and interpreting the success of implementation as a measure of progress. The EU, in particular, has very explicitly positioned itself as the only door to development for ECE. For instance, one of the EU's progress reports, the 2008 *Western Balkans: Enhancing the European Perspective,* states, "The countries of the Western Balkans have moved closer to the EU. This reflects *progress,* albeit uneven, in reforms and in meeting established criteria and conditions … In December 2007, the European Council reaffirmed that 'the future of the Western Balkans lies within the European Union'" (European Union 2008b, 2, emphasis added).

The resulting heavy-handed EU involvement has amounted to finding ways to bring ECE into the fold of the EU, while maintaining control over the design of policy and political frameworks of the newly capitalist states. The requirements of membership have proven nonnegotiable, and trade and production for export are at the forefront of every government's planning. At the same time, the EU's economic and political clout has taken the membership from desired to necessary. Working with the new political and economic elites in ECE, the EU has ensured that the membership is seen as the only option for a prosperous future.

Enlargement

Several ECE states have already joined the EU (the latest two being Romania and Bulgaria in 2007). Others remain "candidates" or "potential candidates,"[5] and their transition processes are marked by intimate involvement on behalf of the EU. Established in 1993, only a year before the World Trade Organization, the EU grew out of the former European Economic Community (also formerly known as the Common Market), a trade organization whose singular purpose was to facilitate *economic* integration of Western Europe.[6] That entity, on the other hand, was an outgrowth of the European Coal and Steel Community. In other words, the EU was founded on the premise of expanding markets, trade, and common economic interests. Nowadays governed by the Parliament and the Council of Ministers (legislative), and the Commission (executive), the twenty-seven EU member states also cooperate in judicial and security matters. While the member states are still autonomous within the union, the EU law overrides national laws. In essence, the entity that was originally conceived as an economic institution now has superlative governmental and judicial powers. The sea of its bureaucratic measures, offices, directorates, reports, and agreements is daunting, but its official policies still betray the primacy of economy, and more specifically trade.

The acceptance of new members into the union falls under the Enlargement policy. At the heart of EU's enlargement strategy is a nonnegotiable set of conditions, also known as the Copenhagen Criteria, which encompass three broad aspects of membership criteria: political (democratic form of government, human rights and protection of minorities, and institutional stability), economic (free market economy, competitiveness on the European market), and legislative criteria (absorption of Acquis Communautaire into national law).

The overarching legal framework of the EU is Acquis Communautaire, or the whole of laws and policies of the EU. Acquis, which includes the Common Agricultural Policy, is colossal, consisting of around 30,000 legal acts adding up to over 100,000 pages of documentation. The Kafkaesque apparatus is an intimidating instrument of political control buried under the layers of formality and vagueness. The term is difficult to translate into English, but it implies that 'the EU "legal and political structure is a given ('acquis') which the new Member State must accept, not challenge or call into question" (Goebel 1995, 1141). By way of illustrating, Goebel's assessment of the accession of Austria, Finland, and Sweden (in 1989, 1992, and 1991 respectively) explains how any difficulties arising from enlargement are seen as the responsibility of the new member states, who then need to adjust their harmonization process rather than even consider the possibility of revisiting EU requirements. In other words, the accession is a process of approval, rather than bilateral negotiation. Such positioning of the EU is cemented in the nature of Acquis, and has been interpreted as rooted in the European "standard of civilization" once used to justify colonial rule (Silvia and Beers Sampson 2003). Silvia and Beers Sampson detail the functions of that "standard of civilization" as both a legal principle and a hegemonic ideal, a standard that has been codified into laws and treaties, which "effectively invalidated the possibility of other 'civilizations' or other 'standards'" (10). As a hegemonic ideal, the standard conceptualizes "European civilization as universal" (13) and is the basis upon which to judge everyone else. During colonial times the European standard was associated with civilization, but presently it is linked to liberal democracy, with the central assumption still being the same – that the European standard is superior and unquestionably desirable.

The second requirement, however, seems to carry the most weight in betraying EU's economic origins. The free-market priorities are clearly identified in the individual Stabilization and Association Agreements, which spell out the accession conditions for each country that hopes to become an EU member. Trade measures and reconstruction are main concerns of the agreements, which also include macro-financial assistance (in the hundreds of millions of euros) provided to candidate and potential candidate countries but only following "the satisfactory implementation of [International Monetary Fund] backed programmes and the fulfillment of economic policy conditions" (Commission of the European Union 2003, 7). Aside from facilitating International Monetary Fund involvement in the region, the stabilization agreements also require harmonization with World Trade Organization rules of trade and eventual membership in the organization: "Accession to the World Trade Organization is fundamental for fostering economic and trade reforms" (European Union 2008a, 15). While outside of Europe the EU is sometimes perceived as protectionist, in ECE it has in fact acted as a catalyst to global capital – as will become apparent later in this chapter, transnational food processing and distribution mega-corporations benefit the most from the transition facilitated by the EU.

Enlargement, Food, and Agriculture

Within this trade-based and painfully bureaucratized policy framework, food is generally treated as an issue of economic and trade development. Provisions for food security and citizen participation in shaping the food system are completely absent. The EU has no comprehensive food policy and, as in most neoliberal states, handles food issues through agricultural policy and food safety law. Its agricultural programs are enormous, however, and the Common Agricultural Policy has consistently accounted for nearly half of the EU's total budget. The Directorate General for Agriculture and Rural Development is the EU overarching body in charge of the thirteen agricultural and rural development directorates.[7] The directorate's mission statement seems a progressive one and includes concerns of environmental sustainability, fairness and quality of rural life, and support to membership candidates and potential candidates. The first and foremost objective of this directorate, however, is "promoting a robust and competitive agricultural sector," and, delving only a bit deeper into its other commitments, one is again faced with the largely market-driven agenda (European Commission n.d. a). For instance, the "Health Check of the Common Agricultural Policy" (European Union 2008a) initiative, despite its name suggesting otherwise, is an *economic* initiative designed to streamline producers' responses to market demands.

Food security concerns are then predictably absent from policy, particularly given that the availability of food in the EU's founding nations are generally good. As Schmidhuber[8] (2007) informs us, the calorie intake in the EU has consistently risen since the 1960s. However, Food and Agriculture Organization's (2000) statistics show that while the undernourished population in the EU may be low in proportion to the overall population, it is not entirely absent. This is particularly true for new member states, and even more so for candidate and potential-candidate countries, where the dietary deficit in 2000 ranged from 130 to 250 calories per person per day (Food and Agriculture Organization 2000) and where poverty rates skyrocketed after the fall of socialism. Wehrheim and Weismann's 2006 study, for instance, indicates that between the late 1980s and mid-1990s, the number of poor in ECE and the former Soviet Union increased tenfold, from some 14 million to 147 million. Yet nothing in the Enlargement Strategy document (European Union 2009) indicates that poverty and food security are even being considered as issues for potential members. The omission of such concerns is in some ways more telling than what the policy includes. The absence of such considerations shows a lack of interest for those aspects of the ECE food system that do not fit the EU vision for the region.

Equally troubling is the fact that the EU fails to acknowledge that transition itself has delivered new challenges to food security. The transition and gradual opening of trade with the EU was supposed to result in larger markets for ECE's primary commodity producers exporting to the EU, but in practice has mostly been characterized by an influx of processed goods from industrialized countries into ECE, as well as the introduction of transnational supermarket chains. The regulation initially designed for the Western European food system is now being applied directly to transition states, along with the EU-style bureaucracy and food safety and quality standards. In the region where the majority of farmers still cultivate small and diverse parcels of land, the one-size-fits-all regulation has proven challenging to many producers.

The EU assistance programs ensure that there are resources for the specific type of reform, and though the assistance is sometimes referred to as "aid," the programs are intended merely to facilitate harmonization with Common Agricultural Policy and EU food law (European Commission 2002, 1). The "aid" is distributed through the Special Accession Programme for Agriculture & Rural Development (SAPARD), which between 2000 and 2005 had an annual budget of over €500 million and has served essentially as an agency in charge of propagating the EU's Common Agricultural Policy. Since 2006 the budget has been decreasing as some of the beneficiary states became full members, and in 2007 it was renamed Instrument for Pre-accession Assistance, but the purpose has remained the same: "to help the beneficiary countries of Central and Eastern Europe deal with the problems of the structural adjustment in their agricultural sectors and rural areas, as well as in the implementation of the acquis communautaire concerning the Common Agricultural Policy and related legislation. It is designed to address priorities identified in the Accession Partnerships" (European Commission n.d. b, 1).

The goal of the EU is then simply to ensure that ECE countries can play by the rules already established. The rules are non-negotiable, and the creation of transition countries' new agricultural and food policy has amounted generally to simple translation of existing EU documents. In Croatia, for instance, the guiding agricultural document is the Instrument for Pre-Accession Assistance for Rural Development plan.

The pre-accession deal with the EU is *the* policy for Croatian agriculture. The approach, including use of the phrase "structural adjustment," harkens back to the 1970s International Monetary Fund and World Bank regime change projects that sent many countries in the global South into a spiralling trap of debt and political powerlessness. As with those institutions, the EU also insists that harmonization with the Union brings progress, and promises expanded markets and opportunities (European Union 2004). Realities of new membership, however, paint a different picture. Gross domestic product of the southeast European members of the EU is the lowest in the EU, with the newest EU members at the bottom: "In 2007 twelve of the fifteen weakest regions were located in Bulgaria and Romania," the two countries that joined earlier that year, indicating that they had met the EU requirements (Roth 2007, 29). While subsidies programs make financial support available to Bulgaria and Romania, many farmers are now struggling to meet EU regulations, and under the Common Agricultural Policy even national support programs have to be in line with EU rules. Consequently, in Romania only 7 per cent of properties classified as agricultural are commercial farms actually producing for markets that can qualify for support payments (Luca 2005).

EU accession alone, however, cannot be blamed for this grim landscape. The transition process itself, with or without EU membership plans, has been challenging throughout ECE. Measured by neoliberal instruments, transition has in some ways been good – a 2006 report for the World Bank indicates that the region "now sends and receives more than two-thirds of its goods and services to and from the rest of the world ... and, since the mid-1990s, trade growth has been faster than in any other region worldwide. The Region's exports have tripled and imports increased two and one-half times" (Broadman 2006, 2). But the growing trade has been beneficial only to some, as social inequality has been a major side effect of transition, particularly affecting the agrarian sector: "In the 1990s the impact of capitalism and globalization, combined with inadequate national policies ... increased the disparities between the urban centres and rural peripheries" (Roth 2007, 30). Broadman's 2006 report indicated that with all the trade growth in ECE, "the share of food and agricultural raw material exports of the total of the Region's exports has declined from 22 percent in 1996 to 16.7 percent in 2003" (81) and that "net overall short-term effect in agriculture is likely to be negative" (157). While other factors have to be considered, such as the corrupt process of privatization, and pre-existing inequalities, the growing inequality and the uneven gains of transition seem to generally be necessary by-products of neoliberalism. As Serova (2007) proposes, for the policymaking process in post-socialism the typical challenge is "the contradiction between efficiency and social justice" (1).

The EU's vision for ECE reveals that contradiction as well, and this is glaringly evident in its progress reports for the potential future members. While poverty, inequality, and food insecurity grow, these reports reveal that the EU is much more concerned with the imperfect land ownership records and lack of modern approaches to farming (European Union 2006a, 2006b, 2006c). Moreover, in a place where poverty and economic insecurity are so significant, the ability of citizens to at least partially produce their own food should be welcome. Yet the EU sees subsistence farming as a problem. For instance, while the report on Croatia acknowledges the importance of subsistence and semi-subsistence farming for bare survival (European Union 2006b, 11), it also suggests that this is an impediment to development: "Key problems that Croatia faces in rural areas include the high number of small-scale subsistence and semi-subsistence farms, the lack of competitiveness of existing commercial farms and the lack of rural economic diversity" (59).

In Croatia, and in Bosnia and Herzegovina, farmers still have to deal with several million uncharted landmines hidden in the soil since the 1990s civil wars, but the EU's official documentation repeatedly ignores this issue and insists on neoliberal ideals of production, efficiency, and competitiveness. Perhaps the truth is that, despite its declarations of humanitarian position on ECE, the EU's work in the region is more self-interested than it would seem at first. The 2008 *Western Balkans: Enhancing the European Perspective*, states, "It is in the interest of the European Union, and of Europe as a whole, that the region should go ahead as rapidly as possible with political and economic reform, reconciliation among peoples and progress towards the EU. Accordingly the EU is mobilising all available policy instruments to support the achievement of these goals" (European Union 2008b, 2). In other words, it is the interests of the EU that have shaped and will continue to shape the process while the actual benefits of EU membership, and reform in general, to ECE countries remain debatable.

Foodscape

Travelling around Serbia's countryside, it is hard to miss the fields close to the road (mostly cornfields) that boast Pioneer Seed signs marking the use of (often experimental) hybrid seed corn. Stores across Serbia are filled with Milka chocolate bars (manufactured in Germany and owned by Kraft), despite Serbia's successful chocolate and candy manufacturer Soko Štark. At bulk stores in Sarajevo, Bosnia, and Herzegovina, there are sacks of chickpeas, an ingredient introduced to the local cuisine with shipments of food aid during the 1990s civil war and now apparently there to stay. In corner stores in Zagreb, Kraš – Croatia's main chocolate and candy manufacturer for almost a century – is being pushed to the sides of displays so that Mars products like Orbit gum (since Mars bought out Wrigley's) and Snicker bars can have the prominent spots.

In a small town set in the heart of Bosnia's most fertile agricultural land along the northern border, farmers are still hesitant to return to their fields because of the thousands of landmines that remain uncharted, years after the civil war ended. Yet at the edge of the town there is an Interex supermarket, which is the name for Intermarché's operations in the Balkans. Intermarché is a 2,000-store transnational supermarket chain based in France, and its shelves here are filled with PepsiCo, Nestlé, and Unilever products. There are even bars of Cote d'Or, the famous Belgian chocolate now also owned by Kraft Foods. In Croatia and Serbia, Interex is not necessary, as home-grown supermarket chains – Konzum and Maxi, respectively – hold virtual monopolies.

Croatia's largest grocery chain, Konzum, has nearly seven hundred stores across the country, from corner stores to supermarkets. Konzum is a subsidiary of Agrokor, Croatia's largest corporate conglomerate, and it boasts a number of store brands for products that include preserves, baby food, and cosmetics. Agrokor also owns several dozen subsidiary operations that include a drugstore chain, filtered and mineral water brands (and bottling plants), flour mills, oil presses, a seasalt plant, an ice-cream brand (and production facility), and many others. Its investments are also found in the primary production sector, as Agrokor owns several agricultural companies as well. Its commercial reach stretches beyond the Croatian borders, as Agrokor's subsidiaries are found in Bosnia and Herzegovina, Serbia, and Slovenia as well. The distribution power of Konzum has granted the company much control over its suppliers and food pricing, leading consumers, suppliers, and politicians to accuse it of monopoly and exploitation (Vujisic Sardelic 2009).

In the Serbian food sector, Delta Holding[9] is by far the most important player and has subsidiaries in primary production, processing, and retail. Delta is involved in "crop improvement" projects with agro-chemical and biotechnology giants such as Syngenta, Pioneer, and BASF, it owns dozens of processing plants, and it runs Serbia's main food retail chain Maxi, with hundreds of stores ranging from corner stores to "hypermarkets."[10] It has recently expanded to run a chain of coffee shops, and its president, Miroslav Mišković, is the region's largest landowner.

Concentration is also seen in Bosnia and Herzegovina, where Croatia's Konzum dominates the market after having acquired dozens of local stores (including Super Nova, Velpro, and VF Komerc super-market chains). The second most significant retail chain is Serbian Delta. Slovenian Mercator owns eight supermarkets and nine massive hypermarkets across Bosnia and Herzegovina, and French Interex boasts twenty-two outlets around the country, eighteen of which are hypermarkets.

Across the western Balkans, store shelves are stocked with value-added products from the EU, particularly processed foods and house-hold products such as cosmetics and cleaning supplies, despite the fact that in those countries there is already a range of processing plants. This free flow of goods sometimes results in substandard products sold in the region, which is partly due to the rushed efforts to open up the markets and partly due to the lack of governmental capacity and will-ingness to control the influx of goods. For example, while Bosnia and Herzegovina has legislation to regulate what food products enter the country, the state has not been able to place inspectors at border cross-ings, so the legislation is not enforced. While the promise of develop-ment is at the foundation of EU membership proposals, the expansion of markets into ECE as well as access to cheap primary commodities seems to be the more palpable result that increasingly benefits corpo-rate agri-food giants such as Kraft and Pioneer.

All three of these states used to be a part of former Yugoslavia where, unlike in most of the Eastern Bloc, land ownership stayed largely in private hands throughout the socialist regime. But agrarians who owned the land also participated in strong farmers' co-ops, which then worked with social enterprises for processing and distribution. Under the socialist regime, social enterprises played multiple roles in the com-munity (addressing a variety of social needs directly linked to social reproduction, such as child care, health benefits, fair price for suppli-ers, etc.), but now in the free market framework, few firms provide that, and if they do, it is entirely voluntary. In other words, not only is control over the food system increasingly concentrated, the system now also provides fewer social benefits and less local financial security. While the diversion of local financial and social benefits is a threat to local food security, the overall trend is a direct challenge to food sovereignty, as the concentration of control over the food means fewer people make decisions about the food system and the associated benefits, including how profit is distributed and used.

Meanwhile, the effects of transition have not been only economic. Throughout ECE, the associated cultural changes have been significant. With the region's entry into the global food economy, new foods, particularly processed, pre-packaged products, have appeared (Harper and West 2003). Introduction of hypermarkets has been promoted as "shoppers' utopia" but has concomitantly shifted citizens' relationship with food and its sources (Smith 2003). Combined with global media's reach, this has also introduced the Western body ideal, including restrictive diets (Thiessen 2002), and eating disorders, previously unheard of in the region. Traditional cuisine is increasingly devalued, as the symbolic role of food requires new foods to represent the new times. Ries (2009) explores the role of the potato in the social, cultural, and political life in post-socialist Russia: "People rising above subsistence cut their connections to potato labor in practice and in narrative. The banker who told me she no longer eats potatoes, said 'We were poor as kids, and I ate so many potatoes my whole life, I told myself that was *it*, I will never eat another potato.' This kind of shift in diet marks class detachment as well as a deliberate dividing of past and present, socialism and capitalism" (202).

The decrease in demand for traditional foods threatens the producers of those foods as well – from traditional farmers, to food processors (such as cheese-makers and butchers), to cooks and chefs. Yet new foods have not corrected social inequalities. Haukanes (2003) found that the responsibility for feeding a family in transition societies was primarily still the domain of women, but the significance of that role was now undermined. In other words, gender inequalities were maintained, but the position of women was seen as less valuable because of the availability of what are considered to be convenience foods: "The capitalist offer of domestic leisure may actually threaten [women's] position within the family" (Passmore and Racine Passmore 2003, 5). This dramatic change of foodscape, however, has not taken place without resistance. With official political channels not a welcoming venue, citizens in ECE have simply distanced themselves from formal politics *and* economy. In many ways they have opted, albeit only partially, out of the system. The following section discusses this in more detail.

Tensions

This chapter's opening quote illustrates the tensions created between the EU's (and global) increasingly neoliberal food regime and the agricultural realities in transition states. Coelho's 2007 segment for CBC Radio describes the frustrations Polish farmers have been facing since the economic reforms began in 1989. At that time the British *Farming Press* announced upcoming changes with a headline that read, "Poland: Up for Grabs" (Coelho 2007). Over the last twenty years, three-quarters of Poland's two million farms remain of the small, family kind, and their stewards now face myriad bureaucratic obstacles, which in addition to being complex, are also proving to be expensive to small producers. The country's experts claim that "Poland's economic progress outweighs lifestyle questions facing small farmers" (Coelho 2007) and that the number of agricultural producers will have to continue to shrink in order to meet the state's economic goals – which are by default those of the EU, the goals of unfettered trade and flow of capital.

Poland is an example of what has been taking place in ECE, as many formerly socialist states continue to experience the growing pains of economic reform. While some form of a democratic government remains a requirement for EU membership, the purpose of such a government becomes elusive once accession has begun. The EU rules apply unquestionably, and there is no instrument for democratic participation in shaping the economic and political system in the new and future member states. Moreover, the rules are applied selectively. For instance, subsidies are discouraged in the transition process, and in some cases their curbing or disappearance is an explicit condition of trade negotiations. At the same time, ECE countries are pressured to accept heavily subsidized products from Western Europe and beyond. Serbia's agricultural strategy document best explains how this is justified: "Although [Common Agricultural Policy] provides much higher support payments per hectare than the current agricultural policy in Serbia, they represent only 0.5 per cent of the EU's GDP, whereas the existing handouts for agriculture in Serbia's budget constitute 2 per cent of the GDP" (Government of Serbia 2005, 6). In relative terms, the subsidies are higher in Serbia and hence need to be curbed, yet Serbia's farmers are at the same time expected to increase efficiency and compete with EU farmers who receive much higher absolute subsidies. This puts a disadvantaged ECE economy at an even more unequal footing, as the cost of land and agricultural inputs in ECE countries is on the rise but their subsidies are being slashed – the market is supposed to be an even playing field, yet farmers in the ECE are essentially being penalized for their countries' relatively low GDP.

Such imbalances shed a great deal of doubt over the EU's vision of "progress." Furthermore, all the claims of democracy that the EU makes cannot hide the simple fact that for transition countries there are no democratic procedures involved in the EU membership preparations. This also implies that there is no democratic forum in which to discuss how the preparations and the eventual membership will affect the food systems of future members or to make democratic decisions about which of the changes are desirable and how they should take place. Citizens of candidate and potential-candidate countries hand over all political power once their desire to be a part of the union has been declared. Of course, a state can choose not to pursue EU membership, but that would equal economic suicide for any European state unless it is prepared to give up all trade. Moreover, by rejecting the EU, a state risks more than just economic isolation. Political isolation in what is already mostly a "visa-free" Europe also makes rejection of EU-oriented future virtually impossible.

Still, just as Polish farmers continue to secretly welcome sparrows (as vividly described in the quote that opens this chapter), subversive ways of maintaining autonomy seem to have taken root in ECE. Despite their governments' powerlessness before the free market forces, the citizens of transition countries continue to maintain a unique form of sovereignty over their daily meals. Food sovereignty efforts have globally been only partly about food, while also being about political and economic autonomy (see Menser; Wright; Massicotte, all in this volume). ECE is no exception here, and the daily foodways fit neatly into the larger food sovereignty efforts, even when not explicitly identified as such. Political sovereignty in the continuously uniting Europe has proven impossible – for nation states in ECE as well as for citizens within those states. Unless willing to risk political and economic isolation, ECE states have no choice but to subject themselves to the EU designs. Unable to politically participate and shape policy, however, citizens make their daily purchases and participation in food production continue to act as a rejection of the EU's, and more broadly global, food regime. This resistance is not organized and is rarely seen as political, but its scope is significant. It is widespread and it takes place at multiple everyday sites, and it is concerned, as James Scott would argue, with immediate gains (1985, 33). Nevertheless it is powerful, particularly where formal channels for challenging formalized governance are absent. These acts, Scott observes, are "institutionally invisible ... [but when] multiplied many thousandfold ... make an utter shambles of the policies dreamed up by their would-be superiors in the capital" (35).

While the EU offers expertise needed to shift production to the industrial model, many are simply not interested. The majority of producers continue to farm on a small scale, and at least in Bosnia and Herzegovina, the numbers of subsistence farmers is growing (European Union 2006a). In Croatia, the EU estimates that "65% of all agricultural holdings are smaller than 2 ha and characterized by mixed production systems" (European Union 2006b, 3). The EU's assistance programs are aimed at commercial producers, yet the majority of production remains outside the neoliberal framework. For many who farm those parcels, farming is not the only, and for some not even the primary, economic activity and is simply a way to supplement either food supply or income or, most often, both. While the EU framework attempts to phase out subsistence farming and dismisses it as economically insignificant, citizens have taken advantage of this marginalization by continuing and in some cases increasing this agricultural activity away from the watchful eye of regulators and policymakers.

Moreover, many producers who do operate commercially choose to opt out of the system all together and operate in the informal market. Official statistics in Serbia, for instance, indicate that a full 81 per cent of all grain, 93 per cent of potatoes, 78 per cent of apples, 79 per cent of milk, and 68 per cent of pork are either used on the farms where they are produced or sold to family and friends (Government of Serbia 2005, 60). This not only flies in the face of official GDP numbers, but it also alludes that the way in which the food economy is conventionally assessed is out of touch with how the social relations and *culture* of food in the region influence the local foodways. As these numbers suggest, most primary production does not even show up in accounting estimates of the agricultural sector. Estimates may not be as high in other potential member states, but are still significant: "Agriculture in Bosnia and Herzegovina plays a considerable role in grey economy and several informal economy activities, which contribute an *additional 40 per cent* to the GDP" (Bojnec 2005, 4; emphasis added). Where the EU regulation and the international markets have made food production technically and bureaucratically difficult, citizens have found ways to bypass these new challenges by simply staying out of those markets.

Farmers' markets exchanges are only partly formalized, if at all, and despite the encroaching supermarket chains, the lively markets remain packed with both sellers and buyers across the western Balkans. The enduring preference for homemade and home-grown products purchased directly from producers is seamlessly mixed with consumption of imported, branded, convenience products from supermarkets. The homemade foods seem to exist quite happily with industrial products, as if these combinations were embodiments of the contradicting results of democratic aspirations and the vortex of the free market. How this hybridization takes place is determined ultimately by the consumers themselves, and, while far from being a movement or a formally politicized force, this decision-making power at the individual and community level remains the greatest challenge to the EU and the most intimate form of food sovereignty.

As Diana Mincyte (2009) describes in her study of an informal dairy market in Lithuania, "EU standards are acting as agents of social engineering that are transforming [post-socialist citizens] into self-disciplined citizens" (83). Participation in informal markets as a form of resistance is a way to create identities "outside of the EU's supervision" (95). As such, the activity is "not a reflexive risk-management practice, but an embodied experience of sovereignty. This is because the risks lie not in the food but in the new economy" (95). As a whole, the activity represents a powerful resistance movement, but it is decentralized and practised individually by producers and consumers alike and therefore virtually impossible to control. Caprice or innovation, this economy is a parallel universe to the EU enlargement efforts – the two models operate virtually independently, though the informal market is fuelled largely by the EU's disconnect from the region's realities. The ECE states' inability to make political and economic decisions independently from the EU has downloaded sovereignty claims to individuals and communities.

Conclusions

Despite the EU's growing political and legal role in Europe, the economic origins of the union are still evident in the free-market principles that define it. The first of the three requirements of EU membership addresses democratic government and human rights. The other two requirements, however, those of a free market and absorption of Acquis Communautaire, have not only overshadowed the first requirement but have also jeopardized it. The recent expulsion of Roma from France speaks to priorities embedded in the foundation of the union. The Roma were sent back to Romania and Bulgaria, despite the free-movement pillar of the EU. The legal loophole is found in the fact that the freedoms of the EU are in reality market freedoms, and the free movement is granted not to citizens but to labour. If unable to find work, migrants can be deported, and with the recent resurgence of nationalism in Europe, this is a growing threat to minorities and racialized groups.

Yet both of those conditions (free market and absorption) are non-negotiable, indicating that the EU is uninterested in democracy unless the democratic process leads to expansion of international trade and harmonization with the existing rules of trade. Accession process stipulations for each potential future member leave no room for citizen participation in food policy development or any other way of shaping the food system. Transition and accession are presented as win-win scenarios for ECE countries, but the foodscape of the region and the growing social inequalities speak for themselves. In the western Balkans, the foodscape reveals that the benefits of transition are being reaped by global capital with ease. The likes of Intermarché continue to expand in ECE, local tycoons establish new regional empires, and the control of the food system becomes increasingly concentrated. The economic changes bring with them social and cultural consequences that are felt by both producers and consumers but seem to not be seriously considered by EU leaders and many governments in ECE.

On the other hand, local producers and processors face growing challenges in the marketplace. They are either treated as too small and therefore irrelevant, or are required to adjust to new and inflexible rules that were fashioned somewhere else and for an entirely different way of producing food. The bureaucracy that surrounds the changes is increasingly complicated, making the system inaccessible to most and therefore impossible to change. Faced with political impotence, citizens resist in ways that are impossible for the EU to control – through grey markets and only partial participation in the formal economy. Food sovereignty, in this case, is an individual and community practice, one that circumvents formal barriers to sovereignty (food and otherwise) by avoiding making formal claims to it. While political and food sovereignty are being dismantled through the bureaucratic channels, subtle everyday practices are rebuilding them by preserving local foodways and thus food sovereignty. The rejection of the EU model of food production and exchange is in itself a rejection of neoliberalism, albeit a covert one and far from being defined as such by its participants.

It should also be noted that in addition to new economic inequalities, the EU model has also been observed to at times reinforce disparities, particularly for women and racialized groups. Those issues are still under-explored in the ECE context and are only mentioned in this chapter, but they remain significant. Social and economic marginalization increases the likelihood someone will participate in the informal sector. Future research that explores how gender, race, and ethnicity play out in the informal food sector in ECE will be invaluable for a better understanding of that sector as a function of everyday resistance.

Neoliberal pressures have inadvertently motivated producers and consumers alike to turn to their communities. Andrée (this volume) describes how Australian farmers have looked to local food networks to alleviate challenges of global trade and liberalization. Similarly, Massicotte (this volume) portrays the stealth that Latin American peasants have shown in organizing and demanding a political voice. Their activism has found resonance in the industrialized world as well (see Ayres and Bosia, this volume). But, as the introductory chapter of this volume suggests, food sovereignty is not a monolith and the case of the western Balkans shows that resistance is sometimes more subtle than that. There, the informal economy is neither very organized (at least not in *formally* recognized ways) nor explicitly politicized, but as Rao and Waldon (2004) point out, "the lack of overt activism by subordinate groups does not necessarily reflect acceptance of the existing social order" (23). Animated and politicized activism has more to do with perceptions of what is possible than with views on justice. A sense of injustice provokes, among those who feel disempowered, more subtle "everyday" forms of resistance. Where the EU pushes for implementation of exogenous policy that attempts to eliminate an entire class of food producers, citizens are circumventing what their state and the EU are prescribing and contributing to a flourishing peasant economy. As McMichael (this volume) indicates, these practices of resistance are not about resurrecting a fantastic peasant utopia; instead, they are commonly borne of crisis.

In the neoliberal project, contradictions are many, and it should not be surprising that the most common form of resistance in ECE is consumer choice – the proverbial "vote with your dollar" action or its informal iteration. Citizens may have no say in what the political process and policy creation will bring next, but they have maintained at least partial autonomy when it comes to their dinner plates – within but without united Europe.

ACKNOWLEDGMENTS

This research was financially assisted by the Social Sciences and Humanities Research Council of Canada, the Ontario Graduate Scholarship program, York University's Fieldwork Cost Fund, and the E.B. Rowe Politics and Policy grant. I owe thanks to Peter Andrée, Marie-Josée Massicotte, and the anonymous reviewers for their thoughtful comments on earlier drafts of this chapter.

NOTES

1 Anthony Winson defines *foodscapes* as physical sites of food purchasing and consumption (2004, 299 and 301), but the term can be used more broadly to refer to the multiple levels of food environments, or the landscape of food production, consumption, and the interventions between those two.
2 The western Balkans region includes Albania and the states that outgrew from former Yugoslavia: Bosnia and Herzegovina, Croatia, the former Yugoslav Republic of Macedonia, Montenegro, Serbia, and Kosovo. Slovenia, the first to split from former Yugoslavia, is already a EU member and not included in the formal western Balkans designation.
3 In Croatia, it has been estimated that three-quarters of firms privatized in the 1990s were privatized in an illegal and fraudulent manner (HRT – Croatian Radio-Television, *Evening News*, 22 June 2007).
4 It is of note that the study was prepared for USDA's Economic Research Service and is explicitly in favour of transition. For instance, for the two transition countries where agricultural production did not fall, namely Uzbekistan and Turkmenistan, the report argues that this "reflects failure to reform, rather than reform success" (Liefert and Swinnen 2002, 12)!
5 A *candidate* country is in the final stages of harmonization and already receiving support payments. A *potential candidate* may have already signed a Stabilization and Association Agreement but is still years away from becoming a full member.

6 The organization also established the European Parliament, members of which were appointed until 1979, when the first election was held. The purpose of both the European Economic Community and its Parliament still remained economic until the introduction of the EU in 1993 which broadened the scope of its international judicial and political powers.

7 The thirteen directorates deal with multilateral negotiations, enlargement, markets, subsidies, four different aspects of rural development, resource management, audits, inter-institutional relations, economic analysis, and agricultural legislation. The complete list is available at ec.europa .eu / dgs / agriculture / who-is-who / who-is-who.pdf .

8 Schmidhuber's study is, in fact, a critique of the Common Agricultural Policy, in that it implies that the policies have had a negative effect on European diets, resulting in unhealthy types and levels of consumption, including over-consumption, high intake of fats, sugar, and salt, and unprecedented levels of overweight and obesity.

9 Delta conglomerate is Serbia's second-largest company, second only to the National Oil Company, which is still in the process of privatization. Delta owns shopping centres, insurance companies, banks, car dealerships, international retail franchises, and so on, and operates in Serbia, Bosnia and Herzegovina, Slovenia, Macedonia, Montenegro, and Bulgaria.

10 *Hypermarket* is the preferred term in Europe for what in North America is known as superstore, and, as in North America, it is usually located in a town's outskirts and therefore accessible only to those with access to a vehicle.

REFERENCES

Bojnec, Stefan. 2005. "Agriculture in Post-war Bosnia and Herzegovina: Social Buffer vs Development." *XIth European Association of Agricultural Economists Congress Proceedings*, Copenhagen.

Broadman, Harry G., ed. 2006. *From Disintegration to Reintegration: Eastern Europe and the Former Soviet Union in International Trade*. Washington, DC: World Bank. http://dx.doi.org/10.1596/978-0-8213-6197-9.

Coelho, Saroja. 2007. "Dispatches: Poland's Old Time Farming." CBC Radio. Aired 13 August. 9 min 43 sec.

Commission of the European Communitie. 2003. *The Stabilisation and Association Process for South East Europe*. http://ec.europa.eu/enlargement/pdf/ enlargement_process/accession_process/how_does_a_country_join_the_eu/ sap/sap_composite_paper_annex1_en.pdf.

European Commission. N.d. a. *Directorate-General for Agriculture and Rural Development Mission Statement.* http://ec.europa.eu/dgs/agriculture/.

– N.d. b. *SAPARD – Programme for Agriculture and Rural Development.* http://www.delhrv.ec.europa.eu/?lang=en&content=1286.

– 2002. *EU Agriculture and Enlargement: Fact Sheet.* http://ec.europa.eu/agriculture/publi/fact/enlarge/2002_en.pdf.

European Union. 2004. *Enlargement and Agriculture.* http://ec.europa.eu/agriculture/publi/enlarge/text_en.pdf.

– 2006a. Bosnia and Herzegovina Country Report in *Study on the State of Agriculture in Five Applicant Countries.* http://ec.europa.eu/agriculture/analysis/external/applicant/bosnia_herzegovina_en.pdf.

– 2006b. Croatia Country Report in *Study on the State of Agriculture in Five Applicant Countries.* http://ec.europa.eu/agriculture/analysis/external/applicant/croatia_en.pdf.

– 2006c. Serbia Country Report in Study *on the State of Agriculture in Five Applicant Countries.* http://ec.europa.eu/agriculture/analysis/external/applicant/serbia_en.pdf.

– 2008a. "Health Check" of the Common Agricultural Policy. http://ec.europa.eu/agriculture/healthcheck/index_en.htm.

– 2008b. *Western Balkans: Enhancing the European Perspective.* Communication from the Commission to the European Parliament and Council. COM (2008) 127.

– 2009. *EU Enlargement Strategy and Main Challenges 2009–2010.* http://ec.europa.eu/europeaid/infopoint/publications/enlargment/43f_en.htm.

Food and Agriculture Organization. 2000. *Undernourishment around the World: Depth of Hunger: How Hungry Are the Hungry?* http://www.fao.org/DOCREP/X8200E/x8200e03.htm.

Goebel, Roger J. 1995. "The European Union Grows: The Constitutional Impact of the Accession of Austria, Finland and Sweden." *Fordham International Law Journal* 18 (4): 1092–190.

Government of Serbia. 2005. *Agricultural Development Strategy.* Belgrade: Author. http://www.minpolj.gov.rs/index.php?id_menu=18.

Harper, Krista, and Barbara West. 2003. "Editors' Notes: Food and Foodways in Postsocialist Eurasia." *Anthropology of East Europe Review* 21 (3): 5–7.

Harrison Schwartz, Andrew. 2006. *The Politics of Greed: How Privatization Structured Politics in Central and Eastern Europe.* Lanham, MD: Rowman and Littlefield.

Haukanes, Haldis. 2003. "Ambivalent Traditions: Transforming Gender Symbols and Food Practices in the Czech Republic." *Anthropology of East Europe Review* 21 (3): 77–82.

Just, Sine Nørholm. 2007. "Deliberative Process and Bargained Positions: The Public (Re-)Presentation of the European Convention." *Critical Discourse Studies* 4 (3): 257–82. http://dx.doi.org/10.1080/17405900701656866.

Liefert, William, and Johan Swinnen. 2002. *Changes in Agricultural Markets in Transition Economies*. USDA Economic Research Service, Agricultural Economic Report No. 806. Washington, DC: USDA.

Luca, Lucian. 2005. "Agricultural Policy: Agro Policies, Electoral Cycles and the EU Accession; What the Current Administration Can and Should Do in Agriculture." *Policy Warning Report* 2:18–24.

Macours, Karen, and Johan F.M. Swinnen. 2000. "Causes of Output Decline in Economic Transition: The Case of Central and Eastern European Agriculture." *Journal of Comparative Economics* 28 (1): 172–206. http://dx.doi.org/10.1006/jcec.1999.1643.

Mincyte, Diana. 2009. "Self-Made Women: Informal Dairy Markets in Europeanizing Lithuania." In *Food and Everyday Life in the Post-Socialist World*, edited by Melissa L. Caldwell, 78–100. Bloomington, IN: Indiana University Press.

Passmore, Ben, and Susan Racine Passmore. 2003. "Taste and Transformations: Ethnographic Encounters with Food in the Czech Republic." *Anthropology of East Europe Review* 21 (1): 37–41.

Rao, Vijayendra, and Michael Waldon. 2004. "Culture and Public Action: Relationality, Equality of Agency, and Development." In *Culture and Public Action*, edited by Vijayendra Rao and Michael Waldon, 3–36. Stanford: Stanford University Press. http://dx.doi.org/10.1596/0-8047-4787-3.

Ries, Nancy. 2009. "Potato Ontology: Surviving Postsocialism in Russia." *Cultural Anthropology* 24 (2): 181–212. http://dx.doi.org/10.1111/j.1548-1360.2009.01129.x.

Roth, Klaus. 2007. "What's in a Region? South-East European Regions between Globalization, EU Integration and Marginalization." *Ethnologia Balkanica* 11:17–41.

Schmidhuber, Josef. 2007. *The EU Diet: Evolution, Evaluation and Impacts of the CAP*. Paper presented at the Global Perspectives meeting in Montreal. http://www.fao.org/fileadmin/templates/esa/Global_persepctives/Presentations/Montreal-JS.pdf.

Scott, James. 1985. *Weapons of the Weak: Everyday Forms of Peasant Resistance*. New Haven, CT: Yale University Press.

Serova, Eugenia. 2007. "Farm Restructuring in Transition: Land Distribution in Russia." *Food Policy for the Developing Countries: The Role of government in the Global Food System*. Ithaca, NY: Cornell University. http://cip.cornell.edu/DPubS?service=UI&version=1.0&verb=Display&handle=dns.gfs.

Silvia, Stephen J., and Aaron Beers Sampson. 2003. "*Acquis Communautaire and European Exceptionalism: A Geneaology.*" American Consortium on European Union Studies Working Paper Series. http://www1.american.edu/aces/Working%20Papers/2003.1.pdf.

Smith, Jeff. 2003. "From *Hazi* to Hypermarket: Discourses on Time, Money and Food in Hungary." *Anthropology of East Europe Review* 21 (3): 179–88.

Sutcliffe, John B. 2010. "Critical Interpretations of Integration in North America and the European Union: A Comparative Evaluation." In *Comparative Regional Integration: Europe and Beyond*, edited by Finn Laursen, 63–82. Surrey: Ashgate.

Thiessen, Ilka. 2002. "Body Alterations and the Creation of the Other: A Macedonian Case." *Anthropology of East Europe Review* 20 (2): 55–9.

Vujisic Sardelic, Snjezana. 2009. "Linic prozvao Agrokor za monopol." *Poslovni Dnevnik*, 22 April. http://www.poslovni.hr/hrvatska/linic-prozvao-agrokor-za-monopol-114180.

Warner, Mildred E. 2009. "Civic Government or Market-Based Governance? The Limits of Privatization for Rural Local Governments." *Agriculture and Human Values* 26 (1–2): 133–43. http://dx.doi.org/10.1007/s10460-008-9181-6.

Wehrheim, Peter, and Doris Wiesmann. 2006. "Food Security Analysis and Policies for Transition Countries." *Electronic Journal of Agricultural and Development Economics* 3 (2): 112–43.

Winson, Anthony. 2004. "Bringing Political Economy into the Debate on the Obesity Epidemic." *Agriculture and Human Values* 21 (4): 299–312. http://dx.doi.org/10.1007/s10460-003-1206-6.

PART THREE

Food Sovereignty in Contentious Politics

9 Feminist Political Ecology and La Vía Campesina's Struggle for Food Sovereignty through the Experience of the Escola Latino-Americana de Agroecologia (ELAA)

MARIE-JOSÉE MASSICOTTE

What we need is a more profound debate [about food and agro-fuel] with society as a whole ... on what is our energy sovereignty, our food sovereignty? ... [W]hat model of society do we want? ... What are we going to use our territories, our lands, and our natural resources for? To produce fuels for exportation?

MST member, personal interview, Belém, Brazil, January 2009

There has always been a crisis of distribution in Brazil, not a food crisis. But what exists now is the large proportion of ethanol production, for example. If you walk in the north and southeast in Rio Grande do Sul, you can see the proportion of soya ... The role of small agriculture has changed, but it is crucial. Because today the big fazendeiros are mostly producing sugarcane, soya, and celluloses from large extensions of eucalyptus – that's among the key struggles of the movement, of La Vía Campesina – and beef production that causes deforestation in Amazonia to introduce these cultures ... But in reality, we don't eat paper; we don't live only with alcohol or soya. So today, who guarantees the production of food in Brazil? It is the small agriculture.

MST member, personal interview, Sao Paulo, Brazil, July 2009

Food is a vital element for social reproduction, and its quality and quantity depends on *Pacha Mama* (Mother Earth) and people's wisdom and practices, especially among rural communities. However, only recently (since the 1990s, following mass mobilizations and protests, and especially since the 2007–8 food crisis across the globe) have public opinion and the often-myopic disciplines of political science and economics begun awakening to the contentious nature of food politics. For their part, family farmers and peasants have long understood the risks and felt the multiple impacts of the globalizing model of agro-industrial development, which is based on export-oriented and capital-intensive monocultures. Their livelihoods, their modes of farming, and their cultures have been under threat since the so-called Green Revolution of the post–Second World War era that pushed for greater "productivity" through increased agrochemical, technological, and energy inputs. In many parts of the world, they use more sustainable methods not because it is trendy or more profitable, but because it is their traditional way of farming (Altieri 2010) and / or because they lack the resources to incorporate expensive agro-toxics (i.e., pesticides), energy-intensive methods (i.e., petroleum), and genetically modified seeds into their production. This is still, too often, especially true for rural women.

Hence, peasant activists around the world have a tough row to hoe. Not only are they dedicating themselves to the demanding field of small-scale agriculture, but they are also fighting inequalities and struggling for a piece of land that they can call theirs. These common travails sometimes culminate in grassroots resistance movements, repoliticizing the public sphere by inciting peasants to organize and participate in national movements, campaigns, and transnational networks (Dal Maso 2004; Wittman 2009; Wolford 2004, 2010). In so doing, they are contesting and redefining the politics of place and scale – that is, they are challenging the socio-political construction of the "local," the "national," and the "global," concepts that usually confine rural movements to a bounded local place associated with traditional (read pre-modern or backward) ways of life, identities, and cultures (Massicotte 2010b; Escobar 2001, 2008).

Despite a historical lack of mass media and academic attention to peasant organizations – yet we have witnessed a renewed interest in recent years – small farmers, rural women, and peasants continue to innovate and defend their modes of living and social reproduction at multiple scales. They have been key players in mass mobilizations since the early days of what are now associated with alter-globalization movements, from opposing the World Trade Organization (WTO) in Seattle in 1999 to the more recent mobilizations held in parallel with the international climate change meetings in Copenhagen in 2009 (COP15), Cochabamba in 2010 (Mother Earth Summit), and Cancun in 2010 (COP16). Indeed, in light of recent international trade negotiations that included agriculture within the WTO regulatory system, despite intense protests and resistance against it, many peasant organizations feel an urgent need to build stronger alliances at the national and transnational levels.

La Vía Campesina,[1] one such transnational peasant network, was founded in 1993 to articulate and defend the position of small- and medium-sized producers. Operating in opposition to the main institutions that promote neoliberal development and governance (e.g., the WTO, the International Monetary Fund, and the World Bank at the international level, and NAFTA, the EU, and the Asia-Pacific Economic Cooperation at the regional level), La Vía Campesina is now active in sixty-nine countries, representing about 150 organizations, and its numbers continue to expand. La Vía Campesina members build solidarity links among small-farmer organizations that fight for social justice and people's food sovereignty. These efforts translate into a call for gender equity as well as decentralized, democratic, and sustainable models of agricultural production that prioritize the needs of local communities while respecting cultures and ecosystems (see La Vía Campesina 2010).

This chapter examines contentious food politics and the experiences of peasant activists and small-scale food producers by exploring the meaning and potential of food sovereignty as an emerging norm of global governance, developed by La Vía Campesina and their allies in Brazil and Latin America. I begin by discussing global governance as an analytical framework. I then introduce feminist political ecology as a complementary approach to critical political economy, for the former can yield a better understanding of the needs and practices of the locally grounded peasant organizations that promote food sovereignty and gender equity. In the final sections, I further examine the meanings and practices of food sovereignty through an analysis of the Latin American School of Agro-ecology (Escola Latino Americana de Agroecologia, or ELAA hereafter), which is based in Brazil and coordinated by members of La Vía Campesina–Brazil and the Landless Rural Workers Movement (MST).

The objectives of this discussion are to better understand such experiences, to show how they are not only challenging the dominant model of agro-industrial production and distribution, but also bringing today's neoliberal model of development and governance under scrutiny, and to call upon researchers to rethink their own epistemological framework of analysis to learn from local actors. Following the work of Gibson-Graham (2006), I argue that such experiences have the potential to democratize agricultural governance from the ground up, by working from within rural communities to experiment with agro-ecological practices and to create opportunities for interaction with allies on different scales. Through their localized actions and struggles, peasant movements are producing relevant knowledges and practices, as well as non-statist forms of governance that connect across borders.

Theorizing Global Governance: Insights from Movements and Feminist Political Ecology

Global governance has emerged as a new framework of analysis more inclusive than state-centred regime theories. The term *global governance* generally refers to regulatory mechanisms, both private and public, formal and informal, used for coordinating socioeconomic relations (Massicotte 2010b; Rosenau and Czempiel 1992; O'Brien et al. 2000). Since the mid-1970s, numerous analysts have recognized that the state is no longer the only source of regulation, nor is it a very effective one. That is where the model of global governance comes in, for it encompasses evolving interactions from the local level and beyond, to state policies and transnational norms and institutions. It also has the potential to extend to new but often neglected actors and processes, such as peasant organizations that call for food sovereignty as an emerging norm (Pimbert 2008), which contest the dominant model of agricultural governance.

Susan Strange (1999) was among the first scholars to discuss the "Westfailure system" – that is, the collapse of the Westphalian system that most political scientists associate with the modern state system. Following a wave of debt and financial crises during the 1980s and 1990s, Strange (1986) denounced the impact of growing financial speculation, referring to it as "casino capitalism." She further highlighted the incapacity of territorially bounded "sovereign" states to control their financial systems, to properly manage their environments, and to promote greater social justice within their borders and beyond.

Many other analysts have acknowledged the limits of state and interstate institutions, some calling for greater regulatory and enforcement capacity beyond the state and in new areas (Commission on Global Governance 1995; Falk 1995), while others insist on the need for greater autonomy and a decentralization of power below the state level (Blaser et al. 2010). Gustavo Esteva and Mahdu Suri Prakash (1998), for instance, highlight the multiple risks of co-optation for civil society actors engaging with institutions of global governance. Because such engagement could contribute to further legitimizing "global" institutions of power and norm-making, they instead privilege locally grounded activism, self-determination, and a disregard of (inter)state and market elites.

By actively seeking autonomy – or at least diminished dependence upon states and transnational corporations (TNCs) for food production and distribution – grassroots organizations can help to empower local forces and to consolidate alternative forms of governance that are more adequately adapted to the needs and cultures of their communities (Altieri 1995). Hence, a key question for political and social scientists, as well as knowledge producers from social movements and organizations, concerns the proper site(s) and scale(s) of social transformation, and the role and potential of civil society in democratizing and / or strengthening the norms and institutions of global governance.

In the global South, the neoliberal undertaking of global governance often came in the form of the World Bank's stabilization and structural adjustment programs (SAPs), which favoured such trends as intensive export-led monocultures to reduce and reimburse the external debt of many countries. While neoliberalism remains the dominant political project behind global governance, it has always been and continues to be widely contested, especially in light of the widespread financial, political, and socio-ecological crises in recent decades.[2] Indeed, after massive protests in the global South contesting SAPs put in place by interstate organizations – often in partnership with irresponsible state authorities plagued by mega-debts – we have witnessed a resurgence of rural and urban opposition to neoliberal governance (Gills 2000; Juris 2008; Macdonald 2002; Massicotte 2010a). In turn, an increasing number of studies are examining the growing role that civil society forces are playing in domestic and global politics (e.g., Amoore 2005; O'Brien et al. 2000; Held 2006). However, most analyses remain centred on (inter)state institutions and the strategies used by civil society actors to make TNCs more responsible (e.g., Lozano 2008). In contrast, this chapter will examine how rural grassroots movements are governing themselves and seeking ways to make governance practices more democratic and sustainable, in spite of multiple pressures and constraints.

Moreover, social scientists often depend on international political economy (IPE) analytical tools in their efforts to understand the main trends and changing socio-political and economic processes within and beyond states, especially when analysing today's mechanisms of global governance. By adopting macro-approaches that focus on global trends, wide-reaching structural constraints imposed by dominant capitalist and political forces beyond national and local scales (and apart from nature-culture dynamics), many IPE scholars unwittingly tend to reproduce the myth that the state is powerless, an argument often used by state officials to justify their lack of action or deficient regulations. For instance, world-system theorists have highlighted the relations of domination and exploitation-enrichment between different regions of the globe, and have stressed the incorporation of non-capitalist regions and "peripheral" societies into the globalizing market economy led by "core" countries. By so doing, they can neglect to consider how specific ecosystems and social reproduction are fundamental elements in the maintenance of every political-economic model of society and governance.

Hence, my objective is to build on political economy traditions to study the complex interactions between power relations and political economic norms and institutions, in conjunction with (re)productive activities of individuals and communities evolving in specific geopolitical and cultural places, *and* ecosystems. One needs to note here that ecosystems are "significantly but not always entirely socially constructed" (Greenberg and Park 1994, 1). Some insightful works in both "cultural political economy" (CPE) and everyday IPE have drawn from the work of Karl Polanyi (see introduction, this volume) and others to demonstrate how explicit efforts have been necessary to "dis-embed" the economy from socio-cultural and natural life, as part of the modern capitalist development. Indeed, these scholars reject the idea of a naturally self-regulated market and attempt to illuminate the cultural aspects of power relations and / or alternative practices that have survived in parallel with the dominant market economy, or that have emerged in response to problems created by global capitalism (Munk 2007; Hobson and Seabrooke 2007; Best and Paterson 2010; Davies 2006, 2010).

In this vein, the chapter will draw more directly on the works of Arturo Escobar and J.K. Gibson-Graham, as well as Dianne Rocheleau, Barbara Thomas-Slayter, and Esther Wangari – scholars who draw from feminist political ecology and postcolonial studies to make sense of the many aspects of political ecology. These approaches are well equipped to explore the creative developments and adaptations that persist alongside market relations (Gibson-Graham 2006) to make locally grounded initiatives more visible and more relevant. Indeed, such works highlight the role of marginalized actors and spaces in maintaining alternative practices and meeting the challenges that are faced by so many rural communities and ecosystems. Moreover, many political economy studies continue to insist on growth and productivity measures, without paying sufficient attention to the environment, gender, and the quality of life experienced in communities. There is therefore a need for (international) political economists and political scientists to draw from other perspectives, and from activists' own knowledges and practices, that offer complementary tools to make sense of the relationship between nature and culture, and to examine the role and potential of place-based, less-powerful actors, in shaping today's political ecologies.

As Escobar notes, political ecologists examine, among other things, the "relation between environment, development and social movements; between capital, nature and culture; production, power, and the environment; gender, race and nature ... [and] environmental governmentality" (2010, 92). These interrelations allow us to observe the centrality of ecological issues, and localized and gendered practices. They are especially useful in navigating the deficiencies of today's locally dependent but globalizing food systems. These relationships also shed light on the struggles of peasant and women farmers, who are often dealing with food, land, and biodiversity scarcity, as well as genetically modified organism (GMO) contamination and very often the intrusion of market, technology, and state forces that create new imbalances and socio-environmental injustices (McMichael 1994, 2008; Harvey 1996). Indeed, numerous studies have highlighted the growing number of rural communities in which the neoliberal model of agricultural trade and governance translates into dispossession (of land, seeds, and knowledges), displacement, insecurity, and the dislocation of local cultures, economies, and households (e.g., Fitting 2006; Marchand 2008). These processes are experienced differently by men, women, and racialized groups seeking to sustain themselves in an ecologically viable way.

However, while one needs to acknowledge such impacts and the presence of pervasive obstacles for small-scale agricultural producers – especially for those promoting agro-ecological methods – there is also an urgent need for research on alternative practices and discourses that some communities seek to consolidate. This is where the works of feminist political ecology researchers are useful, for they turn our attention to the actors, knowledges, and practices that have been largely marginalized or nullified under the modern liberal canon of Western sciences. This particular approach adds a gender dimension to the analysis of "decision-making processes and the social, political, and economic context that shapes environmental policies and practices" (Rocheleau et al. 1996, 4). It takes seriously not only global contexts and Western sciences, but also local knowledges and practices embedded in specific cultures and ecosystems. Gibson-Graham and Santos similarly offer original insights and a framework of analysis to (re)valorize and illuminate the non-hegemonic agents, practices, and knowledges that have been marginalized by Western sciences and modernity, but that also play a key role in locally grounded governance practices.

In the words of Santos, modernity has created five monocultures (knowledge, linear time, classification, the universal and the global, and capitalist efficiency and productivity) that marginalize, discredit, or render invisible a variety of knowledges, practices, and actors. That is, modernity has generated a sociology of "producing" absences as though certain actors and practices simply don't exist or are insignificant, especially in the global South. However, instead of emphasizing the exploitation and domination of such actors and practices, Santos proposes a "sociology of emergences" that consists of identifying, defining, and thus "making known" alternative practices and discourses that are already emerging without their being fully realized (Santos 2006b, 15–34). The political objective of Santos's new epistemology is "to transform impossible into possible objects, absent into present objects, invisible or non-credible subjects into visible and credible subjects" (15). Santos thus insists on the need to recognize a diversity of relevant and valuable knowledges, arguing that "all ignorance is of certain knowledge, and all knowledge is the overcoming of a particular ignorance" (19).

For feminist political ecologists, diverse knowledges should also include those emerging from "the gendered science of survival," or alternative sciences and gendered experiences, grounded in everyday life (e.g., subsistence farming, unequal access between men and women to natural resources in isolated highland communities), South and North. Discussing gendered science, Rocheleau et al. further ask what science is, who does it, and for what purposes, in order to question "the apparently separate sciences and technologies of production, and reproduction, public and private domains, and home, habitat, and workplace spaces" (1996, 7).[3] Hence, it does not simply call for a valorization of any kinds of localized knowledges and practices, but for a recognition of the very existence of gendered knowledges and practices emerging from within specific communities and ecosystems that mutually shape, adapt, and resist each other, as well as the encroachment of external pressures usually privileging men and exploiting women and nature.

Whereas many analysts usefully examine the constraining power of today's globalizing forces, feminist political ecologists reclaim multiple knowledges and emerging alternatives that are arising amidst a radically democratic utopia, to see how concrete alternative experiences *en puissance* are already being practised and promote the construction of other possible worlds. As Gibson-Graham emphasizes, there are multiple non-capitalist experiences present everywhere that are helping to sustain – and often simultaneously resist – the market economy, based on unequal gendered relations, in important ways (e.g., producer and consumer co-operatives, solidarity economies, unpaid and volunteer work, the retired, etc.; see the iceberg model, 2006, 70). While these local practices are relevant subjects of study, they are also sources of knowledges that can offer ways to go beyond the limits imposed by today's neoliberal model of development and governance.

When discussing the need to transform our food systems, Eric Holt-Giménez and Raj Patel remind us that, "like green grass breaking through the asphalt, local equitable and sustainable alternatives are thriving in the cracks of the global food system" (2009, 98). Such alternatives carve out spaces to invent and reinforce "other possibles" that are worth studying and experimenting with, despite their limitations and the internal contradictions that arise in trying to do so.

The Landless Rural Workers Movement and La Vía Campesina: Peasant Activism for Food Sovereignty and Social Change

Like indigenous movements, peasant resistance forces are uniquely rooted in places and local struggles. This is certainly the case with the Brazilian Landless Rural Workers Movement (Movimento dos Trabalhadores Rurais Sem Terra, known as the MST) created in 1984. Contributing to a sociology of emergence, this movement has empowered peasants to use collective action to take control over the most fundamental resource in their lives: land. Operating in Brazil, one of South America's most unequal countries in concentration of fertile land, the MST has openly challenged the dominant patterns of land tenure, as well as agriculture and trade politics (Branford and Rocha 2002). As one MST organizer in charge of the production sector in the state of Rio Grande do Sul explains, "The MST exists today because of a historical problem of land concentration that privileges a few and discriminates against millions ... To obtain the de-concentration and the democratization of lands ... requires organized people. This is the principal function and raison d'être of the MST" (personal interview, Porto Alegre,

Brazil, June 2009). In the short term, the MST privileges direct action through collective organizing and land occupations. Land occupations provide "an alternative for employment for millions of families ... to live and feed themselves [social reproduction] ... working mainly in the agricultural sector," thus reclaiming the value of subsistence farming as a viable option for the present and the future (MST member, personal interview, Curitiba, Brazil, June 2005). In the medium term, the MST fights for land reform "to modify the level of land ownership concentration [and] to democratize the ownership of land in Brazil," which requires much greater efforts, by men and women within rural and urban movements to address deep-rooted gender and racial forms of discrimination and inequality. In the longer term, it seeks "structural changes ... to build a society that is more just, more human, [and] more democratic" (MST member, personal interview, Curitiba, Brazil, June 2005).

Through its striving, the MST has successfully worked from below to produce innovations in democratic governance through promoting participatory decision-making, collective action, and access to education for all (see Wittman 2009; Wolford and Wright 2003). For instance, in every MST camp and settlement, everyone is involved in various sectors (e.g., health, education, production, cultural activities, leisure, and administration) through *nucleos* – groups of people or families in which decisions and activities are made and implemented collectively – in an effort to respond to the needs of the whole community. Moreover, through their everyday practices and interactions within MST settlements, members are invited to exercise citizenship rights and responsibilities and to govern themselves, what many refer to as promoting *autogestão* (Wittman 2009; Rangel Loera 2010). This is very much in line with the "maximal democracy" and self-determination concepts discussed by Michael Menser (2008; this volume). In order to strengthen the autonomy, capacity, and emancipatory potential of individuals, MST leadership promotes access to education and training as one of its central objectives.

While being territorially grounded in specific locations (Stédile and Fernandes 1999; Wolford and Wright 2003), the MST and other peasant and small-farmers organizations across Latin America are active in transnational networks and initiatives such as La Vía Campesina (Desmarais 2009; Patel 2006; Borras 2008), the Coordinadora Latinoamericana de Organizaciones del Campo (CLOC, or Latin American Coordination of Rural Organizations), and the World Social Forum.[4] They also mobilize to protest the widespread acceptance of norms and practices that are against their interests, such as the use of GMOs and the dominant model of trade agreements.

As mentioned earlier, La Vía Campesina is a young and expanding transnational network that mobilizes grassroots organizations of small-scale farmers, rural women and youth, indigenous people, and agricultural workers. Its main goal is to transform today's agriculture using the principles of food sovereignty by providing its members with a platform from which to voice their experiences and demands. This powerful network self-identifies as an "autonomous, pluralist and multicultural movement, independent of any political, economic, or other type of affiliation" (La Vía Campesina 2010) and strives for global justice, food sovereignty, gender equity, and sustainable agriculture and communities. While La Vía Campesina is making modest strides towards these goals, much remains to be done to realize them within La Vía Campesina and in today's society as a whole. While the MST is one of the key founders and participants in La Vía Campesina, it is mostly women's groups within the transnational network that have insisted on and continue to fight for greater gender equity. The following section will examine the Escola Latino-Americana de Agroecologia as a concrete way in which members of La Vía Campesina are trying to democratize knowledges and to put the principles of food sovereignty into practice via mutual learning and solidarity among rural communities in various regions. But first, we need to clarify the concept of food sovereignty, as defined by the peasants themselves.

Food Sovereignty

As Michael Menser (this volume) also explains, for La Vía Campesina and its allies, "Food sovereignty is the right of peoples to define their own food and agriculture; to protect and regulate domestic agricultural production and trade in order to achieve sustainable development objectives; to determine the extent to which they want to be self-reliant; [and] to restrict the dumping of products in their markets ... Food sovereignty does not negate trade, but rather, it promotes the formulation of trade policies and practices that serve the rights of peoples to safe, healthy, and ecologically sustainable production" (La Vía Campesina et al., quoted in Rosset 2003).

Here, La Vía Campesina is responding to the Green Revolution's limited version of "food security," focused mainly on access and distribution as the means to safeguard sufficient food for everybody that has been used to justify large-scale monocultures and the use of GMOs to feed the "poor" (see Shiva 1997; Martin and Andrée, this volume). In contrast, the campaign for "people's food sovereignty" emerged from the experiences of small producers. It calls for a radical reorganizing of food production, distribution, and consumption patterns that contests the common understanding that large-scale agriculture is necessarily better and more efficient than small-scale farming, as is implied within the WTO regulatory framework of agricultural governance.

Food sovereignty advocates also demand that peasants and small farmers be recognized as full citizens with rights and responsibilities by virtue of the major contributions they make towards the well-being of people, ecosystems, and social reproduction (Wittman 2009; Woods 2006). As described in Article 1 of the Declaration of the Rights of Peasants and promoted by Lá Vía Campesina members, "A peasant is a man or woman of the land, who has a direct and special relationship with the land and nature through the production of food and / or other agricultural products. Peasants … rely above all on family labour and other small-scale forms of organizing labour. Peasants are traditionally embedded in their local communities and they take care of local landscapes and of agro-ecological systems" (La Vía Campesina 2010). In light of the central role of peasants described above, the proponents of food sovereignty highlight at least three key dimensions that need to be taken into consideration in order to promote a sustainable model of agriculture and communities: socio-economic well-being, ecology, and democratic governance.

The first dimension refers to the productive and reproductive roles of small-scale food producers who resist the dislocation of rural communities by emphasizing peasants' crucial role as workers, and by providing sources of employment and subsistence locally. This is usually the priority when MST families get legal titles from Brazil's National Institute of Colonization and Agrarian Reform (INCRA):[5] they work the land for their own subsistence (MST members, personal interviews, Porto Alegre and *assentamento*, Rio Grande do Sul, Brazil, June 2009). Eco-feminist and political ecology researchers speak to the first dimension of food sovereignty. They have demonstrated, on the basis of empirical analyses, that a significant number of small food producers are helping to preserve and maintain ecosystems and biodiversity while sustaining agricultural production and social reproduction (Rocheleau et al. 1996). Highlighting how rural communities – and especially rural women from the global South – are disproportionately disadvantaged in access to land, formal education, technology, natural resources, and monetary income, the subsistence perspective developed by eco-feminists illuminates the crucial role of women and family farmers in sustaining life itself (Mies and Bennholdt-Thomse 1999). The food sovereignty framework also emphasizes the need for more balanced relations between men and women, as well as between communities and nature. It includes the right of all peoples to a healthy diet, while respecting the diversity of human cultures and ecosystems.

In this vein of research, the second, ecological dimension of food sovereignty, is put forward by activists to demonstrate that small-scale producers act as stewards of natural resources and of a multiplicity of biological cultures and cultural practices, while helping to reduce the pressure on cities and of migration flows by being able to sustain themselves in rural spheres. With the transnational campaign on food sovereignty promoting responsible ecological policies, La Vía Campesina has attracted many supporters and has built coalitions with women's groups, environmental and human rights activists, indigenous peoples advocacy groups, and other socio-political movements that are, as Michel Pimbert notes, "the prime movers behind [this] newly emerging ... policy framework" (2008, 3). For example, since 2007 approximately 150 groups have joined forces with La Vía Campesina to form the Southern-led coalition Climate Justice Now! (CJN!), which aims to reclaim solutions for climate change that promote social, ecological, and gender justice. These activists not only seek to put pressure on formal negotiations about climate change, but they are active "on the ground and in the streets, to promote genuine solutions that include ... sustainable family farming and peoples' food sovereignty." They maintain that small-scale agriculture contributes to "cool[ing] down the planet" by reducing the use of chemical products and long-distance food circuits (CJN! 2010).

The third dimension of food sovereignty, democratic governance, also underlines the capacity and willingness of peasant organizations to assert self-determination and democratic decision-making. Eric Holt-Giménez (2009) argues that food sovereignty activists call for self-governance of the food system by those who cultivate the land. He holds that these farmers should have the capacity to decide what types of food they produce, how they produce it, and where and how it should be distributed or consumed. This does not mean that small farmers can opt for *any* form of agriculture, but that, in line with food sovereignty principles, they should be able to decide for themselves while favouring healthy products and diversified local farming practices. They should also choose proximity markets over export-oriented industrial monoculture, which is described as being energy intensive (production and transportation) and requires the use of pesticides and agro-chemicals, thus reducing the quality of products, soils, and ecosystems. Clearly, the democratic capacity of small producers to control their own production through self-determination (or democratic governance from below) contrasts sharply with the perceptions *and* real impacts of today's globalizing food regime and the concentration of market power and agricultural trade politics in the hands of a few agro-industrial corporations (Otero 2008; McMichael 2006).

To give but one example of the lack of democratic decision-making power on the dominant, globalizing model of industrialized agricultural governance, the case of Pilgrim's Pride Corporation is quite revealing. As of 2010, Pilgrim's Pride was considered one of the fastest-growing companies in the industry; it was ranked 317 on Fortune 500s list of the largest companies in the world, and was the fourth most profitable in the food-production industry (Fortune 500 2010). Pilgrim's Pride is the United States' third-largest poultry company, and the second-largest in Mexico. Active in eighty countries, it takes satisfaction in being a vertically integrated production, processing, and distribution company, controlling every part of the process from breeding, hatching, and raising chickens to processing the meat that ends up on our plates.

Without a doubt, Pilgrim's Pride is running a profitable business. It contracts "shared risk" agreements with small farmers and provides them with "chickens, feed, technical assistance, medicines and in some instances, loans to upgrade their facilities," which, as Gaspar Real Cabello notes, creates a deeply asymmetric relationship between the "partners" (2003, 134). Within such a "partnership," Mexican chicken farmers working with the company receive a salary based on their productivity, and in return they need to carefully follow a prescribed "industrial recipe" and deliver grown chickens following established requirements and standards. In this way, Pilgrim's Pride's farmers are effectively stripped of their self-determination, losing control over the methods and the kinds of food they produce, where it is sold, and at what price.

The Mexican peso crisis of 1994 played a large part in establishing these so-called partnerships between Pilgrim's Pride and small, knowledgeable chicken farmers in Mexico. The company came onto the scene when the farmers were at their most desperate, buying facilities and offering the technology and credit farmers "needed" to avoid bank-ruptcy. This "help" was furthermore presented as an effective way to face the increased competition introduced by NAFTA and the eventual opening of North American borders to poultry trading. In concrete terms, Pilgrim's Pride ushered into Mexico an increased dependency on technology, a decreased dependency on agricultural workers, and a notable drop in the price of compensation for farm work.

These "partnerships" are representative of the general shifts that have taken place in the agricultural sector. For many Mexican farmers facing the peso crisis and rapid trade liberalization, the options were often limited to "modernization" through unequal partnerships with large TNCs, or else disappearance. Cabello notes that the introduction of technology into the Mexican poultry industry has vastly transformed the sector, and today only about 30 per cent of the overall chicken pro-duction in Mexico comes from traditional producers, and 70 per cent makes full use of technology in a TNC-dependent fashion (Cabello 2003). As David Harvey (2005) argues, this is a new trend of "accumula-tion by dispossession," an arrangement in which farmers are forced to forfeit their self-determination and their capacity to use their expertise and techniques. While they remain partial owners of the land and some of the capital, they make no management or production decisions and they do not own the product of their paid labour (here, the chickens).

Nonetheless, this is not the only story that needs to be told about small food producers. As one member of the MST explained when asked about what strategies the movement will use to face economic and food crises,

> One of our strategies is what you saw in our *asentamentos*, where people try to obtain as much autonomy as possible, from production until the agro-industrialization of all our products. We put a lot of effort not to produce and sell only primary products to anybody in any market ... We don't want to just sell seeds, but produce and sell ecological seeds, pro-duce in a correct way in terms of both ecological management and the human beings that are working and producing them. This is a central ele-ment of our struggle, that we can gain this autonomy, which is not easy ... Seeds are the patrimony of the peoples, in the service of humanity. So we can talk of food sovereignty only from the moment that we have in our hands the means to produce. (Personal interview, Sao Paulo, Brazil, July 2009)

As this quotation suggests, there is a palpable urgency to promote and consolidate alternative models of agriculture and self-governance from below. Some alternative experiences already exist and peasants are struggling to sustain themselves amidst global monoculture and the abandonment of small-scale rural producers by most states. These new initiatives are promoting democratic governance and sustainable agricultural production via those who work and live on the land. In this respect, Michel Pimbert argues that the notion of food sovereignty might be "best understood as a *transformative process* that seeks to recreate the democratic realm and regenerate a diversity of autonomous food systems based on equity, social justice and ecological sustainability" (2008, 3). The food sovereignty campaign can therefore be understood as a flexible mobilizing tool around a highly political project that opposes the commodification of food and seeks ways to open new spaces to revalorize smaller-scale agricultural practices that offer viable alternatives, and that are socially and ecologically more just and sustainable. Holt-Giménez and Patel (2009) add that attaining food sovereignty requires both individual and collective actions to reclaim popular control over all aspects of the food system, from the very ownership of land and seeds to the food that we eat. Indeed, numerous aspects of the food system have been largely, but not completely, captured by large corporations, which limit the choices that consumers can make at the grocery store and fail to provide adequate information and products that nurture socially and ecologically responsible options (Smythe, this volume).

Food sovereignty thus calls for a democratization of governance and decision-making about food production and food policies by small-scale farmers themselves as local experts, often the most knowledgeable ones to make decisions on local ecosystems and their adaptability. Even though "most of the world's food is grown, collected and harvested by over 2.5 billion small-scale farmers, pastoralists, forest dwellers and artisanal fisherfolk" (Pimbert 2008, 3), (inter)state policymakers all too often raise barriers instead of supporting and creating opportunities for these small producers. In such a climate, Pimbert argues that the only way for small farmers to regain control over their food and lives is to initiate a food sovereignty policy framework, in partnership with urban citizens, that includes "several mutually supportive national and international policies to strengthen the autonomy and resilience of more localised food systems" (3). Despite intense debates among proponents of food sovereignty about types of national and international regulations that need to be implemented (and whether such regulations need to be implemented at all), a growing number of analysts and citizens recognize that current norms and policies need to be challenged because they are unsustainable and often run against the very efforts of those promoting food sovereignty and environmental justice. Food is *not* just another commodity, but a human right. Like water, it is essential for sustaining life itself.

In this vein, agro-ecology practices respond to unsustainable norms and policies by promoting forms of agriculture that are environmentally and socially responsible. As Miguel Altieri (1995) explains, advocates of agroecology seek to reduce chemical and energy inputs in agriculture, while relying on the interactions between biological elements to maintain or revitalize the quality of soil, seeds, and productivity. Agroecology also emphasizes the central role that many women and small producers play as knowledgeable actors, contributing to sustain life and diversified ecosystems. The following section turns to the case study of the ELAA, one of La Vía Campesina's schools of agro-ecology, in order to better understand the meanings and practices that give form to the concepts of agro-ecology and food sovereignty among small farmers and peasant movements.

Putting Food Sovereignty into Practice: The Escola Latino-Americana de Agroecologia (ELAA)

In June 2005, I first visited the site of the Latin American School of Agroecology (ELAA) in the southern municipality of Lapa, Paraná, Brazil. I was there to meet with activists from approximately seventy families affiliated with the Landless Rural Workers Movement (MST) and had recently received formal title for the *Contestado* settlement located in the area. While the site had no infrastructure at the time of my initial visit, the school was inaugurated in August 2005 and today can accommodate approximately two hundred people with beds, hot showers, and a collective kitchen. Most importantly, it is now training its third cohort of agro-ecology technicians,[6] who will earn a nationally recognized university degree for their study of sustainable agriculture and food sovereignty.

What makes this still-fragile experience, full of challenges, such an inspiring case of alternative (and in many ways, non-capitalist) economy within which peasants themselves carved out a space for alternative knowledge production by fostering democratic governance from below? Or in Santos's project for a sociology of emergence, what makes the ELAA an experience calling on researchers and peasant-activists to adopt a new epistemology and to convey the diversities of relevant knowledges and (re)productive activities?

Building on the work of Gibson-Graham (2006, 2008), I refer to alternative, or diverse, economies to emphasize the diversity of ways in which individuals, communities, and private and public associations continue to engage in productive, reproductive, and distributive activities, in parallel to the market-based economy (e.g., public health and education services, unpaid labour, worker and consumer cooperatives, and subsistence farming, among others). In this way, as Wright's chapter (this volume) highlights, value is placed not only on competitiveness and profit but also on solidarity, reciprocity exchanges, and the well-being of communities *and* ecosystems. I thus seek to examine how alternative knowledge production can foster alternative norms and socio-economic practices based on solidarity and participation, and how such practices may help to democratize the dominant model of agricultural governance and development.

The ELAA represents a direct attempt to translate the concept of food sovereignty into concrete action. The ELAA is a La Vía Campesina international school that welcomes student producers from a variety of peasant and farmers movements, mostly from Brazil and the Southern Cone countries. The school emerged as a partnership through the Intention Protocol signed during the fifth World Social Forum in Porto Alegre, Brazil, in January 2005. The agreement was between La Vía Campesina–Brazil and La Vía Campesina International, the Federal University of Paraná (UFPR), the government of Venezuela, and the state of Paraná, Brazil, all of which agreed to cover the cost of the course on an equal basis between the institutions and the movements (internal document obtained from the MST-Paraná Headquarters, signed 30 January 2005). Embedded within the Brazilian socio-political and economic context, La Vía Campesina leaders thus had to innovate and find ways to materialize their project. They succeeded, despite continuing difficulties, in gaining the support of allies and government institutions to obtain the much-needed resources (e.g., professors, land access), the funding (from the Programa Nacional de Educação na Reforma Agrária [PRONERA]), and the official university stamp to lend legitimacy to the training offered by the ELAA. Nonetheless, the success of the school depends largely on other resources, beyond formal institutions and conventional market circuits.

The location of the school itself is a first sign of its alternative econo-my connections, for no capital was traded to obtain it and no financial institutions were directly involved in its setup. Land access was negoti-ated with the *Contestado* settlement families who had already obtained legal titles from the government with the support of MST leadership. Thus the new school did not have to buy land or buildings and was al-lowed to use a large house that had once been part of a slave-trading operation. The development of the school also represents an alternative economy in the sense that the participants attend the program for free, and the new buildings and facilities have been constructed mostly through the voluntary labour (i.e., work brigades) of affiliated move-ments. Moreover, many improvements and infrastructure upgrades were made possible because of a solidarity alliance with the Brazilian petroleum trade union, Federação Única dos Petroleiros, which held its national convention in the settlement in July 2009. Instead of paying hotel fees for their annual convention, the Federação Única paid an equal amount of money ahead of time to allow for the construction of new infrastructure at the ELAA, which was then used by the conven-tion participants during their event. ELAA students and coordinators volunteered their time and energy to service the convention, and today the permanent installations remain for the benefit of the school.

Through embracing an alternative economy, it has been made possi-ble for the ELAA to put the concept of food sovereignty into practice via its unique form of learning and knowledge sharing. Indeed, the ELAA's three-and-a-half-year agro-ecology course is intended to train "activist-technician-teachers" (Hadich and Tardin 2009, 4) rather than simply training farmers. In general, agro-ecology techniques "tend to be knowl-edge intensive rather than input intensive" and are often site-specific, which means that these techniques are "grounded in peasants' ratio-nale and knowledge" (Altieri 2010, 124). In practice, the ELAA's agro-ecology program allows young Latin American peasants from the MST and other La Vía Campesina movements to share their learning time back and forth between the ELAA school (sixty to seventy-five days) and their community (ninety days) (author's fieldwork notes, June and October 2009; Hadich and Tardin 2009). Both facets are integral parts of the curriculum and are meant to enable students to put their newly ac-quired knowledge and technical skills into practice and to share them with other farmers back home.

During school time, training and learning methods also combine theory and practice and include various activities to ensure the continued functioning of the school. This is a way to sustain the school as well as to encourage cooperation, self-management, and participation beyond school life. On a rotating schedule, different groups take care of cooking and kitchen duties, administration, production, and infrastructure maintenance. The rest of the school day is generally divided between interactive learning in the classroom, reading and homework periods, sharing in group discussions, and practical activities in the field, such as experimenting with compost-making, pest control, or beekeeping. The students are also in charge of organizing leisure and social activities, during which they are invited to share their talents as musicians or to teach their indigenous languages.

Once they return to their villages, each activist-technician-teacher has a community mentor to help experiment with new practices and continue learning. Students are encouraged to share their knowledge and experiences with other members of their community and thereby become agro-ecology experts and teachers themselves. Based on the pedagogy of Paulo Freire (1970), and building upon the *campesino a campesino* training methodology where farmers share and exchange knowledge and techniques, the ELAA program harnesses the knowledge and experience of each student-producer, and then invites all to improve their own practices and to share their knowledge and skills.

Vis-à-vis the ELAA, then, we can see how agro-ecology training in its essence goes far beyond the usual academic formation in its goal to improve small-scale farming. The school embraces the principles of food sovereignty, both fundamentally and in practice. As Miguel Altieri explains, "In addition to providing a scientific basis for sustainable and enhanced productivity, agroecology promotes the capability of local communities to innovate, evaluate and adapt themselves through farmer-to-farmer research ... Technological approaches emphasizing diversity, synergy, recycling and integration, and social processes that value community involvement, point to the fact that human resource development is the cornerstone of any strategy aimed at increasing food production" (2010, 121).

Agro-ecology training thus explicitly promotes the full development and emancipation of individuals and communities from socio-economic, political, cultural, and biological perspectives. The ELAA agro-ecology program further promotes self-determination through political activism as a way to strengthen peasant organizations, foster greater autonomy, and encourage social transformations in harmony with nature. As one ELAA activist-technician-teacher emphasizes, the school's training program can have deep transformative impacts and can contribute to transformations in social relationships between men and women, as well as in society more generally: "'The small habits that we used to do at home and that we do not do here already have big results; for example, this is turning us into a different kind of citizen,' said Giovane Gonçalves, an activist of the MPA [the small farmers movement, in Brazil] in Rio Grande do Sul, and 'student' [*educando*] of ELAA. He continues, 'From how to take care of our clothing, which is a small detail that I was not doing and that many people were not doing, and like this, you start to value the gender question, you start to value the work of women, and in this sense, [before] we did not do this, and thus we did not value it. This is a very important point that I will carry with me all my life'" (translation, quoted in Hadich and Tardin 2009, 6).

In this vein, the ELAA makes strides to promote gender equality by facilitating the participation of all activist-technician-teachers – especially females – by enabling their children to attend the same elementary school and day-care centre as the children of the settlement families, free of charge. In this way, too, the ELAA is putting the concept of social responsibility and the framework of food sovereignty into practice.

Rural women from the Movimento de mulheres camponesas, who are also members of La Vía Campesina-Brazil, are taking part in the ELAA school and similar courses in growing numbers. These women further emphasize how peasant movements allow participants to not only share experiences and learn more about ecological techniques, but also to strengthen their organizational skills and their self-determination. As one Movimento interviewee from the north of Brazil points out, "We learn a lot, and with this [agro-ecology course], already we are better organized in the region. We have developed some ... activities, not only grassroots work but also consciousness raising" (personal interview, Belém, Brazil, January 2009).

Jornada de Agroecologia, Paraná, Brazil

One of the ways in which agro-ecology perspectives and practices have directly contributed to carving out spaces for different kinds of economies to exist in parallel with conventional markets is through the Jornada de Agroecologia, a transnational gathering that takes place in the Brazilian state of Paraná. Indeed, since 2002, this annual La Vía Campesina event has attracted participants from different regions of

Brazil and beyond, and has brought together producers and researcher-activists from various backgrounds.[7] The Jornada represents a permanent articulation of entities that share a common objective and vision: to promote ecological family farming that recognizes the key contribution of small producers and the need to work in partnership with nature (see Jornada de Agroecologia 2010).

Such events and articulations have contributed to creating new spaces for multiple exchanges and mutual learning. Participants come to share and celebrate the knowledges, skills, experiences, and strategies used to develop and expand alternative (re)production models in the face of the constant pressures exerted by conventional markets linked to seed industries and other agribusinesses. Some small-scale producers come to the Jornada to exchange or sell seeds and products. Others come to meet with other small producers, expand their networks, or to learn about agro-ecology for the first time in response to the increasing debt and lowering revenues they face as the result of rising production, seed, and agrochemical costs. As MST activist-poet Ariulino Alves Morais explained during the 2010 Jornada de Agroecologia, agro-ecology is "a refuge" for small producers who are non-viable under the conventional model – and the actual conditions – of the market. In his view, "There is a forced transition towards agro-ecology" (author's translation, as quoted in Torinelli and Carrano 2010), and the Jornada is there to act as a midwife for this change and to advocate for food sovereignty as the goal of family farming, and not simply a means of surviving during hard times.

Indeed, as Ines Burg (2005) points out, the promotion of agro-ecology by movements and NGOs has opened new spaces for the rethinking of agricultural models of production and the rescue of local knowledges and practices. What's more, as we have seen with the ELAA model, agro-ecology also has the capacity to slowly transform gender relations. Burg demonstrates that women engaging in agro-ecology – and especially those attending local markets to sell their products – have significantly increased their participation and visibility in public spaces. In doing so, even though they have increased their workloads, they have also expanded their access to different training and reinforced their participation in family decision-making. That is, because selling their produce helps to raise the family income, their men are more willing to value these women's work and to give them a greater voice in the household.

Those who promote agro-ecology and food sovereignty generally insist on building equal relationships and respect between people and nature (in terms of needs, life cycles), as well as between men, women, and children. In that sense, locally grounded peasant movements are also fighting for greater inclusion (as relevant political actors, "citizens," and food producers), contributing to the well-being and social reproduction of their families, their community, the movement, their country, and society as a whole, through interaction with other locally grounded peasants and popular forces across state and cultural boundaries (personal interviews, Brazilian peasants, June 2005 to May 2009). Far from waiting for state officials or theorists to respond to their needs, many small producers are organizing and sharing knowledges. They are the ones who know best what is needed to protect their land and provide for their people. As feminist political ecologists remind us, "Theory is made more relevant, accurate, and compelling when it incorporates the perspectives, knowledges, and voices of those who are struggling for change 'on the ground'" (Mallory, quoted in Salleh 2009, 6).

Traditionally, most rural women in Brazil, like in many parts of Latin America, have few opportunities to participate in the community beyond attending church and family activities. By participating in agro-ecology (i.e., production, training, fairs, and markets), women gain confidence, dignity, and greater autonomy through earning their own revenue, and they simultaneously expand their social networks beyond the family circle (Burg 2005). Yet gender equality is far from being fully realized, despite the strides being made.

While agro-ecology clearly has a lot to offer peasants and small-scale producers in ecology as well as personal and political empowerment, as shown by the success of the ELAA and the annual Jornada, a sizable number of small-scale farmers and peasants still look to the agro-industrial model to deliver profit and success (Andrée, this volume). Field research has shown that, for lack of resources, *acampados* (camped people) and recent *asentados* (settled people) adopt agro-ecological practices by default; while some dream of maintaining such practices after they stabilize, others hope to gain access to agro-industrial technologies as soon as they are able to. Furthermore, some participants in agro-ecological fairs and markets also look for industrial-style commercial venues for their products, which adds to the tensions and challenges that many grassroots movements and rural communities still face in a Brazilian society deeply marked by individualist and consumerist values. These tensions thus highlight the need for further research and for seeking concrete ways to make such alternative practices more visible and viable. For some, this might be best pursued through policy reforms that support small-scale sustainable agriculture and avoid raising further barriers; for others, it requires a radical delinking from dominant structures of power and governance. However, among peasants and small food producers, a mix of strategies and tactics tends to be the norm.

Conclusion

From the creation of the MST in 1984 until 2000, its leadership and many family farmer organizations adopted the dominant view that even small agricultural operations needed to "modernize" and adopt agro-industrial methods, including new technologies and agrochemicals. As one MST / La Vía Campesina leader mentioned, at that time most people in the movement believed that such methods could increase efficiency and productivity and therefore ameliorate the life of poor rural families (personal interview, Lapa, Paraná, Brazil, June 2009). However, this same interviewee argued that, over time, it became clear that such methods were ecologically and socially unsustainable, and that this unsustainability largely explains the failure of many settlements. Green Revolution practices increased the economic dependency of small farmers upon market forces to gain access to credit, seeds, machinery, and agro-chemicals.

Therefore with the turn of the twenty-first century, and in parallel to the strengthening of La Vía Campesina and global campaigns rejecting the neoliberal model of governance, many leaders and participants of both the MST and La Vía Campesina became convinced that agro-industrial methods were sustainable for neither small farmers nor for the environment or the well-being of urban and rural communities. This is the context in which linkages between peasant organizations North and South, and the diffusion of emerging norms of agricultural governance (anti-GMOs, food sovereignty, slow food, etc.), rooted in local experiences and small farmers' expertise, expanded in Brazil and across borders. Indeed, during the fourth National Congress of the MST in 2000, about 11,000 delegates decided to adopt agro-ecology as a part of the movement's political program. As a result, agro-ecology is becoming an integral part of every course taught within the Brazilian MST, at every grade level and within every subject, from agriculture to political leadership (Hadich and Tardin 2009, 8). Moreover, food sovereignty was adopted by La Vía Campesina representatives as a main objective of its organization in 1996, and it slowly but surely has become one of La Vía Campesina's main campaigns to defend peasants' rights and way of living.

In today's context of multiple and interconnected crises (food, energy, state, financial, and ecological; see Leite in Beaudet, Canet, and Massicotte 2010), the campaign for food sovereignty and agro-ecological production methods represents a key opportunity to affect social change that acutely responds to the urgency of democratizing today's food systems and governance mechanisms, from the local to the global. As strategic tools to mobilize and promote concrete changes, the food sovereignty and agro-ecology frameworks contribute to addressing the needs of producers and consumers in the short term in specific locations. Yet these tools also enable us to engage in a longer-term critical reflection and debate on how to effectively challenge the root causes of these global crises, and on ways to consolidate alternative models of agricultural governance to avoid the exacerbation of social and ecological problems.

Through an analysis of specific discourses and practices, this chapter has argued that peasant organizations and networks are deeply involved in contentious agricultural politics, as well as in formal and informal governance mechanisms, in order to coordinate socio-economic, ecological, and cultural relations. Without a doubt, grassroots movements are carving out innovative, dynamic meeting places where peasants, rural women, small farmers, and their allies can learn and build from each other's expertise and experiences within and beyond a neoliberal landscape. By seeking to implement the principles of food sovereignty, their alternative socio-economic practices around small-scale agriculture are displacing dominant forms of governance from above and calling for greater self-determination to maintain and improve the peasant way of life and to reclaim their rights. Nonetheless, in order to envision other modes of governance and development, it is essential to expand our theoretical framework as researchers and to listen to the voices of those who are already engaged in alternative practices and epistemologies.

Despite very unequal power relations, some peasants are refusing to give up their land to industrial agribusinesses or hedge fund speculators. In various ways, small farmers and landless rural workers are challenging today's trade policies and agricultural governance mechanisms locally, nationally, and globally. By directly engaging with, and sometimes defying, political and economic rules and actors, they have

demonstrated their determination to prove that other agricultural practices are possible – and are already in existence, in parallel with industrialized monocultures. Some of the processes discussed in this chapter are
not only reactions to the pressures of neoliberal governance, but also
examples of the wisdom and multiple knowledges of rural people – that
is, of peasants who have worked and lived on the land for generations.

Many activists involved in the day-to-day struggles and social organizing of small-scale agriculture do not romanticize the local or opt out
of globalization and regionalization. At the local level, for example, they
continually need to address problems of credit, access (to land, water,
and seeds), pollution, and pests. What's more, peasant farmers know
about insecurity and violence, as those living in marginalized rural
communities without formal land titles generally fear expulsions. The
harsh conditions in which they live often make it difficult for peasant
families to come up with democratic and respectful decision-making
processes to "govern" themselves and to organize collective life.

Nonetheless, many rural organizations insist on greater participation
and inclusion – that is, democratization – of their needs and hopes within local, national, and / or international agricultural policies and governance. They claim that their small-scale, sustainable agricultural models
are not compatible with the priorities of free trade negotiators, agribusinesses, and international financial institutions pushing for greater neoliberal integration. Through such strategies, we can see that, despite the
unfavourable correlation of forces, peasant activists are far from passive
victims. Today they are at the forefront of contentious trade politics, and
they are set on bringing about change.

Indeed, not only do food sovereignty principles and values already
shape and regulate socio-economic and cultural relations locally and
regionally, they have been recognized and promoted by formal, rule-
based institutions of governance. Jean Ziegler, former special rapporteur of the Right to Food, and the Food and Agriculture Organization
(FAO), of the United Nations, have acknowledged the need to promote
food sovereignty and small-scale food production (Wittman, Desmarais,
and Wiebe 2010, 6–8). Moreover, in 2008, the new Ecuadorian constitution included a specific article (281) on food sovereignty, as "a strategic
objective and an obligation of the state to guarantee that individuals,
communities, peoples and nations reach self-sufficiency in healthy and
culturally appropriate food on a permanent basis" (author's translation
from Spanish, Carrera 2010, 79). Of course, as Wittman et al. also point
out, these steps forward and the "discursive recognition" of such norms
by some states and interstate institutions do not easily translate into

practices. In fact, even in Ecuador, and in other states that have endorsed at least some elements of food sovereignty in their judicial systems, competing norms and legislations (on mining and the use of GMOs, for example), as well as socio-economic and cultural pressures, go against implementation of this emerging norm of food sovereignty.

This chapter has highlighted how peasant activists are putting up resistance against the mass commercialization of their livelihoods as a clarion call to invite other researchers to rethink their own analytical frameworks surrounding food and trade politics, and to reconsider the possibility of less-powerful forces being influential actors and knowledge producers in their own right. Through empirically grounded research, it becomes possible to dig into the very practices and discourses of grassroots organizations that are rejecting the neoliberal order and developing their own practices and expertise, both locally and across state and cultural boundaries. By participating in broad campaigns, agro-ecology trainings, and networks such as La Vía Campesina, grassroots organizations are learning from one another and bringing different lessons and strategies back home to their own communities.

Overall, it is essential to not only highlight the strengths and weaknesses of alternative experiences and practices, but also to recognize them as valid approaches. By so doing, the dominant institutions and global forces will be obligated to recognize and respond to the contributions of these "other possibles," at least in part. Giving visibility, credibility, and space to emergent practices and alternative knowledges may in turn destabilize the legitimacy of existing norms and institutions and / or bring about significant policy reforms that could promote further innovations, thereby giving greater incentives to various actors to try to pursue, deepen, or reverse such changes. This chapter has argued that the idea of agro-ecology as a transformative process and a life-long project to implement food sovereignty extends well beyond the trainings offered to small farmers like those attending the ELAA school. It also called for theorists to expand their understanding of global governance as more inclusive of a variety of practices and norms at multiple levels, such as those associated with food sovereignty. Indeed, the seeds of both agro-ecology and food sovereignty take a lifetime to sow: "The Green Revolution was a process that took a few years to be implemented and was accelerated afterwards, with the adoption of policies. We are in the same process with agro-ecology. We are planting the seeds, and after a certain time we begin to pick up the fruits that are the results of agro-ecology" (Giovane, ELAA activist-student, quoted in Hadich and Tardin, 2009, 10–11).

ACKNOWLEDGMENTS

I would like to thank all interviewees and activists for sharing their knowledge and experiences on small farming, agricultural politics and peasant organizing, during multiple field research trips, between June 2005 and March 2011, funded by the Social Sciences and Humanities Research Council of Canada. These pages have also benefited from constructive feedback by Peter Andrée, Arturo Escobar, Janet Conway, April Carrière, Dan Furukawa Marquez, and Catherine Walsh.

NOTES

1 La Vía Campesina translates as "The Peasant's Way," but the majority of member organizations use the Spanish title. For a definition of *peasant*, see the epigraph, above.
2 For more in-depth analyses on "global governance" as a political project that promotes the neoliberal norms and policies privileging market efficiency above the democratic rights and practices of people, see, for examples, Brodie (2005), Gill (2003), and Santos (2006a).
3 Discussing an emergent approach in political ecology, Escobar explains how "flat" or "relational ontologies" reject binary thinking (e.g., culture vs nature, universal vs particular, global / macro vs local / micro, subject vs object, human vs non-human) in order to examine the complex interactions between human and non-human inhabitants that define the content and the contours of spaces and sites of struggles. This approach "discards 'the centering essentialism that infuses not only the up-down vertical imaginary [e.g., global economy / WTO → state →local communities] but also the radiating (out from here) spatiality of horizontality' [e.g., from the metropolis to rural areas, core capitalist economies to peripheries, or even from the Lacandon forest to other rural and urban areas]" (Marsden et al. quoted in Escobar 2010, 99).
4 For analyses of the World Social Forum, see Santos (2006b), Conway (2013) and Beaudet, Canet, and Massicotte (2010).
5 In Portuguese, Instituto Nacional de Colonização e Reforma Agrária.
6 Many other schools in Brazil graduate agro-ecology technicians (there are thirteen such schools within the MST), although they are shorter programs that do not lead to a university diploma. The ELAA is the only one offering university degrees after three and a half years of theoretical, political, and technical training.

7 The main participants are landless and family farmers, including rural
   women and youth, but also professors, agronomy engineers, NGO and
   environmental activists, *quilombolas,* and indigenous peoples. *Quilombolas*
   are ex-slave communities that have often been expropriated from their
   land in the interest of "modernizing agriculture," which led to further
   land concentration.

REFERENCES

Altieri, Miguel A. 1995. *Agroecology: The Science of Sustainable Agriculture.*
   Boulder, CO: Westview.
– 2010. "Scaling Up Agroecologial Approaches for Food Sovereignty in Latin
   America." In *Food Sovereignty: Reconnecting Food, Nature and Community,*
   edited by Annette Desmarais, Hannah Wittman, and Nettie Wiebe, 120–33.
   Toronto: Brunswick Books.
Amoore, Louise, ed. 2005. *The Global Resistance Reader.* London: Routledge.
Beaudet, Pierre, Raphäl Canet, and Marie-Josée Massicotte, eds. 2010.
   L'altermondialisme: forums sociaux, résistances et nouvelle culture politique.
   Montreal: Éditions Écosociété.
Best, Jaqueline, and Matthew Paterson, eds. 2010. *Cultural Political Economy.*
   New York: Routledge.
Blaser, Mario, Ravi de Costa, Deborah McGregor, and William D. Coleman,
   eds. 2010. *Indigenous Peoples and Autonomy: Insights for a Global Age.*
   Vancouver: UBC Press.
Borras, Saturnino Jr. 2008. "La Vía Campesina and Its Global Campaign for
   Agrarian Reform." *Journal of Agrarian Change* 8 (2–3): 258–89. http://dx.doi
   .org/10.1111/j.1471-0366.2008.00170.x.
Branford, Sue, and Jan Rocha. 2002. *Cutting the Wire: The Story of the Landless
   Movement in Brazil.* London: Latin American Bureau.
Brodie, Janine. 2005. "Globalization, Governance and Gender: Rethinking
   the Agenda for the Twenty-First Century." In *The Global Resistance Reader,*
   edited by Louise Amoore, 244–56. London: Routledge.
Burg, Ines C. 2005. "As mulheres agricultoras na produção agroecológica e na
   comercialização em feiras no sudoeste paranaense Curso de Pós-Graduação
   em Agroecossistemas." MA thesis, Florianópolis, Universidade Federal de
   Santa Catarina, Brazil.
Cabello, Gaspar Real. 2003. "The Mexican State and the Agribusiness Model
   of Development in the Globalisation Era." *Australian Journal of Social Issues*
   38 (1): 129–39.

Carrera, Javier. 2010. "La soberania alimentaria en la constitucion." In *Soberanias*, edited by Alberto Acosta and Esperanza Martinez, 75–90. Quito: Abya-Yala.

Climate Justice Now! (CJN!) 2010. http://www.climate-justice-now.org/.

Commission on Global Governance. 1995. *Our Global Neighbourhood: The Report of the Commission on Global Governance*. Oxford: Oxford University Press.

Conway, Janet. 2013. *Edges of Global Justice: The World Social Forum and Its "Others."* London: Routledge.

Dal Maso, M. 2004. "Movimentos Sociais: a longa viagem para o mesmo lugar." PhD diss., Universidade Estadual de Campinas.

Davies, Matt. 2006. "Everyday Life in the Global Political Economy." In *International Political Economy and Poststructural Politics*, edited by Marieke de Goede, 219–37. New York: Palgrave Macmillan.

– 2010. "Works, Products, and the Division of Labour: Notes for a Cultural and Political Economic Critique." In *Cultural Political Economy*, edited by Jaqueline Best and Matthew Paterson, 48–63. New York: Routledge.

Desmarais, Annette A. 2009. "Building a Transnational Peasant Movement." *NACLA Report*, May–June, 24–6.

Escobar, Arturo. 2001. "Culture Sits in Places: Reflections on Globalism and Subaltern Strategies of Localization." *Political Geography* 20 (2): 139–74. http://dx.doi.org/10.1016/S0962-6298(00)00064-0.

– 2008. *Territories of Difference: Place, Movements, Life, Redes*. Durham, NC: Duke University Press.

– 2010. "Postconstructivist Political Ecologies." In *International Handbook of Environmental Sociology*, edited by M. Redclift and G. Woodgate, 2nd ed., 91–105. Cheltenham, UK: Elgar.

Esteva, Gustavo, and Madhu Suri Prakash, eds. 1998. *Grassroots Post-modernism: Remaking the Soil of Cultures*. New York: Zed Books/St Martin's Press.

Falk, Richard. 1995. *On Humane Governance: Towards a New Global Politics*. University Park, PA: Pennsylvania State University Press/World Order Models Project.

Fitting, Elyzabeth. 2006. "Importing Corn, Exporting Labor: The Neoliberal Corn Regime, GMOs, and the Erosion of Mexican Biodiversity." *Agriculture and Human Values* 23 (1): 15–26. http://dx.doi.org/10.1007/s10460-004-5862-y.

Fortune 500. 2010. "Pilgrim's Pride." http://money.cnn.com/magazines/fortune/fortune500/2010/snapshots/884.html.

Freire, Paolo. 1970. *Pedagogy of the Oppressed*. New York: Herder & Herder.

Gibson-Graham, J.K. 2006. *A Postcapitalist Politics*. Minneapolis: University of Minnesota Press.

– 2008. "Diverse Economies: Performative Practices for 'Other Worlds.'"
     Progress in Human Geography 32 (5): 613–32. http://dx.doi.org/10.1177/
     0309132508090821.
Gill, Stephen. 2003. *Power and Resistance in the New World Order*. New York:
     Palgrave Macmillan.
Gills, Barry, ed. 2000. *Globalization and the Politics of Resistance*. Basingstoke,
     UK: Palgrave. http://dx.doi.org/10.1057/9780230519176.
Greenberg, James B., and Thomas K. Park. 1994. "Political Ecology." *Journal of
     Political Ecology* 1:1–12.
Hadich, Ceres, and José Maria Tardin. 2009. "Escola Latino Americana de
     Agroecologia: Experiências Camponesas de Agroecologia." Author's
     collection.
Harvey, David. 1996. *Justice, Nature & the Geography of Difference*. Oxford:
     Blackwell.
– 2005. *The New Imperialism*. Oxford: Oxford University Press.
Held, David. 2006. "Reframing Global Governance: Apocalypse Soon or
     Reform!" *New Political Economy* 11 (2): 157–76. http://dx.doi.org/10.1080/
     13563460600655516.
Hobson, John M., and Leonard Seabrooke, eds. 2007. *Everyday Politics of the
     World Economy*. New York: Cambridge University Press.
– 2009. "From Food Crisis to Food Sovereignty." *Monthly Review* 61 (3), online.
Holt-Giménez, Eric, and Raj Patel. 2009. *Food Rebellions! Crisis and the Hunger
     for Justice*. Oakland, CA: Food First Books/Pambazuka.
Jornada de Agroecologia. 2010. "9a Jornada de Agroecologia." *Jornal Liberal*,
     19 April. http://www.liberalonline.com.br/index.php?option=com_
     content&view=article&id=167:9o-jornada-de-agroecologia&catid=37:
     geral&Itemid=56.
Juris, Jeffrey. 2008. *Networking Futures: The Movements against Corporate
     Globalization*. Durham, NC: Duke University Press.
La Vía Campesina. 2010. "What Is La Vía Campesina?" http://viacampesina.
     org/en/index.php/organisation-mainmenu-44/what-is-la-via-campesina-
     mainmenu-45/1002-the-international-peasants-voice27.
Lozano, Joseph M. 2008. *Governments and Corporate Social Responsibility:
     Public Policies beyond Regulation and Voluntary Compliance*. Basingstoke, UK:
     Palgrave Macmillan/ESADE.
Macdonald, Laura. 2002. "Globalization and Social Movements: Comparing
     Women's Movements' Responses to NAFTA." *International Journal of
     Feminist Studies* 4 (2): 151–72.
Marchand, Marianne. 2008. "The Violence of Development and the Migration/
     Insecurities Nexus: Labour Migration in a North American Context."

Third World Quarterly 29 (7): 1375–88. http://dx.doi.org/10.1080/
01436590802386575.

Massicotte, Marie-Josée. 2010a. "Confronter la mondialisation." In
L'altermondialisme: forums sociaux, résistances et nouvelle culture politique, edit-
ed by Pierre Beaudet, Raphaël Canet, and M.-J. Massicotte, 21–43. Montreal:
Éditions Écosociété.

– 2010b. "La Vía Campesina, Brazilian Peasants, and the Agribusiness Model
of Agriculture: Towards an Alternative Model of Agrarian Democratic
Governance." *Studies in Political Economy* 85 (Spring): 69–98.

McMichael, Philip. 1994. *The Global Restructuring of Agro-Food Systems*. Ithaca,
NY: Cornell University Press.

– 2006. "Peasant Prospects in the Neo-Liberal Age." *New Political Economy*
11 (3): 407–18. http://dx.doi.org/10.1080/13563460600841041.

– 2008. "Peasants Make Their Own History, But Not Just as They Please."
Journal of Agrarian Change 8 (2–3): 205–28. http://dx.doi.org/10.1111/j.1471-
0366.2008.00168.x.

Menser, Michael. 2008. "Transnational Participatory Democracy in Action: The
Case of La Vía Campesina." *Journal of Social Philosophy* 39 (1): 20–41. http://
dx.doi.org/10.1111/j.1467-9833.2007.00409.x.

Mies, Maria, and Veronika Bennholdt-Thomsen. 1999. *The Subsistence
Perspective*. London: Zed Books.

Munk, Ronaldo. 2007. *Globalization and Contestation: The New Great Counter-
Movement*. New York: Routledge.

O'Brien, R., A.-M. Goetz, J.A. Scholte, and M. Williams. 2000. *Contesting Global
Governance: Multilateral Economic Institutions and Global Social Movements*.
Cambridge, UK: Cambridge University Press. http://dx.doi.org/10.1017/
CBO9780511491603.

Otero, Gerardo. 2008. *Food for the Few: Neoliberal Globalism and Biotechnology in
Latin America*. Austin: University of Texas Press.

Patel, Raj. 2006. "International Agrarian Restructuring and the Practical Ethics
of Peasant Movement Solidarity." *Journal of Asian and African Studies* 41
(1–2): 71–93. http://dx.doi.org/10.1177/0021909606061748.

Pimbert, M. 2008. *Towards Food Sovereignty: Reclaiming Autonomous Food Systems*.
London: International Institute for Environment and Development (IIED).

Rangel Loera, Nashieli. 2010. "'Encampment Time': An Anthropological
Analysis of the Land Occupations in Brazil." *Journal of Peasant Studies* 37 (2):
285–318. http://dx.doi.org/10.1080/03066151003594930.

Rocheleau, Dianne, Barbara Thomas-Slayter, and Esther Wangari, eds. 1996.
Feminist Political Ecology: Global Issues and Local Experiences. London:
Routledge.

Rosenau, James, and E.O. Czempiel, eds. 1992. *Governance without Government*. Cambridge: Cambridge University Press. http://dx.doi.org/10.1017/CBO9780511521775.

Rosset, Peter. 2003. "Food Sovereignty: Global Rallying Cry of Farmer Movements." *Food First Backgrounder* 9 (4). http://www.foodfirst.org/node/47.

Salleh, A., ed. 2009. *Eco-Sufficiency & Global Justice: Women Write Political Ecology*. New York: Pluto.

Santos, Boaventura de Sousa. 2006a. "Globalizations." *Theory, Culture & Society* 23 (2–3): 393–9. http://dx.doi.org/10.1177/026327640602300268.

– 2006b. *The Rise of the Global Left: The World Social Forum and Beyond*. London: Zed Books.

Shiva, Vandana. 1997. *Biopiracy: The Plunder of Nature and Knowledge*. Cambridge, MA: South End.

Stédile, Joao Pedro, and Bernardo Mançano Fernandes. 1999. *Brava Gente: A trajetória do MST e a luta pela terra no Brasil*. São Paulo: Editora Fundação Perseu Abramo.

Strange, Susan. 1986. *Casino Capitalism*. Oxford: Blackwell.

– 1999. "The Westfailure System." *Review of International Studies* 25 (3): 345–54. http://dx.doi.org/10.1017/S0260210599003459.

Torinelli, M., and P. Carrano. 2010. "Encontro no Paraná propõe produção de alimentos sem agrotóxicos," 20 May. http://www.mst.org.br/node/9895.

Wittman, Hannah. 2009. "Reframing Agrarian Citizenship: Land, Life and Power in Brazil." *Journal of Rural Studies* 25 (1): 120–30. http://dx.doi.org/10.1016/j.jrurstud.2008.07.002.

Wittman, Hannah, Annette Aurélie Desmarais, and Nettie Wiebe. 2010. *Food Sovereignty: Reconnecting Food, Nature and Community*. Halifax: Fernwood Publishing.

Wolford, Wendy. 2004. "This Land Is Ours Now: Spatial Imaginaries and the Struggle for Land in Brazil." *Annals of the Association of American Geographers* 94 (2): 409–24. http://dx.doi.org/10.1111/j.1467-8306.2004.09402015.x.

– 2010. "Participatory Democracy by Default: Land Reform, Social Movements and the State in Brazil." *Journal of Peasant Studies* 37 (1): 91–109. http://dx.doi.org/10.1080/03066150903498770.

Wolford, Wendy, and Angus L. Wright. 2003. *To Inherit the Earth: The Landless Movement and the Struggle for a New Brazil*. Oakland: Food First Books.

Woods, Michael. 2006. "Political Articulation: The Modalities of New Critical Politics of Rural Citizenship." In *Handbook of Rural Studies*, edited by P.J. Cloke, T. Marsden, and P.H. Mooney, 457–72. London: Sage. http://dx.doi.org/10.4135/9781848608016.n33.

10 Food Sovereignty, Trade Rules, and the Struggle to Know the Origins of Food

ELIZABETH SMYTHE[1]

Introduction

As the introduction to this volume indicates, the "globalizing food system" or what McMichael has called a "globalizing food regime" has generated abundant and affordable food for some and paradoxically crises, hunger, and destruction for others, particularly peasant and small-scale food producers in the global South. As a system it features industrial-style food production that is an export-intensive monoculture with globally organized systems of production, distribution, and processing dominated by large corporate entities of ever-increasing size and market dominance. A key element in the development of this system has been a trend to liberalization of agricultural trade based on rules and standards negotiated globally. The system's impacts have included a changing role for the state in many countries vis-à-vis agriculture, a growing distance between food producers and eaters, rising food imports, new technologies, and a growing unease (Blay-Palmer 2008) of many food eaters about the nature of the food they are eating. Fuelled by well-publicized food scares, especially in Europe and North America, deep concerns have emerged about the methods by which the food we eat is produced.

One lens through which we can study the response to this food system is Polanyi's concept of protection (chapter 1, this volume) where society seeks to protect itself from a too-powerful market, often through the state. In the case of food eaters, as this chapter will show, one response has been to demand, in reaction to two decades of deregulation and trade liberalization, greater state regulation of food safety and food standards. In particular, greater regulation of food labelling is seen by food eaters as a means by which they can better understand how their food is produced and what it contains, allowing more informed choices. As chapter 1 indicates, a second lens through which we can study the societal response to the globalizing food system is social movements that have emerged in the global North and South to challenge it and develop alternative food systems. In some areas of the North, this has manifested in a variety of food movements, many of them oriented to local food. In countries in the global South, but also in Western Europe where strong peasant economies are present (see Bosia and Ayres, this volume), a major challenge to the globalizing food regime has emerged around the concept of food sovereignty. This concept is complex, multifaceted, and contested (Menser, this volume) but one that increasingly resonates in both the North and the South. While the initial concept and discourse around food sovereignty as articulated by La Vía Campesina focused on food providers (Rosset 2003, 1), its broader emphasis on re-localizing the food system profoundly challenges current international trade rules that both demand liberalization of market access and legitimize the dumping of agricultural products (McMichael, this volume). One key demand of food sovereignty advocates is to reclaim control over food policy and local practices in states and communities. The role of non-producer groups in building and supporting alternative food systems and challenging the prevailing export-oriented, agri-business industrial model of food production is less clear and one that remains contested, as I indicate below.

This chapter examines the struggle over mandatory labelling of food (a form of protection in Polanyi's sense) through case studies of labelling for country of origin and genetic modification. In the process of this struggle at both the national and global level, the interests and positions around food labelling become visible. The array of movements and activists seeking a right to know the provenance of food have contributed to politicizing food issues and highlighting the problems and contradictions in norms and food regulations. Most importantly, they have challenged key aspects of trade rules that limit the policy space at the national level that might support some aspects of food sovereignty. These movements and activists also raised the question of knowledge and power, another lens through which we can view the globalizing food system. International standards and national regulations that privilege Western "science-based risk assessment" (often based on data controlled by powerful corporate actors), to use the language of international trade regulations, raise questions about whose views and whose knowledge matter. Movements have challenged the assumption that such knowledge can be separated from material interests and argued for a broader justification for eaters' rights to know the provenance of their food. Despite the limitations of focusing on food consumers, the struggles over food labelling can form an important part of building a movement to promote greater food sovereignty.

While citizens are increasingly attentive, for a variety of reasons, to the provenance and quality of food and sustainable food production and thus could contribute to the global struggle to achieve food sovereignty, they face a multilevel complex structure of public and private governance that limits their knowledge about the provenance of what they are eating. To re-localize the food system then requires action globally, nationally, and locally involving food producers and non-producers. Challenging national and international rules that impede the capacity of food eaters to privilege the local, or act in ways that support diversified alternative food systems and smaller-scale food producers is important, I argue, to the realization of food sovereignty.

I begin with a discussion of the concept of provenance and the debate about the role of consumers in challenging the globalizing food system and building alternatives. As Morgan, Marsden, and Murdoch indicate, the concept of food provenance encompasses much more than just place, including

> a spatial dimension (its place of origin), a social dimension (its methods of production and distribution), and a cultural dimension (its perceived qualities and reputation). The social dimension is particularly important because it helps consumers to deal with the ethical issues in globally dispersed food supply chains, including the employment conditions of food production workers; the welfare of animals farmed as food animals, such as battery hens and veal calves for example; the integrity of some food production methods, such as adding hormones to beef for instance; the environmental effects of certain production methods, such as the use of pesticides and the destruction of flora and fauna. To the extent that a new moral economy is beginning to emerge around food issues, this question of provenance assumes a central importance in food chain regulation. (2006, 3)

Issues of provenance, they note, are part of current political struggles over food labelling policy and "whether consumers have the right, or even the need to know the spatial history of their food" (3). Labelling thus could provide multiple tools for environmentalists and food activists to support small producers and alternative, just, and sustainable models of food production.

The focus on labelling, however, has been seen by many critics of the globalizing food system to be problematic. Local food movements in North America and efforts to promote ethical consuming through third-party certification and labels for fair trade or environmental sustainability have come in for much criticism for their limitations in building an alternative food system (Zerbe, this volume; McMahon, this volume). Guthman (2007) argues there are contradictory and troubling aspects of relying on market mechanisms and individual consumer initiatives to build an alternative to neoliberalism. Voting with our dollars reduces our role as citizens to that of consumers, creates justice issues, and, it could be argued, further embeds rather than challenges neoliberalism. The growing popularity of local food and local food movements, DeLind (2011) claims, may lead to ignoring broader issues of participatory democracy and empowerment and, in the case of locavores, emphasizing consumption and personal behaviour as the route to transformation of the system. These concerns are certainly valid, but here I argue that struggles over the right to know the provenance of our food, while not the sole way to realize an alternative food system, can play a role in bridging the distance between producers and food eaters within the food sovereignty movement – a challenge that the movement itself recognizes – and thus contribute to building alternatives to the current food regime. As my cases show, corporate agri-businesses, and U.S. and Canadian governments, at various points have tried to stop mandatory labelling, claiming that consumers do not need to know the provenance of their food. In contrast, consumer groups, small farmers, environmentalists, and global justice and local food activists are allying their forces and claiming a right to know the provenance of food. The reality is that the "right to know," despite the echoes of neoliberalism, is a frame that resonates broadly with food eaters, especially in the global North, where small producers are so few (Kneen 2010). Far from a technical issue, food labelling is a "key site of the quality battleground in the contemporary food chain" (Morgan, Marsden, and Murdoch 2006, 3). Within this battleground, spaces have emerged where new knowledge and awareness about the food system can be generated and smaller producers can engage with food eaters. In addition, these struggles over labelling highlight for citizens the extent to which international rules and standards have limited national and local policy space to privilege local food and thus create the potential for more pressure to challenge these rules. For all these reasons I would argue that the issue of mandatory food labelling is linked to the issue of food sovereignty and the realization of alternative food systems.

Transnational Movements and Food Sovereignty

In the 1990s, transnational networks emerged challenging aspects of corporate globalization. One of the most significant, La Vía Campesina, emerged out of a network of peasant- and farmer-based organizations from South, Central, and North America, as well as Europe (Martin and Andrée, this volume; Borras 2008). It has now grown to 148 peasant and small farmer organizations in sixty-nine countries, including the National Farmers Union (NFU) in Canada, the Quebec-based Union paysanne, and the National Coalition for Family Farming in the United States. Since its creation in 1993, La Vía Campesina has played an important role in challenging the neoliberal food regime and international trade rules and in articulating an alternative vision of agricultural production (Martínez-Torres and Rosset 2010, 149) that focuses on what food is produced, how it is done, and the scale of production. Its fierce opposition to organizations like the WTO and regional trade agreements are well known. The first key principle of food sovereignty La Vía Campesina articulated in 1996 was one of "placing priority on the production of healthy, good quality and culturally appropriate food primarily for the domestic market" (Desmarais 2007, 134), which has clear trade implications. This is reflected in the coalition Our World Is Not for Sale, formed in 1999 in opposition to the WTO, which includes La Vía Campesina as a member. This coalition has integrated food sovereignty into its demands, arguing that "governments … acknowledge the flaws in the 'free market' principles that underpin perceived comparative advantage, export-led agricultural development and 'structural adjustment' policies; and replace those policies with ones that prioritize and protect local, subsistence and sustainable production, including use of import controls and regulation that ensure more equitable sustainable production methods" (OWINFS 2009, 3).[2] The declaration also calls for rules allowing states to control food trade, especially imports and exports, and for agriculture to be taken out of the WTO altogether. La Vía Campesina has also challenged transnational corporations, intellectual property, and the control of seeds and genetically modified organisms (GMOs) and addressed a broad range of issues on gender and human rights. The scope of its concerns has allowed the organization to work with other development, environmental, and global justice networks.

As chapters 1 and 2 of this volume indicate, food sovereignty is a multifaceted concept that allows for a variety of ways of framing food issues that resonate with actors, North and South, who are challenging the globalizing corporate food system and promoting alternatives that are more adapted to each context. Thus food sovereignty has a number of manifestations, including demands for strong and better state regulation, normative discourses that challenge the WTO as indicated above, and calls for more local control over the food system. In 2002, the International Planning Committee on Food Sovereignty, of which LVC is also a member, identified "the need to give primacy to food security and food sovereignty principles when considering trade measures" (International Planning Committee 2002, 3).

In 2007, six pillars of food sovereignty (outlined in Martin and Andrée, this volume, and the Peoples' Food Project) were identified, one of which is localizing food systems and reducing "the distance between food providers and consumers," indicating an increased attention to building coalitions with consumers and others concerned about the global food system. Again, focusing on local control, the International Planning Committee emphasized the priority of national and local markets and "transparent trade that guarantees just income to all peoples and the rights of consumers to control their food and nutrition." It recognized the need to strengthen the political power of those advocating for food sovereignty by "expanding the debate outside producer groups to consumer groups and workers' trade unions" (Pimbert 2008, 47).

The aspect of food sovereignty that argues for reasserting local and national control over food systems challenges international rules of the WTO that prohibit the privileging of the national and the local. WTO agreements have limited the policy space for measures and regulations that would facilitate local food systems in the name of trade liberalization. Among those regulations are ones on food standards and labelling. Thus if those who are not food providers are to play a role along with governments in supporting food sovereignty, as outlined above, they must challenge these rules at multiple levels of governance involving a complex struggle over food regulations. I now turn to a discussion of these rules and that struggle at the national and international level.

Global Governance Mechanisms

Globalized food production dominated by large corporate conglomerates, the rapidly increasing level of food imports, and differing national food regulations made harmonizing standards an important part of the neoliberal trade liberalization project. This was reflected in WTO agreements on Sanitary and Phytosanitary (SPS) Measures (1995) and Technical Barriers to Trade (TBT) (1995).

The SPS and TBT WTO Agreements

Two agreements, key parts of the establishment of the WTO in 1995, deal with food regulations, including product labelling. Both are intended to ensure that national regulations do not impede trade liberalization. The agreement on Sanitary and Phytosanitary (SPS) Measures does, along with Article 20 of the GATT, allow for a state to set its regulatory bar as high as it likes on safety and human health "to protect human, animal or plant life or health," but such measures must be "based on scientific principles and not maintained without sufficient scientific evidence" (Article 2.2 WTO Agreement on Sanitary and Phytosanitary Measures (WTO, SPS, 1995, 2), and, in the interests of harmonization, states "shall base measures on international standards, guidelines or recommendations, where they exist" (Article 3, WTO, SPS, 2) . States may go beyond international standards, but only if the justification is supported by scientific evidence. All such regulations should be transparent, notified to the WTO, and use the least trade restrictive measures possible. The SPS agreement does not reference any broader societal or environmental concerns, nor does it recognize any justification that is not rooted in scientifically-based risk assessment.

The WTO Technical Barriers to Trade (TBT) covers non-safety aspects of product labelling and seeks to harmonize national labelling requirements on the basis of standards so as not to create "unnecessary obstacles to international trade." It affirms the right of countries to take "measures necessary to ensure the quality of its exports, for the protection of human, animal or plant life or health, of the environment, or for the prevention of deceptive practices" (WTO Agreement on Technical Barriers to Trade).

While the protection of the environment is recognized to lie within the ambit of the SPS, measures undertaken "shall not be more trade-restrictive than necessary to fulfill a legitimate objective" (Article 5.6,

WTO SPS, 1995, 3). And, as noted above, what constitutes a legitimate objective does not necessarily encompass providing consumers with full information about the provenance of their food. As a result, neither agreement provides much guidance on how labelling measures enacted to achieve other social objectives might be viewed. While national security is a legitimate reason to label, a consumer's right to know is not, especially as it relates to the way in which food is produced. Given the level of public concern about food and its provenance, it is not surprising that there is pressure on states to label for reasons that go beyond those identified as legitimate in either the SPS or the TBT. The European Union's 2003 labelling and tracing regulations for GM products, including food and animal feed, offer a case in point.

Responding to growing concerns in the late 1990s about the implications of GM crops and consumer demands for tighter regulation and more information about their food after the BSE beef crisis, these EU regulations sought to "ensure that accurate information is available to consumers to enable them to exercise their freedom of choice in an effective manner" (European Parliament and Council Regulation No. 1830, 2003). They enshrine the consumers' right to know and "ensure that consumers are fully and reliably informed about GMOs and the product, food and feed produced therefrom so as to allow them to make an informed choice of product." Tracing GM products is also seen in the regulations as integral to effective monitoring of the impacts of such products on both human health and the environment.

From the outset, these EU regulations were seen as a major trade irritant for the United States, Canada, and other countries exporting GM crops and food, and the resultant conflict over them highlighted for the state and non-state actors on each side of the issues the need to influence international food standards (as enshrined in the SPS and TBT agreements in particular) in order to either facilitate market access for food exports or preserve national policy space for food regulation.

The Codex Alimentarius and the Struggle over Food Standards

The standards of the Codex Alimentarius, a joint body of the UN Food and Agricultural Organization and the World Health Organization established in 1963,[3] are referenced in the SPS and TBT agreements and thus since 1995 have served as a benchmark and justification to the WTO for national food regulations. As a consequence, the Codex Commission since 1995, along with the WTO, has become a site of struggle around states' rights to regulate food, food eaters' rights to know the provenance of food, including where and how it is produced, and to what extent such regulations constitute unjustifiable barriers to trade. Nowhere is this more graphically illustrated than in the long struggle over regulations on the mandatory labelling of foods containing GMOs, discussed briefly below. This struggle preoccupied the Codex Committee on Food Labelling for almost twenty years as a range of state and non-state actors sought to influence the Codex standard to closely reflect their national labelling policy preferences. The reason is that national rules that deviate (i.e., exceed) Codex standards in response to consumer demands could become the subject of trade disputes and targets for WTO-authorized trade retaliation. On the other hand, as Buckingham points out, "Once international standards emerge, their employ is very difficult to challenge under the WTO dispute resolution mechanism. With a Codex standard on labelling, clearly WTO panels would be obliged to accept the standard once enacted into any national legislation. Such legislation would be a legitimate exception to WTO rules set up to facilitate international trade" (Buckingham 2000, 210).

Codex standards thus can reduce or expand the policy space for national food regulation and, as a result, Codex rule-making processes have become even more politicized. Membership has grown (186) with the increased involvement of trade officials, the WTO, and non-state actors (both corporations and non-governmental organizations) (Veggeland and Borgen 2005). The last have sought to play a greater role in the setting of standards, through their direct involvement in the work of the Codex and its committees, as they seek to influence the negotiating positions of state actors. The Codex was founded with a mandate to develop food standards protecting the health of consumers and harmonize them to ensure "fair practices in the food trade" (Codex Alimentarius Commission 2013). The Codex Commission is in session for two years, culminating in a biannual meeting held in Rome (FAO) or Geneva (WHO). Committees carry out much of the work on functional issues (such as general principles, labelling, limits on pesticide residues) and commodity areas (such as milk, milk products, or meat), as well as geographic regions. National chairs of Codex committees host the committee's work, that is, fund the secretariat and annual committee meeting costs. Canada has chaired and hosted the food labelling committee's work for many years. The development of new food standards follows an eight-step process of proposals, discussion papers, and decisions by relevant committees. Once a new standard is developed, the draft standard is circulated to members for comment and may be revised and ultimately adopted. Given the increasing demand for, and complexity of, food production standards and the small size of the Codex secretariat, the process can take years.

The Codex process allows for input (written and oral comments) from non-state actors, especially food producers and processors, and is more transparent than the WTO. But like the WTO, it operates on consensus, and state members rarely vote on issues. The reality behind the consensus, however, is that Northern major food-exporting countries, along with a few in South America, play important roles hosting and chairing many of the key committees. Funding and assistance have slowly increased the representation from the global South, but on food labelling issues major food-exporting countries tend to dominate. Given the trade significance of Codex standards, openness has provided a direct channel for corporations and others to try to influence international standards. By 2007 the number of International Non-Governmental Organizations (INGOs – the Codex term) numbered 157. Observers' numbers have increased more rapidly than state membership (Huller and Maier 2006), and the Codex Committee on Food Labelling has followed a similar pattern. In the May 2007 meeting, twenty-one of the twenty-seven INGOs present represented producer or corporate organizations. Moreover, national delegations often include industry representatives and other organizations as observers. In the 2008 committee meetings on labelling, for example, Canada's delegation included the umbrella organization BIOTECanada, which calls itself "the national voice for industry leadership for Canada's biotechnology sector" (GrowCanada 2013), represented by a Monsanto executive, along with representatives of Kraft, Nestlé, and Mead Johnson.

Consumer, environmental, health, and nutrition NGOs, despite limited resources, have also been active at both national and international levels trying to influence regulations on food labelling. Consumers International, a federation of 220 member organizations in 115 countries, has been very active, along with Friends of the Earth International and Greenpeace, in challenging the introduction of GM crops and demanding the labelling of foods produced with them. These groups have used their capacity to access committee and commission meetings to report on, and to try to influence the proceedings, either themselves, or as part of national, state-led delegations. Their reports on Codex activities are shared with other transnational coalitions, making the work of the Codex and who seeks to influence its standards better known. In terms of how food standards are developed, the scope of risk assessment within the Codex has been largely restricted to human health.

Given its small secretariat and limited resources, the Codex relies heavily on "independent experts" for scientific advice on questions of health risks. Determining what is independent, disinterested scientific knowledge is not always easy. Corporate actors enhance their authority and legitimacy on controversial issues in food or product safety by the creation of what Buse and Lee have called "institutionalized nonprofit industry established and funded scientific networks" (2005, 13) such as the International Life Sciences Institute, which claims to be nonprofit, worldwide organization whose mission is to provide science that improves public health and well-being (ILSI 2013). Founded in 1978 by food and beverage firms such as Coca-Cola and linked to the tobacco industry (Sell 2007), it also has extensive links to the FAO and is active in the work of the Codex, including the Committee on Labelling. That certain knowledge and rationales for regulating food standards are acceptable within the Codex and others are not is a reflection of power (chapter 1, this volume). While the Codex does allow for "other legitimate factors" (aside from food safety) to be considered in making decisions on labelling standards, these have been the subject of disputes within the Codex committee on General Principles. In countries where these other concerns might be driving national food labelling regulations or where there is scientific uncertainty, major divisions have emerged within the Codex that have proven difficult to resolve, as the case of GM food indicates.

The Battle over GM Food Labelling in the Global North and in the Codex

In the case of GM food products, the negotiating positions of many state delegates reflect their interests in GM commodities. GM production is concentrated in soybeans, maize, canola, and cotton. Major producers are the United States, Canada, Argentina, Brazil, and China. As early adopters of biotechnology, the United States and Canada became heavily invested in GM crops and food, with close links between the biotechnology industry, government departments (especially agriculture), and regulatory agencies (Smythe 2009). The Grocery Manufacturers of America estimate that over 70 per cent of food on the shelves of U.S. supermarkets contain GMOs (Hallman and Aquino 2005, 217). In contrast, Europe has been slower to adopt these crops, more hesitant to approve them, and has gone in a different direction on regulations.

With Canadian and U.S. support for this industry and their influence came limited regulation based on the concept of "substantial equivalence," which assumed that if the GM product, in its components, was the same as those products already deemed safe, the product would, in its entirety, also be considered safe. Despite limited regulation and the pervasive presence of GM crops in the United States and Canada, concerns in these countries about their safety, environmental impacts, especially around crop contamination, accidental releases, and the growing stranglehold that strong intellectual property rules and market concentration have afforded biotechnology corporations over access to seeds have persisted (Prakash and Kollman 2007; Smythe 2009).

Numerous surveys show that consumers in Canada and the United States want to know which foods contain GMOs and prefer mandatory labelling (Consumers Association of Canada 2003; Hallman and Aquino 2005, 219). In both countries, the influence of biotechnology and food industries and the weakness of consumer groups (especially in Canada) resulted in voluntary labelling. In practice this has meant no labelling of GM food products, leaving those who seek to avoid GM food with limited options, one being to buy organic food. Despite the limited regulation, environmental groups such as Greenpeace have continued to oppose GM crops in Canada, the United States, and elsewhere and encourage consumers to avoid them by publishing shopping guides to GM-free products.

In contrast, since 1998, as a result of food scares, public distrust of regulators, and strong consumer and food retailer opposition, the European Union had not approved any new GM products. Two had been approved earlier – corn and canola – but growing public concern and division among EU members led to a moratorium on further approvals until mandatory labelling and traceability rules were put in place. On 2 July 2003 the European Parliament approved two laws requiring the labelling of GM product discussed above. As a result, European food retailers anticipating strong consumer resistance sought to avoid foods with GMOs, affecting, in turn, the decisions of food processors and limiting export opportunities to the EU for GM crop producers. Strong consumer, environmental, and small-scale food producer movements have continued to counter the push from biotechnology corporations to gain a greater presence in EU member countries.

Given the negative impact of the EU's GM moratorium on food exports, the United States (June 2003) and then Canada (August 2003) launched a trade dispute at the WTO. Differing regulatory regimes, the potential for limited market access for GM products, and existing and potential trade disputes meant that both sides had strong incentives to advance their interests through the Codex. The EU sought to block Codex standards, as in the case of bovine growth hormones when the emerging standard did not support EU regulatory practice limiting the use of such hormones. When that effort failed, the EU became the subject of a WTO challenge over its ban on U.S. and Canadian beef. On the other hand, when U.S. attempts to gain Codex acceptance of synthetic hormones to increase cows' milk production failed, the basis of another trade challenge against the EU disappeared. In these cases, the central issues have been the scientific justification for the regulations and processes of risk assessment and management.

In 1991 the Codex Commission recognized a need to address biotechnology and GM foods. A U.S. paper on labelling was developed and formed the basis for the first major debate at the Commission on Food Labelling in October 1994, which centred on whether labelling should be required only when there were health and safety concerns and whether it should be required if the food products in question did not differ substantively from traditional equivalents.

Consumers International (CI), a non-government organization made up of consumer groups from around the world, favoured a system of comprehensive labelling based on the consumers' "right to know." Others argued in favour of labelling that indicated how food was produced in order to permit consumers to make choices based on values other than those of health and safety, such as environmental sustainability. In the absence of a clear consensus, the issue was ultimately referred back to the commission's executive committee. By April 1997, the secretariat had produced a set of draft guidelines, but after delegate complaints about the short time frame in which to consider the guidelines, the committee decided to solicit more member comments. The draft guidelines would have limited labelling to GM foods that were not considered equivalent to traditional foods and were supported by major producers of GM foods, including the United States, Brazil, and Mexico, along with the major players in the biotechnology industries. Norway, supported by consumer organizations, advocated a broader approach that reflected the right of consumers to know and choose. These divisions would be replicated in subsequent meetings of the Committee on Food Labelling as a consensus became ever more elusive.

In 1999, an alternative set of draft guidelines emerged that would allow for all foods containing GMOs to be labelled. Consumers International supported this more inclusive approach. In opposition, the United States and Argentina argued that labelling was unnecessary, given the equivalence of GM foods to conventional foods and should be required only when there were health and safety concerns (e.g., allergens) or if the foods differed substantively from traditional equivalents. The United States, supported by a number of food processing industry associations and biotechnology companies, claimed that labelling based on the method of production would imply that GM foods were unsafe and deter consumers. In the absence of consensus, the committee opted to create a working group, coordinated by Canada, to rewrite the draft and develop the two options. By 2001, the working group's revised draft included three labelling options, but no consensus was found, and another working group was established, whose report was reviewed in the 2004 meeting.

U.S. opposition to labelling based on the "method of production" was shared by Canada, a strong ally in opposing mandatory labelling. Both argued that such a policy would constitute an unfair trade practice and a barrier to exports, since consumers would perceive the label as a safety warning. The United States argued that only cases where significant changes in the product composition had occurred were legitimate candidates for mandatory labelling. The European Union, which had just developed its own labelling and traceability regulations (see above) and had been subjected to a U.S. and Canada trade challenge on its earlier moratorium on GM approvals, opposed the U.S. position.

Over time, the U.S. position opposing anything other than voluntary labelling has lost ground as more countries have opted to develop systems of mandatory labelling. Environmental organizations such as Greenpeace had been working at the national level in many countries, raising concerns about the safety of GM food and the environmental risks posed by GM crops. In addition, it worked for mandatory labelling, and where it was absent provided its own published guides to GM-free foods designed to encourage citizens to avoid them. Mandatory labelling from the perspective of Greenpeace was but one part of their anti-GM strategy, designed to make GM products less profitable by limiting the market for them. For consumer organizations, the push for labelling was part of a broad commitment to the consumer's right to know. This position was argued consistently at the Codex and by 2005 was gaining ground. Countries supporting a more comprehensive labelling of GM food included the EU members, China, Japan, Korea, Thailand, India, Nigeria, Kenya, Cameroon, Malaysia, Australia, and New Zealand. Non-state actors included Consumers International, the International Federation of Organic Agriculture, Greenpeace, and the Erosion, Technology and Concentration (ETC) Group.

Those favouring very limited or no labelling included the major biotechnology organizations such as CropLife, the Biotechnology Industry Organization (a U.S. industry advocacy group), BIOTECanada, the
International Association of Plant Breeders for the Protection of Plant
Varieties, and the International Council of Grocery Manufacturers
(Public Citizen 2005). Recognizing that its more restrictive view of labelling was losing support, the United States at the May 2006 meeting
argued that the Codex should abandon the search for guidelines on labelling altogether (Codex 2006), fearing any development of mandatory labelling standards would limit their push for more export market
access for GM food via the WTO.

Some smaller countries lined up behind the EU and Japan, partly
because they feared the implications for their own exports to these markets if they accepted GM products without labelling or traceability. At
meetings of the Codex Committee on Food Labelling in 2006 to 2010 a
major issue, once again, was GM food labelling. The United States continued, despite the new Obama administration that initially seemed to
be sympathetic to mandatory labelling, to argue over the growing domestic opposition of eighty consumer, environmental, and food activists groups (Consumers Union 2010) that GM labelling was misleading
and inappropriate, even for organic food, because of the "substantial
equivalence" of GM and non-GM foods. However, in the face of growing concerns and popular pressure, the majority of state delegations at
the Codex favoured allowing countries to opt for mandatory labelling
if they chose. Further attempts to reconcile the two sides in a meeting in
Brussels in November 2010 failed. The sixteen-year battle came to an
end in May 2011 at the thirty-ninth session of the Committee on Food
Labelling when the U.S. delegation – seeking to weaken wording and
further marginalize the text in its placement within the labelling guidelines[4] – faced defeat. Even staunch allies of the United States in the
Canadian delegation gave up the fight. The committee approved the
compilation of texts on GM labelling, which, while not strong on mandatory labelling, does acknowledge a variety of national approaches to
labelling, including mandatory ones and thus implicitly accepts and
permits such approaches (Consumers International 2011). This recom-
mendation went forward for expedited approval at the full Codex
meeting in Geneva in July 2011. To the surprise of many, the United
States abandoned its opposition at that final meeting.

The debate over comprehensive labelling has centred on the consumers' "right to know" how food is produced in order to make choices

based on values not limited to health and safety. Both Canada and the United States had argued that labelling based on process or production methods violates trade rules. Moreover, they claimed the consumers' right to know was not a legitimate basis on which to require labelling. The stalemate at the Codex committee did not end the conflict over GM food labelling – rather it continues on a number of fronts, including through the trade dispute system of the WTO and the SPS and TBT committees, as well as at the national and sub-national levels.

As this case indicates, the power of the biotechnology industry and influence over its champion, the United States, was not enough to stop GM mandatory labelling in many countries or enable it to ensure that the Codex guidelines would condone only voluntary standards. Rather the strong consumer demands for labelling in Europe created a wedge of division at the Codex, which allowed over a long period of time for the erosion of the U.S. position. The consistent demands by NGOs for a right to know shifted the ground away from scientific risk assessment. While the outcome permits national mandatory labelling, it does not mean, even where state regulations mandate such labels, that consumers will necessarily avoid GM foods or corporate efforts will not continue to manipulate or weaken regulations. What it will do, however, is create a context in which education on the implications of biotechnology and GM crops can occur and potentially lead to consumer action. If that action, along with state regulation, lead to limits on the development and profitability of GM crops and foods, space again will be created for alternative and sustainable agriculture. I would argue that such steps can move us towards greater food sovereignty.

European labelling regulations have continued to create problems for U.S. exporters. Despite pressure from the biotechnology and agricultural sectors and some members of Congress to launch another trade complaint against EU regulations, uncertainty about its likely success based on the TBT obligations and the need for European cooperation to rescue the sinking Doha negotiations led to U.S. restraint (Schramm 2007, 96). More recently a major biotechnology company, BASF, has left Europe, citing the difficulty of regulation. Within the United States the push for GM labelling has continued and the coalition arguing for it has broadened, partly because of a sense of betrayal by the Obama Administration's actions at the Codex and in the appointing of biotechnology executives to key positions in the U.S. Administration, including the Trade Representative's Office. Most recently, California food activists have created a broad-based Right to Know campaign, which put the question of mandatory GM food labelling on a state ballot initiative for the November 2012 election.

Country-of-Origin Labelling

The provenance of food, especially where it is produced, has been recognized historically and often celebrated for creating distinctive and desirable food qualities. Many European foods were and are intimately connected to place, often a region, a locale, a *terroir*. In those cases food producers and distributors want to label the place of origin and often extract a price premium for the product from consumers. With food products that are interchangeable, however, sourcing is done globally on the basis of price, and other qualities such as durability in the case of products shipped over long distances. The current globalized and integrated food production system makes it difficult in such cases for consumers who are far from sites of production and processing to identify or determine the place or method of production of the food they are eating, especially if it is highly processed. Consumers might desire such information if they wish to purchase food produced closer to home or if they harbour concerns about how food is produced in other countries or regions. Yet they are totally reliant on the information contained in the food label to know what they are eating and from where it comes. If requirements to label for geographic origin, such as country, are voluntary, it means that the labelling of origin will be used by food retailers, or even governments, as a marketing tool at their discretion. That is, they will label for origin only when it will give advantage to their product against competitors in the marketplace. Thus control over what is on the label, if voluntary, rests with corporate entities and is, in most cases, market-based. Having the right to know where food comes from is obviously important for those eaters who wish to privilege the local, however defined, in their food purchases. And, as noted in the introduction to this chapter, the concept of food sovereignty has within it a notion of privileging local food production.

Both the WTO and the Codex have guidelines on food labelling in terms of origins. The WTO does permit the labelling of a product's origin under Article 9 referring to marks of origin. But labelling requirements are subject to WTO principles including non-discrimination, which requires that like products, be they domestic or foreign, be treated equally. The SPS and TBT agreements cover matters of labelling and accept certain justifications for labelling, but these justifications do not include the "right to know" unless the information is necessary to avoid deception.

In the case of the Codex, labelling for origin is covered in the General Guidelines on Labelling of Prepackaged Foods, section 4.5, which states that origin must be declared only when its omission would mislead a consumer. Origin is defined, in the case of processed food, in terms of where the processing occurred (Codex 2007, 13). Thus there is no standard requiring mandatory country-of-origin labelling and in the case of processed goods could involve voluntary labels that identify a product as domestic, that is, "made in Canada," even if the food being processed, such as olives, was clearly not grown in Canada.

Beyond ensuring that consumers are not misled, the Codex currently has little to say on the issue. That is the result, however, of successful efforts by the United States to stop work on country-of-origin labelling (COOL). Consumer demands and experience with BSE led the newly created U.K. food standards agency to argue that the Codex should look at COOL since many countries were seen to be moving in that direction. Delegates proposed that the Commission on Food Labelling engage in new work on COOL revising the guidelines. The Committee on Food Labelling asked the United Kingdom, along with Malaysia and Switzerland, to prepare a paper setting out issues and identifying areas where provisions were lacking, such as in dealing with the sources of ingredients in processed food. However, disagreement among delegates led the full commission to withhold approval for new work and encourage further committee discussions. In 2002 a paper summarizing the issues was discussed in Halifax, and the extent of disagreement among delegates became clear (Codex 2002). Despite the looming passage in the U.S. Congress of the 2002 Farm Bill, which had mandatory COOL requirements for meat in it, the U.S. (G.W. Bush) Administration was unsupportive of such labelling. Claiming that mandatory COOL labelling would provide no benefit to consumers, would be difficult for the food industry to implement, given global sourcing, and might violate provisions of the WTO, especially the TBT Agreement, the United States argued for the status quo (Codex Alimentarius Commission 2002, 13).

In contrast, the U.K. delegation argued that many countries had already begun introducing either voluntary or mandatory labelling and that consumers' demands for more information on country of origin had been increasing, especially for meat. Once again the debate centred not on food safety but on providing consumers with the "information needed to make a choice of products" (Codex Alimentarius Commission 2002, 13). A number of state delegations, Malaysia, Korea, Switzerland, India, Japan, Norway, the European Commission and consumer and public health NGOs Consumers International, International Association of Consumer Food Organizations, and International Baby Food Action Network wanted Codex work on COOL to continue. Opposed were largely food-exporting countries of North and South America, along with New Zealand. Consumers International and a number of other NGOs argued that consumers were confused about the origins of their food (Codex 2003). The United States, in contrast, argued that labelling should be required only if its omission would mislead or deceive the consumer and that expanded mandatory COOL would "create an un-necessary obstacle to trade with no legitimate or internationally recog-nized justification" (Codex Alimentarius Commission 2002, 13). Siding with the United States against work on COOL was the International Council of Grocery Manufacturers Associations, the International Fro-zen Food Association, and the European Association representing the food and drink industry. Canada supported the U.S. position, rejecting a proposal to identify the country of origin for meat as the place of birth, rearing, and slaughter, arguing to maintain the existing definition based on where the last significant production operation occurred, thus permitting meat from Canadian animals shipped to the United States for slaughter to be labelled as U.S. meat. Continuing divisions led the committee to abandon work on the issue in 2004 (Codex Alimentarius Commission, 2004), which means that mandatory labelling continues to be justified only if omitting it would mislead the consumer.[5] Nonethe-less, the failure to develop a new Codex standard on mandatory COOL did not put an end to public pressures for mandatory labelling; rather, it continued at the national level, even in the United States. The failure at the Codex, however, came back to haunt the U.S. Administration and those U.S. activists who advocated for mandatory labelling. As we will see below, international rules have come into conflict with U.S. Administration efforts to satisfy an array of demands to know more about the origins of food and created challenges for those who want consumers to have access to information allowing them to privilege local food producers.

The Battle in the United States over COOL

U.S. regulations on labelling the origin of goods go back to the Tariff Act of 1930, but the current issue dates from the Consumer Right to

Know Act of 2001. The bill introduced by South Dakota Democratic Senator Tim Johnson required that beef, lamb, pork, fresh fruit, and vegetables be labelled at final point of sale according to their country of origin. Similar bills were introduced by North Dakota and California Democrats in the House of Representatives and were later incorporated into the U.S. Farm Bill, which in a final compromise contained a broader list of products, including meat. Favouring COOL were groups of smaller-scale livestock producers, small farmers, and environmental and consumer organizations. The latter pointed to several public opinion surveys, which showed a desire of the public for mandatory country of origin labels.

Food processors, retailers, meat packers, and large agri-business, along with the G.W. Bush Administration and the U.S. Department of Agriculture, opposed these labelling provisions and, during a two-year phase-in in implementation, were able to mobilize powerful forces of opposition. Similar to the GM food labelling case, U.S. opponents of mandatory COOL labelling had the advantage of close links to the Administration through the revolving doors of corporations and senior administrators and deep pockets for lobbying and campaign contributions (Smith 2003; Food and Water Watch 2010). Twenty-one corporations and trade associations, such as the Grocery Manufacturers of America, spent over $29 million from 2000 to 2004 on lobbying Congress, and 160 lobbyists worked to oppose COOL (Public Citizen 2005, 2). In the same period, these organizations donated $12.6 million to congressional campaigns. USDA and the food industry also exaggerated the costs for implementing COOL, which they claimed would be passed on to consumers with little benefit, but their figures were challenged by the General Accounting Office in a 2003 study (US GAO, 2003).

Opponents effectively used the implementation delay to organize sympathetic members of Congress to pass an appropriations bill for the USDA, which further delayed implementation until 2007. This allowed opponents from outside the United States to provide comments in opposition, including the Canadian government, Canadian meat producers, and processors. The United States notified the WTO's TBT committee of the measures on meat labelling on 26 June 2007 as the clock on delaying COOL ran out. The United States justified the COOL measures in terms of SPS justification of "protection of consumers and human health" (WTO 2007) and called for comment before the final rule. The Canadian government provided observations similar to those of larger Canadian livestock producers (in opposition to the measure) and U.S. COOL opponents, claiming that regulations would cost US$3.9 billion (the USDA figure) without benefit to consumers. Canada also claimed that the U.S. and Canadian governments had been working hard for eighteen years towards trade integration to "make national origin irrelevant in business and consumer decisions" (Government of Canada 2008, 6). The Canadian submission noted that the definition of processing in the act did not conform to the Codex standard.

With over 10 per cent of Canadian agri-food exports being meat and a tightly integrated continental system of production, the industry perspective (represented by organizations of beef and pork livestock producers, corporate meat packing and processing firms, and the Canadian Federation of Agriculture) and that of the Canadian government were shaped by the high level of cross-border industry integration and the extensive movement of live animals, carcasses, and meat products across the border. Canadian producers feared that meat that needed to be labelled as product of Canada or Canada and the United States would suffer at the hands of U.S. meat packers and consumers in comparison to U.S. products. In contrast, consumer groups and smaller livestock producers in the United States argued that the voluntary system of labelling was misleading U.S. consumers who did not realize that USDA-inspected meat originated in Canada or Mexico and had only been slaughtered in the United States. Others in Canada such as the National Farmers Union did not oppose COOL, seeing the problem as corporate concentration and excessive dependence of Canadian livestock producers on the big meat processing companies.

In June 2008 the Food Conservation and Energy Act (the "Farm Bill") passed, replacing the 2002 Farm Bill, after a drawn-out battle that included a presidential veto and override. At 673 pages, the bill contained much political pork and trade-offs among interests, including those of agri-business, recipients of massive subsidies, as well as local and organic farming. Title XI included measures to implement COOL, effective 30 September 2008. Again similar forces opposed the COOL provisions. Canada raised concerns to the USDA in September 2008 and indicated it would launch formal consultations with the United States under the provisions of the WTO. The Canadian government objected to the three labelling options and the definition of processing, and claimed discriminatory treatment under the WTO, arguing that the resulting labels would only confuse consumers and be costly. COOL opponents in the United States and Canada lobbied to have the act implemented in a way that allowed vague labelling of meat products as derived from a number of national sources. While this compromise raised concerns among consumer activists, it reassured the Canadian government, which felt confident enough to suspend its WTO challenge in January 2009. In the interim, a president supportive of COOL[6] and a new secretary of agriculture took over the administration. The USDA final rule on COOL was preceded by a letter on 20 February 2009 from U.S. Agriculture Secretary Vilsack who "suggested" to the industry that they voluntarily go beyond the rules and indicate specifically to consumers what production steps occurred in which country, signalling a move, if they failed to do so, to tighter mandatory rules. Labels should note that the animal was born in Canada, and raised and slaughtered in the United States (Vilsack 2009). Canadian producers feared that if compliance costs increased and led to a need to segregate Canadian cattle and meat, U.S. meat processors would be reluctant to purchase Canadian livestock, or there would be discounted prices for Canadian producers in the U.S. market. At that point Canada restarted the WTO process.

What had changed in the period from the U.S. Administration's opposition to COOL at the Codex in 2003 and the Farm Bill in 2008? A simple answer might be a new Democratic administration. However, there is little evidence that previous Democratic administrations had been supportive of such labelling. Rather the answer might be found in changing attitudes about the food system. As Michael Pollan has argued, "The American people are paying more attention to food today than they have in decades, worrying not only about its price but about its safety, its provenance and its healthfulness. There is a gathering sense among the public that the industrial-food system is broken. Markets for alternative kinds of food – organic, local, pasture-based, humane – are thriving as never before. All this suggests that a political constituency for change is building" (Pollan 2008, 6).

By 2008 small-scale producers had been joined in the battle for COOL by over 100 other local food, environmental, and consumer activist organizations. In fact the COOL case reflects a broader trend that poses challenges for the globalized system, including the development of local and transnational movements such as slow food, local food, and groups concerned about food security and climate change. All of this has converged around demands to know the provenance of food. Despite these pressures, however, international trade norms continue to exert a powerful influence, as the U.S. dispute with Canada and Mexico over COOL shows, when it moved to the formal panel stage at the WTO in the spring of 2010.

The first U.S. submission to the panel is indicative of how the United States justified these measures. While the initial notification to the WTO spoke of measures "to protect consumers and human health," the formal U.S. submission to the WTO panel was much more limited and circumspect. The United States was careful to argue that the measures complied with WTO obligations by not discriminating against foreign products (all meats must be labelled) and were necessary to avoid misleading consumers, part of the Codex Criteria and the TBT justification. The U.S. submission included survey data showing confusion of U.S. consumers about the origins of meat under voluntary labelling systems. The submission also noted, in response to Canadian and Mexican demands that the United States retain only voluntary labelling, that previous voluntary guidelines had resulted in an absence of clear labelling. According to the United States, "The primary problem with voluntary labelling is that many businesses will not voluntarily make the choice to label their products with origin information when given the option" (United States 2010). This comment could well be used to describe voluntary U.S. rules on labelling GM food.

In May 2011 the WTO panel released a preliminary ruling followed by a final report on the dispute, which, while it did not dismiss the right to label origin of food or the justification of providing more information to consumers, found the measures too trade restrictive (WTO 2011). As the International Centre for Trade and Sustainable Development (ICTSD 2011) noted, this was the third U.S. regulatory measure strengthening consumer protection and access to information found too trade restricting by the WTO in the past year. The U.S. response to the WTO was to note that "the panel affirmed the right of the United States to require country of origin labelling for meat products," but disagreed with the specifics of how the United States designed those requirements (USTR 2011). The United States left open the possibility of appealing the ruling at the WTO. The result, while it has disappointed and angered U.S. activists who supported COOL, has reopened a debate at the level of trade law about the legitimacy of consumers' right to know as a basis on which to regulate (Ross 2010) and brought home once again the extent to which trade rules have limited regulatory policy space regarding citizens know how (e.g., GM labelling) and where their food is produced.

Linking the Local and the Global: Food Sovereignty and the Right to Know the Provenance of Food

As the introduction and chapter 1 of this volume have argued, the concept of food sovereignty has resonated with many groups and movements in the global South and the North. In the United States this has been reflected in efforts since 2007 to use cross-movement gatherings such as the United States Social Forum (USSF) to bring activists from an array of food, agriculture, climate, and other movements together, using food sovereignty as their entry point (Aziz 2010). This initiative culminated in the launch of the U.S. Food Sovereignty Alliance in New Orleans in October 2010. In Canada, networks like Food Secure Canada and the Canadian Biotechnology Action Network (CBAN) also reference the concept of food sovereignty. In 2009 the Peoples Food Policy Project (see Martin and Andrée, this volume) developed a food sovereignty policy for Canada, which includes positions on labelling (Peoples Food Policy Project, 2011). Beyond creating alternative food systems that shrink the distance between smaller-scale producers and food eaters, many movements and organizations have demanded the right to know more about the provenance of food than what large corporate processors and retailers choose to reveal. Many of these organizations have been involved in campaigning in both Canada and the United States for mandatory labelling of GM foods and country-of-origin labelling.

In Canada, food scares and confusion around misleading labelling of products (such as Chinese apple juice labelled as "Product of Canada") led the government in April 2008 to introduce new guidelines, which would require that both the contents and processing be Canadian if a "Product of Canada" label is used. Debate and discussion around the issue of "Made in Canada" and "Product of Canada" have led consumer and producer groups, local food activists, food retailers, and processors to become engaged. A parliamentary committee has held hearings (Standing Committee on Agriculture and Agri-Food 2008) and the Canadian Food Inspection Agency has held public consultations. The Canadian government continues, however, as does the food processing industry, to resist the idea that such labels should be mandatory. Given the investment of Canadian governments in an export-oriented corporate model of the food system and the international trade rules that support it, this is not surprising. For the past decade, Canadian officials have questioned at the Codex and the WTO whether consumers have a right to know the provenance of their food beyond a set of justifications based on human health and safety defined under scientifically based risk assessments. Yet consumer organizations, environmental activists, and some farmers represented by the National Farmers Union continue to argue for such labelling. The National Farmers Union argues, "Citizens have a right to know where their food comes from; to know if their dinner roast is from Canada or New Zealand or Uruguay.

Most people would prefer to know even more: i.e., whether their Canadian roast is from Southern Alberta, Central Manitoba, or Eastern Ontario. Canada can use country-of-origin labelling to meet the information needs of consumers, help build diversified local markets, reduce food miles, and move our meat system toward increased social, economic, and environmental sustainability" (National Farmers Union 2008, 21).

As this chapter clearly shows, however, achieving that right can involve a long and drawn-out struggle at both the domestic and international levels.

Conclusion

As consumers, or more accurately,[7] food "eaters," demand to know more about the provenance of their food, pressure has increased for states to do more to regulate food labelling. These demands from movements of food, environmental, and other activists represent a reaction to the globalizing food system and a demand for protection of society from the excesses of the market. However, my two case studies of GM and country-of-origin labelling show clearly the extent to which international trade rules that seek to harmonize regulations to further liberalize global food and agricultural trade not only destroy sustainable peasant-based agriculture but also limit domestic policy space to create regulations and policies that support more domestically oriented food systems. National standards that support the right of eaters to know the provenance of their food, under existing trade rules, could incur costly trade retaliation. If alternative food systems are going to survive and challenge the dominant agri-business model, they "will have to engage with, and draw support from, the multi-level governance system that regulates the agri-food system" (Morgan, Marsden, and Murdoch 2006, 192). Thus the struggle over protection from the market must occur at the international level of the Codex and the WTO as well as at the domestic level. That struggle, as my cases indicate, has been occurring around the issues of food labelling.

This focus on labelling, as I indicated at the beginning of this chapter, has come in for criticism. Ethical consuming, whether it be fair trade or local food, is seen as part of a reformist project based on individual consumption where an emphasis on consumer sovereignty, as Friedmann and McNair (2008) point out, risks reinforcing the existing food system. Embedded in networks of capitalist production, as Zerbe's case study of fair trade in this volume shows, ethical consuming may be open to co-optation by corporations, especially by food retailers. Similar concerns arise in the case of local food in Europe (McMichael, this volume). Yet developing alternative, more localized food systems, an aspect of food sovereignty, involves engaging not just food producers but also eaters who support local and sustainable food systems.

As my case studies show, the struggles over food labelling have provided a broad frame that has generated coalitions of small producers, consumers, environmentalists, public health, and local food activists who can and do work together to challenge rules that limit the capacity of consumers and states to support alternative local food systems. In the process they are generating greater knowledge and awareness about the food system, where and how the food we eat is produced, as well as how international trade rules and standards and the power structure underlying them have limited domestic policy space. This knowledge is significant, as it forms the basis of a dialogue between consumers and food producers about the existing system, who benefits, and who makes the rules and alternatives, as identified by advocates of food sovereignty. In this context, the struggle over labelling can strengthen the movement challenging the current system of global food governance. Mobilizing support for local food systems and food sovereignty is more than a local or even a national matter; it involves transnational movements. In the process, and despite the pitfalls, it must involve a wide array of actors going beyond food producers to include the more numerous food eaters and their desire to know the provenance and quality of their food.

NOTES

1 The support of the Social Sciences and Humanities Research Council of Canada is gratefully acknowledged.
2 "Stop Corporate Globalization: Another World Is Possible! A Statement of Unity from the Our World Is Not for Sale Network," 21 November 2005, 7.
3 See Codex Alimentarius (2013).
4 Author's observations at CFL meeting, Quebec City, 10 May 2011.
5 For example, if a product in North America were called Florida Fresh Juice but were in fact made from Brazilian orange juice, the omission of the origin on the label might mislead a consumer. On the other hand, a product of Boston Baked Beans might not be required to label, since few

consumers would be likely to think the beans or the preparation occurred in Boston or even the United States.

6 Under Plans to Support Rural Communities, in his campaign platform Obama committed to "establish country of origin labeling" (2008).

7 Nettie Wiebe often uses the term *eaters* when speaking to audiences about food issues to counter the "notion that food is just another standardized commodity where unit price determines customer choice" (Wiebe and Wipf 2011).

REFERENCES

Aziz, Nikhil. 2010. "US Food Sovereignty Alliance Launches in New Orleans." Grassroots International, 19 October. http://www.grassrootsonline.org/news/blog/us-food-sovereignty-alliance-launches-new-orleans.

Blay-Palmer, Allison. 2008. *Food Fears*. Aldershot, Hampshire: Ashgate.

Borras, Saturnino M. Jr. 2008. "La Vía Campesina and Its Global Campaign for Agrarian Reform." *Journal of Agrarian Change* 8 (2–3): 258–89. http://dx.doi.org/10.1111/j.1471-0366.2008.00170.x.

Buckingham, Don. 2000. "The Labelling of GM Foods: The Link between the Codex and the WTO. *Agbioforum* 3 (4): 209–12.

Buse, Kent, and Kelley Lee. 2005. "Business and Global Health Governance." Discussion Paper #5, December. London: Centre on Global Change & Health London School of Hygiene & Tropical Medicine.

Codex Alimentarius Commission. 2002. *Report of the Thirtieth Session of the Codex Committee on Food Labelling*. Halifax, May.

– 2003. *Consideration of Country of Origin Labelling, Comments from Brazil, Costa Rica, Denmark, France, Italy, New Zealand, Spain, United States, CIAA, and the European Community*.

– 2004. *Considerations of Country of Origin Labelling, Committee on Food Labelling*. Montreal, 10–14 May.

– 2006. *Report of the Thirty-Fourth Session of the Codex Committee on Food Labelling*. Ottawa, 1–6 May.

– 2007. *Food Labelling*. 5th ed. Rome: Food and Agriculture Organization.

– 2013. "About Codex." http://www.codexalimentarius.org/.

Consumers Association of Canada. 2003. "Consumers Want Mandatory Labelling of Genetically Modified Foods." News release, 3 December.

Consumers International. 2011. "Consumer Rights Victory as US Ends Opposition to GM Labelling Guidelines." 5 July. http://www.consumersinternational.org/news-and-media/news/2011/07/gm-labelling-victory-as-us-ends-opposition.

Consumers Union. 2010. "Letter to Taylor and Merrigan." 20 April. http://
consumersunion.org/pdf/Codex-comm-ltr-0410.pdf.

DeLind, Laura B. 2011. "Are Local Food and the Local Food Movement Taking
Us Where We Want to Go? Or Are We Hitching Our Wagons to the Wrong
Stars?" *Agriculture and Human Values* 28 (2): 273–83. http://dx.doi.org/10
.1007/s10460-010-9263-0.

Desmarais, Annette Aurélie. 2007. *La Vía Campesina: Globalization and the Power
of Peasants*. Halifax: Fernwood.

European Parliament and the Council. 2003. Regulation (EC) No. 1830. http://
eur-lex.europa.eu/LexUriServ/LexUriServ.do?uri=OJ:L:2003:268:0024:0028:
EN:PDF.

Food and Water Watch. 2010. "Food and Agriculture Biotechnology Industry
Spends More than Half a Billion Dollars to Influence Congress." http://
www.foodandwaterwatch.org/briefs/food-and-agriculture-
biotechnology-industry-influence/.

Friedmann, Harriet, and Amber McNair. 2008. "Whose Rules Rule? Contested
Projects to Certify 'Local Production for Distant Consumers.'" *Journal of
Agrarian Change* 8 (2–3): 408–34. http://dx.doi.org/10.1111/j.1471-0366
.2008.00175.x.

Government of Canada, Canadian Ambassadors to the United States. 2008.
"Letter to Lloyd Day, USDA, and Attached Government of Canada.
Comments on the Interim Final Ruling Mandatory Country of Origin
Labelling." 5 September. http://www.regulations.gov/contentStreamer?obj
ectId=09000064806f435d&contentType=pdf&disposition=attachment.

Grow Canada Conference. 2013. Partners. http://www.growcanadaconference
.ca/2013/about.php.

Guthman, Julie. 2007. "The Polanyan Way: Voluntary Food Labelling as
Neoliberal Governance." *Antipode* 39 (3): 457–78.

Hallman, William, and Helen L. Aquino. 2005. Consumers' Desire for GM
Labels: Is the Devil in the Details? *Choices: The Magazine of Food, Farms and
Resource Issues* 20 (4): 217–21.

Huller, Thorsten, and Matthias Leonhard Maier. 2006. "Fixing the Codex?
Global Food Safety Governance under Review." In *Constitutionalism,
Multilevel Trade Governance and Social Regulation*, edited by Christian Jeorges
and Ernst-Ulrich Petersmann, 267–99. Portland, OR: Hart Publishing.

International Centre for Trade and Sustainable Development (ICTSD). 2011.
"Canada, Mexico Defeat US Country of Origin Labelling at the WTO."
Bridges 15 (40). http://ictsd.org/i/news/bridgesweekly/119343.

International Life Sciences Institute (ILSI). 2013. "About ILSI." http://www
.ilsi.org/Pages/HomePage.aspx. http//ilsi.org.

International Planning Committee. 2002. "Developing a New Relationship between the Food and Agriculture Organization and Non-Governmental and Civil Society Organizations: A Summary of Principles and Action Proposals." Presented to Jacques Diouf, director-general of FAO, 1 November 2002, NGO/CSO Forum "For Food Sovereignty," Rome. http://www.foodsovereignty.org/Portals/0/documenti%20sito/IPC%20Fao/2002-En-Regional%20Consultation%20Guidelines-Principles%20and%20actions.pdf.

Kneen, Cathleen. 2010. "Grassroots Voices: Mobilization and Convergence in a Wealthy Northern Country." *Journal of Peasant Studies* 37 (1): 229–35.

Martínez-Torres, María Elena, and Peter M. Rosset. 2010. "La Vía Campesina: The birth and evolution of a transnational social Movement." *Journal of Peasant Studies* 37 (1): 149–75. http://dx.doi.org/10.1080/03066150903498804.

Morgan, Kevin, Terry Marsden, and Jonathan Murdoch. 2006. *Worlds of Food: Place, Power and Provenance in the Food Chain*. New York: Oxford.

National Farmers Union. 2008. "The Farm Crisis and the Cattle Sector: Toward a New Analysis and New Solutions." November.

Organization for Action. 2008. "Obama Supports Immediate Implementation of the Country of Origin Labeling Law so That American Producers Can Distinguish Their Products from Imported Ones." http://www.mega.nu/ampp/obama_agenda/rural.html.

Our World Is Not for Sale (OWINFS). 2009. "The OWINFS Statement of Political Unity," 17 July. http://www.ourworldisnotforsale.org/en/signon/owinfs-statement-political-unity.

Peoples Food Policy Project. 2011. http://peoplesfoodpolicy.ca.

Pimbert, M. 2008. *Towards Food Sovereignty: Reclaiming Autonomous Food Systems*. London: International Institute for Environment and Development.

Pollan, Michael. 2008. Farmer in Chief, the Food Issue. *New York Times Magazine*, October 9.

Prakash, Aseem, and Kelly Kollman. 2007. "Biopolitics in the US: An Assessment." In *The International Politics of Genetically Modified Food: Diplomacy, Trade and Law*, edited by Robert Falkner, 103–17. Basingstoke City, Hampshire: Palgrave.

Public Citizen. 2005. *Tabled Labels: Consumers Eat Blind While Congress Feasts on Campaign Cash*. Washington, DC. http://www.foodandwaterwatch.org/reports/tabled-labels-consumers-eat-blind/.

Ross, Carrie. 2010. "In the Hot House: Will Canada's WTO Challenge Slaughter US COOL Regulations." *Brooklyn Journal of International Law* 36 (1): 299–336.

Rosset, P. 2003. "Food Sovereignty: Global Rally Cry of Farmer Movements." *Food First Backgrounder* 9 (4): 1–4.

Schramm, Daniel. 2007. "The Race to Geneva: Resisting the Gravitational Pull of the WTO in the GM Labelling Controversy." *Vermont Journal of Environmental Law* 9:93–129.

Sell, Susan. 2007 "Lobbying Strategies of Multinational Corporations in Biotechnology." Paper presented at the International Studies Association, Chicago, 4 March.

Smith, Jeffrey. 2003. *Seeds of Deception*. Fairfield, IA: Yes! Publishers.

Smythe, Elizabeth. 2009. "In Whose Interests? Transparency and Accountability in the Global Governance of Food." In *Corporate Power in Global Agrifood Governance*, edited by J. Clapp and Doris Fuchs, 93–124. Cambridge, MA: MIT Press.

Standing Committee on Agriculture and Agri-Food. 2008. "'Product of Canada' Claims: Truth and Transparency Are Necessary." June.

United States. 2010. *Certain Country of Origin Labelling (COOL) Requirements: Executive Summary of the First Written Submission of the United States of America*. 24 August. WTO document WT/DS348/386. http://www.ustr .gov/webfm_send/2292.

United States General Accounting Office. 2003. *Country of Origin Labelling: Opportunities for USDA and Industry to Implement Challenging Aspects of the New Law*.

United States Trade Representative Office (USTR). 2011. "Statement by the Office of the U.S. Trade Representative in Response to WTO Panel Decision on Country of Origin Labelling." 18 November. http://www.ustr.gov.

Veggeland, Frode, and Svein Ole Borland. 2005. "Negotiating International Food Standards: The World Trade Organization's Impact on the Codex Alimentarius Commission." *Governance: An International Journal of Policy, Administration and Institutions* 18 (4): 675–708. http://dx.doi.org/10.1111/ j.1468-0491.2005.00297.x.

Vilsack, Tom. 2009. "Letter to Industry Representatives." 20 February. United States Department of Agriculture. http://www.usda.gov/documents/0220_ IndustryLetterCOOL.pdf.

Wiebe, Nettie, and Kevin Wipf. 2011. "Nurturing Food Sovereignty in Canada." In *Food Sovereignty in Canada*, edited by Hannah Whitman, Annette Desmarais and Nettie Wiebe, 1–12. Halifax: Fernwood.

World Trade Organization (WTO). 1995. "WTO Agreement on the Application of Sanitary and Phytosanitary Measures (SPS Agreement)." http://www .wto.org/english/tratop_e/sps_e/spsagr_e.htm.

– 1995. "Agreement on Technical Barriers to Trade." http://www.wto.org/
  english/docs_e/legal_e/17-tbt.pdf.
– 2006. *Panel Report*, 23 September. http://www.wto.org/english/tratop_e/
  dispu_e/291r_conc_e.pdf
– 2007. "Notification, Committee on Technical Barriers to Trade," 26 June.
  G/TBT/N/USA/281. docsonline.wto.org/imrd/directdoc.asp?.../t/G/
  Tbtn07/USA281.doc.
– 2011. *Reports of the Panel United States Certain Country of Origin (COOL)
  Labelling Requirements*, 18 November. WT/DS384/R. http://www.wto.org/
  english/tratop_e/dispu_e/384_386r_e.pdf.

11 Food Sovereignty as Localized Resistance to Globalization in France and the United States[1]

JEFFREY AYRES AND MICHAEL J. BOSIA

The June 2006 "Chicken Pizza Direct Action" is folkloric. Vermont restaurant-owner George Schenk challenged state authorities by threatening to serve chicken from a nearby farm in his restaurant without proper state certification. Schenk, the founder and president of American Flatbread, qualified what he referred to as his entrepreneurial non-violent civil disobedience (St Peter 2006) as a means of raising greater awareness about regulatory barriers that undercut the rights of citizens to choose where and from whom they buy their food. Schenk's defence of food sovereignty challenged government policies favouring industrial agribusiness and factory-farmed meat at the expense of small farmers and consumers knowledgeable about the source and safety of their food. While the farm in question sold chickens directly to consumers, it could not sell to retail businesses without a state-approved slaughter-house facility. Remarked Connie Gaylord, whose chicken farm lies directly across the street from American Flatbread, "Why force us to do something which means we get bigger ... why can't local just stay local ... why does everything have to come from far away?" (Porter 2006).

Eighteen months later and across the Atlantic, the more renowned José Bové, noted as the "French farmer" from the region of Larzac, launched a hunger strike to win a one-year ban on genetically modified (GMO) crops. A worldwide activist-celebrity and one-time anti-neoliberal candidate for president of France, Bové popularized food sovereignty by associating GMO seeds and other symbols of food's global commodification with threats to the rural way of life and the quality of foodstuffs, concerns widely shared by the French population. Ridiculing the government's proposed temporary ban on the commercial use of GMOs, Bové argued that his action, in concert with a dozen other activists, called attention to research questioning the safety of modified seeds, and more broadly to the public's right to grow and eat food untainted by multinational agribusiness. The ensuing eight-day hunger strike resulted in a political victory when French officials banned the commercial use of MON810, a transgenic maize developed by Monsanto (Kempf 2008).

Does the Vermont story, with its emphasis on local foods, localvore eating (often called *locavore* outside New England), and food democracy, represent a branch of the global food sovereignty movement illustrated by our Larzac farmer's actions in France? Conceptually specific, sharply focused, but vague in its political usage, "food sovereignty," as outlined by Menser in this volume, was originally developed by the international farmer and peasant collective La Vía Campesina at the World Food Summit in 1996, and expanded most recently as the "Nyéléni Declaration" at a global conference of peasants and farmers in Mali in 2007. Generally, food sovereignty is a demand for greater local control over food systems and the proliferation of locally empowered producers and consumers in response to the industrialization and commodification of food under neoliberal governance. In the United States, food sovereignty might be framed as food democracy; nonetheless, the premise and priorities remain the same, whether named democracy in terms of community and popular participation over decision-making, or sovereignty in terms of local and community-based control over food-related decisions. Despite its specificity, food sovereignty (and the North American variant of food democracy) is predicated on a political and social pluralism that allows for the persistence of local differences in the realization of concrete objectives. Considering the tensions between a global framework and its local realization, we call attention to how claims-making and grievance-naming within the Larzac movement and among Vermonters derive from and reinforce some sustained transnational relationships within the food sovereignty movement; and, at the same time, we examine how their roots and organization as a local food movement also clearly predate the founding of Vía Campesina and a food sovereignty movement, a founding in which many of these activists participated. Moreover, actors in the small rural U.S. state of Vermont and this rural region of industrial France engaged in acts of contention that, while sharing ideas with a durable transnational farmer and peasant movement, in fact reflect distinctly local forms of ongoing resistance and alternative contentious politics in reaction to the industrial food system. These illustrate varied processes of contention that differ in degree of local-global interaction and in terms of the invocation of state authority against global institutions.

Nonetheless, the localized actions of farmers in Vermont and the local and global intersections in Larzac together require a reassessment of popular protest strategies as they presage a hinge moment before the long-anticipated structural crisis of global commodity capitalism. Until the 1970s, the political power of the sovereign state served as the main countervailing force against the worst excesses of capital, but increasingly in the post–Cold War era of neoliberal globalization, new patterns of cross-border transnational protest emerged as countervailing pressures to challenge the reigning capitalist market orthodoxy inherent in emerging free trade agreements, neoliberal economic institutions such as the World Trade Organization (WTO) or multinational corporations (Ayres 1998, 2004; Khagram, Riker, and Sikkink 2002; Smith and Johnston 2002; Bandy and Smith 2004).

In this chapter we explore the burgeoning strategy of re-localization and in particular the diffusion of localizing strategies around the concept of food sovereignty. The discussion focuses on what we call "localism" as a means of rearticulating an effective while diffuse platform of resistance to global capitalism evident in agribusiness, and we highlight central organizing themes of this book as identified in the introduction and chapter 1, relevant to food as a source of crisis in the neoliberal market system as well as the emergence of alternative food practices. Specifically, we are interested in illustrating how the concept of food sovereignty is realized and resonates in local practices employed strategically and every day to reject or secede from the global agribusiness model, within the confines of our two cases. For illustration we examine the direct appropriation of the food sovereignty framework within the Larzac movement in France as an issue of governmentality and its use in terms of local autonomy, food sources, and food democracy among food activists in Vermont. Through a descriptive comparative study, we present these two locales as exemplary centres of food movement activity and illustrate how distinct historical developments shaped different manifestations of a shared concern for food sovereignty.

Yet beyond social movement dynamics, the current crisis in the global agribusiness model as well as the deeper structural crisis in capitalism have both affirmed and unsettled traditional state-level as well as more recent versions of transnational methods of popular resistance. In the Larzac movement, we see a deeply structured response to the state's imposition of agribusiness models and the threat of neoliberal globalization. A long tradition of rural preservation, state regulation of food as local, and even the failures of 1968 provide opportunities for organizing as they close off other channels, always with a clear eye to local communities, global actors, and state mediation. As a site of local resistance in the United States, Vermont provides a contrast, especially in its anarchic practices. However, in comparison with the actions of French farmers, we show that it is a more entrepreneurial, local-market-based response to organizing against food commodification, and as a valid form of localism or re-localization, illustrates an accessible and adopted form of small-scale individual or community empowerment, even as the role of the state is limited. We share Zerbe's concerns, in chapter 3, about the limitations of commodity-based responses to the global agribusiness model, whether consumer or producer based, though our comparison between Larzac in France and Vermont in the United States suggests that a shared food sovereignty frame reflects a mutual antipathy to neoliberal market dynamics. Indeed, key contributions to this volume underline the tensions between sovereignty as community participation and sovereignty as personal autonomy, including chapters by Menser, McMahon, and Andrée, and these are at the heart of concerns among many global food sovereignty activists who doubt the compatibility of corporate and participatory decision-making. In our conclusions, we point to some practical limitations of both the localvore market and consumer movement in the United States and the class-based peasant movement in France, issues that are more fully interrogated by Zerbe.

"All Politics Is Local": Diffusion and Food Sovereignty

Recent scholarship has turned towards increased theoretical interest in political practices embracing varieties of localism as strategies to resist neoliberal globalization (Conway 2004; Changfoot 2007; DuPuis and Block 2008; Evans 2008). While cognizant of the hegemonic power that neoliberalism has had in the post–Cold War era over the imaginations of mass publics, they are as well critical that local spaces, local resistance, or re-localization strategies have often been "eclipsed as sites of political engagement with the rise of globalization discourse" (Changfoot 2007, 129, quoting Magnusson 2005). Even so, localism has been especially appropriated by farmers, peasants, and other popular sector groups concerned about the globalization of food systems and attendant food crises (Norberg-Hodge 2002; Starr et al. 2003; Huey

2005; Feagan 2007). For some, localism refers to greater local control and participatory democracy – local production for local consumption, using local resources under the guidance and control of local communities. Others embrace more explicitly anti-capitalist politics, using local strategies and mobilizing local food movements as vehicles to resist or secede from the capitalist system of food production, exchange, and distribution. Regardless of political intentions though, frequently, as Feagan notes, "the place of food seems to be the quiet centre of discourse emerging from these movements" (2007, 23).

While recognizing that similar ideas, tactics, and discourses around the politics of food in different parts of the world might draw attention to protest diffusion (McAdam and Rucht 1993; Tarrow 2005), we consider the relationship between globally inspired challenges and campaigns transformed through culturally acceptable meanings in new local settings as the interaction of global macro-climates and the local micro-climates where globalization is realized and resisted (Bosia 2009). Our jumping off point is the macro-climate of neoliberal globalization that subjugates farmers and peasants globally to the imperatives of large-scale supermarket chains in advanced industrialized markets just as it challenges state sovereignty, as well as the organization of a global response through La Vía Campesina that reclaims sovereignty. But we focus on the micro-climates where re-localization seeks to strengthen rural communities and restore some sense of autonomy or sovereignty. We are interested in exploring the degree to which political and social actors in Larzac and in Vermont, while having only some direct relationships, have developed a similar praxis by targeting agricultural capitalism and industrial agribusiness through either political or economic action. In this way, we juxtapose the more producer-oriented politics in Larzac with the consumer-centred politics of Vermont.

Again, while the local food movements in Larzac and Vermont developed along distinct trajectories, the food sovereignty concept is a useful analytical term for conceptualizing much of the logic behind their activities. From land rights to global trade, food activists at global La Vía Campesina meetings elaborated "food sovereignty" as a set of political claims and rights after 1996 (Desmarais 2005), serving as the immediate predicate to the actions in Vermont and Larzac.[2] According to these charters, food sovereignty encapsulates the "right of peoples to define their own food and agriculture; to protect and regulate domestic agricultural production and trade in order to achieve sustainable development objectives; to determine the extent to which they want to be self-reliant" (Rosset 2003). As Food First Co-director Peter Rossett notes, Vía Campesina draws a critical distinction between economic development models in rural communities: one that gives priority of market access to local producers (food sovereignty) versus the more dominant post–Cold War model giving priority of market access on the basis of market power and subsidized prices for multinational agribusiness (neoliberalism) (Rosset 2003).

Much like the examples explored by Andrée and Martin in chapter 6, the concept of food sovereignty, with its emphasis on the empowerment of the local, sustainability, and self-reliance, has taken root in locales as geographically and culturally dispersed as Vermont and Larzac, even with the former's relative distance from Vía Campesina, as compared to the founding role of French farmers in the international movement. In conjunction with the study of Canadian practices, these cases reinforce the fact that some food activists and producers in wealthy contexts will develop explicit solidarity with similarly positioned farmers and peasants at the margins. Whether solidarity is institutionalized in a shared transnational movement or only discursive in terms of similar values and claims, farmers and activists in our analysis adapted the food sovereignty frame and made it relevant to their own situations, in ways that reflect unique conflict structures – the resources and political opportunities and cultural settings – that provided acceptable environments for food sovereignty to take root in rural regions of both the United States and France. Because we are sceptical about the degree of intensity of transnational integration and connections between these locales, we are interested in how food sovereignty helps us understand the resonance of similar though domestically appropriate actions and tactics.

Moreover, we examine the tactics and ideas surrounding food sovereignty in these different locales to provide insights into what James Mittelman (2004) has referred to as "microencounters" or "microresistance to globalization." Mittelman calls microresistance "countless diverse acts and beliefs that send forth streams of doubt and questions concerning the viability and sustainability of neoliberal globalization" (26). When Vermont farmers, food activists, rural workers, and increasingly knowledgeable consumers prioritize local farms and markets, organic produce, or food grown locally over that shipped thousands of miles, they are participating in acts of resistance that are often hidden below the surface of more widely known mobilizations against multinationals and corporate control. In fact, the comparison between Larzac

and Vermont demonstrates that the variable levels of economic and political effect of such resistance are not analytically determinant, as they
remain vital as local manifestations of both everyday and broader strategies of resistance, even as they might be directed either inward, as in
Vermont, or out towards empowered domestic institutions, as in Larzac.

Indeed, food sovereignty has explicitly and implicitly become a
meaningful and tangible concept for many engaged in daily and strategic local acts of reflection and resistance to an increasingly delegiti-
mized global agribusiness model. In fact, multiple acts of local resistance
feed a subversive, less easily appreciated discourse potentially far more
accessible and acceptable to the many lower- and middle-income people otherwise too occupationally preoccupied or financially constrained
to travel great distances to attend People's Summits and protest summitry. Moreover, the global financial crisis, the underlying structural
crisis of capitalism, and immense and pending global and local environmental challenges (Bello 2008; Wallerstein 2009) have destabilized
social systems and present uncertain challenges to political regimes
such that neoliberalism's hegemonic common-sense understanding of
what is natural and inevitable in the recent era of globalization has been
damaged. Today, the populist outrage and social dissent accompanying this moment of crisis and de-globalization reflects an unsettling of
forms of collective resistance, creating new opportunities to assess appropriate areas for political struggle and alternative politics.

The Larzac Movement: Class Solidarity, Colonialism, and Cuisine

One iconic image from the global campaign for food sovereignty is that
of the 300 farmers under the leadership of "The French Farmer" José
Bové dismantling a yet-to-be opened McDonald's in Millau, France, in
the summer of 1999. "The structure was very flimsy," Bové reported,
noting that it was put together like a kit and easy to take apart (Bové
and Dufour 2001, 6). Demonstrators, including children, loaded the frag-
ments of American fast food culture onto a tractor trailer, and deposited
them unceremoniously on the doorstep of the prefecture. Bové, arrest-
ed with other organizers, refused bail and became a cause célèbre both
at home and among the growing movement against industrial agriculture around the world.

Despite a persistent myth in the English-speaking world that Bové
was just fighting *malbouffe* or "junk food" (Reuters 2008), he in fact was
coming to the aid of friends and neighbours around Millau who

produced Roquefort cheese, who were targeted by the United States for trade retaliation under the procedures of the WTO after the European Union refused to allow the importation of American beef raised with growth hormones. Though global in nature, this event in its genealogy and as it is situated in the French branch of the food sovereignty movement suggests the localization of diffusion necessary for understanding both local responses to agribusiness and how localvores and organic farming in the United States do indeed represent the American branch of a diffused global social movement. Rhetorical similarities between France and the United States tell us as much about their historical-contextual differences as they do commonalities, indicating points of contemporary agreement and departure over food sovereignty and its relationship to the state as a response to global agriculture. Indeed, the Larzac movement in rural France is a more structured resistance with origins in the everyday practices of farmers and regulatory logic of the French state, but reaching through a kind of high-speed network that connects local and global in ways that indicate the authentic resistance as well as the unstructured and profoundly local nature of the American movement.

Both the American and French movements have origins in student organizing in the 1960s as well as responses to the Cold War and Vietnam, in many ways, sharing a romantic attachment to rural life and communal living (from the French word *commune* or town), a fondness for natural over industrial processes, a national and historic obsession with the family farm, and a network of transatlantic experiences and relationships stretching from the hippie communes of northern California to the anti-globalization demonstrations in Seattle in 1999. José Bové, raised in part in Berkeley during the 1960s counterculture, professes a fondness for an American environmentalist icon, Henry David Thoreau.

Nevertheless, the experience of the 1960s are strikingly different, with the Larzac movement tied more to social solidarity and less to an idiosyncratic counterculture. As well, the family farm is politically paradigmatic in both countries, but the peasantry and rural life in France remain a pointedly preserved domain, even through various modernization programs. Further, peasant production is tied to French cuisine, and the self-defence of French farmers is more class- and labour union–based and less personally self-reliant. Instead of cross-national commonalities, surface similarities in trajectory and the diffusions of ideas mask distinctions that help explain why the French movement is more global, while the American is profoundly local. These differences also help us understand why, unlike his American counterparts, conservative French President Nicolas Sarkozy would promise during his 2007 campaign to use the French veto at the WTO to defend French peasants: "The independence of French food is a priority" (Guiral 2007). To understand the differences that characterize French food sovereignty, we highlight the multiple origins of the McDonald's demonstration in 1999 and a uniquely French response predicated on concepts of social class, French cuisine as a system of regulation, and forms of solidarity, universalism, and anti-colonialism inherent in the French left's conception of self.

French Peasants: Was Marx Wrong?

In his analysis of Louis Napoleon's 1851 coup, Marx famously referred to peasants as a "sack of potatoes." In reality, French peasants have been the target of government policy and political organization, from the peasant soldiers who did the heavy lifting for Napoleon's empire to the peasant voters who helped centre a Third Republic torn between the forces of tradition and those of urban labour. Indeed, the peasantry has long been one key to the construction of France as a nation and state as well as the nation's mythic foundation (Hazareesingh 1999). Until the 1930s, the model of governance Hoffman called a "stalemate society" (Hoffmann 1961a, 1961b) promoted stability over robust modernization, preserving rural life and the tie between peasant and land in ways that discouraged rural transformation. While U.S. modernization reduced the ratio of farm population to less than one-third by 1916, France maintained that proportion until the late 1940s, and while urban life had grown to 79 per cent in Britain and 65 per cent of Germans by the 1950s, French urbanization lagged at 55 per cent (United Nations Department of Economic and Social Affairs 2005).

Though Chambres d'agriculture established in 1924 began organizing farmers, only during the "30 Glorious Years" did new philosophies of state promote rapid transformation and modernization, changing peasant life significantly and reducing the proportion of French men and women on the farm. With peasants in mind, French governments transformed rural as they did urban living, modernizing agriculture and promoting farm consolidation through commodified, mechanized, and highly energy dependent agriculture, targeting national self-sufficiency as well as cash-generating exports. While 3.4 per cent of French workers laboured on the land in 2007 (Institut National de la statistique et des Études Économique 2011, 160), the number of farms declined and the average size increased, from 3,847,000 farms in 1979 to 1,100,000 in 2005. Small farms of less than 49.7 acres declined from 1,791,000 in 1955 to 237,000 in 2005 (ibid.). Key segments of the peasantry cooperated in these changes, especially through the Fédération Nationale des Syndicats d'Exploitants Agricole. Younger farmers began their own organizing sections within the broader movement, as many peasants saw commercialization as a way of preserving peasant life. Today, French farms earn the bulk of agriculture subsidies from the European Union and provide the lion's share of produce.

The 1960s: Maoist and Peasant Dissent

The 30 Glorious Years also fostered a reaction to commercialization and modernization that ultimately nourished a food sovereignty movement. While modernization created an urban generation raised with increasing consumer affluence and opportunity, the dynamics of the centralizing state with a bureaucratic and industrial elite created a "blocked society" that sowed the seeds of discontent as it attempted to impose instead of co-opt, both in the cities and on the farm (Crozier 1999; Wieviorka 1984). Modernization improved incomes for many, but state-imposed modernization mimicked colonial relationships of tutelage between the centre and the periphery. Similar to the youth movement in the United States, young French men and women in the 1960s reacted to the policies of the state, particularly in relation to militarism and French neocolonialism, and so willingly bridged the local and the global. Different from their American counterparts, the social orientation of the French students ultimately resulted in an explicitly class-based alliance.

But it was an alliance different from the one they envisioned during the events of May 1968. Despite a massive general strike that capitalized on the student movement, and the spontaneous occupation of factories by workers, organized labour and the Communist Party remained indifferent if not hostile, cooperating with police to lock the factory gates at Renault and block 4,000 students marching to support the workers occupying the facility without union approval. After May, the anti-consumerist, anti-authoritarian, anti-bureaucratic, and anti-war consensus that inspired the students propelled a segment of them into the countryside, borrowing heavily from Maoist strategy and their own disillusionment with organized labour.

Instead, students imagined an alliance with peasants. In Larzac, they found peasants facing the expropriation of vast tracts of land for expansion of a military base to be used as grounds for missile and tank exercises to replace outposts lost in the former colonies. Historian Herman Lebovics provides an analysis of the Larzac movement, focusing on the interventions of a French version of Mao's Red Guard, with urban students "settling down" among peasants as the new organic intellectuals (Lebovics 2004). Because local leaders of the right-wing UDF party had been buying up farmland on the cheap in anticipation of a military takeover, students who came down to help awaken a peasant movement found peasants already sharing a similar antagonism to the state. There was distrust at first, as students became squatters on the newly nationalized lands yet to be occupied by the army, a bit ragged, like their peers on communes in the United States and often called "dirty hippies" by the locals. Nevertheless, according to Lebovics, the assault represented by the expansion of the military base provided a shared soil upon which students and peasants could meet.

While peasants were anxious and frustrated, young people objected to the neocolonial French presence in West Africa as well as cooperation with the United States, while farmers were concerned primarily with the loss of land and the disregard of both the military and the party officials who profiteered from the decisions made in Paris. But peasants and students came to share a sense that the French administration was an occupying force, and conceptualized the local struggle as part of an anticolonial movement located at the same moment in Larzac, the colony of New Caledonia, the former colonies in West Africa, and Vietnam. This coalition reflects what Lebovics characterizes as postcolonial regionalism, calling attention to the historic relationship of Paris to the countryside that has modelled and been modelled on the colonial project. In the colonies, the mission of French officialdom was to civilize through language and education, and modernize through the commercial expropriation of resources (Conklin 2000). French peasants, as the preoccupation of the state administration, were to be similarly civilized through education in the nineteenth century and agricultural exploitation (called modernization) in the twentieth. Increasingly, Larzac became a site for resistance, with peasants from the remaining colonies, the former French colonial empire, and increasingly from the expanding network of activists throughout the global South arriving in Larzac, and celebrating bonds of global class solidarity. At the same time, French peasants positioned themselves as opponents of a militaristic neocolonial and commercial state, universalizing the interests of French peasants and crafting the rural struggle as an expression of a global movement.

However, the peasant reaction to the state as a rural occupying force predates the arrival of the students, as indicated by French historian (and former peasant organizer) René Bourrigaud, who reveals a fertilization of the soil earlier in the 1960s, so that when students came down from the universities, they had suitable ground in which to take root (Bourrigaud 2008). While the FSNEA and Jeunes Agriculteurs (JA – Young Farmers) had cooperated in the professionalization and commercialization of farming, in the 1960s young farmers – particularly in the Loire not far from Larzac – became distinctly more radical, turning against commercialization to organize peasants along class and not professional lines, in the tradition of industrial unions. Bernard Lambert was one, joining the Jeunesse Agricole Chrétienne in 1947 before taking over the family farm in the Loire. By 1967, peasants working within the FSNEA and in the JA were organizing as well with the dominant socialist and communist labour unions in Paris, and in 1968 peasants in the Loire marched with workers and students in sixteen towns of the rural west. Lambert, a veteran of the Algerian War, published the influential *Farmers in the Class Struggle* in 1970.

Bové joined the students and peasants organizing in Larzac and squatted on a parcel of expropriated land. Denied credit as well as electricity, harassed by authorities, he and other squatters faced a formidable task in rehabilitating abandoned farms beyond the level of subsistence agriculture. Bové and Lambert met in 1973, and they founded the Confédération Paysanne in the 1980s, the second-largest association of farmers in France, organized as a labour union of peasant-workers. Through electoral organizing and direct action, the confederation targets an agricultural model it considers responsible for "overproduction, public health crises, the degradation of the natural environment, gross inequality across local, national, and global borders, and the sharp decline in the number of peasants."[3] By joining a consortium of European farmer groups that ultimately became the European Farmers' Coordination, Bové and the Confédération Paysanne lead in La Vía Campesina.

The unfinished McDonald's in Millau provided a convenient and loaded target when the U.S. government launched a trade war on local cheese-makers. Bové and his allies are cautious in distinguishing between an American political-industry complex, on one hand, and the American people and American farmers on the other. As Kuisel explains, the question of American economic influence in France implicates culture and politics (Kuisel 1993). From the authorization of Coca-Cola in the 1950s to the later expansion of McDonald's and the importation of· industrial food products, the American model threatens incomes and a distinct way of life, social solidarity, and a distaste for profit. By the 1990s, the threat posed by American culture became a veil for economic reform, as Socialist and conservative governments associated American multiculturalism with Arab tribalism as the real threat to French culture at the same time they adopted Wall Street investment and profit models that began to undermine French notions of social solidarity.

It is the false anti-Americanism of the political elite – attacking American multiculturalism as they embrace American profit motives – that the peasant-workers often clarify their position against. Bové's assault is on *malbouffe*, which is not a form of American dominance but corporate dominance, dangerous to peasants in France and to the family farmer in the United States, a threat to economic survival and the distinctly peasant nature of French culture. François Dufour, a leading peasant with Bové in Millau, explains their outreach to Americans at a film festival that year: "We wanted to explain to the American festival-goers that it was not their culture we objected to: that it was very welcome in our regions, but that the multinational companies had to respect our differences, our identity" (Bové and Dufour 1991, 20).

Malbouffe as a product of multinational globalization is inextricably in contestation with cuisine as a cultural field in France (Ferguson 1998). French food – state authorized, institutionally as well as culturally empowered, framed through expertise – is a highly articulated and densely packed network of relationships, norms, rules, and regulations. Even as the state commercializes agriculture, it makes legible the production and attribution of historically and distinctly French products through the authority of the state bureaucracy. This ambiguity fuses the French desire to promote the superiority of French products like wine and Roquefort in global markets, with the promotion of larger and larger systems of production and mechanization, dismantling the very logic of local production that constitutes French cuisine. Even in its contradictions, however, French cuisine represents the height of taste and authenticity as both the haute cuisine of the jet set and the hearty food of *cuisine grand-mère*, against the poisonous nature of *malbouffe* represented not just by McDonald's but all systems of industrialized agriculture.

This sense of the local is distinct from the American. For Americans, the local often responds to a post-industrial world threatened by global warming and peak oil; in France, the local returns to the pre-industrial heart of French culture. French cuisine is crafted through careful and cautious assimilation and authorization that is inherently a celebration of the local and the national against the global. The dismantling of the McDonald's at Millau is at one moment an intensely local reaction to a global threat, a national response to globalization, a French rejection of American profiteering, the preservation of distinct cultures against the monotony of industrial food, a call for state protections in support of peasant life globally, and a call to history in order to reach forward. Imbedded in economic and cultural politics, the Confédération Paysanne, in its advocacy of food sovereignty, recalls the industrial protectionism that dominated the French post-war political economy until the 1980s. As well, the elaboration of cuisine as a distinct field of sociopolitical life is integrated in the notion of the local, and the return to local artisan expertise is an adaptation to but not rejection of the expertise tied to the legitimacy of the French bureaucratic elite. Despite shared origins in the student movements of the 1960s and the reliance on local reactions to global industrial practices – even the emphasis on the artisan over the mechanized – French food sovereignty differs from the American in its decidedly peasant orientation with global linkages resulting from colonial and neocolonial experiences. It calls for state action even as it promotes local self-reliance, reinforcing the nation state at the same time it reinforces transnational solidarities.

Green Mountain Localvores: A Long Way from Mao's Red Guard?

"Food sovereignty" among farmers and activists in Vermont may not be directly associated with class struggle or state intervention, or even with Vía Campesina, as it is in the Larzac movement. Indeed, social and political actors are more likely to speak about food democracy than sovereignty, or in terms of local food systems. The scale of resistance is smaller and involves for many a proactive response to imminent chaos associated with accelerating climate change, U.S. imperial overstretch, and economic collapse.[4] Moreover, Vermonters are not immune to the pop culture "return to the local" as it has been increasingly highlighted nationally in a variety of settings, from the new organic garden on the White House lawn (Martin 2009), to left-leaning blogs and publications such as the *Nation* and *Yes! Magazine*, from Michael Pollan's (2008) *In Defense of Food* to Barbara Kingsolver's (2008) *Animal, Vegetable, Miracle*. However, food sovereignty has analytical resonance across Vermont more directly through a mix of narratives similar to those targeting multinational agribusiness practices in the Larzac region of France, including fears over GMO seed contamination and state collusion with globalization.

The Vermont reaction also shares with that of the Larzac movement a desire to protect unique local culture against large market forces and the blandness of suburban life. Contentious, claims-making activity in Vermont around food sovereignty, then, is similar to the French but strikingly different as it mirrors the sort of under-appreciated micro-level anti-globalization activity often overshadowed by global summitry protests, invocations of state authority, and the overtly transnational organizing like that in Larzac. Armory Starr and Jason Adams (2003), in an analysis that links local action to anti-globalization contention, point out the importance of a local food cycle in the form of cooperatives, farmers' markets, community bartering, and the establishment of local currencies. Additional acts of resistance to corporate agriculture that they document – "slow food," urban gardening projects, permaculture, purchasing food when it is "in season," and agricultural land reform – have been taken up by Vermonters across the state, albeit out of sight from the sorts of mega-protests covered by the national or international media (McDermott 2007).

At the same time, however, there has been considerable room in Vermont for the development of a grassroots rebellion in defence of food nurtured by a political and cultural tradition that has for centuries emphasized small-scale frugality, local citizenship, and direct democracy. This sense that Vermont remains distinct pervades contemporary culture across the state: the first to ban all commercial billboard advertisement along its roads; the last to have a Walmart; the only one never visited by former U.S. president George W. Bush; represented for over a decade in the U.S. House of Representatives, and now in the U.S. Senate, by a self-proclaimed independent socialist; the largest city is nicknamed the People's Republic of Burlington. Vermont today is experiencing a quirky, albeit not widely known, movement to secede and form the Second Vermont Republic.[5]

Beyond this independent-mindedness, Vermont in more recent decades has developed a social infrastructure that would prove especially hospitable to the ideas diffused through the food sovereignty movement. Vermont was an early destination in the "back-to-the-land" movement, attracting those hippies and others embracing the 1960s counterculture and later the "voluntary simplicity" movement, as well as modern-day local-food homesteaders and "downshifters" seeking escape from the stresses of modern life (Blumenthal and Mosteller 2008). The Institute for Social Ecology (ISE) in Marshfield is an activist-education and research centre in the vanguard of ecological approaches to food production, holding summer workshops to provide first-hand experience in organic gardening, eco-feminism, and alternative technologies.[6] Founders and students of the ISE played important roles from the 1980s in Green political organizing across the United States, and more recently in global justice, anti-capitalist protests, and mobilizing opposition to GMOs through the ISE Biotechnology Project (Tokar 2008).

Farmers and rural activists in Vermont clearly and vocally identify with the goals of Vía Campesina, as well as with the plight generally of small farmers facing both global market forces and industrial agriculture. Many of the ways in which food sovereignty has become a collective action frame in Vermont demonstrate that the concept is appropriated differently within local environments: there is not an advanced, durable, or tightly integrated connective tissue linking the Larzac peasants and Vermont activists in a cross-national social movement per se, but there is still a higher degree of domestic-international fusion in cross-national references that encourage food sovereignty to resonate in these different settings.

Rural Vermont and the Diffusion of the Food Sovereignty Frame

In some ways similar to the mediating role played by the French Confédération Paysanne, Rural Vermont is affiliated through the National Family Farm Coalition with La Vía Campesina, and the organization's actions and organizing principles draw from the same chords of concern and resistance as Vía Campesina, though distinctly American in flavour: "Our vision is for a Vermont local food system which is self-reliant and based on reverence for the earth ... Economic justice for family farmers is the foundation of a health rural economy. Towards this end we strive for fair prices for farmers and we work to counter corporate consolidation of agriculture and the food supply" (Rural Vermont 2013).

While Rural Vermont does not have a spokesperson as internationally known as José Bové, it nonetheless has been recognized by Vía Campesina and the non-governmental organization Grassroots International as "leading efforts at the local level to build legal and organizing capacity for food sovereignty initiatives" (Grassroots International 2008, 19). Moreover, Rural Vermont's national affiliations have facilitated the diffusion of collective action frames and tactics, and it has embraced similar targets and campaigns with Vía Campesina, encouraging mobilizations and contentious food politics in support of rural farmers and against multinational corporations and trade and investment deals. These solidarity actions in conjunction with Vía Campesina have included such Global Days of Action as an April 2004 event in which over fifty Canadian and American farmers rallied at the Quebec-Vermont border to mark the seventeenth International Day of Farmers' Struggle. "We are here at the border to demonstrate the global solidarity of farmers in the face of corporate globalization," said Burlington farmer Hillary Martin, amidst a collection of puppets, signs, and a large banner hung from an interstate overpass that read "No to Genetically Modified Organisms (GMOs)" in English, French, and Spanish (Common Dreams 2004). In addition to direct advocacy, Rural Vermont lobbies for policies favourable to local farmers and markets, and engages in such micro-level actions as a Bioimperialism and Food Sovereignty speaking tour and a "hot chocolate social" in 2007 under the theme "Farmers and Consumers Unite to Strengthen Local Food Systems" (Rural Vermont 2009).

Through its advocacy and education campaigns, Rural Vermont is in solidarity with farmers around the world in resisting corporate agribusiness, and has consciously viewed Vía Campesina and food sovereignty as models for Vermont agriculture and activism. Rural Vermont's former program director, Linda Setchell (2005), has written of the parallels between the struggles of Vermont dairies and farmers in the developing world in the face of "chemically-dependent agriculture of the 20th century which is not only environmentally destructive, it's also economically unsustainable." She notes an 81 per cent decline in the number of Vermont dairy farms between 1964 and 2004, and links this to the "increasing corporate control of the food supply, whether it is consolidation of processing facilities into the hands of a few, the dumping of cheap commodities or the subsidizing of factory farming at the federal level" (2005). Setchell then compares Rural Vermont's vision to that of Vía Campesina's, detailing the latter's food sovereignty principles and linking the agribusiness model and the WTO and FTAA-style agreements to the destruction of local control and markets.

One incident illustrates this direct relational link between Rural Vermont and Vía Campesina: in September 2001, Rural Vermont hosted the Fertile Ground Festival under the theme, "The World Is Not for Sale," with invited guest José Bové speaking on the Vermont state-house lawn in Montpelier on the theme "Reclaiming Our Food and Our Future."

More often and despite a formal association, the link is more non-relational through primarily Internet-diffused claims, ideas, and targets around food sovereignty and against corporate agribusiness that resonate and take hold in the politically and culturally receptive setting state-wide.

Vermont as the Epicentre of the Defence of the Commons

Beyond direct comparisons between Rural Vermont and Confédération Paysanne, including the strategic actions, targeting, and framing inspired by Vía Campesina, Vermont, possibly more than any other state in the United States, has a decentralized political environment extremely conducive to the transplantation of an informal ethic supportive of food sovereignty. Brian Tokar has written that a sustainable future of genuine food sovereignty may work well with traditions of self-reliance and working collaboratively with one's neighbours, which are less pronounced in other regions of the United States today: "Vermonters are very concerned about the quality of our food, and share a concern and identification with those who grow our food that has been all but obliterated in much of the U.S. In this respect, by moving toward a more conscious culture with respect to food, Vermont may have more in common with Europe than almost any other place in the U.S." (Tokar 2006).

In 2005, for example, an ethos of self-reliance was embraced by a small group of women in Vermont's Upper Valley, who as consumers chose to eat only local food for a month.[7] A local Community Supported Agriculture (CSA) farm, Luna Bleu, provided much of the food, as did the local Upper Valley Co-op. In the past several years since, a wider food movement inspired by their actions – localvores – has spread across the state as hundreds of Vermonters have accepted the "Eat Local" challenge, from large groups in the cities of Burlington, Montpelier, Rutland, and Brattleboro, to only a small handful of participants in smaller villages (McDermott 2007). Another indication of this ethos, Vermont today has the most farmers markets per capita in the United States and ranks first in per capita direct sales from farmers to consumers (Calta 2008). As well, many Vermont schools have active food gardens and horticulture programs, while winter farmers' markets have begun to flourish in smaller cities such as Burlington and Montpelier as well.

As these localvore practices and forms of self-reliance require that the actual production and storage of food in home and professional kitchens change to accommodate re-seasonalization of food markets, they represent a return to alternative forms of knowledge similar in structure and possibility to those examined by Massicotte in her study of Brazilian peasant movements for this volume. Indeed, some of the economic practices that might be grouped as a kind of social commons or systems of mutual support for new local food producers draw from the everyday frugality and survival strategies long evident in Vermont's rural communities (Hewitt 2010).

Since 2003, the Vermont Agency of Agriculture has become much more active in promoting a "Buy Local" campaign. It distributed large inserts in state-wide newspapers in 2007, promoting dozens of farm stands and farmers' markets as well as listing "10 Great Reasons to Buy Local." The state's campaign (Vermont Agency of Agriculture 2008) concluded that if "Vermonters shifted just 10 percent of their food purchases to locally grown food products, [this] would add more than $100 million to Vermont's economy" (Johnson 2007). The Vermont Fresh Network fosters direct relationships between farmers, food producers, and chefs (Vermont Agency of Agriculture 2007) that contribute to a more vibrant local food system. Diners can locate the green Vermont Fresh Network sign and support the Buy Local effort when eating in participating restaurants.[8] And the Northeast Organic Farming Association of Vermont has been promoting local farms through educational programming since 1971.

Vermont's largest city is well known for a citizenry committed to the availability of local food. From "freegans" dumpster-diving for thrown-out restaurant food, to Burlington Bread, an attempt at a local currency, from the prevalence of organic community potlucks and peace groups such as the Burlington chapter of Food Not Bombs, to the three different farmers' markets held weekly in the city, Burlington actively resists corporate agribusiness (Kohut 2007). The large cooperative City Market supports locally grown foods and carries over a thousand Vermont-made products on the store's shelves. Members and volunteers from City Market are involved in a number of programs across Burlington, including a Going Local Colloquium, the School Food Project (where local students are educated on the benefits of local food), an annual harvest festival, and the Lunch with Neighbors senior meal program. The Intervale Center holds over a hundred acres adjacent to the middle of the city, hosting thirteen independent organic farms and four CSA farms, and contributing to a widely embraced ethic of sustainability and local-centredness in and around the greater Burlington area (Intervale Center 2007).

Despite or because of its geographic isolation, Vermont is at the centre of an ethical renaissance relating to food sovereignty though the local-vore movement and small-scale farming. Evolving micro-mobilization efforts suggest a turn towards what some call more meaningful work instead of confrontation, where the large-scale mass protests of the Seattle WTO era are exchanged for a longer-term constructive agenda based on small-scale acts against a broken, global capitalist food system afflicted by E. coli, salmonella, and an atomizing and alienating production and distribution system. Matt Kopka has written on food sovereignty's "radical insistence on community, on the development of a 'defensible life space' against neoliberalism's enclosure of the commons" (Kopka 2008). This description aptly describes the product of the multiple small actions and micro-encounters with local food and farmers by Vermonters who have increasingly insisted on the importance of preserving their distinctive way of life, food supply, and independence from neoliberal policy constraints.

Conclusion: Tensions in the Local While Bridging with the Global

The diverse meaning of food sovereignty provokes tensions that challenge local social and political organizing. The response in Larzac emphasizes organizing among peasants as producers in ways that delayed a consumer response to a commodity-based food system. While class solidarity provided an organizational backbone to challenge both national and global institutions and to support global alliances, only more recently have the French begun to develop the burgeoning organic food movement we see in the United States, nor has class organizing enabled localvore habits popularized in English- and French-speaking North America. Today, French consumption remains largely reliant on industrial practices and agricultural commercialization, while an emerging and still small counter-movement has taken root in cities like Paris in the past five years, with new organic cooperatives and CSA shares as well as flashy natural markets similar to Whole Foods in the United States. A 2012 documentary on French television explored le défi locavore (the localvore challenge) of five families in Toulouse, and one farm even introduced the Vermont favourite kale to the Parisian diet in 2013 as a few market stalls advertised "locavore" and Ile-de-France produce in the capital. However, given the nature of class organizing, urban movements remain more often structured as support for the peasant struggle, while the emerging localvore culture often focused on U.S. expats facing scepticism from a French population that considers local in terms of the appropriate locale for the production of regional artisanal products.

With its focus on individual or community autonomy and away from the state, food sovereignty in the United States risks marginalization as an elite practice that undercuts the message of social change required of a global movement. California, dependent on one of history's largest and most energy-intensive water distribution systems, has made the desert bloom and fostered an easy luxury of localvore abundance often ignorant of the environmental costs of the system. In Vermont, young farmer-entrepreneurs have turned to value-added production like artisan cheeses and specialty vegetables to spur local economies. At the same time, they have risked the exacerbation of generational, class, and gender cleavages in rural communities by, on the one hand, embracing a language of capitalism that irks earlier "back-to-the-landers" as it also diminishes the contributions of those first organic farmers, and on the other, talking in a discourse of rural salvation that mis-characterizes rural communities as desperate (Hewitt 2010). This of course parallels Zerbe's critique, while suggesting the localized limitations of both the more explicit global solidarity examined by Andrée and Martin elsewhere in the volume and the democratic possibility in alternative movements and forms of knowledge explored by Massicotte or Menser.

Nonetheless, we remain convinced that local food sovereignty offers a counterweight to global agribusiness, providing real and analytically important bridges between local and global responses to neoliberalism. While trade and investment institutions, treaties, and multinational corporations have contributed to the diminishment and reformulation of sovereignty, these changes enable resistance to the perceived loss of sovereignty, creating new spaces, opportunities, and targets for cross-border campaigns and transnational movements. While local resistance is much less documented or understood, its practitioners are responding to the same fears, targeting the same policies, and grasping frames similar to those engaged in well-documented transnational campaigns against institutions of global governance and neoliberal trade.

Food sovereignty movements operate at a plurality of social and political scales, from the local grassroots, to the national, and the global. Diverse strategies are used at multiple levels to challenge states, multinational corporations, and multilateral trade institutions, including the WTO, that perpetuate commodified food systems. Thus, since, as Barry Gills (2004) suggests, there are many globalizations and therefore many possible alternatives, local resistance that appropriates meanings surrounding food sovereignty links local and global, offering insights into alternative practices that seek to secede from the unsustainable global capitalist model of mass consumption and unlimited growth.

Food sovereignty campaigns in Larzac and Vermont may seem different, despite similar origins in the 1960s. While both locales emphasize local control and community cohesion, the Larzac movement and French activism in general remain embedded in class and global social solidarity, and Vermonters prioritize environmental and organic practices that sustain "freegans" and Community Supported Agriculture as micro-resistance to global agribusiness. Both cases illustrate how food sovereignty is differently appropriated in local settings, where individuals and groups have embraced it for unique and domestically shaped acts of contention. Thus "alter-globalization" is misapplied when the single focus is large-scale mobilizations, as smaller micro-encounters and localized responses are part of a broader and more nuanced transnational diffusion of resistances, struggles, and reformulations over sovereignty at multiple political and social scales.[9]

NOTES

1 A previous version was published in 2011 as "Beyond Global Summitry: Food Sovereignty as Localized Resistance to Globalization," *Globalizations* 8 (1): 47–63. Revised and reprinted with permission.

2 See as well Desmarais (2007).

3 See for example, http://www.confederationpaysanne.fr / presentation_de_la_confederation_paysanne_2.php.

4 A number of groups promoting food sovereignty are also active in campaigns around "peak oil" and excessive military spending. See Transition Vermont (2013).

5 Sarah Adelman (2006) further summarizes the intangible sense of Vermont's distinctiveness, writing, "Vermont is not 'Anywhere, USA,' but neither were many of these places 50 years ago. Vermont is unique because you usually know that you are in Vermont."

6 See the ISE webpage for information on activism directed by the institute, at http://www.social-ecology.org /.

7 Internet resources include Mad River Valley Localvore Project, http://www.vermontlocalvore.org and Locavores, http://www.locavores.com.

8 See the special issue of *Vermont Life*, "Our Food, Our Farmers" (summer 2008), and see Vermont Fresh Network, http://www.vermontfresh.net.

9 Field research was conducted in Vermont with the assistance of student researchers Dan Hock, Kelly McQuade, Derek Souza, Katherine Downs-Angus, and John Ryan, who interviewed farmers and food producers in April 2009.

REFERENCES

Adelman, S. 2006. "Vermont Must Preserve Creative Economy." *Burlington Free Press*, 8 October.
Ayres, J. 1998. *Defying Conventional Wisdom: Political Movements and Popular Contention against North American Free Trade*. Toronto: University of Toronto Press.
– 2004. "Power Relations under NAFTA: Reassessing the Efficacy of Contentious Transnationalism." *Studies in Political Economy* 74:101–23.
Bandy, J., and J. Smith. 2004. *Coalitions across Borders: Transnational Protest and the Neoliberal Order*. Lanham, MD: Rowman and Littlefield.
Bello, W. 2008. "Capitalism in an Apocalyptic Mood." *Foreign Policy in Focus*, 20 February. http://fpif.org/capitalism_in_an_apocalyptic_mood/.
Blumenthal, R., and R. Mosteller. 2008. "Chasing Utopia: Family Imagines No Possessions." *New York Times*, 17 May.
Bosia, M. 2009. "AIDS and Post Colonial Politics: Acting Up on Science and Immigration in France." *French Politics, Culture & Society* 27 (1): 69–90. http://dx.doi.org/10.3167/fpcs.2009.270104.
Bourrigaud, R. 2008. "L'Ouest a vu émerger un radicalism paysan, précurseur du Larzac." *Libération*, 15 February. http://www.liberation.fr/grand-angle/2008/02/15/l-ouest-a-vu-emerger-un-radicalisme-paysan-precurseur-du-larzac_65044.
Bové, J., and F. Dufour. 2001. *The World Is Not for Sale*. New York: Verso.
Calta, M. 2008. "The Making of a Food Mecca." *Vermont Life* 62 (4): 34.
Changfoot, N. 2007. "Local Activism and Neoliberalism: Performing Neoliberal Citizenship as Resistance." *Studies in Political Economy* 80:129–49.
Common Dreams. 2004. "Farmers Protest at US/Canada Border: Giant Banner Says No to GMOs." News release, 17 April. http://www.commondreams.org/news2004/0419-02.htm.
Conklin, A. 2000. *A Mission to Civilize: The Republican Idea of Empire in France and West Africa, 1895–1930*. Stanford: Stanford University Press.
Conway, J. 2004. *Identity, Place and Knowledge: Social Movements Contesting Globalization*. Halifax: Fernwood Publishing.
Crozier, M. 1999. *La Société Bloquée*. 3rd ed. Paris: Seuil.

Desmarais, A. 2005. "United in the Vía Campesina." *Backgrounder (Washington, D.C.)* 11 (4). http://www.foodfirst.org/node/1580.

DuPuis, M., and D. Block. 2008. "Sustainability and Scale: US Milk-Market Orders as Relocalization Policy." *Environment and Planning* 40 (8): 1987–2005.

Evans, P. 2008. "Is an Alternative to Globalization Possible?" *Politics & Society* 36 (2): 271–305. http://dx.doi.org/10.1177/0032329208316570.

Feagan, R. 2007. "The Place of Food: Mapping Out the 'Local' in Local Food Systems." *Progress in Human Geography* 31 (1): 23–42. http://dx.doi.org/10.1177/0309132507073527.

Ferguson, P.P. 1998. "A Cultural Field in the Making: Gastronomy in 19th Century France." *American Journal of Sociology* 104 (3): 597–641. http://dx.doi.org/10.1086/210082.

Gills, B. 2004. "The Turning of the Tide." *Globalizations* 1 (1): 1–6. http://dx.doi.org/10.1080/14747730412331298851.

Grassroots International. 2008. *Towards a Green Food System: How Food Sovereignty Can Save the Environment and Feed the World.* http://www.grassrootsonline.org/publications/fact-sheets-and-reports/towards-green-food-system-how-food-sovereignty-can-save-environ.

Guiral, A. 2007. "Un président en quête du coup d'éclat permanent." *Libération*, 30 May. http://www.liberation.fr/evenement/2007/05/30/un-president-en-quete-du-coup-d-eclat-permanent_94504.

Hazareesingh, S. 1999. "The Société d'Instruction Républicaine and the Propagation of Civic Republicanism in Provincial and Rural France, 1870–1877." *Journal of Modern History* 71 (2): 271–307. http://dx.doi.org/10.1086/235248.

Hewitt, B. 2010. *The Town That Food Saved: How One Community Found Vitality in Local Food.* New York: Rodale.

Hoffmann, S. 1961a. "The Effects of World War II on French Society and Politics." *French Historical Studies* 2 (1): 28–63. http://dx.doi.org/10.2307/286182.

– 1961b. *In Search of France.* Cambridge, MA: Harvard University Press.

Huey, T.A. 2005. "Thinking Globally, Eating Locally: Website Linking and the Performance of Solidarity in Global and Local Food Movements." *Social Movement Studies* 4 (2): 123–37. http://dx.doi.org/10.1080/14742830500191469.

Institut National de la statistique et des Études Économique. 2011. "Tablaux de l'économie française." http://www.insee.fr/fr/ffc/tef/tef2011/T11F172/T11F172.pdf.

Intervale Center. 2007. "Buy Local Food." http://www.intervale.org/get-involved/buy-local-food/.

Johnson, T. 2007. "Can Vermont Feed Itself? The 'Eat Local' Movement Gains Ground." *Burlington Free Press*, 11 June.

Kempf, H. 2008. "José Bové en grève de la faim contre le maïs transgénique." *Le Monde*, 3 January.

Khagram, S., J. Riker, and K. Sikkink, eds. 2002. *Restructuring World Politics: Transnational Social Movements, Networks and Norms*. Minneapolis, MN: University of Minnesota Press.

Kingsolver, B. 2008. *Animal, Vegetable, Miracle: A Year of Food Life*. New York: Harper Perennial.

Kohut, M. 2007. "Hunger for Sale: Global Agribusiness and Local Resistance Movements." Unpublished manuscript, Colchester, VT: Saint Michael's College.

Kopka, M. 2008. "Defending Food Sovereignty." *NACLA Report on the Americas* (January/February). https://nacla.org/article/defending-food-sovereignty.

Kuisel, R. 1993. *Seducing the French: The Dilemma of Americanization*. Berkeley: University of California Press.

Lebovics, H. 2004. *Bringing the Empire Back Home: France in the Global Age*. Durham, NC: Duke University Press.

Magnusson, W. 2005. "Urbanism, Cities and Local Self-Government." *Canadian Public Administration* 48 (1): 96–123. http://dx.doi.org/10.1111/j.1754-7121 .2005.tb01600.x.

Martin, A. 2009. "Is a Food Revolution Now in Season? In Washington, the Gardner in Chief Embraces the Activists." *New York Times*, 22 March.

McAdam, D., and Rucht, D. 1993. "The Cross-National Diffusion of Movement Ideas." *Annals AAPSS* 528:56–74.

McDermott, R. 2007. "Eat Locally: Growing a Statewide Movement." *Vermont Commons Journal* 20, Fall. http://www.vtcommons.org/journal/issue-20-fall-2007/robin-mcdermott-eat-locally-growing-statewide-localvore-movement.

Mittelman, J. 2004. "Globalization Debates: Bringing in Microencounters." *Globalizations* 1 (1): 24–37. http://dx.doi.org/10.1080/1474773042000252138.

Norberg-Hodge, H. 2002. *Bringing the Food Economy Home: Local Alternatives to Global Agribusiness*. London: Zed Books.

"Our Food, Our Farmers." 2008. *Vermont Life* 62 (4).

Pollan, M. 2008. *In Defense of Food: An Eater's Manifesto*. New York: Penguin.

Porter, L. 2006. "Court Rules Chicken Can't Cross the Road." *Rutland Herald*, 16 June. http://www.rutlandherald.com/apps/pbcs.dll/article?AID=/20060616/NEWS/606160322/1004/NEWS03.

Reuters. 2008. "French Activist Bové to Go on Anti-GMO Hunger Strike," 11 December.

Rosset, P. 2003. "Food Sovereignty: Global Rallying Cry of Farmer
    Movements." *Backgrounder* 9 (4). http://www.foodfirst.org/en/node/47.
Rural Vermont. 2013. "About Us." http://www.ruralvermont.org/about-us/.
Setchell, L. 2005. "'Food Sovereignty': A New Vision for Vermont Agriculture."
    Vermont Commons Journal, 6 October. http://www.vtcommons.org/journal/
    issue-6-october-2005/linda-setchell-food-sovereignty-new-vision-vermont-
    agriculture.
Smith, J., and H. Johnston, eds. 2002. *Globalization and Resistance: Transnational
    Dimensions of Social Movements*. Lanham, MD: Rowman and Littlefield.
Starr, A., and J. Adams. 2003. "Anti-Globalization: The Global Fight for Local
    Autonomy." *New Political Science* 25 (1): 19–42. http://dx.doi.org/10.1080/
    07393140320000071217.
Starr, A., Adrian Card, Carolyn Benepe, Garry Auld, Dennis Lamm, Ken
    Smith, and Karen Wilken. 2003. "Sustaining Local Agriculture: Barriers
    and Opportunities to Direct Marketing between Farms and Restaurants in
    Colorado." *Agriculture and Human Values* 20 (3): 301–21. http://dx.doi
    .org/10.1023/A:1026169122326.
St Peter, B. 2006. "Chicken Pizza and Civil Disobedience: Reclaiming Our
    Food Sovereignty and the Right to Choose What We Eat." CommonDreams,
    7 September. http://www.commondreams.org/cgi-bin/print.cgi?file=/
    views06/0907-30.htm.
Tarrow, S. 2005. *The New Transnational Activism*. Cambridge: Cambridge
    University Press. http://dx.doi.org/10.1017/CBO9780511791055.
Tokar, B. 2006. "Toward Food Sovereignty in Vermont." *Vermont Commons
    Journal*, April. http://www.vtcommons.org/sites/default/files/back-issues/
    vol.12_April_2006.pdf.
– 2008. "On Bookchin's Social Ecology and Its Contributions to Social
    Movements." *Capitalism, Nature, Socialism* 19 (1): 51–66. http://dx.doi
    .org/10.1080/10455750701859430.
Transition Vermont. 2013. "Welcome." http://transitionvermont.ning.com/.
United Nations Department of Economic and Social Affairs/Population
    Division. 2005. "World Urbanization Prospects: The 2005 Revision."
    Geneva: UN.
Vermont Agency of Agriculture. 2007. *Vermont Harvest*. Montpelier: State of
    Vermont.
– 2008. "Food and Markets Buy Local Program." http://vermontagriculture
    .com/buyvermont2.htm.
Wallerstein, I. 2009. "Reply to Reimagining Socialism." *Nation* 288 (11): 17–18.
Wieviorka, M. 1984. "Three Phases in the Emergence of a Student Based Social
    Movement in France." *European Journal of Education* 19 (3): 327–41. http://
    dx.doi.org/10.2307/1502849.

Conclusion: The Food Sovereignty Lens

PHILIP McMICHAEL

Introduction

The chapters in this volume together seek to broaden the concept of "food sovereignty." From its origins in the early 1990s in relation to land rights and trade politics, food sovereignty has captured the imagination of a variety of counter-movements concerned with food justice, human rights, and environmental integrity. What is distinctive about this volume is that many of the chapters grapple with the implications of the growing allegiance to food sovereignty, including identifying common meanings in distinct locales, and whether and to what extent food sovereignty's elasticity endows it with different meanings for different populations, or whether food sovereignty remains anchored in its (authentic) agricultural base. The question of authenticity also concerns in what sense food sovereignty at its core may implicate groups beyond the countryside, and if so, whether its meaning changes through incorporation by urban struggles over food access, availability, and appreciation. This is a debate worth promoting.

From a different angle, and laid out thematically by the editors, this volume examines the implications of the extraordinary contentiousness of food politics in the current era. In this respect, the editors consider the contemporary food crisis as a flashpoint throwing light on numerous contradictions of neoliberal globalization. In particular they note that food rebellions and activists raise questions about state sovereignty, democracy, global inequalities, food security and food safety, trade rules and relations that undermine food cultures, and the role of food in the variety of movements for social protection in a Polanyian impulse to regulate markets – for rural producers or for urban consumers.[1] At base, they note that many of these forms of contention are grounded in local forms of politicization. The question becomes what constitutes and animates the "local"? This, then, revisits the above issues regarding assigning significance, scope, and salience to food sovereignty claims.

This concluding chapter attempts to weave these issues together to situate the different aspects of, and claims for, food sovereignty in a historicized account to try to make sense of food sovereignty's multi-dimensionality – as an expression of a global threshold of crisis and possibility.

What Crisis?

A long-simmering agrarian crisis was decisively signalled in 2007–8, when food prices spiked (rising 75 per cent from 2005 to 2007) and world grain reserves reached their lowest level at fifty-four days (Holt-Giménez and Kenfield 2008, 3). By mid-2009, almost one-sixth of humanity (about one billion) were considered hungry or undernourished, especially women. And almost three-quarters of this world subgroup reside in rural areas – a veritable "agrarian crisis." By 2011, the food crisis returned with a vengeance, food prices surpassing those of 2008. The world's attention has now been refocused on agriculture, following a long period of neglect and seduction by the corporate food regime, claiming to "feed the world" (McMichael 2005a).

In 2008, the World Bank revisited the subject of agriculture after a twenty-five-year hiatus, dedicating its annual *World Development Report* to the subject of agriculture. It certainly spoke to the agrarian crisis, symbolized by a rather stale attempt to equate small farming with poverty in its opening paragraph (McMichael 2009). But the bank was really addressing a different crisis, namely, an accumulation crisis, now requiring agricultural investment to jump-start an overly financialized global economy.[2] The link between the food and financial crises was thereby forged, as a land grab to secure food and fuel supplies has ensued since, with financiers partnering with national governments in the global South, counselled by the World Bank on land titling and other governance matters (GRAIN 2008; Daniel 2009, 2010; Houtart 2010). The problem of course is that this financial reflex is about sustaining affluent consumption and profits for political and economic elites, not addressing hunger or the agrarian crisis at large.

It was the agrarian crisis in the first place that gave rise to the food sovereignty movement in the early 1990s. The progenitor of "food sovereignty," La Vía Campesina,[3] formed from a meeting of farmers' organizations, from Latin America and Europe, in Managua in 1992. As founding member, Paul Nicholson of the International Coordinating Committee of Vía Campesina put it, "At that time, we issued a 'Managua declaration' where we denounced the 'agrarian crisis' and 'rural poverty and hunger' resulting from the neo-liberal policies" (Nicholson and Delforge 2008, 456). Four years later, in Tlaxcala, Mexico, a Vía Campesina working group coined the term *food sovereignty*, which "was adopted by the whole movement and then defended publicly for the first time at the FAO World Food Summit in Rome" later in 1996.[4] Noting that "food sovereignty has become the backbone of our struggle," particularly in proposing ways out of the crisis, Nicholson summarizes, "We propose local food markets, the right of any country to protect its borders from imported food, sustainable agriculture and the defence of biodiversity, healthy food, jobs and strong livelihood in rural areas" (457).

Perhaps what is most telling is that the agrarian crisis identified by the early food sovereignty movement is largely responsible for the recent and ongoing crisis of rising food prices. That is, as a result of the overproduction of U.S. and European agricultural commodities, and their systematic dumping at 30 per cent or more below cost on global markets (a practice legitimized by WTO rules in 1994), small farmers everywhere found themselves unable to compete with such highly subsidized foodstuffs. Peasant dispossession intensified from the mid-1990s, with deteriorating small farming conditions, under the pressure of this "cheap-food regime" (Rosset 2008; McMichael 2005a). Patnaik's investigations suggest that this regime undermined the social reproductive capacity of peasantries, contributing to a stagnation in food supply manifest in particular during the 2007–8 "food crisis," when small farmers suffering "income deflation" were unable to respond by expanding production (2008, 113). At the same time, as even the bank acknowledges in the deep recesses of its *World Development Report*, 2008, privatization also took its toll: "Structural adjustment in the 1980's dismantled the elaborate system of public agencies that provided farmers with access to land, credit, insurance inputs, and cooperative organization ... Incomplete markets and institutional gaps impose huge costs in forgone growth and welfare losses for smallholders, threatening their competitiveness and, in many cases, their survival" (2007, 138). And more recently, "In the food crisis, for example, the governments didn't have any political mechanisms for recognizing the crisis, of controlling the crisis, or reacting to the crisis. All the instruments were privatized" (Nicholson 2010, 40).

While certainly food speculation and biofuels production contributed to the food inflation, the supply shortfall episode was a product of a long-standing agrarian crisis deepened by neoliberal disregard for agriculture, and it will continue so long as neoliberal policies and land grabbing endure. Both are responsible for the devaluation of farming everywhere, as a toxic combination of debt and offshore production drives farmers to the wall. In a subsequent interview, Paul Nicholson observes, "The bad news is that we are losing a lot of farmers day-to-day. And not only small family farmers, but big farmers also cannot compete. And in fact, very often, because of the debt levels, they are closing down faster than the small farmers … In the European Union, it's one farmer every minute. And this is happening in the face of policies which support agro-industry, the big industrial farmers, the consolidation of food production and the lowering of prices at farm gate" (2010, 40).

A similar fate has confronted farmers in the Balkan states, where, as documented in the chapter by Irena Knezevic, European Enlargement policies enlist IMF and WTO rules for accession of new states to the EU – in particular in planning for the reduction of small farming. In an intriguing examination of resistance by citizens, Knezevic shows how informalization, including the proliferation of farmers' markets, constitutes an incipient form of food sovereignty appropriate to this episode of shock therapy.

The point is that "food sovereignty" was born of crisis. That is, it is not about restoring a peasant utopia; rather it is about countering the catastrophic social and ecological effects of the neoliberal assault on the agrarian foundations of society. It stems from mobilization in / of the countryside, but has broader implications. As this volume's editors note in chapter 1, the crises of the global food system (security, safety, displacement, peak oil and peak soil, climate change) "are clearly connected, then, to the persistence of neoliberalism as a motivating ideology legitimating the unfettered commodification of food production and distribution and undermining national and local control over food policies." Neoliberalism draws on modernist assumptions that labour-intensive ("peasant") agriculture is anachronistic, while deepening the long-term fracturing of nutrient cycles by capitalist agriculture (metabolic rift) and fossil-fuel dependency. In this sense food sovereignty, as a counter-movement against neoliberalism, serves as a critique of the modernist narrative at the same time as it advocates solutions to the human-ecological crisis confronting the world (McMichael 2008).

The Epistemic Intervention

As Marie-Josée Massicotte observes in her chapter, food sovereignty is originally about rural mobilization, and, as such, challenges modernist epistemology that would discount rural self-identification and self-organizing. In this sense, her appeal to Santos's *sociology of emergences* (rendering the impossible possible) is appropriate to this subject. In the modernist narrative, peasants are supposed to disappear via the gravitational pull of city lights and through their inability to "compete" with modern, capital-intensive agriculture. By contrast, food sovereignty mobilization by smallholders, farm labourers, pastoralists, fisherfolk, and forest-dwellers champions values other than unit productivity and profitability, offering a counter-narrative of solidarity and collective well-being – for Massicotte expressing a feminist political ecology. Central to this project are knowledge-intensive practices that reduce chemical and other commercial inputs to farming and restore local ecological knowledges as essential to democratic and sustainable food systems. Massicotte's engagement with the Latin American School of Agro-ecology reveals how agro-ecology becomes a way of restoring the value of informed farming labour (the target of elimination of capitalist agriculture) and the centrality of women to this way of life.

This kind of intervention underscores the epistemic implications of the food sovereignty movement, in viewing the right to farm as both a democratic claim (Wittman's "agrarian citizenship" [2009, 805]) as well as an assertion of the integral relations between food, environment, and social justice. Whereas capitalist modernity promotes "agriculture without farmers" (La Vía Campesina) – extensive monocultures highly dependent on energy and mechanical and chemical inputs – the food sovereignty movement demonstrates the multi-functionality of farming as a cultural and ecological practice premised on skilled labour and the solidary economy of seed sharing. In this vision, restoring and sustaining soil and biodiversity are foundational to modern civilization. Perversely, capitalist agriculture is premised on undermining this foundation in the rush to realize profit upon alienation of the products of agro-industrialization. Worse, because of commodification and now financialization, the products are not necessarily foodstuffs, as agro-fuels and general bio-mass become the objects of investment for profit and speculation (Houtart 2010; McMichael 2010).

These more recent developments, epitomized by the land grab, reveal the process of abstraction of agriculture as just another industry serving an unsustainable market imperative, rather than a socio-ecological imperative. Sustaining profits rather than natural processes and cycles shapes an episteme in which development is measured in monetized output, abstracting from sensuous socio-natural labour practices. Dispossession of small producers, elimination of the commons, chemicalization, rising greenhouse gas emissions, and reduction of biodiversity follow – characterized as "economic externalities." Food sovereignty inverts this ontology by re-centring farming knowledges in agro-ecological practices designed to revalue human labour and its sustaining relationship to the natural world.

Such deliberate food relations become the medium, and product, of an alternative, political ontology. "Sovereignty" is the means by which this political ontology is to be secured. Here, Sarah Wright's chapter on the Philippines' food sovereignty network, MASIPAG, underscores the greater productivity, food security, and resilience of the food sovereignty "method" of farming, based on "food first," restoring biodiversity, diversifying diets, reducing chemicals and the significance of nurturing farmer exchanges. This case study confirms in no uncertain manner Jan Douwe van der Ploeg's long-term study of "re-peasantization" (2009), by which withdrawal from agribusiness dependency (inputs, processing, export markets) improves the condition of farmers, rural communities, and the land, building a multifunctional agriculture.

The Sovereignty Issue

The concept of food "sovereignty" raises the question of the meaning of sovereignty. In the shadow of the continuing world food crisis, export bans are viewed as alarming challenges to multilateralism and the ability to provision food deficit states. Land grabbing offshore, by food importing states, to ensure food (and biofuel) supplies is one result (McMichael 2013), expelling producers from common lands (sold / leased by indebted governments) and deepening patterns of food insecurity. Under these conditions the pursuit of food sovereignty, as a national reflex, is double edged. While it appears to undercut the possibility of food transfers to deficit world regions, it offers the possibility of reversing the construction of food deficit nations as a product of the diabolical misapplication of the doctrine of "comparative advantage."[5] The short answer to this seeming paradox is that food sovereignty advocates "food first," meaning ending the agro-export priority that governs the current food regime. But the nationalist implications of "sovereignty" are even more complex.

Michael Menser's chapter raises the question of what constitutes the "territory of self-determination," as implied in the concept of food sovereignty. Noting that states often transgress or contain indigenous territories, he confronts the political question of the space of social reproduction and the role of the state in guaranteeing sovereignty. This focuses attention on the ambiguity of food sovereignty as a political strategy versus a political practice. Arguably, in the first instance food sovereignty is a protective strategy, deploying "sovereignty" as a legitimizing category (given Westphalia, etc.) regarding states' rights to withdraw from the WTO regime of open borders for the food trade. In the second instance, there is the question of scale (political, cultural, and ecological), which, arguably, can be resolved only through cultural and class-based practice – and how that plays out will vary across space (see, e.g., Escobar 2008). In arguing that the food sovereignty movement is class war re-territorialized, Menser notes that states are political conveniences based on violent histories, and that the food sovereignty movement holds out the possibility of a rights- and class-based (including peasant classes) struggle to redefine appropriate and just forms of territory that recognize the universality of food growing and eating (see Patel 2009).

The food sovereignty movement, as above, emerged in response to the global agrarian crisis, advocating land rights as the practical precondition of the right to food. It is important to remember the disproportionate rural location of hunger on the one hand, and on the other to note that most food produced in the world is consumed locally, and that small farmers still produce most of the world's food (Altieri 2008). This is the context for the food sovereignty movement, precipitated by the intensification of circulation of Northern food surpluses under the aegis of the corporate food regime and in the name of "food security." When "food sovereignty" entered public discourse in 1996, it represented the counterpart of the rhetorical claim to "food security" on the part of agribusiness and the development industry. Whereas food security had emerged in the 1970s as a UN-sponsored idea promoting national self-sufficiency (Jarosz 2009; Martin and Andrée, this volume), in the subsequent neoliberal project it was appropriated as a function of market access, facilitated by the combination of Northern granaries and transnational food companies and governed by WTO trade rules (McMichael 2003). Martha McMahon makes a similar observation in her chapter in this volume, namely that "food security" is vulnerable to neoliberal solutions.

In contrast, "food sovereignty" offered an entirely different vision of ordering the world food system, one based first in policies of national and sub-national food self-reliance, essentially inverting the export imperative that defined neoliberal food provisioning (geared as it was to servicing those with purchasing power). And the inversion had significant implications for democratic control over food policy, land rights / use, and questions of food access. In these terms, food "sovereignty" could be understood as a form of strategic essentialism – a particular kind of intervention designed to reverse environmentally and socially destructive, and unjust, food policies, with the immediate goal of recovering and restoring farming as a cultural and ecological practice to provision food-deficient populations.

Under the Vía Campesina vision, trade is not ruled out so much as subordinated to the basic principle of agricultural multifunctionality. La Vía Campesina does not reject the "global" for the "local"; instead it redefines the global in terms appropriate to democratic conditions of food production and distribution. The peasant coalition emphasizes two central premises: first, that the international tensions surrounding the politics of food ultimately derive not from conflict between governments, but between models of production and rural development; and second, that the struggle is global but decentralized in content and leadership. French farmer-activist Jose Bové articulates the latter point; "The strength of this global movement is precisely that it differs from place to place ... The world is a complex place, and it would be a mistake to look for a single answer to complex and different phenomena. We have to provide answers at different levels – not just the international level, but local and national levels too" (Bové and Dufour 2001, 168). Embedded in this quote is the "global" vision represented by La Vía Campesina, namely that an alternative modernity depends on both rejecting the WTO / corporate move to privatize modernity as market uniformity and erase (shared) local knowledges (see Desmarais 2007, and on reinstating "the right of peoples, communities and countries to define their own agricultural, labour, fishing, food, and land policies which are ecologically, socially, economically and culturally appropriate to their unique circumstances" (quoted in Ainger 2003, 11).

Implementation of this model of strategic diversity is the issue at hand. Noting that "the massive movement of food around the world is forcing the increased movement of people" (2000), La Vía Campesina offers a new paradigm based in self-reliance at the national or community scale, as the anchor of an alternative globalization. Here, food sovereignty depends on access to credit, land, and fair prices to be set via rules negotiated in a reformed UN and alternative multilateral institutions such as a Convention on Food Sovereignty and Trade in Food and Agriculture, an International Court of Justice, a World Commission on Sustainable Agriculture and Food Sovereignty, and so forth (Bové and Dufour 2001, 8). Bové asks, "Why should the global market escape the rule of international law or human rights conventions passed by the United Nations?" (165). Meanwhile, food sovereignty as a principle has been inserted into UN discourse, via the UN Commission on Human Rights – in a report viewing food sovereignty as a vehicle of human rights to food security (cited in Desmarais 2007). It has also been officially adopted in national constitutions of Ecuador, Bolivia, Nepal, Venezuela, Senegal, Mali, and in the United States in Vermont, and Sedgwick (Maine).

Realization of strategic diversity through the principle of food sovereignty involves not only struggles for and on the land, as the MST models, with varying degrees of success (Wolford 2010), but also struggles to reverse or contain neoliberal policies protecting corporate rights to agriculture and food. These latter struggles target the state and multilateral organizations. While they draw from sub-national representations of alternatives, their macro-political target is appropriately the domain of a transnational movement, such as La Vía Campesina. The baseline, of course, is "the active participation of farmers' movements in defining agricultural and food policies within a democratic framework." The specificity of this politics is that, while the consumer movement has discovered that "eating has become a political act," articulating the health / transparency relations of food, La Vía Campesina adds the social / ecological and historical dimension: "Producing quality products for our own people has also become a political act ... this touches our very identities as citizens of this world" (1999). In this sense, La Vía Campesina emphasizes that consumption of (quality) food is the outcome, rather than the premise, of food sovereignty. The latter is ultimately rooted in the survival and sustainability of biodiverse ways of farming (currently under assault from the corporate food regime). This is a claim developed more fully in McMahon's chapter in this volume, especially in her deployment of the feminist concept of co-production, reminding us of the relationality of city and countryside in the first place, but ultimately of the strategic importance of the countryside to urban existence.

Scale, Territories, and Resistance

It is here that the contributions of Jeffrey Ayres and Michael Bosia, Sarah Martin and Peter Andrée, and Elizabeth Smythe come into focus. In different ways, these authors examine the extension of the scale of food sovereignty to include alliances with urban labour and urban consumers. Smythe focuses in particular on the right to know the provenance of food – echoing Bové's critique of the neoliberal "food from nowhere" regime (see McMichael 2002). While this is a critical element in food sovereignty, as it demands "food from somewhere" and implies reducing social distance between producers and consumers, and transparency, provenance is arguably a criterion rather than a premise of sovereignty. U.K. supermarkets in particular are already heavily into provenance (Frith 2006), so that how provenance is situated becomes the issue – as expressed in Smythe's treatment of an emerging politics of food labelling in Canada via the rise of the Canadian People's Food Policy Project, alongside the emergence of a U.S. Food Sovereignty Alliance.

Smythe's point is that in order to develop the concept and practice of food sovereignty, it needs extending organizationally from growers to eaters. As McMahon has noted, how eaters are identified and mobilized is itself a matter of (class) politics. Ayres and Bosia's chapter contributes to this question with a comparison between forms of "localization" in Larzac – an organized, producer-oriented and pre-industrial-inspired movement in France identified with José Bové – and Vermont – an anarchic, consumer-centred movement arising from the ruins of a crisis-ridden dairy industry. In each case, local control and community organization were central to the claims for food sovereignty, although the content of claims differed: with the Larzac movement combining class solidarity with a global politics (vs the model of industrial agriculture symbolized by GMOs), and the Vermont movement inspired by a green politics and the proliferation of community supported agriculture. The authors' conclusion that "both cases illustrate how food sovereignty is differently appropriated in local settings, where individuals and groups have embraced it for more unique and domestically shaped acts of contention" emphasizes the flexibility and place-specificity of food sovereignty as a universal principle, and as perhaps a leading edge of the alter-globalization movement.

Flexibility of course is double edged, as networks and questions of provenance are always open to appropriation by neoliberal forces and relations. Peter Andrée addresses this question in his study of the citizen-farmers in Australia, perhaps the most liberalized environment for agriculture. Claiming farmers join alternative food networks as survival mechanisms rather than on principle, his argument that AAFNs reproduce neoliberal practices appears to confirm the suspicions of Guthman's (2004) work on the industrialization of organics. But this study is also about farmers negotiating an intensely competitive neoliberal market with few public supports. In examining the "middle-class food quality" phenomenon from the other side, Andrée provides a window onto the measures taken (and represented) by originary commercial farmers to continue to farm in a hostile environment, sustained (perhaps entrapped) by class purchasing power. In a clever use of Polanyi's double movement dialectic, arguing collective action is a product of neoliberalism, the emergence of alternative food networks is represented as limiting realization of the self-regulating market fiction, but, as such, is a product itself of economic liberalism. The question here is whether Polanyi's metaphorical representation of class politics and ecological degradation is sufficient to sustain an argument that alternatives are condemned to reproduce the system itself. Polanyi, of course, claimed that the counter-movement eventually had its way in substantive market regulation (but see Halperin 2004). Whether or not this is an adequate account, now transcended by global economic liberalism (Lacher 1999; McMichael 2005b), it is perhaps important to keep the baby, if not the bathwater.

Noah Zerbe's chapter is instructive here, as he uses a comparison with fair trade (which he argues reproduces the global market) to claim that local food movements offer a basis from which to articulate a food sovereignty vision, in particular by substituting local for global market relations. With a community-based politics geared to social justice, exemplified in some CSAs, privileged forms of local consumption of quality foods can be transformed in a substantive food sovereignty direction. The lesson is that local food markets in themselves are not food sovereignty, yet.

Andrée claims alternative food networks colonize neoliberal space, but relatively insignificantly. However, the formation of cooperatives, biodiverse agriculture, and the reduction of commercial inputs all represent strategic possibilities that, if recognized as the basis for a sustainable form of farming via public subsidies and class-based alliances geared to food justice and environmental concerns, cannot be dismissed. If the Polanyi example means anything, this is a long-term process of change and positions farmers to inherit a landscape as industrial agriculture collapses under the combined forces of climatic changes (big in Australia) and rising energy costs (see Roberts 2008). What this kind of study allows is a critical examination of the possibilities for food sovereignty in commercial settings (especially settler states) quite unlike those in agrarian societies with large peasantries. Farmers in both settings are under siege from neoliberalism, but their range of possibilities differs, as do the relations of consumption.

With respect to this refocusing, Martin and Andrée ask what new meaning food sovereignty has for Canada, at "the heart of the neoliberal global food system." Food sovereignty for them involves the increasing role of NGOs in service provision associated with food access. Their problematic is aptly phrased in terms of "why food bank workers in Toronto or farmers in Nova Scotia are negotiating change by turning to terminology rooted in international peasant struggles." A reconstruction of the history of food security advocacy in Canada, and its mutation into a food sovereignty politics follows – perhaps the key turning point being in 1999 when the Canadian National Farmers' Union affirmed Bové's point that export agriculture threatens not just peasant farmers in the South, but also Northern family farms and environments. This point was developed by the Union des Producteurs Agricoles in recognizing that WTO rules threaten supply management and therefore domestic food policies. And this has in turn mutated into a broad movement of civil society organizations for farmer protection, Aboriginal rights, and the fight against hunger.

The key development, according to Martin and Andrée, is that food sovereignty in Canada derives from "new sites of governance that have been abandoned by the state" – giving rise in particular to community food governance schemes. In actual fact their narrative of developments in Canada parallels the Southern food sovereignty narrative in recognizing that the nexus between the state and the agro-export complex undercuts domestic (and international) food justice, requiring a challenge not simply to the state system but the state itself (McMichael 2006). While the initial food sovereignty movement had a strategic target to address in the complicity of states in a neoliberal version of market-based food security, the various food sovereignty chapters, like the

MST in Brazil, were busy constructing sub-national communities in the name of "agrarian citizenship"[6] – as an epistemic challenge to the modernist premise of citizenship as urbanity, including a process of transforming the (meaning of the) state by subordinating markets to social and ecological criteria.

Claims that the Canadian food sovereignty movement has a distinct cast certainly underline the specificity of such Northern movements in addressing class / race-differentiated urban consumer needs, but they also register two important points. One is that the initial critique of the neoliberal food order emerged from a besieged peasantry, but developed the vision to situate that struggle in the broader politico-cultural relations of food – as noted by Paul Nicholson above and in La Vía Campesina's variously stated desires to "look after the earth" and to "produce society" (Desmarais 2007). And the other is that food provisioning must depend ultimately on political-ecological alliances between consumers and producers (as agrarian citizens and stewards of the land) as the basis for a healthy community-based food system (Friedmann 2007). Here, McMahon's precautionary note regarding the politics, vision, and horizon of the local food networks is well taken. Where La Vía Campesina's original critique of the displacing effect of the circulation of food conjoined the rural and urban via the proliferation of peri-urban slums (see Araghi 2000), our understanding of "food sovereignty" is only strengthened by recognition of the "centrality of agriculture" to its realization as a substantive and sustainable form of democratic organization (Duncan 1996).

Conclusion

It has become very clear that without land management policies, and farmers of course, food sovereignty is a non-starter – this is as true in Ontario as it is in Brazil as it is in Mali (especially given the land grab). And it is echoed in Paul Nicholson's lament: "We are questioning the deregulation and the loss of control by the governments and the public systems on the food chain … One issue in Europe which is very important is land use. And there the tendency is to liberalize land use: to make land use very market-oriented with very little public conditioning. And that means that land is going into the hands of the rich – the urban rich, who need their second homes, or the savings bank. They use it also as a speculative measure" (2010, 40–1). One might say the same about land use elsewhere, given the phenomenon of an accelerating land grab as states and speculators take matters into their own hands with the prospect of rising energy, water, and food prices and the enabling policies of the development agencies and debt-stressed and / or corrupt governments in the South.[7]

The point here is that the localization of food markets is a necessary but not sufficient condition for food sovereignty. Uneven global developments juxtapose an international peasant movement advocating local markets as a resistance against elimination by global markets, with Northern locavores building local markets to improve food quality, reduce food miles and environmental stress, and sometimes for food justice. Here, CSAs are certainly a positive step where they sustain local farming, but local farming sustainability depends additionally on the politicization of land management relations, including mutual recognition of rural and urban social and ecological relations involved in the production, processing and distribution of food (see, e.g., Friedmann 2011). One might observe that food sovereignty in the South begins in the besieged countryside, while food sovereignty in Northern America tends to be urban / consumer driven.[8] Whether the urban point of departure addresses besieged "eaters" (the malnourished) is critical to the food sovereignty vision, but ultimately the democratic content of food sovereignty is substantiated by close rural / urban alliances around biodiversity and justice.

This collection of chapters offers a wide-ranging commentary on food sovereignty, its origins and evolution as a vision encompassing agroecology, food distribution networks, CSAs, localization movements, political alliances, gender relations, and so forth. A unifying thread is the growing political contention over food, much of which has to do with the conditions under which it is produced and exchanged / distributed, which in turn shape the kind of food available to consumers. Industrial food embodies a variety of unhealthy relations with the land, water, bodies, animals, the atmosphere, micro-climates, and natural processes (from pollination to soil replenishment). While the practice of food sovereignty seeks to counter these relations, the original politics centred on a strategy of politicizing the corporate food regime and its destructive trade rules, as a precursor to reversing such unhealthy relations. Accordingly, food sovereignty needs to be understood as a vision arising from a particular moment when accelerating neoliberal political-economic relations were deepening a global agrarian crisis. It has become more than this, and the progenitors favour its broadening appeal, so long as it is anchored in the twin goals of biodiversity and justice.

Perhaps the most straightforward way of presenting this is in the UN Human Rights special rapporteur's report to the Human Rights Council of the UN General Assembly, 10 December 2010. Without using the term *food sovereignty*, Olivier de Schutter's executive summary captures its essence:

> Drawing on an extensive review of the scientific literature published in the last five years, the Special Rapporteur identifies agroecology as a mode of agricultural development which not only shows strong conceptual connections with the right to food, but has proven results for fast progress in the concretization of this human right for many vulnerable groups in various countries and environments. Moreover, agroecology delivers advantages that are complementary to better known conventional approaches such as breeding high yielding varieties. And it strongly contributes to the broader economic development. The report argues that the scaling up of these experiences is the main challenge today. Appropriate public policies can create an enabling environment for such sustainable modes of production. These policies include prioritizing the procurement of public goods in public spending rather than solely providing input subsidies; investing in knowledge by reinvesting in agricultural research and extension services; investing in forms of social organization that encourage partnerships, including farmer field schools and farmers' movements innovation networks; investing in agricultural research and extension systems; empowering women; and creating a macro-economic enabling environment, including connecting sustainable farms to fair markets.

This approach is fully grounded in practice, including the sharing of agro-ecological knowledges. The notion of scaling up is not simply a spatially vertical process, but also an enriching of institutional relations with a sensibility to recentring sustainable human development on its ultimate foundation: the agri-food system, its ecological underpinnings, and its role in provisioning food.

NOTES

1 Arguably, food riots, contributing to the recent Mideast uprisings, embody questions of moral economy and political legitimacy of states embedded in a corporate food regime geared to provisioning wealthy, rather than civilian, populations (Patel and McMichael 2009).

2 See theme sections on this in both the *Journal of Peasant Studies* 36, no. 3 (2009) and the *Journal of Agrarian Change* 9, no. 2 (2009).

3 An international coalition comprising 148 organizations from sixty-nine countries. In 2000, Vía Campesina joined fifty-one other civil society organizations to form the International Planning Committee for Food Sovereignty, which operates at the international policy level.

4 For elaboration of this history, see Desmarais (2007).

5 Ricardo's original concept did not assume the mobility of capital, which is now able to construct comparative advantage as a corporate competitive advantage – as institutionalized in the WTO regime, which sanctions the dumping of artificially cheapened food via huge subsidies to Northern agribusiness (Peine and McMichael 2005).

6 Hannah Wittman defines agrarian citizenship as "the idea that rural producers have not only rights to the land and the environment but also responsibilities, connected to these rights, for maintaining the diversity of social-ecological reproduction" (2010, 96).

7 See special issues of *Development* 51, no. 4 (2011), and the *Journal of Peasant Studies* 38, no. 2 (2011).

8 Arguably this reflects the settler origins of Northern America, and Australia for that matter, as detailed in Andrée's chapter, in contrast to the European scene, where there is an active food sovereignty movement (Bové and Dufour 2001; McMichael 2011).

REFERENCES

Ainger, Kathleen. 2003. "The New Peasants' Revolt." *New Internationalist* 353:9–13.

Altieri, Miguel. 2008. "Small Farms as a Planetary Ecological Asset: Five Key Reasons Why We Should Support the Revitalization of Small Farms in the Global South." *Food First*, 9 May. http://www.foodfirst.org/en/node/2115.

Araghi, Farshad. 2000. "The Great Global Enclosure of Our Times: Peasants and the Agrarian Question at the End of the Twentieth Century." In *Hungry for Profit: The Agribusiness Threat to Farmers, Food, and the Environment*, edited by Fred Magdoff, F.H. Buttel, and John Bellamy Foster, 145–60. New York: Monthly Review.

Bové, Jose, and Francois Dufour. 2001. *The World Is Not for Sale*. London: Verso.

Daniel, Shepard. 2009. *The Great Land Grab: Rush for World's Farmland Threatens Food Security for the Poor*. Oakland, CA: Oakland Institute.

– 2010. *(Mis)Investment in Agriculture: The Role of the International Finance Corporation in Global Land Grabs.* Oakland, CA: Oakland Institute.

De Schutter, Olivier. 2010. *Report to the UN Human Rights Council.* 10 December.

Desmarais, Annette Aurélie. 2007. *La Vía Campesina: Globalization and the Power of Peasants.* London: Pluto.

Douwe van der Ploeg, Jan. 2009. *The New Peasantries: Struggles for Autonomy and Sustainability in an Era of Empire and Globalization.* London: Earthscan.

Duncan, Colin. 1996. *The Centrality of Agriculture: Between Humankind and the Rest of Nature.* Montreal and Kingston: McGill-Queen's University Press.

Escobar, Arturo. 2008. *Territories of Difference: Place, Movements, Life, Redes.* Durham, NC: Duke University Press.

Friedmann, Harriet. 2007. "Scaling Up: Bringing Public Institutions and Food Service Corporations into the Project for a Local, Sustainable Food System in Ontario." *Agriculture and Human Values* 24 (3): 389–98. http://dx.doi .org/10.1007/s10460-006-9040-2.

– 2011. "Food Sovereignty in the Golden Horseshoe Region of Ontario." In *Food Sovereignty in Canada,* edited by H. Wittman, A.A. Desmarais, and N. Wiebe. Halifax: Fernwood.

Frith, M. 2006. "Ethical Foods Boom Tops £2bn a Year and Keeps Growing." *Independent,* 13 October.

Grain. 2008. "Seized: The 2008 Land Grab for Food and Financial Security." *Briefings,* October. http://www.grain.org/article/entries/93-seized-the-2008-landgrab-for-food-and-financial-security.

Guthman, Julie. 2004. *Agrarian Dreams: The Paradox of Organic Farming in California.* Berkeley: University of California Press.

Halperin, Sandra. 2004. *War and Social Change in Modern Europe: The Great Transformation Revisited.* Cambridge: Cambridge University Press.

Holt-Giménez, Eric, and Isabella Kenfield. 2008. "When Renewable Isn't Sustainable." In *Agrofuels and the Inconvenient Truths behind the 2007 U.S. Energy Independence and Security Act.* Food First Policy Brief No. 13, 1–4. Oakland: Institute for Food and Development Policy.

Houtart, François. 2010. *Agrofuels: Big Profits, Ruined Lives and Ecological Destruction.* London: Pluto.

Jarosz, Lucy. 2009. "The Political Economy of Global Governance and the World Food Crisis: The Case of the FAO." *REVIEW* 32 (1): 37–60.

Lacher, Hannes. 1999. "Embedded Liberalism, Disembedded Markets: Conceptualising the Pax Americana." *New Political Economy* 4 (3): 343–60. http://dx.doi.org/10.1080/13563469908406408.

La Vía Campesina. 1999. "Seattle Declaration: Take WTO Out of Agriculture." http://www.viacampesina.org/en/index.php?option=com_content&view=

article&id=57:seattle-declaration-take-wto-out-of-agriculture&catid=24:10-years-of-wto-is-enough&Itemid=35.

– 2000. "Bangalore Declaration of the Vía Campesina." 6 October. http://www.viacampesina.org/en/index.php/our-conferences-mainmenu-28/3-bangalore-2000-mainmenu-55/420-bangalore-declaration-of-the-via-campesina.

– 2001. "Our World Is Not for Sale." 17 November. http://viacampesina.org/en/index.php/actions-and-events-mainmenu-26/10-years-of-wto-is-enough-mainmenu-35/323-statement-network-qour-world-is-not-for-saleq-owinfs.

McMichael, Philip. 2003. "Food Security and Social Reproduction." In *Power, Production & Social Reproduction*, edited by S. Gill and I. Bakker, 169–89. New York: Palgrave Macmillan.

– 2005a. "Global Development and the Corporate Food Regime." In *New Directions in the Sociology of Global Development*, edited by F.H. Buttel and P. McMichael, 229–67. Oxfordshire: Elsevier.

– 2005b. "Globalization." In *The Handbook of Political Sociology: States, Civil Societies and Globalization*, edited by Thomas Janoski, Robert Alford, Alexander Hicks, and Mildred Schwartz, 587–606. Cambridge: Cambridge University Press.

– 2006. "Reframing Development: Global Peasant Movements and the New Agrarian Question." *Canadian Journal of Development Studies* 27 (4): 471–83.

– 2008. "The Peasant as 'Canary'? Not Too Early Warnings of Global Catastrophe." *Development* 51 (4): 504–11. http://dx.doi.org/10.1057/dev.2008.56.

– 2009. "Banking on Agriculture: A Review of the *World Development Report* (2008)." *Journal of Agrarian Change* 9 (2): 235–46. http://dx.doi.org/10.1111/j.1471-0366.2009.00203.x.

– 2010. "Agrofuels in the Food Regime." *Journal of Peasant Studies* 3 (4): 609–29.

– 2011. "Food System Sustainability: Questions of Environmental Governance in the New World (Dis)Order." *Global Environmental Change* 21 (3): 804–12. http://dx.doi.org/10.1016/j.gloenvcha.2011.03.016.

– 2013. "Land Grabbing as Security Mercantilism in International Relations." *Globalizations* 10 (1): 47–64.

Nicholson, Paul. 2010. "Seeing Like a Peasant: Voices from La Vía Campesina." In *Food Sovereignty: Reconnecting Food, Nature and Community*, edited by Hannah Wittman, Annette Aurélie Desmarais, and Nettie Wiebe, 169–89. Halifax: Fernwood.

Nicholson, Paul, and Isabelle Delforge. 2008. "Vía Campesina: Responding to Global Systemic Crisis." *Development* 51 (4): 456–9. http://dx.doi.org/10.1057/dev.2008.51.

Patel, Raj. 2009. "What Does Food Sovereignty Look Like?" *Journal of Peasant Studies* 36 (3): 663–706. http://dx.doi.org/10.1080/03066150903143079.

Patel, Raj, and Philip McMichael. 2009. "A Political Economy of the Food Riot." *REVIEW* 32 (1): 9–36.

Peine, Emelie, and Philip McMichael. 2005. "Globalization and Governance." In *Agricultural Governance: Globalization and the New Politics of Regulation*, edited by Vaughan Higgins and Geoffrey Lawrence, 19–34. London: Routledge.

Roberts, Wayne. 2008. *The No-Nonsense Guide to World Food*. Oxford: New Internationalist.

Rosset, Peter. 2008. "Food Sovereignty and the Contemporary Food Crisis." *Development* 51 (4): 460–3. http://dx.doi.org/10.1057/dev.2008.48.

Wittman, H. 2009. "Reworking the Metabolic Rift: La Vía Campesina, Agrarian Citizenship and Food Sovereignty." *Journal of Peasant Studies* 36 (4): 805–26. http://dx.doi.org/10.1080/03066150903353991.

Wolford, Wendy. 2010. *This Land Is Ours Now: Social Mobilization and the Meanings of Land in Brazil*. Durham, NC: Duke University Press.

Index

Studies in Comparative Political Economy and Public Policy